FIRE WITH FIRE

Naomi Wolf was born in 1962 in San Francisco. She studied at Yale before becoming a Rhodes Scholar at New College, Oxford, and working in Edinburgh. She was catapulted to success in 1990 by her first book, *The Beauty Myth*, which was an international best-seller, published in fourteen countries. She lectures and writes on women's issues all over the world, and lives in Washington

BY NAOMI WOLF

The Beauty Myth

Fire With Fire:
The New Female Power and
How it Will Change the 21st Century

Naomi Wolf

FIRE WITH FIRE

The New Female Power and
How It Will Change the 21st Century

Published by Vintage 1994

2 4 6 8 10 9 7 5 3 1

Copyright © Naomi Wolf 1993

The right of Naomi Wolf to be identified as the author
of this work has been asserted by her in accordance with
the Copyright, Designs and Patents Act, 1988

First published in Great Britain by
Chatto & Windus Ltd, 1993

Vintage
Random House, 20 Vauxhall Bridge Road, London SW1V 2SA

Random House Australia (Pty) Limited
20 Alfred Street, Milsons Point, Sydney
New South Wales 2061, Australia

Random House New Zealand Limited
18 Poland Road, Glenfield,
Auckland 10, New Zealand

Random House South Africa (Pty) Limited
PO Box 337, Bergvlei, South Africa

Random House UK Limited Reg. No. 954009

A CIP catalogue record for this book
is available from the British Library

ISBN 0 09 932961 1

Printed and bound in Great Britain by
Cox & Wyman, Reading, Berkshire

For David

*The master's tools will never
dismantle the master's house.*
— Audre Lorde

Fight fire with fire.
— Proverb

Contents

CONTENTS

Acknowledgements

There are many without whose help I could not have written this book.

The following people took time from pressing schedules to grant me interviews: Katha Pollitt of *The Nation*; Marie Wilson of The Ms. Foundation; Nancy Woodhull of 'Women, Men and Media'; Holly Ainbinder and Jim Naurekas of Fairness and Accuracy in Reporting; and Andrea Berman of Mayor David Dinkin's office.

I am grateful to the audiences of men and women across the country who shared with me their concerns about and hopes for the women's movement. And I thank the groups of young women (particularly the WAC members of SUNY Geneseo, Jenna Soleo, Serena Morse, Noël Raley, Kirsten Konefal, Jill Scheltz, Nicole Montagna, Caycee Cullen, Anna Fleshler and Tammy Schultz) who allowed me to record their feelings about their relationship to the issues of power and leadership. Their voices stay with me.

Friends' and colleagues' work has enriched my understanding. Elizabeth Alexander of the University of Chicago discussed identity politics, race and feminism, and provided in her teaching and her poetry a role model for combining the progressive curriculum with intellectual rigour and broadmindedness. I also thank writer Susie Bright; novelist and safe-sex educator Karen Cook; Judy Coyne of *Glamour*, a consistently challenging 'ideal reader' in general; and Rhonda Garelick, of the University of Colorado. Catharine MacKinnon and Jeffrey Masson discussed some of the themes; Marcia Ann Gillespie, executive editor of *Ms.* magazine was an inspiration early in the writing process; Barbara Findlen and Julie Felner, also of *Ms.*, gave me extensive, salient notes on early drafts; Ann Godoff was the ideal interlocutor for this project; Ann Hornaday, author of the original 'PC/PI' article, gave manuscript readings that have been unfailingly sharp and Susan Faludi made valuable suggestions. Nancy Frank and Susan Roxborough; Suzanne Levitt of Yale University; Tom Molner, Donna Minkowitz, Will Schwalbe, Amruta Slee, Dan and Tara Goleman, John Brockman, Katinka Matson, John Stoltenberg, Carmen Callil and Frances Coady all offered important insights. My mother and father, Deborah Goleman Wolf and Leonard Wolf, and my grandmother Fay Goleman, provided their reliable combination of vital critical commentary and general psychic nourishment.

Gloria Steinem merits special acknowledgement. She read and commented on a draft while under a deadline of her own.

Many people helped me meet this and other commitments: Enrika Gadler, Beth Pearson and the production staff at Random House (who made miracles of order from my cryptic notations and baroque system of inserts); Alison Samuel, my editor at Chatto & Windus; Helen Churko, Lucy LePage and Carlton Sedgley of Royce Carlton, and Bethany Saltman. Joan and John Shipley made their hospitality available to me, as did The Virginia Center for the Creative Arts. Finally, my gratitude to Anastasia Gochnour, who assists me, is profound. She oversaw the needs of the office with foresight and creativity and contributed in many other ways.

I would also like to thank Candida Lacey and the following organizations for their help in providing me with information for the British edition: The Association of University Teachers (AUT); The Broadcasting, Entertainment, Cinematograph and Theatre Union (BECTU), especially Jane Paul, the Equality Officer; The British Film Institute; Nigel Dyckhoff of Spencer Stuart and Associates Limited; Emily's List, UK; The Equal Opportunities Commission; Equity; The Institute of Directors; The Institute of Management; The Institute of Manpower Services, University of Sussex; The National Union of Journalists (NUJ); The 300 Group; Women into Business; Women in

Management; Women in Film and Television; Women in Publishing; and The Women's Broadcasting Committee.

Readers may be surprised to see that I appreciate on some pages thinkers or publications with whom I argue on others. Let this book be read with the thought in mind that drove me to write it: dissenting from another's ideas is a form of honour, and taking a critical look at one's own cherished movement is an act not of sacrilege but of love.

Introduction

The 1980s were the height of the backlash years, but from the autumn of 1991 to the present, a new era has begun – the era of the 'genderquake', in which the meaning of being a woman is changed for ever. The 'genderquake' started in America with the eruption of Oklahoma law professor Anita Hill's charges of sexual harassment, rocked through 1991–2's famous rape trials, flung into the light of day allegations of Senator Bob Packwood's sexual harassment of colleagues, and of the sexual abuse of US Navy women at the Tailhook Convention; and provided the impetus for 52 new women legislators to take their seats in the House of Representatives and the Senate. From these beginnings, and with the election of pro-feminist President Clinton in the USA, the election of the first female Prime Minister of Canada, and the re-election – with the women's vote – of socialist Prime Minister Paul Keating in Australia, a train of events has been set in motion that leads to one conclusion: women have become the political ruling class. And they have the historical distinction of being the only ruling class that is unaware of its status.

During this short time, contributions to women's groups reached record highs in the USA; Emily's List, the Democratic Women's Political Action Committee, which funds the women candidates who have the best chance of winning, became the biggest lobbying force in the country, garnering millions of dollars for women office-seekers; advertising changed, with women depicted in positions of power, being worshipped by men; self-abnegating self-help books for women fell by the wayside, to be replaced on the bestseller lists by *Women Who Run with the*

Wolves and *Revolution from Within*; a million women over-whelmed the Capitol in the largest pro-choice rally in a decade; and a spate of new women's groups, with a media-conscious, take-no-prisoners attitude, mobilized at the grassroots in a frenzy of organizing unseen since the early 1970s: the Women's Action Coalition (WAC), the Women's Health Action Mobilization (WHAM!), YELL, the Riot Grrls, and the Third Wave Organization, all were born.

Even in Britain, where there has been less cause for electoral celebration, several significant feminist victories have changed the climate of the times. Alison Halford's courageous stand against sexual discrimination in the police force opened the door for other women and prompted an independent investigation that revealed, among other things, that nine out of ten policewomen had experienced sexual harassment; Barbara Follett launched Emily's List UK which aims to help ten women stand for parliament with every £30,000 raised; the Labour party elected a woman as deputy leader and passed a resolution that women must represent the party at the next general election in 50 per cent of its target seats; and, in the depths of the recession, in 1992, four feminist magazines were launched – *Second Shift*, *Body Politic*, *Bitch* and *Bad Attitude*.

In Australia, Prime Minister Paul Keating employed advisers on women's policy to help him win his 1993 election and announced a campaign for judicial re-education to combat prejudice against women in the law courts. In May 1993 Senator Rosemary Crowley launched *Women in Australia*, the Australian Bureau of Statistics' most comprehensive social report on the status of women.

But will women consolidate their gains? We have entered a time of great awakening and lightning-fast learning, as female perceptions begin to take their place alongside male perceptions in the daylight of public life. But while the new female power can feel like an unstoppable force, we cannot count on its momentum. Forward motion is up to us.

We will either understand that we are in the final throes of a civil war for gender fairness, in which conditions have shifted to put much of the attainment of equality in women's own grasp or we will back away from history's lesson, and, clinging to an out-dated image of ourselves as powerless, inch along for another several hundred years or so, subject to the whims and wind shifts of whatever form of backlash comes along next.

The decision is ours.

In *Fire with Fire: The New Female Power and How It Will Change the 21st Century*, I will argue that we are at what historians of women's progress call 'an open moment'. Twenty-five years of dedicated feminist activism have hauled the political infrastructure into place, enough women in the middle classes have enough money and clout, and most women now have enough desire and determination to begin to balance the imbalance of power between the sexes. But three obstacles stand in our way: many women have become estranged from their own movement; one strand of feminism has developed maladaptive attitudes; and women lack a psychology of female power to match their new opportunities.

Part One, 'The Decline of the Masculine Empire: Anita Hill and the Genderquake', tells the story of how male prestige began to tarnish just as female psychology became emboldened. These two trends set the stage for the recent upheavals that brought us to this turning point.

Part Two, 'What Went Wrong? How So Many Women and Their Movement Parted Ways', came out of my experience of listening to audiences across the country explain why they often have strong negative feelings about the idea of 'feminism', and warns that we must heal the breach that has opened between millions of women and the movement to secure their rights. While a strong majority of women passionately endorses the *goals* of feminism, a large number avoid identifying with the movement *itself*. This estrangement impedes women from attaining the equality that they desire.

Old habits left over from radical feminism's rebirth from the revolutionary left of the 1960s – such as a reflexive anti-capitalism, an insider-outsider mentality, and an aversion to the 'system' – once necessary and even effective, are now getting in our way. I will examine the other factors that led to many women's estrangement from feminism: dyke-baiting; economic silencing; media omission of debate on 'women's issues' so absolute that it amounts to a virtual news blackout; a tendency towards intellectual rigidity, and an 'insider' clubhouse mentality in some circles; mistranslated feminist theories that 'trickled down' into popular debate sounding bizarre; and a perception that the movement is anti-family, anti-male, exclusively white, and middle class. All of these contributed to many women's resistance to what had become 'the F word'.

Part Three, 'Victim Feminism versus Power Feminism', looks at 'victim feminism', a version of feminism that has come to dominate popular debate, and shows how destructive it is to women, and how wrong it is for the new era at hand. I'll confront the growing voices of critics who are charging that *all* feminism is puritanical, man-hating, and obsessed with defining women as 'victims', and I will separate the nugget of truth in those charges from the destructive, categorical hype. I will explore what is indeed unhelpful about the way a small minority of feminists have phrased the theme of victimization. I will look at how women must recount the all too real ways in which they are often victimized, without creating an *identity* from that victimization. There are and have always been two different approaches within feminism. One – what I define as 'victim feminism' – casts women as sexually pure and mystically nurturing, and stresses the evil done to these 'good' women as a way to petition for their rights. The other, which I call 'power feminism', sees women as human beings – sexual, individual, no better or worse than their male counterparts – and lays claim to equality simply because women are entitled to it. Victim feminist assumptions about universal female goodness and powerlessness, and male evil, are unhelpful in the new moment for they exalt what I've termed 'trousseau reflexes' – outdated attitudes women need least right now. The reactionary reflexes of this feminism are understandable; feminists have been faithfully tending the fires for all women – including those most victimized – during the backlash years, with little thanks and more than their share of abuse. Given these conditions, it is not surprising that one narrow but influential strand of feminism has tried to help women survive the retrenchment by turning suffering into a virtue, anonymity into a status symbol, and marginalization into a mark of the highest faith. While we can sympathize with those who need this approach when times are bad, we must also realize that it proves dangerous when times change.

Victim feminism is obsolete because female psychology and the conditions of women's lives have both been transformed enough so that it is no longer possible to pretend that the impulses to dominate, aggress, or sexually exploit others are 'male' urges alone. I will discuss why it is both empowering and moral for women to look honestly at the 'dark side' within them, emerging now into light.

Part Four, 'Towards a New Psychology of Female Power', asserts that our new opportunities will be wasted unless we develop a vision of femininity in which it is appropriate and sexy for women to use power. The fragility of many women's self-esteem means that we might fail to attribute the genderquake to our own will and strength. And the penalties that many women associate with the use of power keep us convinced that leadership, or even winning, is not 'really worth it'.

I will look at how girlhood social organization leads us into a situation in which, in Gloria Steinem's phrase, 'Men punish the weak while women punish the strong.' Each of us, I believe, has a regal, robust, healthily self-regarding 'will to power' that has been submerged. I will argue that little girls start out with much more than the pre-adolescent 'authenticity' that researchers such as Carol Gilligan and Lyn Mikel Brown have pinpointed; they start out with a desire to rule the world. I will look at how we can retrieve that wild child – the inner *bad* girl – in order to embrace those qualities of leadership and sexual self-possession, and the solid sense of entitlement that we are conditioned to disavow in ourselves, and to resent in other women.

The final section, 'What Do We Do Now? Power Feminism in Action', demonstrates that the feminist successes of the genderquake era have embraced the use of money, the electoral process and the mass media, and rejected a rigid, exclusive ideology. These successes point the way to a flexible feminism for the 1990s that can reclaim the majority.

I will propose specific strategies to make pro-woman action

something that is effective, populist, inclusive, easy, fun, and even lucrative. Rather than relying on 'converting' mainstream women into a subculture that can sometimes feel as if it is for activists only, this approach brings the movement smoothly into most women's – and men's – everyday activities.

It is my passionate hope that these ideas can spark debate about how to close the gap between those women and men who long for gender equality, and the only movement that can win it for us. Only by closing this gap can we consolidate the clout of the un-labelled resurgence of power feminism that has already rocked our world.

Part One

The Decline of the Masculine Empire: Anita Hill and the Genderquake

Chapter One

Fault Line

Those who study earthquakes know that they are not sudden, unpredictable events, but the result of aeons of silent tectonic pressure. The events that exploded with the Anita Hill hearings in Washington in October 1991 were the result of pressure that had been building up for years.

For a decade and a half, American women's anger had been driven underground, to smoulder under the weight of the Reagan–Bush years of reaction. But while that weight kept the lid on their anger, women's psychology was changing rapidly, even as masculine power was beginning to erode.

Anita Hill's testimony merely ripped open existing chasms, driving the continental plates of gender assumptions against one another, freeing locked-up energy and bringing down landslides. As the quake subsides, we find we inhabit a new landscape that we have yet fully to understand. The story is now engraved on the international psyche as surely as the Boston Tea Party or the Tiananmen protests – like any myth of origin for the turning point of an insurrection.

As the hearings preceding Clarence Thomas's confirmation to US Supreme Court drew near, rumours circulated in Washington: a young woman, it was said, had been sexually harassed by the nominee when she was his associate at the Equal Employment Opportunities Commission a decade before. On 10 September 1991 the hearings to confirm Judge Thomas began. On 12 September, according to Timothy Phelps in *Capitol Games*, Anita Hill, a law professor at the University of Oklahoma, telephoned Harriet Grant, the committee's nominations counsel. Hill told the story of what she alleged had happened during her time at the EEOC, and gave Grant the name of her friend, Susan Hoechner, now a judge in California, to whom she had described her difficulties. She was assured that her statement would be given to members of the committee, but that her name would be kept confidential.

The hearings proceeded. When, after six days had elapsed, Thomas had ended his testimony and no one had contacted Hill, Judge Hoechner spoke to the committee and assured them she could vouch for Hill's charges. On Friday 20 September, the final day of the hearings, the FBI was asked to investigate. Hill would have to come forward. On Monday, 23 September, she agreed to do so, and faxed a four-page statement to the committee.

On Wednesday, 25 September, Senator Strom Thurmond, on behalf of the Republicans, decided to ignore the report. Senator Biden scheduled a committee vote for Friday, leaving no time to examine Hill's charges. On Friday, 27 September, after having seen Hill's sworn statement, Biden declared, 'For this senator, there is no question with respect to the nominee's character, competence, credentials or credibility.'

But by 6 October, Timothy Phelps, a reporter, had tracked down Hill and run the story in *Newsday*. Nina Totenberg interviewed Hill for National Public Radio. On 7 October, Hill herself held a press conference in Oklahoma, which was broadcast by CNN. The senators were outraged – not by the charges, but by the leak.

But then the phones began to ring. Senator Daniel Patrick Moynihan's office was deluged by 3,000 infuriated calls; indeed, enraged constituents barraged every senator's switchboard. The Senate phone network could not handle the number of calls. By early Tuesday, the place was in turmoil. Belatedly, the senators moved to delay the vote.

This is Phelps and Winternitz's account of the palace insurrection:

> At lunchtime, seven congresswomen marched from the House side of Capitol Hill ... [and] climbed the steep steps to the Senate. The Senate Democrats, fifty-six men and one woman, were having their weekly luncheon and could not be disturbed. Twice the women of the House knocked on the closed door of

the luncheon room, and twice they were shooed away ... Undaunted, the congresswomen – led by Louise Slaughter of New York and Patricia Schroeder of Colorado – marched over to the office buildings in search of senators to lobby. Women staffers came out into the hallways and shouted encouragement to the representatives on their mission in the bastion of male power. 'Right on! Right on!' they yelled.

The vote was delayed, Professor Hill testified, the hearings were televised, and the balance of power as it relates to gender changed, possibly for good. The 'story' of sexual harassment and how men and women saw it differently shook the country; the 'he said/she said' dialogue went national.

We may never know the truth or falsehood of what was alleged in the hearing room, but what is certain is that something critical to the sustenance of patriarchy died in the confrontation, and something new was born. The sight of a phalanx of white men – notably Senators Arlen Specter, Alan Simpson, Orrin Hatch and Joseph Biden – showing at best blank incomprehension, and at worst a cavalier, humiliating disregard for women's reality and testimony, was a revelation to the nation's women of the barrenness of democracy without female representation, as well as being an unmasking of male authority.

During the McCarthy hearings, Joseph Welch, who represented the Army, stood up to the Senator and said, 'Have you no sense of decency, sir, at long last? Have you no sense of decency?' The whole room stood still, and then everything was changed. The power of the witchhunts began to evaporate at that moment, even as the Senator was still speaking. In terms of the aura of patriarchy, the 1991 hearings served the same purpose.

The following two years were rocked by unprecedented struggles over gender issues, notably the William Kennedy Smith rape trial, the Mike Tyson rape trial, and the scandal of the Tailhook Convention, at which Navy men, after watching pornographic videos, sexually assaulted Navy women. The rage of insulted women ricocheted from the headlines to produce political repercussions, which came to be known as 'the Anita Hill effect'.

Elections 1990s-style

In 1992 record numbers of women ran for office in the US elections, many of them because of anger at the hearings. Retaliation was an open, palpable theme. The Democratic Senator Brock Adams withdrew from his race after eight women went to the press with accusations of sexual harassment. He was succeeded by Patty Murray, who called herself 'the mom in tennis shoes', an ironic riposte to a putdown from a male legislator who had told her, 'You can't change anything, you're just a mom in tennis shoes.' Lynn Yeakel, a newcomer, fought for Arlen Specter's seat in Pennsylvania, campaigning on an explicit platform of anger at Hill's treatment; her opponent had been one of Hill's most heavy-handed interrogators. Senator Alan Dixon of Illinois, who had turned away from his party to vote for Thomas, found himself beaten by a former county recorder of deeds, an African-American woman named Carol Moseley Braun. Californians Barbara Boxer and Dianne Feinstein both used pro-Hill campaign literature to beat their male opponents, 'who were reduced,' as Phelps put it, 'to arguing that they had better feminist credentials than the women candidates'. Women voters nationwide followed the campaigns of the newcomers with the intensity born of a mood of retribution.

The genderquake rattled and reoriented the presidential election. Throughout the campaign, the figure of Hillary Rodham Clinton, the Democratic front-runner's lawyer/activist wife, became a central symbol of the convulsion, a symbol to be used both by her supporters and her detractors. The press, early on, was still unaware of how far-reaching the effects of the genderquake were to become. So the media tended to put the Governor of Arkansas' wife in a harsh light, reiterating that 'the country was not yet ready' for a First Lady who was a prominent attorney. 'For better or worse, an awful lot of Americans have taken a negative image away from their experiences with her. How do you explain that?' Bryant Gumbel asked on the *Today* show, inadvertently providing the explanation himself. Barbara Bush, with her more traditional persona, was treated with relative warmth.

This media misjudgement of the intensifying anger among

women led the Republicans into a grave tactical error: they took their own female supporters for granted. They interpreted Republican women's political orientation from a male point of view, and failed to understand that conservative politics does not mean that a woman is willing to be treated with disrespect. From a woman's point of view, the seriousness of sexual harassment cuts across party lines, as does the wish to be heard by one's representatives. The Republicans' failure to listen to Republican women may have cost them the White House; throughout the campaign, polls showed Bush scoring lower with women than with men.

The bungling of gender issues within the Republican camp moved into a critical phase with the summer campaign. By then, it was evident even to Republicans that the country was poised for a major Zeitgeist shift, and that the gender issue was the major faultline. But they chose the wrong side upon which to stand. They made their appeal to men – or rather to that group of men, the political 'patriarchalists', who were most threatened by the inroads being made into their domain. They cast the Houston Convention as a referendum on patriarchy, and lost.

Their strategists represented the Republican party as the last line of defence against the invading hordes of those who would level the traditional gender hierarchy. The tone had been set by Dan Quayle's 'family values' speech, which attacked TV's fictional single mother Murphy Brown. Misreading the press warmth towards Barbara Bush and hostility to Hillary Rodham Clinton as a reflection of the feelings of the electorate, rather than as a reflex of the male-dominated press, they cued their themes to that contrast, and did not understand that a significant proportion of Republican women – such as those who joined Ann Stone's group, Republicans for Choice – saw their own lives reflected more fully in the lives of the Arkansas governor's wife and of TV's Murphy Brown, than in the lives of Barbara Bush and Marilyn Quayle.

Right-wing commentator Patrick Buchanan laid out the battle lines with his convention warning of a 'cultural war', spearheaded by 'feminists' (like Hillary Rodham Clinton). Reacting belatedly to the Democratic Convention's well-received showcasing of women leaders, the Republicans condescendingly trotted out their wives. Marilyn Quayle, the Vice-President's wife, a lawyer by training, made the disastrous misstep of appearing to attack mothers who held jobs, and stressed that women did not wish to be liberated from their 'essential natures' as women. Unfortunately for the Bush camp, no more sensitive nerve than the guilt experienced by working mothers – Republicans as well as Democrats – could have been found. Mrs Quayle could not have done more damage even if she had struck deliberately.

Clumsier still, Republican strategists depicted George Bush as the reassuring arch-patriarch, the promised redeemer of the Masculine Empire that was losing its stronghold. The President was actually blessed on television by a Greek Orthodox patriarch with a flowing beard, while Bush's children, grandchildren and conspicuously supportive, non-professional wife were massed around him.

By playing these cards, the Republicans were addressing themselves to the patriarchalists' deepest fears, while trusting the women of the party to remain docile.

Male blindness to the reality of women leads to faulty politics, and the Bush White House went down largely because it paid too little attention to its female constituents, and because it neglected to notice what was on daytime talk shows which women, including millions of traditional homemakers, were watching. Commentators pointed out that in 1992, in a departure from earlier years, voters were getting their political information directly from candidates who were bypassing the traditional news media by going to radio phone-in shows and on TV. But this thesis failed to account for the enormous socio-political influence on women viewers of shows like *Oprah* or *Donahue*. For years, while the male strategists were looking elsewhere, these shows had been providing a forum for the deconstruction of the patriarchal family. In spite of the opprobrium heaped upon them, despite their tendency to individualize social problems, these shows did more to bring the feminist issues of incest, and violence against women and children into the consciousness of the mainstream – and to frame them as intolerable wrongs rather than life as usual – than the entire feminist activist community could manage to do. The talk shows also raised the sense of political entitlement of the ordinary woman by doing something unique to our cultural institutions: they treated the opinions of women of all classes, races and educational levels as if they matter, and as if the dissent among women about 'women's issues' matters too. That daily act of listening, whatever its shortcomings, made for a revolution in what women were willing to ask for; daily these shows conditioned otherwise unheard women to believe that they too were entitled to a voice.

By the time the Republicans made their pitch for the patriarchal family, the entire country of *Oprah*-watching women knew exactly what the injustices and dangers of that family structure looked like. As many Republican as Democrat women had experienced sexual harassment, domestic violence, paternal abdication, non-existent child support payments. They were unlikely to be led blindly by appeals to the glory of the patriarchal family and social structure. The Republicans, obviously, lost.

Bill Clinton, in contrast, understood the genderquake with more sophistication. He pitched to the 'egalitarians', male and female. He presented his wife as a respected partner: 'You do not have to tear a woman down to build a man up.' In his acceptance speech at the Convention he made history by using the image of a young *girl* as his central metaphor, and he thanked female mentors and teachers. He also, of course, championed abortion rights. Responding to his tactics, women voted to elect him, finally, by a slightly higher percentage than did men: 46 per cent to 41 per cent. In the presidential election, women were 54 per cent of the voting public. Many analysts now agree that abortion and social issues played a crucial role in the outcome, leading pro-choice Republicans to defect from their party.

This genderquake is not just a US phenomenon, although the US is the epicentre. It is ripping at the seams of power structures worldwide. In October 1991 John Major, the UK Prime Minister, launched Opportunity 2000 to increase the proportion of senior public appointments held by women; in the same year he launched a Citizen's Charter for women; Neil Kinnock, then the leader of the opposition Labour party, promised to outdo him by creating a Ministry for Women; Labour MPs are now required to vote for at least three women in the annual Shadow Cabinet elections; and the party whips on both sides have been eagerly packing their women MPs on to the benches most visible to the TV cameras, as a way to woo women voters. Why the abrupt flurry of respect? The nervousness in the UK follows from the same shift that caused the quake in the US; as the *Guardian* put it, 'The fact that male politicians have suddenly discovered feminism is, of course, related to the imminence of a general election at which women voters will outnumber men.' The UK version of Emily's List was immediately castigated by opposition politicians as 'yet another example of designer socialism'.

In Australia Paul Keating won the 1993 election because he took women's issues seriously. A year before the general election, in May 1992, a Morgan poll showed that Keating was unpopular with 59 per cent of women voters. At a time when 87 per cent of Australia's one-parent families (a tenth of all families) are headed by a woman, when women make up 41 per cent of the Australian workforce, when 33 per cent of small businesses are owned by women, women in Australia were angry about his apparent lack of attention to the issues that directly concerned them: childcare, health insurance and equal pay. Several pre-election commentators warned that women might well cast their vote on childcare concerns alone. To rectify the situation, Keating immediately appointed as his adviser on women's issues Dr Anne Summers, ex-editor of *Ms.* magazine (now editor of *Good Weekend* magazine) and the architect of the Hawke government's pioneering sex discrimination and affirmative action legislation. He launched a women's policy, a $630 million childcare package, a $30-a-week payment for women who stay at home to look after their children, a Medicare rebate for bone density tests to provide advance warning of osteoporosis, and an injection of cash for women's organizations to lift their operational grants to a total of $1 million. He talked about equity, access and a fair deal. As feminist writer Dale Spender summed up: 'Paul Keating went out for the women's vote. He got it. He won.' In his victory speech, Keating gave 'an extra special vote of thanks to the women of Australia'.

In Ireland, three years earlier, Mary Robinson, a barrister, long involved with women's rights campaigns and outspoken defender of abortion, divorce and the rights of single mothers, had become, in November 1990, the first woman President in Irish history. As she said in her acceptance speech, 'I was elected ... above all, by the women of Ireland ... Instead of rocking the cradle, they have rocked the system.'

While parties elsewhere courted women and won, in Britain the Labour party could not get its message across to women and lost the 1992 election. Its redistributive tax proposals and benefits, targeted at women voters, hardly entered public debate. As journalist and author Beatrix Campbell commented: 'One of the more eccentric features of the general election was that while women were perceived to be precious, their issues and priorities were irrelevant.'

In Canada, Defense Minister Kim Campbell became the first woman Prime Minister of that country in 1993, campaigning on a platform of 'the politics of inclusion'. As in the United States, the stage had been set by a high-profile 1991 rape trial. After a controversial acquittal in a rape trial, Canadian women raised an outcry that Canadian rape laws did not adequately protect them. Campbell, then Minister of Justice, pushed to remove sex bias in criminal laws, and proposed changes in the criminal code that made it easier to convict rapists.

In her 1993 campaign, her supporters were swept up in a wave of 'Campbellmania'. An older stateswoman, Flora MacDonald, who had run for the leadership of the Tory party 17 years before only to find the voters unready for a woman leader, publicly supported the younger candidate. 'Many Tories were worried,' explained one report, 'that if they rejected another woman, the party would be fatally branded.'

Campbell's opponents played the losing 'patriarchalist' card much as the US Republicans had tried to do. In the final days of the hotly contested campaign against male challenger Jean Charest, anti-Campbell partisans raised insinuations about Campbell's 'stability' and drew attention to Charest's attractive wife and children to show up Campbell's status as a twice-divorced childless woman. In her victory speech, Campbell confronted the backfired allegations by Charest's supporters that Canada might not be prepared for a female Prime Minister: to a mass of waving pink signs reading 'Kim!' in feminine cursive, she avowed that 'Our choice as a party is clear: We can respond to the winds of change or we can be swept away.' To laughter at a meeting of her female supporters, she remarked, 'There's a Chinese proverb that women hold up half the sky. Yeah, the heavier half.'

In Norway, with its female Prime Minster, Gro Brundtland, 7 of 17 ministers are female and 50 per cent of the police force is female. An Equal Status Act was passed to ensure that 40 per cent of all public boards are made up of women. In 1990 Dr Carmen Lawrence became the first state premier in Australia. In Canada, pressure from women led to the Pay Equity Act which ensures that women are paid comparable worth for the work they do. In Turkey, Tansu Ciller, whose husband took her last name, became leader of the governing coalition, and the country's first female Prime Minister, on a platform that stressed her commitment to promote women's rights. In Italy, there has been a revival of feminism following proposals to tighten abortion laws, the news of Bosnian women's rapes and the suggestion that married women should accept social security payments in lieu of jobs. In Spain in 1992, the main opposition leader, Jose Maria Aznar of the People's Party, brought his wife, Ana Botella, a lawyer and civil servant in her thirties often compared by the press to Hillary Rodham Clinton, into the limelight to try to catch the reflected glow of 'the Hillary factor.' In Sweden, the high-powered feminist networking group *Stödstrumporna* (Support Stockings), led by writer and campaigner Maria-Pia Böethius, has the ear of all the main political parties and their criticisms of government policy make front-page news. In Uganda, an unexpected spin-off from Uganda's AIDS epidemic is that women are establishing a place for themselves in what has always been a male-dominated society: the Uganda Association of Women Lawyers (UAWL) has started a vociferous campaign for women's rights, from inheritance to domestic violence.

Worldwide we are challenging the media, the academy and the law. Australian women put male judges on trial, where they were found guilty of gender bias in rape cases; Irish women have begun to overturn centuries of Roman Catholic dogma to allow women in Ireland the right to have abortions; Danish women voted against the Maastricht treaty at the first referendum to ensure that their maternity rights and abortion facilities would be safeguarded; British women demanded and gained the right for divorced women to be included in their ex-husbands' pension benefits.

What made the genderquake years different from all the years, even the 'years of the women', that came before it? There have been outrages and scandals in the past as well. It was not the chain of scandals that was unusual – rape and sexual harassment are routine facts of life for women. What made them different was that, for the first time, the distribution of power into some women's hands reached critical mass.

Chapter Two

The Decline of the Masculine Empire

Women's clout reached that critical mass just as the empire that made men – and white men in particular – a ruling elite was sinking into deeper and deeper eclipse. In our commitment to women, feminists – Susan Faludi, Marilyn French and others – have been documenting a war, or 'backlash', against women.

But that analysis is incomplete without a corresponding understanding of the war against men. Women commentators have cast women's incursions as small and the backlash as a disproportionately extreme reaction: 'Women have not hurt or deprived the people who lead the backlash,' wrote psychologist Jean Baker Miller in 1986; Faludi, too, sees the 'backlash' as out of proportion to women's minute inroads.

In frustration at moving ahead so slowly and even sliding back, women tend to misunderstand how grave a threat to men's real power are their claims. But men do not underestimate women's power. The 'backlash' is an eminently rational, if intolerable, reaction to a massive and real threat. We are not simply experiencing a 'war against women' in which women are unthreatening victims. We are in the midst of a civil war over gender, in which there is not one side waging battle but two, unevenly matched though they may be. It is also a war against men.

The language of female progress often merges power-sharing in relationships with power-sharing at the highest level of politics, and presents the issue as a no-lose situation: 'Why don't they understand we just want to share? Equality makes the world better for men as well as women.'

But seizing legislative and economic power is not the same as getting help with the dishes. While equal partnership in heterosexual relationships is surely an advantage for both concerned, we are kidding ourselves if we refuse to recognize the gravity of what parity for women really means to men in political and economic terms. *Newsweek* commentator Eleanor Clift said that the situation 'is as serious as South Africa: men are being asked to share power'. She is right to choose so serious an analogy, but she still understates the case; men are not being asked to 'share' power, the way, in a good marriage, they are being asked to 'share' the housework. They are being forcefully pressed to yield power. The recent recognition of women is being interpreted by women as 'respect at last' – a friendly offering. Unused to the weight of power, women are largely overlooking the base note of fear.

Evidence that female power has turned a corner, and that 'the opposition' is far more clear about the situation than women are themselves, is provided in David Brock's 1993 account of the Thomas–Hill hearings, *The Real Anita Hill*, which used debatable evidence to try to demolish Hill's reputation. Ironically, the book provides a sharper and more persuasive account of women's new political power than a feminist writer could have achieved. Brock paints an ominous picture of a 'Shadow Senate' of feminists and their sympathizers. He offers a scenario in which Hill was 'induced to file a complaint by Senate staffers and interest group partisans who wanted to defeat the nomination regardless of the charge's truth or falsehood, and then "outed" Hill when the plan did not work'. He refers to feminists and to Hill's supporters as 'the opposition'; he describes the heads of the National Abortion Rights Action League and the various other groups that mobilized on Hill's behalf as 'deeply hidden operatives'; in his view, the dark forces of 'the feminist groups that demanded a public inquiry on the basis of no evidence' were joined by 'the media' which 'also helped to whip up the feminist frenzy'. Less than two years after backlash theorists were called paranoid, conspiracy-minded and delusional for describing a war against women's rights, Brock has developed a detailed conspiracy theory in which feminists at the highest levels wage war against men's rights. And he is not altogether far from the truth, for he is describing, though with the shadings of a patriarchal nightmare, the first time that women's political power has worked with such efficiency.

Why would Brock go to the trouble of amassing enormous amounts of debatable evidence – allegations of sexual obsessiveness among others – to destroy Hill's credibility? Why would conservative organizations like the Olin Foundation help underwrite the project? Because these men and organizations understand the conflict and all that is at stake. The book is not motivated merely by the desire to clear the name of a potentially wronged man. Brock himself provides the motivation. He details in consternation, much as I do in celebration, the broad advances made by women as a result of 'the Anita Hill effect'. Those who believed Anita Hill, he writes, 'took up the banner in a broader cultural conflict'. A mere two years before the right wing would not have had to go to this trouble to prevent women from taking up certain banners.

What is provoking this new level of defensiveness? What is there for those who endorse male power to be afraid of? A great deal. Right now, the continuing pro-male sex discrimination means that white men receive a mighty unearned power bonus: a fifth to a third more income than women across the board, four times the representation in state government in America, ten times the representation in the House of Commons in Britain and the House of Representatives in Australia, five times the representation in the European Parliament, almost total ownership of the US Senate and the House of Lords, odds of 93 to 7 in their favour for getting to the top of business and legal circles, and, as we shall see, an 76–24 advantage in the struggle for recognition in the press – not to mention the opportunity to cede home responsibilities to women. Truly equal opportunity for women slashes away at those advantages. Who would willingly embrace the loss of advantages such as men enjoy?

Feminists refer to sexist culture as 'reflecting the figure of man at twice its natural size', in Virginia Woolf's phrase, and women often see political parity as something that should be welcome to men, refocusing them on a friendly and realistic human scale, closer to that of women. But when women criticize men's hoarding of power, we rarely concede that, given the same conditioning, any woman would also be convinced that twice her natural size is an appropriate reflection. Any tampering with that reflection would not feel like an adjustment for clarity, but an unjust diminution of scale.

Much female despair of men comes from seeing male sexism as men's personal desire to 'oppress' women. While male dominance is undoubtedly oppressive, and while many men do take personal satisfaction in wielding power oppressively over women, the greater truth is that the majority of the 'oppressors' are simply protecting what they have. When we understand the nature of power, and when women acknowledge our own will to power, men's resistance to women's equality looks every bit as unjust, but less intimately infuriating. Misogyny is all too real; but a lot of sexism, seen in this light, is not the stubbornness of a pig or the oppressiveness of a born monster, so much as the basic logic of politics, a natural human response to a threatened and real loss of status. If the roles were reversed, women would certainly exhibit the same response.

The Crucial Percentage

Those men who are panicking are rightly apprehensive. Though almost all discussions of 'women's equality' presume that the goal of the struggle is 50/50 representation, this assumption is not based on demographic reality. It is actually an arbitrary number in most Western democracies, for the true figures for parity are the terrifying 51 per cent to 49 per cent in the USA; 51.2 per cent to 48.8 per cent in the UK; 51.3 per cent to 48.7 per cent in Europe as a whole.

If voting trends continue, American women will have 10–12 million more votes than will men; according to the Bureau of the Census they now have 7 million more. Throughout the 1980s exit polls showed a gender gap in both statewide and national elections. In most elections, a 2 per cent advantage, a potential voting bloc of 7 million, means that that side wins.

Once we see the significance of the female balance of power, another pattern becomes evident. It is naïve to hope that 'in a matter of time' women will 'be equal'. At the current rate of increase for government representation in America, women will have parity with men in just 342 years. If we trust to 'progress', women will languish in the low forties of representation for ever. For anti-feminists are no fools. There are already signs that even when there is no justification for it, a careful imbalance of power, in the form of the crucial few percentage points, is maintained.

When there is no good reason not to represent women in a demographically accurate way, the opposition routinely under-represents them. Advertisers use a formula for a 'mixed group' shot of three men to two women – they say that *if the numbers are equal, it looks as though women predominate*. This is exactly the insight that images of equal numbers of women will unavoidably inspire: the realization that they do predominate, and that, in political and consumer terms, the ball is in their court.

The *New York Times* 'person in the street' stories are almost invariably slanted towards men. 'Children of the Shadows', a series on the plight of inner-city teenagers, a group both sexes of which society considers equally unimportant, featured six boys and four girls. Women, Men and Media cites a journalist Sidney Blumenthal in a conference on women in the media saying that 'women's issues' 'are ones that can benefit not just women, but the majority of Americans'. In Britain the BBC sets 'equal' opportunity targets – of 30 per cent of women in senior management and 40 per cent in middle management positions by 1996. The number of women professors at Oxford remains at 3 per cent when nationally the university average has risen to 5 per cent. Yale admission numbers for women hover, unchanged for a decade, three to six points just under parity. Women in the British Civil Service make up nearly half of 'fast stream' applicants, one of the most important avenues to the top grades, but fewer than a third of those selected. 'Patriarchalists' in power routinely refer to 'women' as a special interest, or refer to 'women and minorities' as if women were a minority. There is a comically convoluted effort to keep women thinking of themselves as a small and tangential group; to keep women, in short, from even beginning to consider the implications of their majority status, and the minority status of men.

The female mind colludes in maintaining this mythology. There is just as strong and unconscious an effort by women as by men to sidestep the fact of women's majority status. Women are working like hell to avoid knowing that we are in charge. Even feminist organizations go along with this comforting fiction: 'The Feminization of Power' brochure of the Fund for the Feminist Majority is entitled *50/50 by the year 2000*, and its table projecting when women will achieve parity as elected officials stops at that halfway mark.

While men's description of women as a minority is a hopeful conjuring act and a deliberate mystification, women's own attachment to the goal of equality is a polite fiction we tell ourselves, and a symptom of women's fear of their own power as a majority. As we so often adjust our expectations downwards in a demonstration of a sort of feminine political delicacy, one woman in a Ms. Foundation study, 'Women's Voices '92', when presented with the phrase 'First woman president', responded, 'I'd settle for a woman vice-president.'

I understand this reflex. Merely looking at the true figures of 51/49 fills me with anxiety, makes me wish on a deep, subconscious level to bury them away. Like most women, I have learned to visualize political interaction with men in personal terms; I want to be equal partners, and no more. Whenever the crucial 2 per cent is mentioned, this is what I unconsciously do with it: I give it away in my head. I wave it off, waive it, like the offer of an after-dinner mint, in a gesture that I think of as gracious. In effect, I immediately give it back to men as a peace offering, for I do not want to be in charge; I don't want men to worry that they are dependent on my power. ('I don't want to run the world,' says the Virginia Slims model. 'I just want to take it for a little ride.')

Women's claim to parity does not just represent an immediate doubling of the competition and halving of the positions of power available to men. It goes even further. Accurate as is Susan Faludi's insight – that men fear feminism because they fear the loss of the breadwinning role – that loss is only one of a hail of blows raining down on the Masculine Empire. While that loss dislodges man from his position as ruler of the home, other events combine with it to dislodge him from a place he has occupied throughout recorded history: his position at the centre of the universe, his position, in metaphor if not in fact, as ruler of the world. The astronomer Copernicus provoked a hostile reaction when he said that the sun does not revolve round the earth. A shift of Copernican proportions is taking place around men as they lose the centrality of their gender.

Twilight of the Gods

'A few more old fat bald men wouldn't hurt the place.'
(Marlin Fitzwater on the Clinton administration)

Over the last twenty years women have infiltrated every male cultural or political domain. The building site and the boardroom were breached; then female academics questioned men's central role in the canon; female athletes are gaining on male records and may even match them in our lifetime; women soldiers have challenged man's identity as warrior; in the Church of England, women won the right to be ordained, overturning 2,000 years of tradition; female theologians have even questioned the maleness of God.

Men are seeing their empire crumble; their world is indeed dying. Feminist colleagues will laugh at this assertion and point to the unmoving structure of male dominance. But we are at a point where men, and especially the traditional elite of white men, have lost their *authority* before they have lost their *power*. And, in an unjust system, the loss of authority inevitably foreshadows the loss of power.

Men know their empire is threatened, and they are fighting for their lives, or the lives to which they are accustomed. As they would for heirs of any lost empire, no matter how unjust its foundations or how cruelly run its colonies, the old order's obsolete social forms and rituals of entitlement are taking on, in the eyes of men, a wild glamour, and provoking a fierce nostalgia akin to the nationalism of a people entering exile.

In *Male and Female*, anthropologist Margaret Mead found that in pre-industrial societies, when women start to do 'men's work', men anxiously stake out some unmarked labour, call that work exclusively male, and redefine it as the act which makes males men and not-women. Mead's findings suggest that such behaviour is a cultural inevitability, one that mirrors the resentment that some women would feel if men took over their habitual roles and territory. If so, this distress deserves insight and maybe even compassion, rather than simplistic mockery and condemnation. If they want dialogue that can move the sexes beyond this crisis, women might want to understand the current retreat of men on an emotional level, even as they mobilize hard against its political fallout. Let us take our share of the empire as swiftly and gently and fairly as possible.

The 'gender civil war' is the undercurrent of most public discourse since the genderquake. Men's resentment at the implications of the genderquake accounts for many of President Clinton's early troubles, as he opened his term by brazenly flaunting his imperfect loyalty to his own gender; a man in power who gives so many posts away to women, and so much power to his wife, must be made an example of. Mythologies of the civil war include the apocryphal scene, passed along as rumour in British tabloids and in *Newsweek*, of Hillary Rodham Clinton's throwing a table lamp at her husband. Articles may run on the President's expensive haircut; or on Hillary Clinton's china patterns; or Speaker of the House of Commons Betty Boothroyd's brief career with the Tiller Girls; on Attorney-General Janet Reno's 'mishandling' of a cult massacre; on Norma Major's appearance; or on 'male bonding' in the armed forces, but the gender civil war is always the true struggle behind the words, the news behind the news.

Patriarchy's foundation has rested for millennia on the unwritten but rigorously enforced rule that women and children keep the secrets of men, and suffer abuse in silent shame. The development that breached the wall of patriarchy in the 1980s and eroded male authority was the success of the victim's-rights movement. As more and more studies confirmed the staggering frequency with which many men beat and rape their wives and girlfriends, and sexually assault children, the myth that such behaviour was exceptional evaporated. The studies documenting these abuses were dramatized by a new development: women and even children began to tell men's secrets.

That wall of secrecy had hairline cracks in the 1970s; by the

1980s, women's disclosures brought it down. Oprah Winfrey and Roseanne Arnold asserted that they were victims of child abuse. In 1989, a Minnesota ruling held that adult survivors of child abuse could bring charges retroactively against their assailants. In 1992, even Miss America declared that she had been beaten by her boyfriend.

As more testimony came out about child abuse and domestic violence, and increasing numbers seemed to implicate the gender as a whole, the more offended grew men who knew themselves to be innocent of wrongdoing, and the more resentful grew men who knew themselves to be guilty. The deeper plunged the status of masculinity, and the more flyspecked grew the aura that had dazzled women into silence and acquiescence for the duration of recorded history.

Male culture is playing out its anxiety about the barbarians at the gate. The tone of a TV review of anchorwoman Connie Chung's first night as co-host of the *CBS Evening News* unconsciously reveals many men's sense of loss of status when a male preserve is breached. After casting Chung as 'Miss Perk' to Dan Rather's 'Mr Serious', and stressing the physical touching between the anchors, Tom Shales of the *Washington Post* described the change in terms that fended off the implications of women's raised status even as they revealed his anxieties. He quoted a comment about Hollywood stars, 'He gave her class and she gave him sex', and applied it to the pairing, barely masking his concern that Rather conferred his male class on Chung's female sex. 'What is also happening . . . is that Rather is diminished by the arrangement and Chung is elevated by it. . .' Finally, Shales's anxiety got the better of him as he focused on the seating arrangements: 'The way their chairs were adjusted, the very tall Rather and the quite short Chung looked of equal height. . . Though Rather's stature in the news business dwarfs Chung's, her camera savvy and pizzazz may make her his equal, perhaps even his superior, in terms of coming across like gangbusters on the air. . . If it is another step in the decline and fall of virtually everything,' Shales concluded gloomily, 'it's probably too small a step to be lavished with much dismay.' In a follow-up review of Chung's first interview, one with the President's brother, Shales laid bare his angst: he accused

Chung of stepping 'over the line' when she reprimanded the interviewee. 'You half expect her,' wrote Shales, 'to start slapping the guy around, or maybe get him in a choke hold of her own.' Shales's belief in 'the decline and fall of virtually everything' and his seeming fear of men taking women's place as battered victims are shared intuitively by many men at the end of the last century that is truly their own.

In Tom Wolfe's 1987 bestseller, *Bonfire of the Vanities*, a sexy dream mistress turns traitor to her white, rich lover while the democratic hordes unseat the Masters of the Universe. In the movie *Falling Down*, Michael Douglas's character finds himself barred from visiting his ex-wife and family because he can no longer afford support payments, and his ex-wife thinks he 'might be' violent. Blasting his way through what is portrayed as a multicultural wasteland, the white man asks, '*I'm* the bad guy? When did *I* become the bad guy?' In *Made in America*, a restaurant scene has a chorus of women and men of various races laughing at Ted Danson's character, a bumbling white guy who has just eaten a ball of Japanese mustard. In an advertisement for Apple Powerbook computers, an African-American waitress laughs uproariously at two grey-suited white guys who are fumbling with a computer. 'Are you *sure* you guys know how to work that thing?' she asks, guffawing.

It is a question that is being asked about white men's management of the world in general. *Time* magazine ran a cover on 'White Male Paranoia: Are They the Newest Victims – or Just Bad Sports?' *Esquire*, that confident bible of white-manliness, ran a cover depicting singer Marky Mark bound, clutching his groin and screaming, as the cover line read, 'It's not easy being the scion of a dying WASP culture when women have more confidence, gay men have more style, and everyone seems to have the right to be angry with you.' The story's author, Lynn Darling, wrote, 'It is the evening of the American male.' Her subject, a prototypical white guy, describes his workplace as a setting 'where a man threads his way through knots of conspiratorial women talking about men, blaming every man for the sins of all men'. Weekend magazines run elegies about baseball – the game of white men's childhood, whose rules they understand.

Men have traditionally assumed the right to create language and define its meaning. Now, men are bemoaning the incursions of the barbarians' literature into the canon. They are astonished to find that the rules have suddenly changed so as to make the very language capable of hanging them. It is as if the rights conferred on Adam at the dawn of creation – the primal male rights to define women and reality in general – are being revoked by a mutinous population intent on the despoliation of Eden.

Masculinity, for so long the uncriticized norm and self-evident ideal against which femaleness was measured and found to fall short, is suddenly, for the first time in history, stripped of its cautionary taboos and itself held forth as an object of general inspection, for female critique. Medical history is the record of clothed men examining naked women and calling their natural processes a problem. Suddenly male dominance and aggression are being blamed for causing heart disease; men's hormonal cycles are being studied, and hormone replacement therapy for male menopause advocated. There is even a growing academic field for the study of masculinity. The power loss implicit in becoming an object of curiosity, rather than the norm, imbues a comment made by a gruff older cock-of-the-walk when he first heard about the notion. 'Masculinity?' he growled. 'It doesn't sound very masculine once you write about it.'

Male sexuality, once cloaked in prohibitions that kept women from making comparisons, is under scrutiny, and the secrets of male virility are on display. Beefcake photos run regularly in women's magazines and the ubiquitous Marky Mark's substantial bulge adorns bus stops. A 1993 study of male sexual habits, the Janus Report, was published to vociferous male criticism; many respondents told the researchers they were having sex ten times a week, data which raised sexual pressure. *Vanity Fair* ran a cover story by Gail Sheehy on how male potency almost inevitably fades over the course of a lifetime.

This sexual scrutiny elicits male responses whose tone would have been unimaginable a mere two years ago: Peter H. Engel, in a letter to *Vanity Fair*, referred to Gail Sheehy's polemical skill as 'dangerous'. Then he emitted a primal wail for lost dominion:

Who created the phenomenal technical advances of the past 50 years, may one ask? Who created the miracles of a global economy? Who fostered the educational, social and medical conditions that made it possible for women to emerge from the tyranny of kids and kitchen and start to take their rightful place among the power elite? Who . . . put a stop, perhaps forever, to wars between nations? Men. Men who are today aging but who remain strong, virile, knowledgeable and wise . . . So what if we cannot always get an erection?

With that not quite rousing conclusion, Engel rings in the changes. Men never had to pose such questions before, even rhetorically; nor did they have to publicly defend their sexual capacity.

Certain types of interaction which many men saw as normal ways of relating to their families are being redefined as domestic violence and marital rape. Courtship behaviour that was once deemed acceptable (or at least, those who objected kept quiet about it) now earns men who practise it the epithet 'date rapist'. (In September 1993 a UK solicitor was sentenced to three years' imprisonment for attempted rape of the young woman he had taken to a ball.) Many of the behaviours now under criticism are so embedded in the sense of masculinity learned by many men from infancy on that the thought of excising them must feel like being asked to scrape away a skin. What would be left? What would one be but bleeding, mute, unrecognizable? Is that a man? These developments are a healthy sign of a culture evolution. But we must realize that it is traumatic when the cloak of authority, safe for thousands of years, is ripped from the male body and masculinity's soul.

The inchoate despair and rage in men come from lacking an alternative, positive image of masculinity. There is no fully articulated new male language with which to seek sex and love, feel self-mastery, communicate, have stature among other men, and recognize oneself as a successful member of one's gender.

Part of the collective male imagination – the part that is convinced of the worthiness of making a new kind of manhood – is urgently trying to piece together a composite made up of better images of masculinity. Recent popular movies like *Field of Dreams, A River Runs Through It, Patriot Games, Awakenings,*

The Bodyguard, In the Line of Fire and even *Jurassic Park* all provide a model of the 'good father', and reimagine masculinity as virile strength deployed to defend, protect and parent.

This ideal of manhood substitutes 'responsible stewardship' for dominion. It comprises images as diverse as Vice-President Gore's stance as steward of the environment, and the US Army's deployment to bring food to children in Somalia. But those images, resonant as they are to men who long for a masculine stance that is responsive and connected but not 'wimpy', are still forming. The women's movement had years to examine traditional femininity, and it was clear from early on that women stood to gain far more than they had to lose. Men have only begun to examine traditional masculinity, and the promised rewards for doing so are still faint while the treasures to be lost and the punishment threatened are far more vivid and immediate.

Under this pressure, the world of men is dividing into egalitarians and patriarchalists – those men who are trying to learn the language and customs of the newly emerging world, and those who are determined to keep that new order from taking root. The former group welcomes these changes, seeing that though they are painful in the short term, over the long term they provide the only route to intimacy and peace. But the latter group sees only loss. When I speak about those men and male-dominated institutions that are actively resisting women's advancement, I refer to 'the opposition', because it is neither accurate nor fair to lump all men together as being intent on obstructing women's progress. The civil war of gender does not involve 'men against women' in two distinct sides. The patriarchalists' worldview, shared by women as well as by men, is battling against the emerging egalitarian worldview, which is also shared by people of both sexes. Of course, certain issues will polarize women and men because of their experience and perceptions and needs; and, of course, all men stand to lose a great deal if egalitarianism wins the day. But it is just as foolish to assume that all men are opposed to women's equality as it is to assume that all women are in favour of it.

Many men, perhaps most, waver between being egalitarians and patriarchalists (and most relationships with such men involve learning how to identify this wavering), just as many women waver between the desire for independence and a desire for passivity. Some men are egalitarians at home and patriarchalists at work, or egalitarians with their daughters and patriarchalists with their wives. But many, perhaps most, are groping towards citizenship in the new world and making progress, if in fits and starts, in learning 'how to speak egalitarian'.

The egalitarian men are indeed finding joy in the range of intimacy that the emerging world promises. The US *Redbook*'s 1992 surveys find that more men are citing family at the top of their list of concerns. At the same time, however, patriarchalists are retreating into a maleness beyond the criticism or claims of women. The alumni of Yale's secret society Skull and Bones threatened to put padlocks on the door of their building to keep newly elected women out, and the men of London's prestigious Garrick Club, a traditional bastion of male chauvinism, voted by an overwhelming majority to continue to bar women as members. Finding themselves in a workplace of female colleagues and even bosses, these men are seeking solace in a growth industry that ritualistically puts women back in their place – with topless car washes, topless shoeshines, topless housecleaning, and the burgeoning, suddenly respectable male-guests-only topless clubs. Rush Limbaugh, the rotund American white male talk-show host who calls feminists 'feminazis', has built a media empire consisting of a top-rated radio show, a bestselling book and a TV show. As soon as the egalitarian White House adminstration took over, the fringe figure Limbaugh was crowned with a new status as respectable commentator.

This growing distinction between egalitarian and patriarchalist men was evident even in the depths of the Reagan–Bush years, making the old distinctions of 'left' and 'right' irrelevant in this regard. In 1988 a political survey, *The People, the Press and Politics* described voters under the heading 'Tolerance/Intolerance Coalitions': This breakdown referred to those voters who, the authors believed, were most clearly defined by their attitudes towards the role of women. The authors, Norman Ornstein, Andrew Kohut and Larry McCarthy, determined that 'Moralists, New Dealers and the Passive Poor', totalling 35 per cent of voters, were more likely to agree that 'women should return to their traditional role', and more likely to want to make it more difficult for a woman to get an abortion. Another group, 'Seculars, 60s Democrats and Upbeats', totalling 38 per cent, were more likely to maintain opposite views. This division suggests that the fight for women's rights can no longer be seen simplistically as female versus male.

If women want men to continue the journey into the Egalitarian Era, they will have to establish that it is safe for men to divest themselves of the traditional armour of dominance. The patriarchalists are withdrawing because they realize before women do that women have already begun to 'win', and they are frightened that women will do to them what men have traditionally done to women.

At this notion, many women will laugh in disbelief. How could anyone imagine that women could have that power, let alone that wish? Well, that power is available to them now.

It is because women have begun to use the power of their majority status that we must complete the transition into a gender-fair world swiftly and unwaveringly, but also with absolute fairness to men, with consciousness of women's own capacity for oppressive deeds, and with a cogent set of ethics.

Chapter Three

Genderquake: The Evidence

As men's power was under siege, the power of some women in the professional classes was reconfiguring in newly effective ways. When the Thomas–Hill scandal erupted, a number of professional women used their power in fresh ways, and proved the potency of the emerging female power structure.

NPR reporter Nina Totenberg secured her interview with Hill. Congresswomen marched. Women journalists had the stature to recognize and treat the charges as news. Enough of the feminist political infrastructure had been built, and enough women had garnered the political experience to run for office in greater numbers than before. Other women had enough money and clout to support the candidates' bids for power.

Without the women in the media, all these parties could not have linked up in the unstoppable chain reaction that ushered in the new era. By 1992, 40 per cent of news and editorial workers at American daily papers were female. For general management and administrative staff, the figure was 46 per cent. The female reporters and editors were able to take the newsworthiness of the Anita Hill issue back to the street. Since the hearing was a he-said/she-said situation, the stories had to have a structure unusual in the media – they had to present as many women's opinions as men's. What changed women's sense of their voice was not that they found they had a single opinion, but that their diverse opinions mattered.

Of course, Anita Hill did not prevail. But women felt galvanized. While the media's focus sets national priorities, it is also responsive to the national mood. Women's angry state of mind set the stage for the subsequent trials' coverage being unusually respectful of women's sensibilities. So many readers showed vociferous interest in the various court proceedings and scandals that male editors could not ignore the importance of women's perspectives. The effect radiated outward from there.

This time, enough women had attained enough power so that scattered, unsupported individuals became part of an electrified network. When there are only a few women at the top and the thrust of power is anti-woman, many women must adopt the perspectives of those whose agenda they serve. In dark times, there is a female forgetting of a sense of injustice, since it is too painful to be angry and helpless. But when enough women are in place and the winds shift, we see that women do indeed promote their own interests.

After the hearings and the autumn election, the change in the political atmosphere was sustained. On the political level, women in the USA won one victory after another in what was a storm of woman-sensitive appointments, decisions and legislation, compared with the doldrums of the previous twelve years.

North American women won:

- The Family Leave Act. Passed after a twelve-year battle, this legislation grants parents four months' leave, without pay but with job security, to tend a baby or ill relative.
- The end of the gag rule, and of most of twelve years' worth of anti-abortion legislation.
- A doubled budget for breast cancer research.
- Appointments of women as Attorney-General; head of the Department of Health and Human Services; chair of the Council of Economic Advisers; heads of the Environmental Protection Agency and the Energy Department; Surgeon-General; AIDS czar and ambassador to the UN. The administration, finally, was 37 per cent female.
- The right to fly combat planes. Military advisers concede that the Tailhook scandal, and women's outrage about it, forced their hand in ending the ban.
- The introduction of the anti-stalking bill, which would make stalking women a federal crime.
- A 1993 budget for research on women's health that is double

the budget for 1992, and the inclusion of women subjects in medical research that had previously excluded them.

- The Senate Judiciary Committee's unanimous approval of the Violence Against Women Act, which would bolster penalties for federal sex offences, offer about $500 million of grant money to research attacks against women, and allow victims of gender-based crimes to sue their attackers for civil damages without having to wait for a criminal trial. The committee also provided a study that confirmed that almost half of all rape cases in the US are dismissed without trial, and that nearly half of the rapists convicted spend less than a year behind bars, penalties that are lighter than those for burglary. Senators Biden and Hatch co-sponsored the bipartisan measure and clamoured to voice their support for women ('a landmark bill that should make a difference in our society,' said Hatch). In the interrogation of Professor Hill, of course, Biden and Hatch had represented the two extremes of cluelessness and malice.

- The Senate investigation of Senator Bob Packwood from Oregon, charged with having sexually harassed twenty-three women, an internal inquiry that represents a major departure from traditional boys' club rules.

- Leadership by Deborah Tannen, Professor of Linguistics and author of two bestselling books on the gender divide, of a discussion with Senate members and their wives about gender dynamics.

- The Supreme Court's agreement to decide on whether sex offenders can be required to undergo therapy as a condition of staying out of jail if the therapy requires the offender to acknowledge the guilt denied at trial.

- A Supreme Court justice, Ruth Bader Ginsburg, who made her reputation as a crusader for women's rights and mentor, heroine and role model for feminist lawyers. Called the 'Thurgood Marshall of the women's movement', Ginsburg argued and won the cases that established modern sex-equality law. The judge used her acceptance speech to thank her husband for having done the household chores, and proclaimed that her appointment was significant because 'it contributes to the end of the days when women, at least half the talent pool in our society, appear in high places as one-at-a-time performers'. In her confirmation hearings, she came our strongly in favour of abortion rights.

- The assignment of Lieutenant-Colonel Patricia Fornes as the first woman to command an air squadron. In her acceptance speech, she thanked her female military predecessors who 'took great strides to get us to the point where the United States [Military] can now assign women to combat positions'.

- A new head of the Education Department's Office for Civil Rights, Norma Cantu. Observers predicted that the civil rights office would be more sympathetic to women.

- A strong endorsement of women's rights by Secretary of State Warren Christopher at the Conference on Human Rights. Women's groups pressed for a special international criminal court to protect their rights, a stronger UN role in fighting abuse of women, and the recognition of 'gender perspective' in all human-rights treaties. They won an unprecedented resolution devoted to the 'Equal Status and Human Rights of Women', and the conference called for a UN monitor of violence against women.

- A $264,242 sex-discrimination award to New York City policewoman Karen Sorlucco, who charged another officer with raping her at gunpoint.

- The Dinkins administration's immediate intervention when groups of boys were found to be molesting girls by 'whirl-pooling' around them in city pools.

- An investigation into allegations of sexual harassment of female agents at the Bureau of Alcohol, Tobacco and Firearms.

On the cultural level as well as the political, a hundred thousand fresh images of women taking and using traditionally male power showed which way the new current was flowing. The changes ranged from the lightweight to the profound.

The first woman hockey player, Manon Rhéame, joined the National Hockey League; *Time* magazine had a cover on 'God and Women': 'A second Reformation sweeps Christianity'

('Admission to the priesthood is just one issue as feminism rapidly emerges as the most vexing thorn for Christianity'); the FDA warned diet companies to end their misleading advertising; a Stanford professor was charged with sexual harassment after Dr Frances Conley resigned from the university's Medical School and spoke to the press about her years of harassment by colleagues; *New York Times Magazine* ran a serious cover story on girls in Little League; even Hollywood paid a nervous tribute to 'Women in Film'; 'Equal Pay' badges were displayed in the windows at Bloomingdale's; the Ms. Foundation's 'Take Our Daughters to Work Day' was given national coverage; an in-depth examination of unequal pay appeared in *Ladies' Home Journal* ('It's not only interesting. It's illegal'); a portrait of Ellen Malcolm, guiding light of Emily's List, showed her holding a thick cigar heavenward, cocked at the angle of Franklin D. Roosevelt's well-known cigarette holder; a woman became co-host of a prime-time network news broadcast for the first time, there was a sudden willingness on the part of news magazines to do in-depth stories on women's views of current events; a new talk show, *Equal Time*, featured female pundits; of movies in development for stars like Sharon Stone and Geena Davis, two are about a female pirate and a woman gunfighter, and one is a female-driven Western (the trend, according to the Hollywood wisdom, is due to the belief that 'a woman with a gun in her hand is sexy and therefore potentially big box office'); autumn 1993's American TV show, *My So-Called Life*, is told from the point of view of a 15-year-old girl, and produced by the creators of the retrogressive *thirtysomething*; ABC's *Sirens* is a series about three female rookie cops; in Lifetime TV's drama, a woman general became the first female President; the new women in Congress and Senate were treated as media darlings, their clothes and schedules lovingly chronicled; and the US national media from *Glamour* to *Vanity Fair* to *Time*, ran a feature on the 'Year of the Woman' or the 'Women of the Year'.

Throughout the late 1980s women producers in Britain, like Verity Lambert (producer of *Widows* and *Minder*), Philippa Giles (*Oranges Are Not the Only Fruit*) and Sophie Balhetchet (*The Manageress*), made some of the most popular and innovative programmes. Successful drama series, written by women, have followed, each showing women in strong, independent roles: Lynda La Plante's *Prime Suspect*, starring Helen Mirren as the ambitious Detective Chief Inspector who becomes a target for sexual discrimination, won audiences in their millions as well as several industry accolades; Lynda La Plante also wrote *Seekers*, a two-part drama produced by Sarah Lawson and starring Brenda Fricker and Josette Simon, about two women joining forces to take over their bigamist husband's detective agency; Sophie Balhetchet produced Mary Wesley's *The Camomile Lawn* to great acclaim; Antonia Bird directed Harriet Walter in *The Men's Room* by Ann Oakley; and Lavinia Warner of Warner Sisters maintained her excellent track record of exciting series and real roles for women (*Tenko*, *Wish Me Luck*, *Selling Hitler*) with the hugely popular *Rides*, written by Carole Hayman and exploring the lives of several women running an all-woman minicab company.

Advertising reflected the changes too. DKNY ran a series of ads that followed a woman President to her swearing-in; an ad for the American Medical Association deplored violence against women; an ad for US Healthcare featured Rosie the Riveter: 'She symbolized everything good about American workers'; a Timex ad showed a woman who saved her husband's life by whacking a grizzly bear on the nose and then using her bra as a tourniquet to stop the man's bleeding; a Toyota ad proclaimed the achievements of a female student playwright. Pirelli spent a reported £20 million on a new advertisement starring Sharon Stone appearing to seduce her chauffeur but in fact relegating him to the back seat as she takes over the steering wheel. Even the exhibitors at the 1992 British International Motor Show stopped draping scantily clad models over their cars after a study showed that car sales to women are growing four times faster than sales to men. And after a Lex report confidently forecast women in 37 per cent of supervisory and managerial positions by the year 2000, Citroën launched an executive car with special features for the female driver.

Phallic objects began to appear in ads aimed at women. But these phalluses were *different*. Traditionally, phallic objects in ads are licked, worshipped, or otherwise cosseted by adoring women. But after the genderquake, phallic objects began to emerge, rather startlingly, from women's *own* groins. 'Not Just for Dancing,' proclaimed a Danskin ad of a tough young woman in hip-hop gear and men's jockey shorts, her index finger pointing out from between her defiantly spread-apart legs, her other fingers curled before two shirtcuffs dangling between her thighs. For Matrix skincare, a model in a man's cutaway morning coat and trousers gripped the heavy gold handle of an ebony walking-stick. Virginia Slims put together an entire series of women-sprouting-phallic objects, and ran quasi-feminist tag lines with them. In one, a model holds a fishing line aloft with a tight right-handed grip. The line is attached unquestionably to herself, and projects jubilantly skyward from between spread thighs (bare to the crotch, but encased in thigh-high rubber fishing boots). At the fishing line's base, nestled against her thigh, is a scrotum-sized leather pouch. The sentence, 'Women aren't opposed to a good line – it just all depends on what it's attached to' makes explicit the connection between fishing line and male organ. In another, the model straddles a motorcycle; and in still another, the model plays an enormous electric guitar, its neck projecting up from her crotch area at a 45-degree angle.

It became clear that, while women did not actually want penises, they were fascinated by the drama of women's capture of 'male' authority and power, rather than traditional images of femininity.

It was because of a basic misunderstanding of the difference between this 'male' authority and power and traditionally 'female' revenge, that Vauxhall's £3 million campaign failed to impress the women it set out to woo. The series of advertisements featured several supermodels attacking the new 'supermodel' Vauxhall Corsa in fits of jealousy. The company was inundated with complaints that its advertisements were degrading to women, and the campaign backfired.

The metamorphosis in ad-land went beyond women-with-phalluses to turn on their head conventions about the representation of women that were as old as the industry itself. Kotex showed a heavyset 'real woman' playing baseball, with the caption, 'We know what it means to be a woman.' No-Nonsense pantyhose profiled half a dozen prominent women, including a surgeon, a pilot, a fire chief, a billiards champion, a college dean and a stock-broker. The face of Governor Ann Richards of Texas even appeared inside the 'women's power symbol'. George Lois, the advertising agency chair who created the campaign, said, 'No-Nonsense is synonymous with women who don't take any s——; women who get the job done.' *Cosmopolitan* decided to abandon its trademark, full-length body shots featuring décolletage, in favour of head-shots, and it qualified its trademark phrase 'Cosmo Girl' ('the fun of a girl') with the term 'young woman' ('and the power of a woman'). An ad for Lilyette bras showed a young woman confronting a mirror. The caption read, 'Am I still pretty? . . . And then it hits me. Maybe I'm the one who's unforgiving. And not the mirror.'

In a Bloomingdale's catalogue, the standard Madison Avenue pose of men standing erect with women at their feet was reversed; a woman towered over supine men. Romance novels made a radical reversal of convention when they produced jacket covers with a fully clothed, tempestuous romance heroine bending force-fully over a swooning, beautiful, half-stripped hero. An ad for Versus perfume by Gianni Versace, the designer who had pioneered bondage clothing six months earlier, offered up a model lying confidently backwards astride a huge motorcycle, leaning, as if on furniture, on a half-naked man. The woman was surrounded by the bulging biceps of three other men, their faces hidden, their eyes in shadow; as women's faces and eyes had traditionally been seen in such depictions.

Women's boxing became a fashionable trend, and female boxers often appeared in the US press. A fierce-looking Reebok model pounded a six-foot, cylindrical, rounded-on-top (and even evi-dently circumcised) boxing dummy with her big black Champion gloves. The caption read: 'I believe there's a place where your head, and lungs, and ambition, and drive, do lunch together.' For Revlon's 'Knock Out Eyes', top models brandished even bigger black gloves than their Reebok sister. Supermodel Claudia Schiffer, not a hair out of place, taped up her knuckles, and five of the 'most unforgettable women in the world', who, during the 1980s, had shown the camera expressions of vapid passivity, now posed beside male boxing champion, Sugar Ray Leonard. They peered menacingly at the viewer, and held up their shiny assault mitts, sewn with Revlon logos. Most famously, several manu-facturers of athletics shoes produced immensely popular quasi-feminist ad campaigns: Nike's resonant campaign encapsulated one important face of the genderquake: not that women were ex-pressing a given option, a feminist 'line', but that women were reclaiming the right to voice their own opinions, whatever they might be. The 'I believe' campaign presented list after list of a woman's idiosyncratic convictions, some political, some personal: 'I believe high heels are a conspiracy against women.' Ryka shoes started a campaign – 'Regain One's Self Esteem' – to deliver a share of their profits to help battered women escape domestic violence.

I have heaped up these fragments of evidence, some serious and some, seemingly, superficial, not to suggest that political parties have had a true conversion to feminism, or that ad-land has seen the error of its ways – the same self-interest drives the political machine and the consumer machine as always – but to show that when women begin to speak up about what they want, powerful institutions in the realms of politics and commerce – the very same institutions that manipulated and insulted women without compunction when they were silent – *have* to court them. Look back just a few years, and see, with the historical self-conscious-ness that women are usually denied, how much *better* this sort of accumulation of victories, petty and profound, really feels. If we can bring about changes like these in a spontaneous, unorganized uprising – without really trying – then what could we not do with a concerted, unified effort?

When women look at their unequal status, they wonder, 'What can I do? Nothing really makes a difference.' But the events of the early 1990s have given us many answers to that question. If we look at these political and cultural shifts, we can see how it is pos-sible to make the assertion that women already have the power to bring about the conditions that can begin to secure equality.

The first lesson is that when women voice their opinions, it makes a difference. Obviously, women's groups have been saying this for years. But women as a whole must see from the gender-quake that the conditions of our lives can be drastically changed for the better when we do that simple thing so contrary to female socialization: believe that our viewpoints count. Women might vote as a bloc on certain issues; the gender gap is verifiable. But even if they don't, it's clear that when women rattle the chains across the political spectrum, legislators ignore them at their peril. And it is good for women to be seen, in a bipartisan light, as people whom one has to consult in order to be safe.

The second lesson is anathema to female socialization. Women must own and use the money they have. Emily's List, the Democratic Political Action Committee that provides women candidates with seed money for their campaigns, won women 25 new female leaders for a cost of $6.2 million in 1992. That money was collected from fewer than 100,000 donors. Those 25 new leaders, and the fund-raising capacity behind them, helped create a new climate in America of respect for women as political agents mobilized in our own behalf. How long before the effect of Emily's List is felt in the UK, too?

The simple economics of the genderquake can make the conditions for equality more attainable than we could have dreamed. But women must see that their movement is not something that leads them from above. They themselves, and they alone, must act as the agents of change.

According to the Census Bureau, there are 99,202,000 women in the United States in 1993. (There are 91,338,000 men.) The $6.2 million that has begun so decidedly to change the political landscape works out at less than 7 cents a woman. If a little more than 6 cents per woman won 25 new women leaders, $6 from every adult woman would raise $600 million and earn the political firepower equivalent to 2,500 women leaders.

We could still reach that figure if one woman in two gave $12; one in four gave $24; or one in eight gave $48. For the price of a few pairs of high-quality pantyhose a year, those American women who can afford the $48 could provide themselves, and every woman and girl in America, with a bipartisan war-chest that could provide legislative parity, and a political voice that it would be suicidal to disregard, by the year 2000.

Sometimes history can outpace consciousness. Knowing that

the actions described above are the right ones to take does not necessarily mean women can take them. They require a change in female psychology. The change, though a long way from completion, has begun; certain turning points in female psychology prepared the way for the genderquake.

Chapter Four

A Change in Consciousness: Women Learn to Imagine Triumph

Diana, Sheba and Nike

The genderquake required women to do three things that had long been alien to female consciousness: to fantasize political retribution for an insult to the gender, to claim and use money, and to imagine and enjoy the act of winning.

Women had begun to experiment in bestselling books and movies, with the female uses of retaliation, money and victory. Paradoxically, though, the more passionately mainstream women were trying on these new characteristics, the more determinedly some of the feminist subculture was distancing itself from them.

While mainstream female imagination was investigating images of newfound worldly power, the imagination of feminism was producing exactly the wrong images for the time: images of helplessness, silence, pain and defeat. When it urged women to vote, Lifetime TV in the US used an ad depicting a woman without a mouth. Planned Parenthood solicited money to fight the rule forbidding federally funded clinics from discussing abortion with an ad showing a female doctor with a gag in her mouth (a gag that looked something like a sanitary towel). NOW distributed coathangers for women to carry at pro-choice rallies, as reminders of deaths from illegal abortions. The Fund for the Feminist Majority sent donors tin bracelets engraved with the name of Becky Bell, a teenager who died as a result of a botched abortion. They asked women to wear a bracelet reading, 'Worldwide, One Woman Dies Every Three Minutes', until the anti-choice laws were repealed. Fundraising letters from women's organizations regularly used a scenario of imminent disaster to mobilize their members. In Britain a TV advertisement for Cellnet mobile telephones featured a woman stranded at night at a railway station. As the wind howls menacingly and leaves rustle she pulls a Cellnet telephone from her bag; within seconds her husband drives up to collect her, complete with family dog. The switchboard of the Advertising Standards Authority was jammed with calls from women complaining that Cellnet were exploiting women's fear of being attacked while alone in the dark.

One reason why these images and 'pitches' did not work well, did not capture women's imaginations as new images of power began to capture them, is that images of women being victimized have so often been made 'sexy', and have been used to sell jeans and record albums, that they have lost all impact. Our subconscious can see little difference between Planned Parenthood's gagged young doctor and the Rolling Stones' gagged billboard babe.

But the other reason is far more significant. Women are at a point in history when they are fed up with the reminders of their oppression, and are moved far more effectively by appeals to their strength, resourcefulness and sense of responsibility than they are by appeals to a sense of being without options. For reawakening in the female psyche are new incarnations of female power that have been foreshadowed in old archetypes. These include such archetypes as the goddess Diana, avenger of insult; Sheba, the responsible politically influential sovereign; and Nike, the female spirit of victory. These archetypes embody the alien qualities that women have been learning to master: a willingness to retaliate when offended; the ability and willingness to acquire money and the political influence it buys; and the buoyant and generous spirit that comes from the knowledge of victory.

Just as the individual mind reacts to and recognizes archetypes, so does the collective or political mind. History does not move purely materially or pragmatically; it also moves, today as much as in the past, in response to narratives, dream-images, heroes, heroines and myths. The great leaders are those who know how to tell a story and use symbols that can resonate on the unconscious level as well as make sense of literal circumstances. In this view, an advertisement that shows the swearing-in of a woman President can have as much or more power to advance women's historical progress on the psychic level as can the passage of the Equal Rights Amendment on the political level.

Retaliation: The Diana Principle

In the Graeco-Roman myth of Diana and Actaeon, the Goddess of the Hunt was bathing one day in a wooded clearing, along with her band of attendants. The mortal Actaeon, a hunter, caught sight of the naked Goddess through the trees. Instead of turning respectfully aside, he treated her as he would mistreat a mortal woman: he knelt down beside his hounds to peer at her nakedness. When the Goddess caught sight of the voyeur who had so insulted her, she declared, 'The hunter shall be prey', and turned the hapless man into a stag. Actaeon's faithful dogs – in fact, the master's tools – turned against their master, and dismantled the man himself; unable to recognize the man trapped in the animal's skin, the dogs chased down the metamorphosed voyeur and tore him to pieces.

This bloody retribution fable embodies a truth about those who are continually victimized: if they have any self-respect left intact, there is a deep chord, a wish for retaliation against insult, that will be struck when circumstances let the sufferer recognize and act upon that impulse.

In the genderquake, female revenge fantasies proliferated. In 1991, Callie Khouri's movie *Thelma & Louise* depicted on a wide screen a drawn-out retaliation fantasy, and the shock it caused was extreme. As editorials denounced the famous shotgun blast at the rapist and the scene in which the two female outlaws blow up the truck of a man who harasses them, female audiences were lustily cheering. They were not applauding the violence itself, for gratuitous violence is not the stuff of catharsis. They were cheering the public affirmation of that part of themselves which was not content to just take it, whatever 'it' may be, in silence any longer.

In 1992, another retaliation fantasy was a national bestseller for weeks. In Olivia Goldsmith's *The First Wives Club*, three neglected and humiliated ex-wives of powerful men plot an elaborate and satisfying revenge. One of the husbands has bankrupted his wife, two have been unfaithful, and one has been physically abusive.

Initially, each woman is depressed and self-pitying ('in such pain, disguising their anger with self-destructiveness'): one drinks, one overeats, and one is a martyr ('Annie identified with victims'). The women are galvanized into action by the suicide of a good friend, whose final letter reveals that her husband had often beaten her.

The women form a club – an 'action committee of first wives' – but the warm and fuzzy expectation of a support group 'to come to terms with themselves and their anger' quickly takes the shape of a pragmatic plan. In one scene this group of gentle, self-effacing Ladies Who Lunch reach a dizzying power-feminist analysis of their condition and switch irreversibly into Diana mode:

'There ought to be some kind of retribution, some way to even the score. We have to show society we can't simply be discarded . . .'

'Don't you see? . . . We're leaking. They've punctured us, and we're leaking and dwindling down to nothing. Society says that's just fine and we aren't even standing up for ourselves.'

'We have to *do* something. We have the resources, the brains, the connections, *and* the imaginations. Let's make sure they pay a price . . . They did it to us. We can do it to them. We've got the leverage . . . I say we wipe these dickweeds out.'

'Are we talking about revenge, I mean Death Wish III here, or what?'

'Not exactly revenge. Something more sophisticated, I thought. Like justice.'

As in the Diana story, each decides that the retribution must fit the offence. They pool their resources – money, stockholdings, insider information and social contacts – and use the powerful men's tools to bring down their antagonists. In the process, they find that wielding power agrees with them: the alcoholic stops drinking and takes a young lover, the overeater accepts herself, grows healthy and moves in with her lesbian lawyer; the martyr finds inner satisfaction, and everyone looks great. In the end, the men are humbled and the women triumphant. The moral of the story? 'Those men, those big, powerful, scary men – they weren't so tough or invincible, not when you really looked at the facts. Sure, they ran the courts, the crime, the corporations, but you could ... you could, perhaps, use their own institutions to bring them down.'

Money and Worldly Power: The Sheba Principle

> And when the queen of Sheba heard of the fame of Solomon concerning the name of the Lord, she came to prove him with hard questions.
>
> And she came to Jerusalem with a very great train, with camels that bare spices, and very much gold, and precious stones.
>
> (I Kings 10:1–2)

A wise and powerful woman makes a brief appearance in the Old Testament: The King greets her with respect and honour; her wealth gives her the influence to enter his court – to judge the wisdom of the King, and hold him accountable. The 'wealth' is literal, but it is also metaphorical. Sheba represents the principle of female material power and politics.

Women lack a positive emotional vocabulary about money. While many of the great stories about men are stories about the romance between men and riches, women have very little narrative relationship to the idea of wealth, or the drama of seeking, building or losing a fortune. During the backlash years women began to fantasize about money in a way that was not a literal fixation on acquiring cash, not crude greed or materialism, but rather an important psychological investigation of the expanded sense of personal importance, choice, mastery and psychic empire-building that money symbolizes. While socialist feminists were holding the marketplace in contempt, mainstream female dreamwork was focused with excited attention on its challenges and dramas. Until recently, the main story formula for women's pop culture was that of the young woman whose marriage to a wealthy man raises her to riches. This is the story of Cinderella, Jane Eyre, and innumerable Mills & Boon romances. Indeed, the heroine's modest origins and the hero's wealth are laid out explicitly in the traditional romance formula guidelines.

But that old story of elevation through marriage has started to change. A new main theme underlay the favourite female dramas of the 1980s and early 1990s – female mastery of riches, of triumph in business, and mastery of the conditions in which one's work is done.

There are precedents for the themes that surfaced in the genderquake. The favourite female fantasy of the modern age in the West – Margaret Mitchell's popular epic, *Gone with the Wind* – pits the angelic victim Melanie against the powerful, bad-girl Scarlett. Melanie is self-effacing and asexual – 'She's a saint and won't see bad in anyone' – and we can't stand her; Scarlett is vain, sexy, power-hungry and bad, and we adore her. The story centres on wealth, insult and retaliation, Scarlett's determination to recreate Tara, building an empire out of her destitution. After the Civil War, Scarlett's newly acquired money buys her vengeance: she expertly runs a lumber mill – 'I won't be poor,' she declares – which gives her the clout to be grudgingly accepted by the society that had disdained her. Though she does not win lasting love, she succeeds in rebuilding a world on her own terms, and becomes a breadwinner for her dependants.

The dormant strains in this beloved story flourished in the 1980s. A new romance plot for women developed in which it was the heroine, and not her man, who built up the wealth. Bestselling books for female readers included Judith Krantz's *Scruples*, in which a young woman recreates herself, becoming the owner of a luxurious Beverly Hills boutiqe. Jackie Collins's *Lucky* and *Lady Boss* are other empire-builders. In Ivana Trump's *For Love Alone*, a poor Czech becomes a thriving international businesswoman.

Critics dismissed such books as 'sex and shopping' novels. But these books cannot be seen as mere escapism. In their pages, readers found better psychological preparation for 'the real world' than in 'victim' feminism, which was withdrawing into increasingly hazy, power-averse utopias. For the formula of the mainstream female dreams of the 1980s was to provide in fantasy form a 'how-to' manual for the heroine to engage with the marketplace, get revenge on the higher-ups who had treated her badly, and finally wield power skilfully and wisely. In many tales, a poor or working-class young woman uses her wit and courage to rise higher and higher up the ladder of professional achievement, and the extra benefits of love, riches and social betterment are celebrated not for themselves alone, but as reflections of how damn good the heroine is at her chosen work. Jo March went to night school; Catherine Earnshaw opened a franchise.

The following stories became test flights for a female psyche intent on winning its pilot's licence in worldly power. *Baby Boom* in 1987, which many feminists hated but many mainstream audiences enjoyed, showed the Diane Keaton character turning her back on a corporate culture hostile to women and babies, and making a killing marketing baby food in Vermont; *Thelma & Louise* included the theme of how naturally good the Geena Davis character was at her new job as a professional outlaw and thief; and in *Fried Green Tomatoes at the Whistle Stop Cafe* (1991) two intimate woman friends rebelled against the abusive husband of one, and escaped him by joining forces to start their own restaurant; the practical details of entrepreneurship were central to the movie's appeal.

The image of a woman having fun managing resources and using power inspired television. Hit TV shows for women included *Moonlighting* in 1987, in which Cybille Shepherd's character ran her own investigative business and employed her love interest; *Designing Women* from 1990 to the present, in which three women friends managed their own design firm; and *Cheers*, whose creators have been so encouraged by their female audience's response to the character Rebecca's management of the bar that they plan a spin-off in which the two lead female characters will run competing saloons. With *L.A. Law* women tuned in to watch highly trained and well-paid women lock horns with others in a battle of wits and to enjoy the drama of female conquest of work and power. The saga of how the Roxanne character recreated herself, changing from insecure clerical worker whose credit-card debt is out of control, into self-confident and better-paid manager, was one of the show's most popular subplots.

In the 1980s, and still in the 1990s, favourite pop heroines included the singer Madonna, producer, director, activist and actress-singer Barbra Streisand, TV entrepreneur Roseanne Arnold, talk-show host Oprah Winfrey and actress-director Jodie Foster. While all are admired for their performing talent, their appeal to women really took off when they formed their own production companies, negotiated $60 million deals, and directed their own movies. Judging from the press coverage, these women's fans are more titillated by the number of zeros in their contracts, and by their negotiations from a position of strength with rich men for more power and control, than they are by the stars' love lives or dieting regimes.

Power-wielding working-women icons included lifestyle entrepreneur Martha Stewart, fashion designer Donna Karan, and Body Shop founder Anita Roddick. These women did not become pop goddesses to other women because they made it to the top in a male corporate environment. Their popularity rests on their having taken products that women are expected to manufacture for free – comfort, glamour, cleanliness – and marketed the hell out of them. Their fans are more interested in the economic narrative of how they built their empires.

During the 1984–5 miners' strike in Britain, the miners' wives won more public support for the miners than most people, especially those in the government, would have thought possible. To the nation's surprise, these women proved themselves to be brilliant entrepreneurs. Lobbying, marching and campaigning for the first time in their lives, they were also handling the kind of money their husbands had never dreamed of: '£85,000 in one week alone at Christmas, not counting a cheque from John Paul Getty II,' as Rosalind Miles said in *The Times* on 9 October 1992.

The most striking feature of the 1993 *Sunday Times* list of Britain's top 50 businesswomen is that women most commonly make it to the top as financial executives: 17 of the 50 were financial directors, bankers or fund managers; only 2 per cent had functions which were not directly related to finance. The list compiler suggested that the reason for this was that 'a superior performance in finance is difficult to dismiss. The same cannot be said of most other management functions.'

Two media metamorphoses, fairy tales of female transformation not through marriage but through divorce, show how women are making romance out of independence. Princess Diana began her story in 1981 in the chrysalis of the unawakened virgin bride – the Cinderella of the pre-feminist imagination, whose life depended on a prince's kiss. For years she was sought out, lusted after and publicly displayed by the telephoto lenses of the world's media. With the 1992 publication of Andrew Morton's biography, she 'fell' into the status of a sympathetic mortal, trapped like many women in an unhappy marriage. When she turned the press hounds on to her oppressor she won the admiration of women in their millions. Upon her separation in 1993, she rose up in a fan-fare of adoration in the women's media, cherished in her new incarnation as cool, powerful avenger, an entrepreneur of her own persona who has handled her 'product' so skilfully that she is strong enough to take on, on her own terms, the corporate board of one of the richest and most influential conglomerates in Europe – the royal family. Now that she has confirmed her place on the international stage, not as the shy beguiling virgin but as an as-sertive ambassador for AIDS victims, children from broken homes, and anorexia and bulimia sufferers, even the most critical feminists have stopped to applaud. Nevertheless, Princess Diana still shows a tendency to use the terminology of the victim – as in her June 1993 speech about bulimia – and her transformation will not be complete until she casts off completely the victim status.

Ivana Trump, while not exactly a feminist heroine, shows how a feminist consciousness is at work in pop culture. She underwent a similar sea-change as a symbol for the female psyche. 'Before' her 1991 divorce, she was the wife who accepted the ultimate capitalist-sexist insult – 'one dollar a year plus all the dresses she could wear' as payment for her work managing the Atlantic City casino – and who underwent a head-to-toe surgical makeover to recapture her husband's roving eye. But 'after', once he cast her off for a woman twenty years younger, Ivana did not get mad; she got even. She posed for *Vogue*, pursued her own interests, and started work on a second book on 'financial management strate-gies for women'.

When we see women transform themselves in this way, we are inspired by their achievements. These stories, and the psychological work they represent, should not be confused with the amoral acquisitiveness of the yuppie 1980s. The stories cast the act of running one's own business, or the mastery of one's own paid work, as a metaphor for exploring the step beyond running one's own life: the step of making the decisions that affect the lives of other adults. Here women move beyond their claim to mastery of the self, and on to the use of power to alter the outcome of events in the greater world.

These dramas reinterpret the classic Horatio Alger, rags-to-riches tale for women. Just as those poor-boy-makes-good stories developed expectations that helped a generation of poor immigrant boys to strive for economic power, so these stories of women entrepreneurs, workers and professionals developed a long-dormant part of female psychology that was eager to rehearse without penalty the still unfamiliar experience of channelling ambition, exerting mastery and generating wealth.

Victory: The Nike Principle

When, in my travels, I asked women who hated the word 'feminism' to describe to me a version of feminism that could capture their aspirations, they replied with striking unanimity, 'That Nike ad. You know – "Just Do It".' (The phrase that was most often cited by 'insider' feminists, in contrast, was Audre Lorde's quote about the master's tools never dismantling the master's house.) The Nike ads present images of successful competition, even victory, and a logo of basic self-reliance. For the past few years, feminism has been selling activism to mainstream women in a way less sensitive to their mood than a footwear company has been selling trainers.

Advertisers may be foolish but they are rarely stupid, and 'Nike', of course, represents victory. The desire that awoke in the female imagination in the 1980s was the desire to win. The most famous statue of Nike, the 'Winged Victory', stands in the Louvre, a fine representation of the idea to which women responded, for she is so strong that you would never dare to show her disrespect; so graceful that one feels dazzled rather than oppressed. Unlike the favourite symbol of the last feminist wave – the Amazon, who lived in an all-female society and cut off her right breast the better to shoot her weapon – the Winged Victory is not torn up by the gender war, but poised in her own mighty balance. It was Nike's play on images of female victory that sparked a response in women's hearts that the mutilated Amazon, with her society purged of men, had never managed to elicit. Nike does not appear to be defensive; she presides in her power, and manifests no conflict between her might and her femininity. Each element reinforces the other. Her great, sinewy, arching wings are no less a part of her than her soft and lightly draped breasts.

Before the genderquake, women seldom saw images of female victory. In fact, there are many reflexes which dilute moments of female victory: press attention that focuses on a candidate's clothing, or an athlete's nervousness serves to ensure that women rarely experience the pure sugar rush of a victory free of equivocation. The opposition knows that the experience of victory, even when vicarious, is dangerously intoxicating.

But the genderquake suddenly provided image after image of female victory. In *A League of Their Own*, Penny Marshall's 1992 hit movie about the Georgia Peaches, a women's baseball league of the 1940s, audiences cheered the excitement of women catching baseballs behind their back one-handed, women effortlessly striking a rival out, women stealing home base, women fighting for the pennant – women, in a word, competing to win, and winning. In Senator Carol Moseley Braun's primary campaign, American women were treated to the sight of an African-American woman winning – not long after Anita Hill had so publicly been made to lose. During the Democratic Convention, Tipper Gore and Hillary Rodham Clinton danced a victory jig together on stage; they won. In *Made in America*, an African-American high-school senior works hard in her science classes and wins a prestigious Westinghouse scholarship – full tuition to MIT. As the award is announced at her high-school graduation, she stands on stage as a chorus sings a rap hosanna, her friends dance around her, and an audience of thousands does 'the wave' – a kind of collective bow with upraised arms.

The fantasy of crowds of people cheering one's personal victory is one that boys keep with them, but that girls are expected to yield. But when offered these images – images of winning not 'the man of one's dreams', but the victory of one's dreams – women devoured them greedily.

Genderquake Images: Vengeance, Money, Victory Come Together

None of these surfacing images stayed safely in female fantasy life. They spilled over and transmitted into the world of real political conflict.

In a media-saturated world, images not only affect history, they are history. Some images change for ever the way we visualize problems, and contain within themselves the seed of a response. The photographs of the 'little blue marble', the earth seen for the first time from outer space, led to an environmentalism that transcended the national boundaries invisible from space. Lennart Nilsson's 1965 photos that showed for the first time the foetus inside the womb influenced legislation on when life begins and thus when it can be aborted. That tiny thumb in the undeveloped mouth created the visual vocabulary of the pro-life movement, who fight, not surprisingly, with pictures as well as words.

In 1991–2, several real-life photographs of women changed the way women saw their possibilities, and – as in the cinema – these were not images of victimization.

The first set of images was thrown up by the debate about women soldiers serving in the Gulf War. As the discussion of women's capable service in the forces transformed all women's ideas about full participation in civic life, and raised their sense of entitlement, images of women wielding real firepower shook loose the blinkers that keep women from imagining themselves as beings that can elicit not just love and attraction, but also respect and even fear. The coverage of women soldiers had to be fairly positive, because the country needed their skills; and this coverage pushed women's status forward not only because of its respectful tone, but because of the very matter-of-factness with which the female soldiers quoted and reported upon approached their work. These images broke down the convention according to which women who can cause physical harm are represented as either saints or demons – Joan of Arc or Medea – but either way, as impossible for ordinary women to identify with. The images followed female lethal force from the killing fields back home to the suburban lawn and the PTA. The women soldiers were depicted returning to children whom they cradled, men who loved them; they were not monsters.

One such image appeared on a magazine cover. A jovial, freckled strawberry-blonde soldier – solidly built, attractive and smiling broadly in her fatigues – comfortably cradled a well-oiled machine gun. If the woman behind you at the checkout at Safeway's can crush a foreign enemy, and probably disable an unarmed domestic assailant, what can you not do? This revelation let women begin to think beyond the thinkable in political terms.

The images that galvanized us into action were images of action, mastery and defiance, rather than of victimization.

The second image is from the Clarence Thomas hearings. But it was not the sight of Professor Anita Hill alone, beleaguered, in a blue dress, seated before the fourteen white men of the Senate Committee, that led to the activism of 1992. That scene is as familiar to our subconscious as dry bread and rough salt. We see it a thousand times a day; it is the story of our own lives, and it told us very little we did not already know. That scene could not have moved us out of our habitual stasis, out of the frustrated rage of active feminists, the depression of aware women generally, and the defensive victim-blaming of female anti-feminists seeking safety.

What made the Thomas–Hill hearings break the mould of standard rituals of female humiliation was that Anita Hill had the master's tools and used them. A tenured law professor who had graduated from Yale Law School, she sat facing her interlocutors, holding the master's own self-professed definition of authority and credibility in her hands. She spoke with the accuracy and measured tone of a well-trained attorney and did not 'play the victim', weep, or recount the destruction of her life to make her case. It was that image which helped to light the fire this time.

The third image was the photo of the seven Congresswomen marching up the Senate steps. Each is intent on the common destination, some carry briefcases, and, uplifted in the hand of the woman at the forefront, in the upright position in which Justice holds her burning sword, is a file folder full of legal papers. A police officer, armed, his hands clasped behind him, stands and watches them pass.

The women in the image are not wailing in a Greek chorus of outraged grief or violated justice. They are climbing up the broad white steps, every line of their bodies angled calmly towards the confrontation, to get to the place where the most serious issues in the nation are deliberated. They are not victims. They are legislators.

The fourth image that fuelled the rebirth of feminism in the USA was one of clear and simple retaliation: an advertisement underwritten by the National Women's Political Caucus. It was a roughly sketched scene of seven women sitting in judgment on Clarence Thomas, who is seated alone, beneath them, looking up, in the dock. Let's not kid ourselves: this was not a pious image of democratic representation. No, the scene was one of vengeance: see what this feels like?

The Diana impulse of retaliation implicit in the advertisement marked the transition from paralysed depression into healing. It galvanized American women not only to have that fantasy acknowledged, but also placed in full view in the *New York Times* for all to see. Had that ad not brought in a penny, it would still have given American women a shot in the arm. Everyone, especially someone who is overworked, underpaid and under stress, needs to be able to imagine what she can do in order to do it. In offering a public symbolism of political retaliation, rather than of everyday pathos, these images further widened the fault lines.

After the Thomas–Hill hearings, American women took out their cheque books. Emily's List grew apace, with the media noting the momentum. The more women read about money being given to fund yet another campaign, the more money they sent in.

With contributions of less than $100 each, donors turned the lobby into a formidable voice for women. For the first time in women's history, female money had a public narrative, a dramatic life story. Women found they took pleasure in using money to teach the legislators this lesson; a pre-inaugural fund-raiser drew 4,600 women to applaud the newly elected female lawmakers their money had helped them to win. For the first time, many women learned that their money visibly mattered, that money could make them stronger as women rather than desexing them. Power didn't take big money, it didn't take men's money; just their money, put together. As this knowledge spread, women sent money flying and knew they were hitting the target. They were high on the Sheba principle.

Finally, the principle of victory took over. Once women experienced what it was like to win, they pressed to keep winning. Their new clout achieved almost at once a series of victories that would have taken 'debate', 'education' and 'changing social perceptions' about a hundred years.

On the US Senator's investigation committee dealing with allegations of sexual harassment against Senator Packwood sat Dianne Feinstein, one of the newly elected women sent to Washington by women's rage. Just as the drawing had foreshadowed, just as the myth depicted, the hunter was hunted and the predator forced on the defensive. Time elapsed: eighteen months. The hounds were loose in the land.

Vengeance, money, victory: as all three principles merged, women discovered a more direct relationship between political acts and consequences – between their hurt and their power to assuage, even avenge, that hurt – than they had ever had the opportunity to witness before.

The Lessons of the Genderquake

Women of all races are not a minority. We are the majority. In the USA, for example, we can cast 7 million more votes than men. But in so far as we are still tangled up in a rhetoric in which others grant us the 'Year of the Woman', and can take such treats back at any time, depending on their whim and our behaviour, we still don't understand.

Women don't need to beg anyone for a ride. We can't even hope to stay safely in the co-pilot seat. Whether we are ready to face it or not, in electoral terms, in Western democracies, women are flying this plane. Our opponents have understood that fact better than we have ourselves, and their control of events depends only on how long they can keep us from grasping this.

In 1992, seventy-two years after American women won the vote, we finally dared to use it properly. Women achieved an unprecedented list of victories, all over the world.

Women made things happen. Women elected Presidents and Prime Ministers. In so far as the majority of citizens – women – used their ballot-box clout to elect their leaders on their commitment to serve the majority, democracy has worked effectively for the first time. Our power, harnessed as the majority, is virtually unstoppable. It was no fluke; we weren't lucky; no one sent victory to us gallantly, wrapped in ribbons and tissue like a dozen long-stemmed roses. There's no point in looking distractedly around us, or playing demurely with our handbags, or saying, as sweetly grateful as we were raised to be, 'Oh, sir, you're too kind!' Because no one else did it for us. We did it.

And since women are used to running with ankle weights – maintaining work, home and family on two-thirds the income we deserve – *it wasn't even that hard*. As one new representative said, Congress is child's play if you've organized a birthday party.

The ease with which women's irritation brought about political change in 1992–3 underlines the single most puzzling condition of women's lives: why is it, after all, that demographic majorities that overwhelmingly favour women's rights are still subordinate? The primary reason is that these majorities have never, until now, had a cogent demonstration of the effectiveness of their use of political power, and so did not really believe in it.

Women tend, in the dreamy, feminine way in which we have been taught to think about our own volition, to have a kind of rescue fantasy about our rights: eventually, when we are somehow made equal – by the unfolding of time, or by government edict, or by whatever means – we can expect to get what we need. But it is not until we take what we need that we can make our opportunities equal. As Helena Kennedy, QC observed in 1991, waiting for women to obtain equality 'when the time is right' is like waiting for a fish to grow feet.

In other words, women are suffering from much subordination for no more pressing reason than that we have stopped short of compelling it to end. In the bad old days, when women could not vote, we were helpless indeed. When we could not earn our own money, independence was a cruel mirage for all, as it still is for so many women struggling financially. When we lacked reproductive choice, civil rights were only partly within our possession. Under those conditions, women were not really living in a representative democracy.

Today, we still have enormous burdens. Subsidized childcare is a rarity; most women have been sexually harassed at work; the court system is almost useless in deterring rape and domestic violence; and women are paid less than men for doing the same jobs. But we tend to talk about these obstacles as if they were insurmountable; as if we lived under a Fascist state in which women can neither earn money nor vote.

Now that reproductive choice and the right to a wage are minimally secure in the democratic West, and now that we have a clear demonstration of the simplicity with which we can bring about the changes that the polls show most of us desire, we must realize that democracy puts our fate squarely in our own hands. If we are slow in lifting those obstacles, it will be for many good reasons, as we become acclimatized to our strength. But if we do not manage to move them significantly by the millennium, and reach parity in the twenty-first century, it will be because women on some level have *chosen* not to exert the power that is their birthright. When we tell ourselves that we are, as women, helpless and at the mercy of events, we are telling ourselves a comforting fable left behind from a world that is already gone.

When I argue that women have enormous unclaimed power, I am not pretending that women are not harmed and held back in every way, or that 'everything's all right now' so we can relax and stop fighting. I am saying rather, that if we understand the events of the recent past and act on that understanding, and if we undergo a sea-change in our own self-image, matters will become increasingly 'all right'. Feminists, including myself, are often anxious when commentators focus on women's achievements, because we fear a return to apathy. My hope is that if we interpret the genderquake rightly, we won't stop fighting. We will fight more intelligently and more elegantly. And we will suffer less of the wear and tear of anger and helplessness while having a lot more sheer fun.

When I say that the genderquake has potentially changed for ever what it means to be female, I mean this: it is no longer necessary for women to ask anyone's permission for social equality.

Women feel they need to spend a lot of time doing PR for their own equality, but it is no longer necessary to focus primarily on appealing to the opposition for justice. In other words, whether it is ready or not, 'society' no longer has the power to keep women in their place. For women now have the electoral clout to create the conditions they need for equality. The question to ask is not whether society is ready to yield to women their rightful places, but whether women themselves are ready to take possession of them.

Equality is no longer something we need to beg for from others. This shift of emphasis demands that women begin to see themselves as potent agents of change with many resources, rather than as helpless victims. Indeed, what is the point of settling for equality when women are entitled to true democracy in which the advantage of our numbers makes us the single strongest force on earth? As Western women, we are, in fact, not just in charge of our own countries, but are also, whether we like it or not, and as truly unjust as it is, in a position to affect what becomes of most of the rest of the world.

This exhilarating, terrifying responsibility for the fate of nations is not waiting to descend on us some day, in some smoky, hazy future of a feminist science fiction novel. It's not even around the corner. It's already here. You've been living it.

If we stay hunkered down, defensive and angry, we waste our energies. We act effectively now if we learn to relax into our power, stand upright, and leave the foxholes that we have almost begun to consider a permanent home. We must stand in a new posture, walking with a loving heart, an open mind, and a very big stick called clout. If we do that, then we can live to see the start of the Egalitarian Era: a reality in which women become something there is no word for – that is, not unequal by virtue of gender.

Today, after thirty years of education against racism have left racial barriers substantially intact, many African-American civil rights activists are turning to the strategies of Malcolm X and the Reverend Jesse Jackson. Their approach mobilizes people's will to self-determination and consolidates their money and influence to force change where anti-racist education and appeals to justice have failed. This approach pressured corporations to disinvest in South Africa, urges African-Americans to support Black-owned businesses, and seeks out public–private partnerships. Gay and lesbian groups are making similar shifts, trading in the plea for tolerance and compassion in favour of PR campaigns, high-profile fund-raising, and a show of political influence. Women, as a group, must make the same psychological transition.

Now that women have begun to steal fire from the gods and use it well is the time to abandon orthodoxy, sloganeering, ideological posturing, and life lived on the margins for marginality's sake. It is time to turn outward in a fair and goal-oriented way, time to trade in preaching to the converted for negotiating with the opposition from a position of strength. And time to forge a new link between sisterhood and capital that offers women the encouragement to get more and the responsibility to give more.

For now is a time in which real change for women depends upon a willingness to engage with power with its seductions and responsibilities, democracy with all its open conflicts, and money with all its pleasures and dangers.

What is power feminism? It means taking practical giant steps instead of ideologically pure baby steps; practising tolerance rather than self-righteousness. Power feminism encourages us to identify with one another primarily through the shared pleasures and strengths of femaleness, rather than primarily through our shared vulnerability and pain. It calls for alliances based on economic self-interest and economic giving back rather than on a sentimental and workable fantasy of cosmic sisterhood.

Power feminism can, without compromising its principles, be reclaimed by the majority. It is flexible enough to make use of its temporary peace dividend: it can adapt much of its wartime economy, based on the struggle for equal rights, into a peacetime economy centred on money and work. It welcomes men and honours their place in the lives of women, straight and gay; and it has no difficulty telling the difference between hating sexism and hating men.

I am not asking us to delude ourselves with the thought that we can move out of victimization into confidence by some sort of individualistic positive thinking. We can only do so by uniting to work towards more power. Frederick Douglass said, 'If there is no struggle there is no progress. . . Power concedes nothing without a demand. It never did and it never will.'

The late feminist poet Audre Lorde wrote that the master's tools would never dismantle the master's house. But the electoral process, the press and money are among the master's tools. The genderquake should show us that it is *only* the master's tools that can dismantle the master's house; he hardly bothers to notice anyone else's.

Now that some women have access to some of his tools, the master has yielded to women the instruments that can rearrange and even open up his stronghold. The question for women now is, 'Do we dare to escalate our use of them?'

Part Two

What Went Wrong? How So Many Women and Their Movement Parted Ways

Chapter Five

Out of Touch?

If you look only at how feminism has transformed our society, and how most women, men, and, increasingly, institutions embrace its principles, the women's movement has won, bringing about the most successful and least bloody revolution in human history.

But even as more and more of feminism's ideals cross over into mainstream culture, more and more women distance themselves from the word 'feminist'. As one reader wrote to me, 'The last wave of feminism in the seventies had a profound influence on me ... However, like a lot of my friends, I hadn't read a 'feminist' book for many long years, because the movement stopped talking to me.' Many women either don't know what feminism means, or don't think it respects their choices, or don't think it addresses their concerns, or don't like the images of it that they see.

In October 1991, *Newsweek* found that only 27 per cent of women believed that Anita Hill had been sexually harassed. This finding led to dismay among feminists and to harrumphing editorials that claimed that feminists were hopelessly 'out of touch' with *real* women. Are they?

Most Women Feel Distant from the Women's Movement

A variety of opinion polls in Britain and the United States illustrate what one writer has called 'these contradictory times, when women recoil from the feminist label while simultaneously donating record sums to women's rights organizations'. A 1992 Ms.

Foundation survey, 'Women's Voices '92: A polling Report', reputedly the first American survey to evaluate women's views across class and racial lines, found that many women are 'personally uncomfortable' with the term 'feminist' even as they endorse the movement's goals. It found that feminists 'are seen by many as being more out for themselves than out for ordinary women and their families'. While women in their survey saw the women's movement favourably – it rated 62 on a scale of 100 – 'many women,' the report concluded, 'feel distant from the term "feminist," which to them does not seem to share their own priority of family nor the daily struggles of many women who are constantly pulled and stretched for time and money'.

A 1989 Time/CNN Yankelovich poll found that 33 per cent of women called themselves feminists, and 58 per cent did not. But women's distrust of the term said little about their wish for equality. Seventy-seven per cent of all women surveyed think the women's movement has made life better, and only 8 per cent think it has made life worse. Ninety-four per cent said that the movement has helped women become more independent; 82 per cent said it was still improving US women's lives. Asked 'Have feminists been helpful or harmful to women?' 62 per cent said helpful and 18 per cent harmful. In spite of that overwhelming support for the goals of the movement, 76 per cent said they pay 'not very much' or 'no' attention to the movement itself. A 1987 Times-Mirror study conducted by the Gallup Organization found that 51 per cent of both women and men identify themselves as feminists. In a 1986 Newsweek-Gallup poll, 56 per cent of all women said they considered themselves feminists while 40 per cent did not and 4 per cent considered themselves anti-feminist.

A similar situation in Britain shows how wide-ranging are feminism's political successes and public relations failures: A 1992 *Cosmopolitan* survey of female students showed that 75 per cent said they were ambitious but only 38 per cent claimed to be feminists. In another survey presented at a British Psychological Association conference, 50 per cent of female students were sympathetic to the aims of feminism but had negative feelings about feminists. A 1991 *Guardian* survey, 'What Women Really Think', found that only 9 per cent of 11,000 respondents thought that feminism was seen positively and only 13 per cent belonged to a women's group, even though 51 per cent of those surveyed who were in management positions believed they were discriminated against and 58 per cent said that sexual discrimination at work had not changed. An ICM poll of the same year, commissioned shortly after John Major launched Opportunity 2000, showed that 57 per cent of women supported feminist goals but 41 per cent did not believe those goals had been achieved.

There are two developments. One is that the number of women willing to identify themselves with the word 'feminist' slipped steadily throughout the 1980s even as support for women's rights steadily rose. The other is that about twice as many women believe in the goals of the women's movement as are willing to use the word 'feminist'. In that 100 per cent shortfall, separating women's expressed wish for equality from the one word we have that describes someone acting on that wish, lies the main reason why women's desire for higher status is not reflected in reality.

The result is a paralysis of women's political will. 'Feminism' should mean, on an overarching level, nothing more complicated than women's willingness to act politically to get what they determine that they need. But between the political weapon of feminism and the great mass of women who should be armed with it lie barriers. The media caricature of feminism, combined with some bad habits in the movement itself, led many women to view the weapon of feminist politics with distaste. The weapon's own rigidity keeps it from adapting itself to the average woman's hand and the female constituency, though it flexes its muscles after long inaction and is astonished to find itself so strong, remains disarmed. For just as a view of feminism divorced from women's lives is sterile, a woman's life divorced from a view of feminism she can act upon is half helpless.

Feminists reassure us with the rationalization that while, yes, most women shun feminism's name, they support its agenda. I certainly have been guilty of backing away from women's hostility to feminism myself. There are few sentiments more painful for a feminist to hear. But such dismissal of women's uneasiness is ultimately a mistake. It can even ascribe some kind of false consciousness to mainstream women ... ('Poor dears, they don't know what's good for them.') The fact that most women of all races and classes – and younger women, in particular – really dislike the word 'feminism' should matter enormously. It matters that more and more women are going into bookshops with feminist books on their reading lists but, according to Sue Butterworth of Silver Moon bookshop in London, 'they are women who wouldn't define themselves as feminists'. By not getting to the roots of this alienation, we lose nothing less than the future.

Many feminists including myself, are so distressed by this aversion that we tend to reach for a fixed set of explanations. 'It's the backlash.' 'Feminism is a process.' 'They'll get politicized as they get older.' Even, 'They're in denial.' Women are certainly lied to about feminism, but they are not clueless. Many of the women I heard from were alienated not because they were brainwashed but because of frustrating experiences with individuals or ideas they encountered. If women have an aversion to 'feminism' it is indeed largely the fault, as the Ms. Foundation report concludes, of a 'persistent and expansive campaign on the part of the mass media, the religious right and others' to discredit the movement. But that is not the entire story.

An image of feminism which is composed of about 80 per cent lies, distortion and caricature, but which includes a 20 per cent nugget of truth, keeps many women disengaged. Let's take a hard look at that 20 per cent.

One of the biggest problems with feminism is that many women fear that it has come to embody a rigid code of required attitudes and types of behaviour. This is a theme I heard so often that I'm convinced there is no more fundamental explanation for the impasse between women and feminism. As strong as their allegiance is to individual women's issues, many women have started to feel uncomfortable merely sticking up for themselves, because they risk being seen as allied to an assortment of convictions they do not necessarily endorse. Just as women resent 'men' – or sexist stereotypes – defining them from one side, they resent what they see as a feminist stereotype defining them on the other. Ironically, it is because most women are strong individuals who respect their own uniqueness – feminists in the best, nearly overridden sense of the word – that they resist being boxed into someone else's overloaded agenda.

One of the women from Fanny Adams, the group of anonymous women artists campaigning for equal representation in galleries around Britain and in the media, maintains, 'Not wanting to be defined in a certain way is linked to not wanting to be defined as an archetypal feminist. There is a persistent problem in art institutions mainly run by men: if you are perceived as a feminist, you are seen as very difficult. There is a one-dimensional view of feminism as seventies separatism. A redefinition is needed in the nineties. It should be up-front, provocative.'

Huggy Bear, the London- and Brighton-based Riot Grrls band, want to reclaim the word 'girl'. Their guitarist, Jo, explained, 'this is a new sort of feminism. "Girl" speaks more effectively to girls who read *Just Seventeen*. Not all feminism has to be Germaine Greer.'

When Huggy Bear was asked whether they sympathized with any particular school of feminist thought, their drummer, Karen, replied, 'I haven't studied enough. I just know if my freedom is restricted.' Like her, north London rap queen Debbie Fagan does not want to be labelled a feminist but she does believe in equal rights: 'Life is short. You've gotta fight to do what you want.'

Many women identify feminism with specific issues that may or may not include them, rather than with a theory of self-worth that applies to every woman's life without exception. *Is it about abortion?* 'Well, I am not certain I know when life begins,' a woman might say. *Is it about lesbianism?* 'Well, I am a married woman.' *It's for middle-class white women, isn't it?* 'I am working class.' *Is it about fighting against men?* 'I am an Afro-Caribbean woman, and there is no way I'm going to put down an Afro-Caribbean man.' *It's anti-pornography, right?* 'I don't believe in censorship, and I don't want anyone telling me what to do in my bedroom.' *Is it about not wearing makeup?* 'I like to look good.' *Is it restricted to women?* 'Well, I am a parent, and I care about my daughter, but I am a man.' *Is it about sexual abuse or rape?* 'That may have happened to me, but I am interested in putting it behind me, and I don't want to define myself as a victim.'

Feminism stopped being seen as guaranteeing every woman's choice – whatever that may be – and fell captive to social attitudes held only by a minority that often could not even reach agreement among its own members. Of course this development might have been inescapable, a result of the abortion wars that demanded an us-and-them worldview. But the ideological hardline, as well as the media's distortion of feminism, has alienated women – and men – in their thousands: women who are not sure about, or who actively oppose, abortion; women who are terrified of being tarred with the brush of homophobia; women who strongly resist identifying themselves as victims; women who are uneasy with what they see as man-bashing and blaming; conservative women; and men themselves.

My friends and I are all self-defined feminists. But we know that if we were to stand up and honestly describe our lives to a room full of other feminist 'insiders' – an act that should illuminate the route to female liberation – we could count on having transgressed at least one dearly held tenet on someone's list of feminism's 'do's' and 'don'ts', and being called to account for it. 'Don't tell the sisterhood,' we often joke, uncomfortably, when we are about to confide some romantic foolishness or unsanctioned sexual longing or 'frivolous' concern about clothes or vulnerability or men. We have all felt pressure to espouse a line that does not conform entirely with our true practices or desires. If you can no longer square your feminism with your real-life experience, then something has gone seriously wrong.

Some feminists have become far too proscriptive of other women's pleasures and private arrangements, and the definition of feminism has become ideologically overloaded. Instead of offering a mighty Yes to all women's individual wishes to forge their own definition, it has been disastrously redefined in the popular imagination as a massive No to everything outside a narrow set of endorsements.

The F-Word

One group of young women I met voiced some of the tensions generated by this situation.

'They assume we hate men. It's perceived as anti-sexual.'

'It connotes a turning away from heterosexuality. People assume if you're a feminist, you're a lesbian.'

'Ugly-dyke-feminist. It's all one word.'

'My image of feminism is very negative – men haters, man bashers. "You can hate sexism and not hate men" – I hadn't ever heard that.'

'[Feminist theologian] Mary Daly hurt us when she spoke here. She was angry, harsh, her jokes were almost all at the expense of the other gender. As a woman who doesn't want to hate men, I felt I was being made to choose, like she was saying, "If you're not with me, you're not a feminist, and you're everything that's making life hell for us women." It's like "Don't make me that. I'm a strong, capable woman. Don't know me as a man hater."'

'Our whole generation refuse to call themselves feminists. Everything's defined by the extremes – you can't think of feminism without thinking of the extremes. That's why we don't identify with it – even if we support its goals.'

'My friends say, "You are *not* a feminist." They see feminism as the opposite of gender bias against women – they see it as women who are gender biased against men.'

'I want to be a revolutionary without being a bitch.'

'Even women who want equal rights won't join a local women's group because they are reluctant to come in and fight for these things and be "seen as a feminist".'

These voices of young women confirm the findings we saw earlier: that the negative image of feminism often outweighs the support for its goals and achievements. As exhilarating as the first upheavals of the genderquake feel to women, this vast obstacle lies before them: as they reawaken to their own power, their relationship to their own political movement is in disarray.

In *Backlash*, Susan Faludi explained how anti-woman forces sought to persuade women that the *goals* of feminism were undesirable. During the same time, though, factors from within the movement as well as from without convinced many women who believed heartily in its goals that the movement *itself* was not for them. Christine Bellini, a 28-year-old secretary, wrote me a letter that summarizes the estrangement many women have come to feel. Her city, she wrote, has

a very strong 'left' group of feminists. They are a strong group that dominates many organizations ... In my opinion, this group is also responsible for sabotaging these organizations that at one point were advocating for the rights of either women's reproductive choices, homosexuals, or all women. It has been difficult ... to get women to mobilize, when other women, namely the left, dump so much criticism and hostility on those very minorities they propose to support.

In this city, many straight middle-class feminists find themselves lost in two very radical worlds. It seems either women can appeal to the left only to find out that men are hated and ignored, or can appeal to the right and find the world of women's organizations centered on their husband's wealth and status. What many of my friends and I have tried to do is find groups and organizations whose mandate is, not to alienate the sexes, but to gain understanding of each other ...

Many of the women [in question] attend many meetings in this city and do the same thing – attack, criticize, and victimize. They almost never offer solutions or constructive criticism and because of the negative feeling they bring with them, they leave many women feeling alienated or confused.

I think women's lack of taking responsibility for their actions and feelings is the main reason feminism has not advanced to the heights it could have by now. I know that some women are truly not in a position to do that (those in abusive relationships, etc.) but those who are, yet continue to victimize themselves into a politically correct corner, are only holding themselves back.

An episode in a Toronto lecture hall in 1991 exemplifies these tensions between women inside and outside the feminist community. The two issues that sparked the confrontation had to do with who owned the basic building blocks of female self-determination: sex and money.

This is how I remember the scene. After a talk I gave, members of the local feminist community asked how I could call myself a feminist while lecturing for the same organization that sponsored a course for men called 'How to Please a Woman Every Time'. When I replied that that course sounded like a feminist victory to me, these women began to react with anger whilst others seemed to start backing away from them. Another woman from the first group said accusingly that my lecture agent would not distribute tapes of the talk for free because, she said scornfully, 'it would interfere with my "market value".' I replied that every woman's work had a market value and that one purpose of feminism was to raise every woman's market value so she could use her own money to determine her own life.

At this, there was a sharper audience division. It was the first time I witnessed the acute resentment of doctrinaire feminism on the part of ordinary women. The majority of women in that lecture hall angrily supported a woman's right to her own money and sexual pleasure without having to justify her actions to a cadre of 'sisters'. 'Do we have the right to look in your wallet?' asked one woman. 'Is that supposed to empower women?' The smaller group, in contrast, seemed to feel that one was not a feminist unless some sort of seal of approval was stamped on one's bed, and one's purse. It was clear to all that we were witnessing a moment in which a social nerve was being struck.

It is not surprising, in retrospect, that the right to sexual pleasure and the right to money should have revealed the divide between the majority of women and this small minority of movement insiders. For both of those rights have to do with women owning their own power and using it to live on their own terms. And this power-feminist impulse is increasingly at odds with the kind of victim feminism which implies that real feminists must renounce power and pleasure in favour of the ideological requirements of a collective identity.

The evidence is all around us: most women support the goals of feminism but cannot identify with feminists. But what brought about this situation?

Chapter Six

Plagues of a Movement: 60s Hangover, Dyke-Baiting, and Silencing on the Job

A number of developments have caused the alienation of the majority of women from their movement. These include:

1. Outdated origins: hangover habits of the revolutionary left of the 1960s;

2. Dyke-baiting, which led to the common perception that feminism and lesbianism are synonymous and reinforced the view that the movement was anti-family and anti-male.

3. Economic silencing. Soon after women entered the workforce in large numbers in the early 1970s, the management ensured that they had to distance themselves from feminism in order to get ahead, or even stay in place. This distance was reinforced by

4. Selective and distorted coverage of the movement in the media, which meant that while working women weren't able to speak clearly about feminism on the job, feminists weren't able to speak clearly to women in the media and on TV;

5. Some feminists' (understandable) consequent hostility toward the mainstream media, which reinforced

6. A tendency to be more comfortable on the margins, preaching to the converted, and a clique mentality. Marginalization was guaranteed by

7. The publication of several theories that, while they looked

good on paper, made no sense as practical propositions for most women and men. These theories and positions, denied debating room in the mainstream, hardened into

8. Rigid proscriptions, which coupled with a fear of debate to weaken the movement's intellectual health and narrow the entry points into it. Added to all this was

9. The relocation of feminist debate from the mainstream press into the university, where the language that developed around it became increasingly obscure to outsiders;

10. The perception intensified the perception that feminism was a white, middle-class or elitist movement.

All of these factors combined in such a way that the feminist movement and its constituency turned to one another in the genderquake years only to find that though they shared common goals, they spoke different languages.

The Hard Left of the 1960s

A small but influential strand of feminism came out of the Marxist-Leninist male left of the 1960s. Alice Echols, in *Daring to Be Bad: Radical Feminism 1967–1975*, tells the story of how groups like Students for a Democratic Society gave rise to splinter groups of revolutionary women who went on to create much of second-wave feminist culture. In that brief, alluring moment, young, mostly middle-class (and mostly white) men and women strove for collectivism; expressed contempt for capital in any form, and for 'selling out' for economic advancement; embraced self-sacrifice; and adhered to doctrinaire precepts, the party line. Though most of the adherents of these beliefs have since moved on and are at best bringing about social change in ways more engaged with real-world problems, the cultural traits of the revolutionary left, old rules of unreconstructed Marxist 'revolutionary' behaviour, survive vestigially in some circles of the women's movement, long after others, including those in socialist countries, had stopped finding them so attractive.

While Marxist analysis was extremely helpful for making connections between issues of gender, money and power, and while the left is realistic in seeing the electoral process as compromised, capitalism as exploitative, and 'the system' as manipulated by an elite, the progressive community, including some feminists, dealt with the despair of the Thatcher years or the Reagan–Bush era by using those insights to justify retreat rather than spark engagement. And in some cases the culture of Marxism was seized upon by feminists as a way to lend a political and even radical hue to the same old power-shy reflexes that were so hard for women to let go. The hangover of this origin shows itself in victim feminism's glamorization of whatever is 'subversive', 'marginal', 'underground', or merely ill-paid, as well as in its contempt for the mainstream media, for women in business and for female individualism. These attitudes, which are passé now almost everywhere else in the world, are foolish burdens to carry when we need to walk unhesitatingly into what lawyer Gloria Allred calls 'the palace of power', and unapologetically use its mighty resources for change. They are responsible for the feminist culture clash which alienates the majority of women, whose commitment to social equality may be just as radical but expressed in an individual, rather than collective, manner.

Dyke-Baiting

Homophobia also widened the gap between feminists and other women. One of the most common reasons women give for avoiding the feminist label is that 'feminist' has become synonymous with 'lesbian'. Many feminists tend to dismiss such women as homophobic and, therefore, to count their alienation as no loss to the movement. But if we look carefully at how dyke-baiting is being used to scare women away from feminism, and if we listen to what such women's concerns really express, the problem becomes more complex.

Ever since women have pushed forward for more freedom, the opposition has pushed back with the insinuation that their sexuality is 'abnormal' or 'perverse'. In short, a woman's wish for a greater public role meant that she was 'un-natural'; she must be a lesbian. As women were making the greatest claims on public life the stigma against lesbianism intensified. 'Women who did not wish to stay in their place were depicted as masculine,' writes historian Lillian Faderman, 'therefore abnormal, i.e., lesbian. The link between feminism and "sexual abnormality" was made not only in America and England but in Germany and France as well.'

In England, in 1911, the writer Edward Carpenter claimed that women embrace feminism when they are abnormal, have poor maternal instincts, and are 'mannish in temperament' and lesbian. In America, psychiatrist William Lee Howard wrote a novel called *The Perverts* that melded feminism, lesbianism and degenerate morality into one 'psychosis'. 'The female possessed of masculine ideas of independence' and 'that disgusting anti-social being, the female sexual pervert' were, he wrote, 'simply different degrees of the same class – degenerates'. During the next decade, the association of lesbianism with feminism in the context of 'degeneracy' would become prevalent. In 1927, a German, Dr E. F. W. Eberhard, asserted that feminism, led by 'men and women', was about to cause nothing less than the destruction of civilization, using lesbianism as its *modus operandi*. Eberhard charged that lesbian leaders converted young women to the movement by seducing them.

Faderman points out that the connection between feminism and lesbianism was made so strongly at this time because the movement in England was growing increasingly confrontational and effective. 'Antifeminists,' she concludes, 'must have considered that whatever would scare women away from the movement was fair play. And to associate feminism with what the experts had called morbid would surely scare women away.'

Throughout the 1920s and 1930s, commentators insisted that women's colleges, with their athletics courses and feminist curricula, produced 'lifelong homosexuality'. In the 1940s the bestselling anti-feminist diatribe, *Modern Woman: The Lost Sex*, was published. It became a handbook for the backlash of the time, which was intent on driving women home, away from the independence and high pay of their jobs in war production. The authors, Ferdinánd Lundberg and Marynia Farnham, called feminism 'an expression of emotional illness, of neurosis . . . at its core a deep illness', and repeatedly depicted feminism as a symptom of 'lesbian sickness'. The association of feminism with 'abnormality' fuelled the 1950s retreat into domesticity and was doubtless responsible for the anxiety about lesbianism that marred *The*

Second Stage, Betty Friedan's breakthrough attack on the back-lash.

Unsurprisingly, this tried-and-true tactic was revived to counteract the Second Wave of feminism in the 1970s. Faderman points out that in 1970 *Time* publicized Kate Millett's bisexuality. In an article entitled 'Women's Lib: A Second Look', it challenged feminists' 'maturity, morality and sexuality', and suggested that Millett's bisexuality 'cast further doubt on her theories, and reinforce[d] the views of those skeptics who routinely dismiss all liberationists as Lesbians'.

Depressingly, if no longer astonishingly, history repeated itself once again twenty-two years later. A 1992 *New York Times Magazine* cover story, under the guise of being a feature on National Organization for Women's new president Patricia Ireland, dwelt at prurient length on 'allegations' of *her* bisexuality.

Beverley LaHaye, president of the right-wing anti-abortion group Concerned Women for America, provided the writer Jane Gross with a chewy anti-lesbian soundbite: 'NOW is a militant fringe whose priorities, such as lesbian rights, are alien to most women.' While LaHaye is entitled to her opinion, Gross's tone extends the anti-lesbian sentiment: 'Tensions over its prominent lesbian cohorts have bedeviled NOW since its beginnings,' she wrote of a NOW march, describing 'prominent lesbian cohorts' – like the 'Yellow Peril' or the Visigoths – as if they were about to burst the bounds of decency and run wild through the Washington Mall, tomahawks flying and nose-rings glinting, 'bedeviling' the law-abiding passers-by. 'Many of the younger, heterosexual women at the Washington march in question said they could not convert others to the cause because of the perceived equation between feminism and lesbianism ... [Said one unnamed NOW member:] "This issue is explosive! It must be defused, within our own groups as well as in the public domain."'

Feminist women have responded to this divide-and-conquer tactic in roughly two ways. One is to give in to homophobia. Some women seek to 'redeem' the feminist label by distancing themselves publicly from lesbians and lesbianism, thus avoiding the stigma but still playing into the hands of the opposition and allowing it to define the terms of the debate. Betty Friedan, for instance, sought to distance the 'lavender menace' from NOW in

1969, causing a still-unhealed rift within the movement (an action about which she has since expressed regret).

Women who deal with the very real problem of the identification of 'feminism' as 'lesbianism' by publicly disavowing other sexualities do not understand the first principle of a backlash: it is not rational. When a straight woman responds to dyke-baiting by more dyke-baiting, she has accepted the opposition's premiss and its weapon: that a woman's sexual choices can discredit her politics. Once you accept this, you have handed over your own sexual self-determination. Heterosexual women would do well to remember that sexual tolerance is a better guarantee of their own freedom of choice. We may delude ourselves temporarily with the warm feeling that comes from knowing that the opposition considers female heterosexuality 'nicer' than lesbianism or bisexuality. But we should bear in mind that the same opposition does not consider self-determined female heterosexuality 'nice' in the least but seeks to control all female sexuality. The conservative moralists, the intolerant and the fanatics will not be satisfied by the act of throwing lesbians or bisexuals to the wolves. The wolves just grow hungrier. They will show up eventually at the doors of straight women as well as gay, eager to meddle in all our sexual lives and use them against us to keep us from making our claims upon the world.

The second way of responding to the feminist-equals-dyke tactic is to welcome the identification of lesbianism and feminism as a way of diffusing the stigma of dyke-baiting. When Gloria Steinem is asked about her own sexuality by hostile press, she sometimes says, 'I try to keep them guessing.' At an early New York meeting, every woman put on a lavender armband to show solidarity with lesbians. The women, gay, straight and bisexual, declared that by standing together under the banner of lesbianism they would outwit the opposition. 'They can call us lesbians until such time as there is no stigma attached to women loving women,' they declared. Historian Faderman concluded, over-optimistically, 'And with that weapon against feminism gone, the movement could advance unimpeded.'

But this tactic, however well-intentioned, has not solved the problem. While it is a clever short-term stand, it still traps women into defining themselves reactively, rather than on their own terms. And it has led many heterosexual women to stay away from the movement – not out of homophobia, but because of legitimate worries about whether their own sexual identity and concerns are represented when 'feminism' and 'lesbianism' are synonyms. For redefining heterosexual identity in a positive way is as legitimate and as central to a straight woman's sense of self as the recognition of lesbianism is to a lesbian woman's identity.

If feminism means choice and self-definition, the collapse of feminism into lesbianism means that many straight women who are not homophobes will still fear that there is little room for their sexuality in the movement. And straight women as well as gay deserve to know the exhilarating process of deriving a politics out of their desire.

Finally, not all women can afford to be seen as gay – and the misidentification becomes a financial, emotional and physical risk few are willing to take. Coming out as a lesbian should be a basic right, but urban, upper-middle-class women suffer fewer penalties for that honesty than do others. If lesbians in many communities feel that they cannot risk coming out, it is unrealistic and condescending for comfortable urban activists to expect straight women in the same communities to shoulder a lesbian identity. Many women who are scared off by dyke-baiting are not themselves homophobic, but are terrified of bearing the brunt of others' homophobia.

Dyke-baiting alienated mainstream women further from a movement that was already having trouble getting across the message that it welcomed all sexualities and was willing to accord heterosexual relationships and family life the respect and support that it tried to win for gay relationships. An image of early-1970s feminism, which had gone through a brief, psychologically necessary but rightly transient stage of criticizing homemaking and motherhood and using mottoes like 'A woman without a man is like a fish without a bicycle', was recycled in the mass media long after its ideas were discarded. And these images persuaded many women that feminism was still anti-male, anti-family and contemptuous of women who did not work outside the home.

Censorship on the Job

On-the-job censorship also silenced women about feminism. The Second Wave feminists of the 1960s, many of them middle class and white, had everything to gain from making a loud feminist noise and comparatively little, in economic terms, to lose. They were united as outsiders, and were clamouring to enter an expanding economy hungry for their services.

But as women entered the workforce they discovered that they could not speak openly about feminism because their livelihoods often depended upon their silence. Barely out of the starting gate, a woman's relationship to feminism was damaged by the fact that if she avowed feminism she stood a good chance of losing her job. Conversely, she soon learned that she could trade in her feminist identification for career advancement.

Women soon found that the workplace that enfranchised them economically was also shutting them up politically. As the divorce rate skyrocketed and women, especially single or divorced mothers, became the new poor, they were also terrorized into silence by the very institutions whose doors the movement had opened for them. The united outsiders became nervous temporary insiders competing with one another for scarce resources in a worldwide recession. The women who managed to get right up against the glass ceiling were pitted against one another for the few token positions at the very top. Not only did the imperative to behave in a 'sisterly' manner towards the woman who wanted your job begin to seem inappropriate, but the act of making feminist waves began to look like professional suicide. As media consultant Nancy Woodhull said to me: 'In the sixties, we could rock the boat because we weren't in it. Now we're in it, but on the edge.' The corporate West discovered that the best way to stop women's revolution was to give them something to lose. And the risk of losing one's livelihood is as good a restraint as any law.

This economic censorship did not just apply to women in the pink-collar ghetto. In fact, the more powerful a woman became, the stronger were the rewards for forsaking feminism, and the harsher the punishments for embracing it. Women at the United Nations, though part of an elite workforce in an organization dedicated to world justice and to the fight against human-rights abuses, had to keep quiet about sexual harassment: 'It's never been politically wise for women here to say boo,' Ceceil Gross, president of the UN women's group, told a reporter in 1992. 'Historically, when there were cries and whimpers heard, the women got fired.' A lawyer for female UN employees warned them that those who complain 'have ended up worse off than before they spoke up'. Even Lynn Martin, Secretary of Labor under Bush, revealed as soon as she was out of office that in the early 1980s she had noticed pay inequities between men and women in Congress. When she brought the data to the chairman of the committee studying work conditions, he told her not to talk to the press, not to embarrass everyone, and to wait. Other chairmen called her names. The inquiry was allowed to languish. The cover-up, she said, was 'part of the "go along to get along" philosophy that senior members made sure you understood'. Dr Carolyn Heilbrun, a popular professor of English at Columbia University, resigned in 1992 because sexism was keeping her from doing her job as a feminist: she had had to warn her graduate students to avoid women's studies courses and keep the word 'feminist' off their c.v.s if they wanted jobs. Even on Capitol Hill in 1992, female legislative aides and policy specialists had to lower their voices, glancing edgily at an open door in a meeting room in the Senate, when they described to me how helpless they were to protest against the absence in their workplace of the laws against sexual harassment that cover other American women. 'If I make a fuss about any women's issue,' one said, echoing the words of other 'powerful' women across the country, 'I'll be blacklisted. And it's a company town.'

In Britain female police officers complain of sexual harassment at their peril. When Eileen Waters was brutally raped by a fellow officer, the Metropolitan Police assigned her to restricted duties and seemed reluctant to pursue the case; Alison Halford, Britain's highest-ranking police officer, complained of sexual discrimination after being turned down for nine jobs as Deputy Chief Constable only to be vilified by the press and suspended on disciplinary charges; WPC Sarah Locker was victimized after complaining about the hardcore pornography she kept finding in her tray.

Even seemingly powerful women are not free of this constraint. A well-known filmmaker told me that despite her success she was apprehensive about her career after having 'come out' as a feminist. She added sadly that a whole stratum of Hollywood women at the top of the power pyramid are secret feminists who dare not show their beliefs too openly. Women sometimes attack apparently powerful women – in Hollywood, in women's magazines, in the media generally – for not taking more risks to produce better material for all women. But without a mandate from below, few women, powerful though they may appear to be, can write their own ticket.

Female politicians also feel this pressure. Margaret Beckett, MP, formerly Shadow Chief Treasury Secretary and now Deputy Leader of the Labour party, told an interviewer: 'Maybe when I've been doing this job for some time it will be possible to make comments about women without people saying: there you are it's only women's issues they want to talk about. But I have a feeling it's too early yet.' Even in Norway, where the three major political parties are led by women, Berit As, a former Norwegian Labour party MP, says that 'as soon as women have access to power they are so afraid of promoting women's issues and being stigmatized by their male colleagues that they deliberately choose neutral issues'.

Many people believe that the secret of Margaret Thatcher's success as Britain's first female Prime Minister, and indeed one of the reasons for her rise to power, was that she managed to distance herself from women and women's issues. For the eleven years of her premiership she kept able women away from the higher echelons of government; she froze child benefit; she insisted 'I owe nothing to women's lib'. A working mother herself, she criticized others for condemning a generation of children to the 'chaos' of workplace crèches – if only there were some, most mothers felt – and, by implication, to an adult life of vice and violence. Ironically, throughout the 1980s every other woman in Britain had to suffer the constant reminder that feminism was redundant and that unparalleled opportunities were open to women: if a woman could occupy 10 Downing Street, she could do anything.

Then, as now, many feminists urged ordinary women to document and confront abuses on the job; but that expectation is founded on an image of feminism that involves falling on one's sword for the good of the cause, since such activism is often a guarantee of unemployment. Telling the truth about women is a luxury of the self-employed, and millions of women in the workplace learned to hide their beliefs and violate their own ethics every day just to survive.

Chapter Seven

Media Omission and Intellectual Polarization: How to Suffocate the Ideas of a Revolution

The Media: Caricature and Absence

A media campaign of omission and ridicule widened the gulf between mainstream women and the feminist movement. With the activism of the early 1970s, caricatures of feminism proliferated. Singling out specific feminist leaders for abuse, journalists attacked their weight, clothing and sexuality. An early seventies magazine cover read, 'Women Are Revolting.'

These caricatures were nothing new, dating back as they did to the Seneca Falls convention for women's rights in 1848, but they were effective. When I ask audiences to describe 'feminists' they come up with physical stereotypes: 'Hairy-legged.' 'Fat.' 'Middle-aged.' 'Scowling.' 'Short hair.' 'Sensible shoes.' 'Big breasts – but the wrong kind.' A British Psychological Society survey found that half of the 500 female students questioned thought of feminists as 'campaigning busybodies; manhaters; lesbian sergeant-major types'. Australian writer Deborah Rechter reported that young women in her country 'are deterred by stereotypes of feminists "with hairy armpits and vicious manners".' As Dr Heilbrun told the *Wall Street Journal*, feminism during the 1980s had 'lost control of its image'.

There is nothing wrong with being the 'image' the audiences describe: feminism should be about looking however one wants to. And the homophobia underlying the stereotype is palpable. The trouble is that audiences came to see feminism as having only one face rather than as many faces as there are women. A sizeable proportion of the young women I heard from truly believe that the main thing that determines feminism is body hair. 'I'm feminine, not a feminist,' one young woman told *Time* magazine in 1989, explaining that feminists don't shave their legs. Many women also believe that a feminist cannot have long hair, wear lipstick or like men. It became commonplace on college campuses for fellow students to look feminists up and down and tell them what was wrong with their appearance. Young women are particularly vulnerable to criticism of their looks, and – once again – the caricatures frightened many away.

Caricatures of feminism became more influential as the real history of the women's movement faded away. Older women are often astonished at younger women's ignorance of the events of the 1970s, but they forget that the media descriptions of the time, which were so vivid to them, are history's ephemera: they vanish. So the story of the women's liberation movement of the 1970s exists only in passing allusions and in a handful of books that few young women have read. When I ask my audiences who has read Germaine Greer or Betty Friedan, usually, out of the several hundred there, fewer than a dozen hands go up. For in spite of critics' cries that feminists are taking over the curriculum only 162 US universities and 16 per cent of universities in Britain have a women's studies programme at all. American students, who are often vague about history in general, are even more so about the recent history of the women's movement. 'Al Capone gets more space in my history textbook,' complained one student accurately, 'than the whole women's movement.'

So college students born after 1960 graduate with little knowledge of Mary Wollstonecraft, the Grimké sisters, Harriet Martineau, the Pankhursts, Sojourner Truth, Margaret Sanger, and the seventy-year fight for the vote, not to mention the facts of life just prior to *Roe* v. *Wade* in America or the 1967 Abortion Act in Britain. A great number of young women are given the impression that the rights they enjoy were granted to them by a naturally evolving society that grows ever more enlightened about women without any pressure from them. 'But why get so worked up?' they often ask. 'Aren't things just getting better?'

Sins of Omission

When we point the camera at one thing, we are pointing it away from another. Thus, one of the first things to look at when viewing the media is what you cannot see.

– Linda Ellerbee

If it were history books alone that deleted the women's movement, women could still turn to contemporary media to document their changing status. But the mainstream media leave out women in general, and the women's movement in particular, with a comprehensiveness that has disturbing implications for a democracy.

In spite of the positive ways in which women have recently been included in the mass media, a willingness to turn a blind eye to even the most historic of upheavals in women's history remains strong. Even in the Year of the Woman, American political magazines and TV shows managed to ignore the significance of the vote with an intentness suggesting that a mysterious virus of gender bias impaired editors' news sense industrywide. The full story of the upheavals sat waiting all year like a vast, ungainly mastodon in the middle of a thousand newsrooms, unremarked by a thousand shapers of opinion as they made broad detours round it on the way to their corner offices.

The media is a key influence on public opinion, as the European Commission Third Medium Term Action Programme recognized in the early 1980s. And the most effective way of influencing programme content and promoting positive images of women is to increase the number of women in decision-making and creative jobs within the industry. Consequently, a Steering Committee for

Equal Opportunities in Broadcasting and Television was established in Britain in 1986, with the specific aim of persuading radio and television companies to promote equal opportunity policies. But a staff survey of the BBC World Service in 1992 showed that many employees felt that equal opportunities was little more than a public relations exercise and that managers lacked any real commitment to significant change. The most recent statistics confirm that equal opportunities is still more of a theory than a practice in the broadcasting industry: 88 per cent of senior executives at the BBC are men; 76 per cent of senior producers and middle managers are men. There are four women and nine men on the Board of Management. Of the twenty-seven producers of BBC documentaries, eighteen are men, of the executive producers seven are male and two female, and none of the five strand editors is female. The vital statistics of Independent Television are even more sobering: of the 48 top-ranking jobs, from controllers to programme directors, not one is held by a woman.

The Institute of Manpower Services 'Skill Search' survey found that men outnumber women in the industry by three to one. Sex ratios vary considerably according to grade: only 5 per cent of technicians in camera grades are women, and 27 per cent of producers, producer/directors and directors. On the other hand, 74 per cent of wardrobe, 79 per cent of makeup and 89 per cent of production assistants are women.

Women also earn less than men. In June 1992 a report by management students at Central London Polytechnic (since renamed the University of Westminster) revealed that ITN's female employees earned on average £10,000 less per year than their male colleagues. Furthermore, men were twice as likely to be promoted. Of the 262 staff at Channel 4 who earn less than £20,000 a year, 194 (74 per cent) are women and of the high earners, with annual salaries exceeding £40,000, 55 are men and 17 (or 23 per cent) are women.

The few women who do have managerial jobs in television often lose out on company perks too. Shortly before bids were tendered in the new system of television franchising, which came into operation in January 1993, London Weekend Television offered 55 of its managers and executives the chance to buy into a lucrative new management share scheme. When LWT retained its franchise the share price rocketed with the result that managers made an amount totalling more than £55 million. What is interesting is that of the 55 names only six are women, and five of these are at the bottom of the league table of profits.

In a survey of the Australian film, television, radio and video industries carried out in November 1992, researchers Eva Cox and Sharon Laura found that they were still as marked by gender segregation as they had been some seven years earlier. Women and men do different jobs, have different skills, and different levels of seniority, pay and training: 21 per cent of producers, 22 per cent of directors and 39 per cent of crew lists are women. Whereas in 1985, 18 per cent of editors were women, seven years later female editors made up only 7 per cent of the total. There are more women writers – 18 per cent in 1985 and 27 per cent in 1992 – and 11 per cent of cinematographers and 14 per cent of camera operators are women; there were no women in these occupations in 1985. At the other end of the industry, they found that women were increasingly ghettoized in traditionally 'female' jobs: all production secretaries and production co-ordinators in 1992 were women compared to 96 per cent and 88 per cent in 1985.

In America a 1990 study by Women, Men and Media, found men reporting 85 per cent of the news on the three commercial networks, and men as 87 per cent of the newsmakers. By 1992 the number of men reporting the news had *increased*: TV nightly newscasts averaged *86 per cent* male correspondents, 79 per cent of the newsmakers. Another study, 'Casting and Fate', sponsored by the American Federation of Television and Radio Artists, looked at the major TV and cable networks and found that in news, women formed 35 per cent of broadcasters, 20 per cent of authorities cited, and 17 per cent of other newsmakers. In the *1992 Transcript/Video Index of TV and Radio News and Public Affairs Programming*, the entire category for 'Women (issues other than abortion, pregnancy, breast cancer)' took up twelve pages – that is, one page *less* than the amount of space devoted to the single category 'H. Ross Perot'.

In an American presidential election year, TV policy and analysis shows are extremely influential, interpreting for millions of viewers the week's history. In 1992 *Face the Nation* had 186 guests. Of these, thirty were women. Of those thirty, one appeared four times and another twice, meaning that twenty-five women were guests out of the total (counting Morgan Fairchild, the soap star). In this historic year, when women elected the first Democrat in twelve years, we had two shows on abortion (both included male guests), and one show on 'Women in Politics' (with two male guests). Other shows that could have had women speaking about the genderquake had few or none: 'The Season of Political Discontent' had no female guests; 'The LA Riots' had none; 'The Moral State of the Union' had one of four; and 'Family Values' had one woman out of five guests. The shows on 'Yugoslavia' and 'US Stance in Bosnia', a trouble zone where mass rapes, part of a pattern of genocide, galvanized women politically, had no female guests. And the two shows that dissected the Republican Convention, at which George Bush lost the White House largely because his platform and party rhetoric insulted women's intelligence, had no women at all.

Meet the Press was worse yet. Sixteen guest appearances out of 118 were by women; but one woman was on six times, and another, five; so eight different women (including those perennials, Jeane Kirkpatrick and Phyllis Schlafly) were guests over the course of fifty shows. Not one show was devoted by title to the topics of abortion, women's political breakthrough or the harassment charges or sex-assault trials that had dominated women's political consciousness throughout the year.

This Week with David Brinkley offered 153 guest appearances; twelve of these were by women, including the high-fashion model Iman. Health care, the Earth Summit, urban revival, crime and welfare reform were all topics of shows that left out women. Eighteen shows on the election were all-male. The show on the Tailhook incident had one woman (Senator Barbara Boxer) and three men. In the show on Bosnia-Herzegovina, the female perspective was provided by Margaret Thatcher. And the show on the Republican National Convention at which Pat Buchanan and Marilyn Quayle helped sink the feminist ship with their potshots at feminists, featured no women guests at all.

Not one leader of a women's organization was featured all year long in any of these shows; not Ellen Malcolm of Emily's List, whose money was reconfiguring Congress; not leaders of NARAL, whose organization's issue was the reason Republican women were going soft in their support of the party platform; not Patricia Ireland of NOW, an organization whose membership had shot up in the wake of the Hill–Thomas hearings.

In 1992's *The McLaughlin Group* we see a fascinating pattern: of 178 total appearances, 51 were by women. This is the highest total of all the shows. But the explanation is the show's format: Eleanor Clift, the sole woman, was responsible for every single one of the female appearances, valiantly slogging through almost every week. The show was hosted by ten pundits, nine of them male.

John McLaughlin's *One on One* show for 1992 had sixty-eight guests. Ten were women. Of these, one was a Republican contributor who had AIDS; one was the Vice-President's wife; one was a reporter invited to talk about the allegations of Bill Clinton's extramarital affair; one was trusty Jeane Kirkpatrick; and one was the omnipresent Iman, whose credentials include that quality so crucial to the solving of international development crises: photogenicity.

There was, to be fair, one show on feminism that interviewed Patricia Ireland; and then there was (for balance, presumably) one show on feminism that interviewed a *Playboy* columnist. There was one show on women in politics, with one woman; and then there was a show that discussed female condoms and breast implants, with no women.

The same absence of women on political discussion programmes in Britain was noted by the *Independent*. The newspaper listed seventy potential women panellists who could be invited to appear alongside the regular weekly line-up of male politicians and commentators on BBC1's *Question Time*. The programme's producer responded by including at least one woman per programme on its four-person panel. But, with the exception of MPs like Edwina Currie and Clare Short, the token woman was often the outsider, pitted against three men from the main political parties. Such disparity gave women little more than a spectacular opportunity to fail.

For the 1992 general election the BBC did not even have a token woman as anchor for the studio interviews. Newsreader

Anna Ford publicly criticized the BBC for sidelining its women journalists: 'I thought it was perfectly disgraceful ... where were the women? We make up 52 per cent of the population. We might have put different questions from those of the middle-aged, middle-class white Anglo-Saxon Protestant men.'

There were more women than men voters and a record number of women candidates standing for parliament in the 1992 general election, but one would never have guessed this from the politicians invited to appear on UK screens. Loughborough University's Media Unit monitored BBC's *Newsnight*, the *Nine O'Clock News*, BBC Radio 4's the *Today Programme* and ITN's *News at Ten* and found that out of the 1,031 appearances by politicians women politicians appeared only 36 times, and 28 of those appearances were by Margaret Thatcher. Shortly after the general election, BBC TV's *Panorama* posed the question 'Why has John Major's election victory promise turned so sour so soon?' The guests were Norman Tebbit, Alan Clark, David Mellor, Tom King, Cecil Parkinson, Andrew Neil and Max Hastings. Among them was one woman: Margaret Thatcher. And at the launch of Bristol Media Women's Group, a woman in the audience asked a senior BBC man why none of the coverage of the Maastricht Treaty had featured childcare, pregnancy, parental leave, minimum pay and rights of part-time workers – all areas that affected millions of women. 'Quite honestly,' he replied, 'I hadn't any idea that Maastricht would affect women any differently from men.'

On the rare occasions when women do have a say in programme-making, they can help to improve the working conditions of other women. Researchers Angela Coyle and Reena Bhauhani, from the Organization Development Centre at London's City University, found that the producer of BBC's highly popular *Crimewatch* series had a very distinctive management style. Unusually in the BBC, Nikki Cheetham used her position to empower others on the team. She also structured the work to avoid late-night and weekend working so that she and her colleagues could spend as much time as possible with their families. In contrast, ITN programme director Sue Caro found that as the company increased its demands on her she was forced to choose between her job and her family. Responsible throughout

1991 for *News at Ten*'s dramatic special editions on the Romanian revolution and Nelson Mandela's release from jail, and for *Channel 4 News'* coverage of Margaret Thatcher's resignation, she was highly paid and highly respected. But with the increasingly long and inflexible hours – her contract stipulated that she had to be on call 24 hours a day, seven days a week – she found that 'there was no effort to understand the obstacles I faced and childcare problems were not considered a good enough reason for changing shifts or rearranging hours'. As she pointed out, 'If this kind of attitude prevails, we will get to a situation where there are simply no women with children working at senior levels in news or any other kind of television, the consequences of which will be reflected in what the viewer sees – or does not see.'

Sue Caro's case was not an isolated one. As the recession deepened, equal opportunity policies came under threat. Jane Paul, equality officer of BECTU, the broadcasting and entertainment union, reported that a 'worryingly high proportion' of mothers and pregnant women were accepting voluntary redundancy packages because of practical difficulties of working longer hours or away from home.

Even Lord Rees-Mogg, the then chairman of the Broadcasting Standards Council, was forced to admit that 'women feel that TV is made by men for men and women feel it is an alien force representing standards, values and interests they don't share'.

All right, one might say, that is television. But unfortunately, the print media is little better.

In America, according to Women, Men and Media's 1992 study, there were three times as many articles on the wives of presidential and vice-presidential candidates as on the women running for office. That year, 72 per cent of front-page newspaper stories bore men's bylines. Of the sources quoted in the stories, 86 per cent were male, 68 per cent of front-page photos were of men.

The White House press corps is 69 per cent male. In 1992 the three biggest news magazines (*Time, Newsweek* and *US News & World Report*) averaged 14 per cent female references in news stories. Even when nine of the eleven medals brought home by Americans from the 1992 Olympics were won by *female* athletes, the sports coverage overwhelmingly featured the men.

The more prestigious the newspaper, the worse the offence: the *New York Times* ranked lowest for women references on the front page (8 per cent); 16 per cent of op-ed pieces ran under a female byline during a one-month survey. Under a new publisher, Arthur Sulzberger, Jr, who has committed himself publicly to opening the paper to women's voices, 70 per cent of the essayists were males over the course of a year. The *Washington Post* also had dismal numbers of women bylined on the front page (29 per cent), as well as the fewest women of all newspapers in the one-month survey on the op-ed page (13 per cent).

Well, one could say, the American daily press is superficial by nature. Let us look, then, at the most important policy and culture journals in the United States to see how they covered the year.

Starting on the left: In the *Nation*, one of the country's oldest and most respected political journals, 23 per cent of articles had female bylines (25 names were gender-ambiguous). Of the female-bylined pieces, all but 66 were poems, regular columns, book or periodical reviews, or letters to the editor. Out of a total of 773, 66 independent articles or editorials were by women.

Harper's magazine, a liberal monthly, ran a total of 249 articles in 1992. Of these, 45, or about 17 per cent, were by women, which sounds promising until one notices that 20 were 'readings' and 4 were fiction. Nine pieces were part of forums that conscientiously included six men. Which leaves 4 independent, originally commissioned non-fiction pieces.

The *New Republic*, a policy journal based in Washington and considered moderate, ran 914 pieces, including poems, in 1992. Of these, 120 (or about 14 per cent) were written by women. Of the 120 female-authored contributions, 10 bylines were for poems and 47 were book and poetry reviews, leaving 63 independent featured articles by women, or less than 10 per cent of the magazine's total.

During the year, the *New Republic* devoted two covers to women. In the 'New Feminists' issue (16 March 1992), three articles – one by me and two book reviews – were written by women. The following week, perhaps to give readers and editors a chance to recover from the shock of all that female prose, it was down to one. In its 5 October 1992 (described to me by an editor as a 'special women's issue') six submissions had female bylines.

The Boston-based *Atlantic Monthly*, ran 64 out of 216 pieces (33 per cent) under a female byline (three names were gender-ambiguous). Of the women-authored pieces 17 were poems, fiction or humour, 39 were reviews of books, art, travel or 'other', such as word games. Eight were independent featured articles, one attacking Feminists Against Pornography.

The *New Yorker* wasn't much better. In 1992, 229 out of 716 bylines (32 per cent) were women's. Of these, most were poems, or fiction, book reviews, other reviews – such as fashion and food pieces – and 35 were independent featured articles on politics, the arts or current events.

In the UK, the scene is as grim. Women comprise 22 per cent of the total staff employed in magazines and newspapers, and most of these women are in magazine publishing. There are very few women in upper management, even in the magazines, and only two national newspapers, the *Sunday Express* and the *News of the World*, have women editors. The worst side of this 'men's club' is revealed when women's issues hit the headlines. Alison Halford was subjected to rumour and counter-rumour in the press when she filed her sex discrimination suit against Merseyside Police. Denise Kingsmill, a solicitor who frequently acts in sexual harassment cases, advises her clients that they will face a media ordeal 'with reporters hanging around their dustbins and following them. British women who allege sexual harassment are pilloried by the press. Americans don't have the kind of media we have.'

The Australians do, though. Female public figures have a particularly hard time. When Dr Carmen Lawrence made Australian history in February 1990 by becoming the first woman premier in the country, the newspapers congratulated her with such comments as: 'Dr Lawrence is no Margaret Thatcher. She hasn't the beauty of Pakistan's Benazir Bhutto. And while she may have the intellect she hasn't the years of Israel's Golda Meir.' It is hard to imagine a male politician being subjected to such comparisons. But women politicians have to suffer this kind of treatment as part of the job. Ex-Senator Janine Haines remembers being subjected to 'an almost continuous and offensive barrage of comments' about her physical appearance. In Britain, MP Gwyneth Dunwoody observed that 'the media treats women Members of Parliament as if they are either to be patted on the head or on the bottom', whilst Teresa Gorman, MP, believes the media treat women 'mainly as a joke'. And in Canada, on the eve of Kim Campbell's election victory as the country's first ever female Prime Minister, newspapers were asking whether 'a 46-year-old, twice-divorced, childless woman who grew up in a broken and embittered home [was] strong enough, sensitive enough to be Prime Minister of Canada'.

A UK survey conducted by Women in Publishing in 1987 of the book pages of national papers found that those which reflected the greatest sex bias were often the ones whose editors were emphatic about the fairness of their own practices:

> It was not particularly surprising, for instance, that the *Financial Times*, which might be expected to have the most specialised readership of all papers, did in fact come near the bottom of the table of women authors (15 percent). But for all their specialised readership ... they still featured more female reviewers than the *Sunday Times* and the *Guardian* and more books written by women than the *Mail on Sunday*. David Holloway, the literary editor of the *Daily Telegraph* who stated quite blithely, 'at a guess I should have thought I use as many women as men reviewers ... but I am certainly not going to bother to count', comes out with a score of 21 percent.

Women in Publishing's follow-up survey, conducted during the last four months of 1991, found little improvement: 24 per cent of the books reviewed in the national newspapers were by women; 18 per cent of the reviewers were women.

Publishers also leave women out. Although women buy more books than men and women read more books than men, women account for just 20 per cent of published authors. This is in spite of the efforts of feminist publishers to raise the profile of women's writing and women's issues. Led by Virago in 1973, and the feminist publishers that followed, a whole industry developed around feminist books, from professional associations like Women in

Publishing, Women in Libraries and Women in Heritage and Museums to women's bookshops and publications devoted to reviewing women's writing. In 1984, under the banner of 'Women's Books Are Here to Stay', the First International Feminist Bookfair was held in London and confounded critics by being both popular and profitable. Now, some 200 years after Mary Wollstonecraft's *A Vindication of the Rights of Woman*, feminist books have become a hot financial property for mainstream publishers. Penguin, for example, launched 300,000 copies of their *Essential Reading for Women* catalogue of 450 titles at the 1992 Fifth International Feminist Bookfair in Amsterdam. So why are there still five times more men than women in print? Nicolette Jones found 'a stunning correlation between the number of women authors on most publishers' lists and the number of women editors on the staff'. In 1990 the Hansard Commission reported that 75 per cent of employees in editorial departments were women, but as Virago founder, Carmen Callil, pointed out: 'There are so few women with any power in British publishing.' Eighty-seven per cent of publishing directors in 1990 were men, and men in the industry were six times as likely as women to be high earners.

Publishing has traditionally rested on its laurels as a paternalistic 'gentlemen's profession' so what about radio, then? For goodness' sake, women are at least supposed to be talkers. But in America, in a year when the call-in show became the nation's town hall, 50 of the National Association of Radio Talk-show Hosts' 900 members were women. (One female talk-show host in Chicago reported to me that when she tries to get tough with her political interviewees, callers tell her to stop bossing the man around.)

How can we be surprised that women question their worth, or that at adolescence girls lose their voice and their sense of entitlement to an opinion? How could girls not doubt the validity of their own concerns? The Western media culture grants women approximately one quarter of its forums in which to try to work out what they think, and indicates again and again that their opinions have one third the value of men's.

By 1993, in the US the press numbers had scarcely budged. Men still accounted for 85 per cent of the front-page quotes. They wrote 66 per cent of the front-page stories and 74 per cent of the opinion pieces. Eighty-six per cent of stories on nightly news programmes were reported by men; 75 per cent of the interviewees were male. Not unexpectedly, given this imbalance, while women's losses were splashed all over the front pages, a victory like passage of the Family Leave Act was dealt with fleetingly, and soon relegated to inside pages.

What are editors' explanations for this gender minority rule in the press? The standard reply is that of Andrew Sullivan, editor of the *New Republic*, who told me, 'It's really hard to get women. Regrettably, opinion journalism is still a boys' club. Women tend not to write opinion pieces.'

But does this explanation ring true? In many fields women's absence at the top is attributable to their status as newcomers, but writing and thinking cannot be counted among the professions that let women in just last week.

Paper is cheap, and sitting still, 'feminine'. Women cornered the writing profession in the nineteenth century to such a degree that the most popularly acclaimed writers of the age were female. Aphra Behn, dramatist, novelist and the first woman to earn a living by her pen, lived in the seventeenth century. Harriet Martineau produced an incisive political and cultural analysis of an entire fledgling nation in 1837; Margaret Fuller was writing essays on the main intellectual currents of the day in 1845. Harriet Beecher Stowe was a bestselling anti-slavery polemicist throughout the 1850s and 1860s; Ida B. Wells exposed lynching in the 1890s. Dame Rebecca West was a crusading social critic in the 1920s. Women have been writing thoughtfully for centuries longer than today's male editors have been on the planet.

Well, are girls *worse* writers today than they have been for the last three centuries? In educational institutions in the Western world, girls are routinely considered the better writers. The National Education Association's data show that 'girls consistently outperform boys on writing-skills assessment'. Other data shows the sexes performing equally. So: press and television journalism leave qualified women out.

Perhaps we should throw up our hands and turn to the escapism of Hollywood. But the pattern is repeated in the film industry. Although women directed some of 1992's biggest hits (such as *Wayne's World* and *A League of Their Own*), *Premiere* magazine's 1992 list of Hollywood's hundred most powerful people is 95 per cent male. Only one woman, Paramount's Sherry Lansing, has the power to give the go-ahead to a movie. Of 400 members of the Producers' Guild of America, just 15 per cent are women. No women have won jobs in the top tiers of the major talent agencies, and a 1991 survey by Women in Film shows that only three women, as opposed to forty-five men, are in top management at the twenty entertainment companies examined; only two of the twenty companies employed women in at least 30 per cent of their senior or executive-vice-president-level positions. Sara Risher, a president at New Line Cinema, one of the smaller movie companies, says, 'It's a white male bastion. They are very reluctant to let outsiders in of any kind that they have not known and worked with for a long time.'

One might look at these numbers in dismay but reassure oneself that women's entry into the media will spontaneously improve the situation. But while women's presence in journalism is a crucial factor in the genderquake, and while many journalists are turning out bold stories about the half of contemporary society that is female, the pressures on such women are intense. It is naïve for women consumers of newspapers, magazines, books, movies and TV to call on women producers of these media to change the situation without giving them support from below to do so. Women who cover politics, for instance, walk an impossibly fine line, under scrutiny from their employers not to report 'as a woman' – a point of view that is considered to be a failure of objectivity, while reporting from a male viewpoint is not – even as they are also expected to produce the 'women's angle' from time to time. Simon Jenkins of *The Times* dismissed women's-issue journalism as 'demeaning to modern women who want to be considered as people not women'. Susan B. Anthony wrote: 'As long as newspapers and magazines are controlled by men, every woman upon them must write articles which are reflections of men's ideas. As long as that continues, women's ideas and deepest convictions will never get before the public.' Over a century later, the same sentiments are echoed by journalist and author Rosalind

Coward: women journalists are popular 'provided they distance themselves from any organised system of thought like feminism and simply fire off witty and opinionated pieces'.

Feminists keep hoping that when 'enough women' work in the media, coverage will change automatically. But that expectation overlooks the fact that women journalists are just as constrained by economic silencing, and just as bound by the carrot-and-stick set of rewards and punishments connected with workplace feminism, as are women in other professions. Indeed, they often experience even more pressure, since their profession plays such a pivotal role in shaping beliefs about women. Unsurprisingly, the Women, Men and Media study showed that women journalists cite women no more often than do their male counterparts.

Like other working women, female journalists are given the message that a sure way to derail a career is to make too much noise about 'women's issues'. They are presented with many examples of this by management: they saw what became of the first openly feminist generation of women at the *New York Times*, who in the 1970s called for more equitable pay scales, but were rewarded in many cases by career limbo. Twenty years later, in 1990, when the *Times*'s female journalists presented the paper's executive editor, Max Frankel, with a study showing the lack of women on the front page, he replied: 'If you are covering local teas' more women would appear on the front page. While the journalists protested about his remark by wearing teapot badges to work, the message from the top was clear.

Even in 1992, in the midst of one of the tremors of the gender-quake, female management was encouraged to analyse the news 'in drag'. *New York Times* editor Soma Golden, the first woman to head the paper's national desk, was confronted by a roomful of journalists – about half female – who had called a standing-room-only meeting to protest at the paper's coverage of alleged rape victim Patricia Bowman's 'wild streak'. She said that she wasn't responsible for 'every weird mind that reads the *New York Times*'. In 1993 Emily Rooney became the first woman executive producer of a nightly network newscast. Anchorman Peter Jennings, who had one of the deciding votes, 'emphasized that "Rooney was never a 'woman' candidate, although she certainly brings an extra dimension."' When Liz Forgan resigned as Channel 4's director of programmes to join the BBC, the *Sunday Times* headline announced: 'John Birt brings in "bossy" woman for top BBC job.'

Almost every woman in television and the press understands that such comments are at once a Freudian slip and a warning: if she presses her newspaper, magazine or TV show to cover 'women's issues' or to interview or hire more women, or even to guarantee equal pay and promotion in the studio, she risks being perceived as a 'woman' reporter or producer or editor, even though her male colleagues do not have to worry about being described as 'men'. And she will not be chosen by the big boys for levitation through the secret trapdoor in the glass ceiling.

The irony is that gender apartheid in the media is killing the goose that laid the golden egg. Newspapers in particular are hurting. For various reasons, in the early 1980s profits plunged from between 30 per cent and 70 per cent. Readership levels have been falling for thirty years. Those in the business are anxiously seeking out the solution, aware that somehow, as media critic Howard Kurtz put it in the *Washington Post*, 'newspapers have become unplugged from their readers'. Male media critics even acknowledge that 'we drive away readers, particularly women, by immersing ourselves in the empty manoeuverings of middle-aged white guys in suits'. But they are tackling this problem in a way that reveals that the male need to own one of the culture's most potent forces – the daily manufacture of history – outweighs even the bottom line.

Newspaper publishers are reluctant to understand that their problem is simple. Many women are no longer reading newspapers that present the white male version of reality, because in the past thirty years women have stopped believing that that perspective *is* the only true reality. Desperately, publishers are courting women with 'light news' and extra tacked-on features. Tabloid editor Peter Hamill argues that the loss of female readership should be remedied with shopping columns, health, education, beauty, food, fashion and lifestyle features. One category he does not mention is news and until newspapermen understand that women newsmakers, and news that is relevant to women, draw women readers, they will continue to lose precious ground.

This segregation of hard news and soft views along gender lines neuters the voices of generation after generation of young women writers. Young women learn that they have a much better chance of being published in the main pages of a national newspaper if they present a viewpoint disdainful of feminist reasoning. Alternatively, if they wish to write regularly about things that matter to women, they must cultivate the frothy touch of so many women's magazines.

'I feel that I'm seeing a segregated mass,' Kendall Anderson, a journalism student in Minnesota, told me. 'It affects me, what I can expect or hope for. If you look at the *Atlantic*, the masthead is 80 per cent men. I go in every month and look at [it]. As a young writer looking at a magazine that's supposed to be progressive, it's discouraging. You see this segregation in politics. But then you see the press – and they're always men. But it's the Fourth Estate! It's not supposed to be segregated. It's supposed to be the watch-dog of society.'

Many feminists advocate rejecting women's magazines, women's pages in newspapers and daytime talk shows on BBC Radio 4's Woman's Hour. This impulse is misguided. Those media are now the heart of feminism – or rather, of the unlabelled power feminism that is shaking the country. Male commentators analysing the 1992 US election understood that daytime talk shows had superseded establishment forums as the source from which people get their politics. The same insight should be applied to the despised 'women's media' of glossy magazines.

But women's magazines are not accorded the respect they deserve as the only regular transmitters of half-substantive debate around women's issues. They operate with neither prestige nor a mandate from their readers – who are critical of them but who have yet to organize the call-in and write-in support the editors need in order to expand serious coverage in the face of advertisers' scepticism.

Consequently, it is rare for a woman's magazine to promote feminism overtly. Those that do, often pay a high price for their politics: when *Honey* increased the feminist content of its articles and featured models wearing little or no makeup, the editor Carol Sarler had to leave. Most women's magazines stick to a tried and tested formula and their contents are dictated, or vetoed, by the advertisers' notion of what is compatible with selling their product, or the magazine proprietor's idea of what will increase circulation figures. For instance, *Cosmopolitan* can boost sales with an ill-advised article on why women should not worry too much about AIDS, and *Elle* can wax lyrical about the Femidom when health officials are still concerned that it is under-researched and when it is still unavailable in the US.

Good investigative journalism in women's magazines increasingly makes way for titillating and voyeuristic articles. Women's magazine features have progressed far beyond the need for women to be informed about the workings of their bodies. In a single month (May 1992), journalist Melanie Phillips found the following on offer: 'Penis envy: why he will always play with himself, even when he's in love with you' (*Cosmopolitan*); 'Why isn't sex like it is in the movies?', 'Free 24-page supplement: a smart girl's guide to men and sex', and 'Exciting, extraordinary sex ... do you have the confidence to get kinky?' (*Company*); 'Sexual ecstasy: dare to go a step beyond' (*New Woman*); 'Tempted by adultery', 'I was married 22 times', and 'I am a thirteen year old prostitute' (*Marie Claire*); 'Get your knickers on! men who prefer lewd to nude' (*She*).

Sociologist Angela McRobbie suggests that while many of these magazines have taken feminism on board 'they are running scared of feminism's didactic, prim image ... they've developed this frank approach which they express in bonking language'.

Even traditional publishers of men's sex magazines are turning their attention to women in an attempt to revive flagging circulation figures. *Penthouse* was among the first to sport photographs of semi-clothed instead of nude models, claiming that this appeals to the 'new man'. At the same time, its publishers, Northern and Shell, have launched three sex magazines for women: *For Women*, *Women on Top* and *Women Only*.

While it would be encouraging to think that women's erotic needs are finally being recognized, the evidence of poorly researched features points to a more cynical explanation: sex sells, but heavy-hitting opinion or investigative journalism is an optional extra.

Women's issues are rarely taken seriously by the media. More often treatment is superficial and underfunded, and they remain the lowest on the list of priorities. Thames TV launched an all-woman talk show in January 1992. Chaired by Eve Pollard, *The Truth about Women* was a potentially exciting current affairs programme. Its guests included politicians Teresa Gorman, Edwina Currie, Diane Abbott and Clare Short; journalists Nigella Lawson and Carol Thatcher; agony aunt Anna Raeburn; actress Geraldine James and Rabbi Julia Neuberger. It should have been an unparalleled success. Instead it was seen to be the experiment that failed. The fact that it went on air at 3 a.m. might explain why the programme was short-lived.

Where women's talk shows do exist and thrive, they can still be left to languish in an ill-researched but nevertheless highly influential ghetto. In the United States, for example, talk-show host Sally Jessy Raphael has said that she believes feminism is 'anti-family', and that when she needs someone to talk about family issues she calls the Moral Majority because they stress that identification. When told that family issues were in fact at the top of women's organizations' agenda, she replied that nevertheless 'the perception is out there that they are not interested in family'. According to polls, American women trust and like Oprah Winfrey more than they do Geraldine Ferraro. But the sexist attitudes that assign these shows such low status keep them unaccountable for the fact that they, more than any other single force, shape the perceptions that lead millions of women to make the political choices they do.

So, in our media-driven culture in which information equals power, second-rate information and space, like second-rate health care and representation, are assumed to be good enough for women. When it comes to mainstream media devoted to women, the situation is clearly 'separate but unequal'. And the unfolding story of women's growing political might must fight for small amounts of space within an eternal orbit of celebrity secrets and hair gel.

The same temptations to trim and shape affect the feminist press. A 1993 *Ms.* cover story about ritual sexual abuse of children – 'Believe It! Cult Ritual Abuse Exists' does not even make the grade of tabloid journalism. Written by a pseudonymous author, the story skimps on locations, dates and corroboration. I am open to believing the author, but why should I? Just because I am a feminist? According to writer Ann Hornaday, a contributing editor of *Ms.*, her interview with performance artist Holly Hughes was edited to delete comments supporting pornography. Similar treatment of readers, in the name of feminism, led to the downfall of Britain's longest-running feminist magazine. Launched in 1972, *Spare Rib* went into liquidation in March 1993 with debts of £100,000. Journalist and ex-employee Eileen Fairweather wrote one of the obituaries, exaggerating the problem, but pointing out a gap between the magazines coverage and its readers' interests. '*Spare Rib* espoused a rigid hierarchy of oppression, blaming the suffering of women worldwide on the smug, over-privileged racist white women who mainly bought the magazine.' So the mainstream media often treat women like children who need not even be addressed, and the women's media sometimes treat women like children who do not even need to be persuaded, but must take things on faith. But if the genderquake has shown us one thing, it is that women are tired of being treated like children.

Women know that they are being cheated. This situation in the media does injustice to the reality that women's dilemmas are, increasingly, not simple and oppositional, but highly ambiguous. And often each side has an equally powerful emotional and intellectual charge. Women want to work *and* raise children; women have misgivings about pornography *and* are interested in sexual self-expression; women like to dress-up *and* hate being required to; women want the right to go to war *and* don't want to kill. But highbrow publications ignore women's issues, women's magazines don't dare get too close to a feminist 'line', and feminist publications don't dare stray too far.

With so many media reluctant to broach these ambiguities – to present substantive, clashing perspectives on erotica, or the sex trade, or mothering – women's concerns erupt in other forms.

Without a conscious, reasonable forum in which to work out these tensions, the female unconscious projects them on to symbols. So during the 1980s symbols arose out of our under-debated anxieties and stood in for real discourse about women's issues. Madonna stood in for 'Can we imagine a vocabulary of sexual imagery in which a woman is powerful?' 'Mothers who stay at home' versus 'Mother who work' stood in for, 'Almost all other industrialized countries have state-funded childcare and family leave. What can we do to get it?' 'Lipstick lesbians' stood in for 'What are our stereotypes about female homosexuality? Why do they exist? What is it about the "ugly dyke" caricature that affects all women?' Attacks on Chelsea Clinton's looks and Hillary Rodham Clinton's headbands stood in for 'Are we ready to make a society in which a woman can be powerful without having herself or her children be punished for it?' And Nannygate stood in for 'Domestic and childcare workers occupy the lowest employment rung in the society, yet they are performing a crucial service that more and more families need. How can we come to terms with their new importance to the nation's wellbeing, and legislate their role in a way that protects them from exploitation?' We never had these conversations with anything remotely resembling the gravity and space that the issues require.

This lack of space in the media tightens further the knots of tension in women's consciousness, but denies the issues room to be untangled. And repercussions of this gender apartheid extend far beyond merely curtailing female experts' careers and annoying women viewers and readers. The situation actually withholds from the nation the tools it needs to solve its own problems, an imbalance that leads to lousy policy debate, and finally to lousy policymaking. ('Come now,' a top-level *New York Times* editor said to me without irony, 'sexual harassment surely isn't a problem for more than a handful of women?') When TV and newspaper editors leave out women experts on women's issues, they leave out the feminist economists who understand that famine and overpopulation result from women's low status and educational levels; they leave out the activists who understand the connection between successful welfare reform and the availability of childcare; they leave out the health-care experts who can point out that you can't have effective medical treatment if the research it is based on has used only male subjects. How can we reason about 'family values' in the absence of the data showing that it was men and not women who abandoned children and home? The gender apartheid in our public forums omits important pieces of the policy puzzle and denies women and men solutions that really work.

Consequence: Slowdown for Women

Maintaining gender apartheid in the selection, interpretation and presentation of the news is central to keeping women from advancement.

The tale of a mighty struggle has tremendous narrative appeal. When victories are broadcast, people feel heartened and connected, and enlist for the fight. But gender apartheid in the news interrupts, shuts down and blocks off the larger story, preventing it building up momentum and taking people forward. Tuning in becomes frustrating – or even downright discouraging. In January 1993, for example, coverage of the recently passed Family Leave Act in the United States – a triumph due entirely to women's new political muscle – was drowned out by Nannygate stories. When the complex, nuanced, interconnected stories of women's struggle are left out of a common forum, it is almost impossible for women to get news from the front: how much ground is being gained or lost? Where should pressure be exerted? The disruption of the news makes women feel as if they are fighting a war in which they are uncertain whether the other soldiers have retreated, been killed, surrendered, or gone home altogether, leaving them foolishly embattled and all alone. The editorial act of detaching female electoral triumphs from their origins in female votes, and then giving women's losses star billing while delegating to female victory the role of mousy understudy, provides an important service to the opposition. It keeps women from perceiving the great secret of the end of the twentieth century: that they can be in charge, and that their clout, when they use it, is untouchable.

So this gender apartheid in the media has four consequences. One, it quenches debate, keeping women politically stalled. Two, when TV and newspaper editors excuse themselves from covering issues that affect more than half of their readership, they fail to inform more than 50 per cent of the population of how to vote in their own best interests. Since the right to vote in one's own interest is part of the basic concept of a democracy, these editors fail to live up to their responsibilities. Three, this press bias specifically ridicules the women's movement, thus alienating women even further from their representatives. Four, since the issues that affect women are given almost no public room for free debate, the public comments that do get through matter too much. Commentators know they will not have the luxury of refinement, cross-questioning and nuance. So their observations are often forced to carry not the light, flexible mass of free mutable ideas, but the hard weight of a solid position under attack.

Feminist Hostility to the Press

This lack of space in turn degrades feminism's relationship to the media and leads some feminists and feminist groups beyond the reluctance to join in the dance to an active stamping on the toes of a sympathetic partner. One talented young organizer wanted to insisted that reporters covering a benefit pay for the expensive tickets at the door. At a 1992 feminist march on Washington, young ushers shoved hapless journalists into a cordoned area like hostages. Some Riot Grrls refuse to speak to the press. Karen Houppert, a sympathetic reporter, covered a WAC meeting at which a fistfight broke out. As the reporter with her took photos, members of the group cried, 'Stop taking pictures!' and, 'Get the media out of here!' One woman said, 'I'm a lawyer ... Give me your film.' Another: 'I think we should demand the right to approve the photos they intend to run with this article.' And another, 'I hope you don't intend to write about this ... You'll only make feminism look bad.' At some feminist meetings, individual members have hissed when journalists identified themselves, in compliance with the group's request.

Feminism's sometimes stormy relationship with the press comes from its experience of being distorted, and is compounded by feminists' insights into the superficial way women are looked at and the seductiveness they must use in order to be seen and heard. This important insight about looking, however, is taken too literally: at the end of the twentieth century, mastering the media is inevitably a form of seduction, no matter who you are or how important the message is. TV, for instance, treats both women and men far more superficially than does print. While it paints women much more heavily than it paints men – it paints men too.

This feminist distrust of the media is also directly related to the experience of date rape and sexual harassment. Women constantly learn that their bodies will be deliberately misinterpreted, their body language used against them. When a woman wears a mini-skirt to 'say' that she controls her own sexuality but she is raped, a court of law will 'read' the skirt as meaning that she ceded control of her sexuality to others. When one feminist group considered a proposal to talk to the press, a member said that it would be better 'not to spread our legs for the media'. This sense that it is impossible to control the meaning of the female body leads some feminists to believe that there is a continuum between public debate in the media and sexual exploitation. They feel that the only way left to exert personal freedom in relation to the press is by withdrawing from it altogether.

The unhappy consequence of the press's relegation of feminist debate to the margins was that some feminists responded by glamorizing, or privileging, the margins of debate, which re-inforced a beleaguered us-against-them mentality. A debate on media coverage in one feminist group illustrates this. *Harper's Bazaar* had undertaken to do a feature on the group. According to reporter Amruta Slee, a faction of women were strongly opposed to this, since *Harper's Bazaar* is a fashion magazine. They argued that their organization should co-operate only with 'honourable' publications such as *Ms.* and the *Village Voice* – 'honourable', in this context, evidently meaning 'left-wing and alternative'. To the group's credit, the majority overruled, and a photographer shot a portrait of several of the activists.

But this in turn gave rise to a round of accusations: the photographer 'should have shot us in action, and not posing'. He 'should not have taken a woman of colour and put her in the front row'. There 'should have been no photograph at all'. Like Victorian invalids who can wield power only through their illness, and therefore refuse to get well, these women were hanging on to the identity of 'those who are excluded' even while their message was in the process of being *included*.

The scene also shows how being left out of free debate creates a mentality that turns marginality into an elitist clique. Any activist movement, especially a marginalized one, is sooner or later also a culture, with its own fashion (even if it is an anti-fashion fashion), its own hairstyles and its own jargon. While it is human nature for people to seek out markers and codes that make them knowledgeable insiders, it is a great irony that a subculture that expresses a commitment to inclusiveness should be so contemptuous of the publications that most women read – and by extension, of most women. The subculture mentality comes perilously close to betraying one of feminism's core truths: every single woman counts.

Who reads women's magazines? Who watches daytime TV? Millions of women do, of every class, background, religion, race and age. Who reads *Ms.* and *Everywoman*? A few thousand people, mostly urban, white, middle class and university educated. When a feminist urges her group to confine its media appearances to what her friends are reading, she is close to saying, 'Women who read *Harper's Bazaar* or *Vogue* are not as important as we are; they're not our kind.' When she doesn't want to bother talking to other groups in their words, about their concerns, that is a snobbery unworthy of feminism, which of all movements should be the exemplar of populism.

Observe a woman trying to bring a strong feminist message into a five-against-one TV panel hosted by some joking chauvinist. It is stressful; it is uncomfortable; it is extremely embarrassing for her. In the white heat of the mass media, saying something as obvious as 'Rape is bad' can position a woman as a fanatical outsider. But power feminism means learning form Madonna, Spike Lee and Bill Cosby: if you don't like your group's image in the media, decide on another image and seize control of the means of producing it. If we don't like the myth we're handed, our responsibility doesn't end with complaining about what's wrong with it. Our responsibility begins with creating better myths. 'If you don't like the news,' reads one feminist T-shirt 'make some of your own.'

Feminist Flatness

So the media leaves women's issues out, and feminism in turn looks away from the media. Consequently, those rare occasions that do include women's issues have a parodic flatness. When the issues are debated, polarization becomes extreme to the point of being surreal. TV and the press love a good cat-fight, but are almost never interested in good-faith debate within feminism. So rather than hearing from Black feminists and white feminists on racism in feminism, or from anti-censorship feminists and anti-pornography feminists we get only this feminist versus A Man, and that feminist versus A Right-wing Woman. In such a situation it becomes intellectually reckless for a feminist to concede ambiguities in her position.

Even media events designed to provide a forum for women's lives can be so truncated that the format is almost an insult to the subject matter. Paramount Pictures is planning a six-part documentary called *Women in the Twentieth Century* (that's right – the whole century). A TV special on Lifetime, an American cable network devoted to women, had to cover the work, family and health of all American women in a grand twelve minutes per segment. The speed required to skim 100 million women's conflicts and viewpoints in forty-eight minutes led to a comical scene of pop-up declarations, but not a serious social or political forum. The pro-choice guest said her sentence, the pro-life one said hers; the woman in the military stood up, and the how-to-reconcile-work-and-family guest sat down. When the show ended, American women were left with their ambivalences and frustrations raw and exposed, but not resolved.

One result is that prominent feminists, tired of biased forums or space offered to them in bad faith, often withdraw from debate. Gloria Steinem decided years ago to avoid appearing on television with an antagonist. Andrea Dworkin and Catharine MacKinnon, almost inevitably invited to debate with pornographers or their hired representatives, refuse to do so. Camille Paglia charges feminism with shutting down debate – calling Gloria Steinem Stalin, and me Little Miss Pravda – but refuses to appear on a Princeton panel with feminist or academic challengers. It is little wonder that so many women aren't sure what feminism means. They rarely hear it articulated, let alone tested and defended in a free forum.

How Discussion Is Blocked and Cartoon Opinions Manufactured: Camille Paglia, FAIR, and the Pornography Non-Debate

Three media journeys show how lack of a forum degrades the level of discourse about feminism and women.

The media journey of Camille Paglia is a good example of the way that a hostile and unbalanced mass media combines with scarcity of real forums to stymie discussion about women's issues. The Philadelphia professor appeared on the scene with a set of opinions that sounded at least superficially provocative and outrageous, and that had the advantage of being packaged in prose much snappier than the academic work she likes to attack. A writer who defines herself as a feminist while she generates some traditionally anti-feminist opinions, Paglia was fêted in the very press that had, over the course of a decade, assiduously neglected to present to the public the currents of thought she indicted.

The absence of space for a critical rejoinder ensured that Paglia's mischaracterizations of feminism went without challenge. For example, her assertion that feminists want men and women to be the same went undebated even though difference feminism and 'the Other' were all the rage in universities throughout the 1980s; her claim that feminism is puritanical was made in the face of a burgeoning feminist erotic vanguard; and her remark that feminists overreact to date rape came as the National Institute of Mental Health in the United States studies showed that many women who experience date rape contemplate suicide. No one seemed to notice, either, the fact that many of her truisms identifying women with nature and men with civilization, and warning that women will become desexed in the workplace, were reiterations of standard anti-feminist rhetoric from an earlier backlash: that of 1890–1910.

In the absence of a serious forum in which to investigate her charges, any debate about the issues Paglia raised were cast as a cat-fight or as an exhibition of personal invective. This ensured that the important, timely points she does raise – What is choice and what is consent? Has feminism become elitist or doctrinaire? Is there a puritanical streak in the women's movement? – were lost, their validity diluted by her undifferentiated assault on feminism as a whole. Thus, Paglia's potentially fruitful challenge to the women's movement was diverted by this appropriation of her persona – an appropriation that is, ultimately, sexist treatment of Paglia herself and that trivializes her seriousness as a thinker.

I saw at first hand an example of how the media distorts the presentation of feminists, and how feminist debate is inhibited in response. At an event at the 92nd Street YMHA in New York City in 1992, which included a range of feminists, Camille Paglia's name came up and the audience hissed. Later, when an entirely unrelated subject was under discussion, the director of a segment for 60 Minutes stood up and, with cameras rolling, asked us about Paglia.

At this, Gloria Steinem stood and demanded that the cameras stop. The director protested, but Steinem insisted, rightly pointing out that it is bad journalistic ethics for a news team to shape an event that is supposed simply to cover. She told the producer that the audience had paid $30 each to come and raise their issues; while the news team was welcome to film the event, it was the audience members' night and their agenda, not the TV crew's.

Those moments were cut. Millions of Americans saw only Steinem shouting to stop the cameras, followed by Paglia saying, in effect, 'See?' The TV audience never heard the discussion; all they got was more 'evidence' that feminists are thought-police; 60 Minutes never apologized for its tactics; the important debate of Paglia's position in relation to the panellists' never took place. Perhaps the most damaging consequence of all was that for the rest of the night we on the panel were almost too careful to support and affirm one another. This might have made the audience feel 'empowered', but maybe not sufficiently provoked or enlightened. 'It was a love fest,' said one critically alert audience member, who understood why it had to be so, but was nonetheless sorry.

Another result of the stifled debate is that some feminists reacted to the fact that Paglia's work is granted space, while no room is assigned to a serious investigation of the issues it raises, by retreating from her challenge. A feminist bookshop in Toronto, for instance, is reluctant to stock her titles. This reinforces the us-against-them mentality, and the fear of dissent, that are damaging feminist intellectual health even as they appear to confirm the opposition's worst charges. The Paglia saga has an important lesson for feminists, if we can bring ourselves to learn it in time: *it is not dissent that is harmful to feminism, but consensus.*

The FAIR saga in America is another example of how media distortion can lead to intellectual defensiveness in those who are fighting the good fight. The formation of a new women's desk at FAIR (Fairness and Accuracy in Reporting), a group that monitors the media for conservative bias, was a hopeful event; a great antidote to the gender apartheid in the press.

FAIR's women's desk swung into an ambitious, hard-hitting campaign to oppose violence against women. Their claims that domestic violence shot up during the Super Bowl generated stories on *Good Morning America*, in the Associated Press, and in the *Boston Globe*. NBC even agreed to broadcast a public service announcement about wife-beating, during the Super Bowl itself.

An Associated Press story reported that Sheila Kuehl, managing lawyer of the California Women's Law Center in Pasadena, cited a finding by sociologists at Old Dominion University which found that the number of women in northern Virginia admitted to hospitals with injuries from domestic violence rose by 40 per cent after games won by the Washington Redskins.

When the *Washington Post* checked with the researchers, it revealed that their findings showed a *slight* increase on win days.

This story, 'debunking' feminists' claims of violence against women on Super Bowl Sunday, was national news; Alan Dershowitz attacked 'self-proclaimed women's advocates' and what he called their 'reliance on hearsay' in the *Los Angeles Times*. The

Wall Street Journal compared FAIR's campaign to Orson Welles's *War of the Worlds*, a notorious hoax about an invasion from another planet.

But after this explosive coverage of FAIR's alleged shortcomings, the other side of the story went largely unremarked. The *Los Angeles Daily News* also found that the number of calls rose significantly at at least two shelters for battered women after the game. When the *Portland Oregonian* investigated at the Portland Women's Crisis Line, it learned that on Super Bowl Sunday the information clearing-house had taken thirty calls – three times the average number. 'We could go to fifty or sixty calls,' said Tess Wiseheart, the crisis line's executive director. 'We've always noticed a climb on Super Bowl Sunday, and we always put on extra help.' (Two other shelters showed no increase.) But the damage had been done. In the minds of millions yet another blow had been struck against female credibility about sexual violence.

A final example of nuance sacrificed to the flatness of feminist debate is the pornography issue. Women are acutely frustrated about how pornography is discussed – or rather, *not* discussed. Daytime TV's ratings-boosting habit of focusing with mock concern on sex workers and pornography is insultingly transparent to women. They are no happier with what seems to be part of feminism's approach. Women in the New York area, for example, spoke often, with much resentment, about how the anti-porn image that people were most likely to see was this: a solitary activist standing on a street corner screaming at passers-by, beside a blown-up photograph of a gagged, bound, naked woman with clamps on her nipples.

Many women feel that extremists on both sides give short shrift to the complexity of their feelings about the issue. In general, women have grave anxieties about the effect of pornography, and particularly about whether it teaches young boys disrespect for women; yet they want to steer clear of anyone else's telling them whether they are entitled to investigate their own sexuality, and they are extremely wary of tampering with the laws of free speech.

The polarization within feminism intensifies the cartoon quality of debate. 'This kind of issue has produced terrible polarization, the kind that says, "How can you think this and say you support women?"' says NOW's Patricia Ireland. Anti-pornography activists see the issue not as a matter of speech but as a matter of harm and believe that pornography is a kind of 'collective defamation'. They are often called censors, but what they primarily seek are financial damages for women who can prove in court that they have been harmed by pornography. Their opponents, the anti-censorship activists, see the pornography issue as a diversion from women's material problems, and a potential threat to women's own freedom of speech and sexual expression. But feminists divided on the issue are rarely able to listen to each other. Says Ireland, they 'cannot even agree to disagree'.

Anti-pornography activists often refuse to debate with 'Pro-sex' women, dismissing them as paid mouthpieces for the pornography industry, and sometimes even impugning their sexual habits. Feminists Against Censorship, on the other hand, relies on semiotics to separate the porn industry from the pornography it produces: 'It is important to remember that pornography consists of images and that they are not just filmed or photographed acts of violence.'

Both stances are rigid because of the scarcity of debate the issue is granted. Both sides use the logic of survivors in a lifeboat deciding what to throw out for ballast. For the anti-pornography movement, the boat is so battered by sexual violence against women that we must throw out women's interest in an erotic culture and their qualms about laws regulating speech, if we are to survive. The assumption is that we don't have the buoyancy to change attitudes and behaviour without the lifeline of legislation thrown down to us from above. Anti-censorship feminists imagine what they could do with all the time and energy that go into fighting pornography. Their assumption is that there are only a few cans of provisions on board, and only a few people left to do the rowing, so the obstreperous passenger who believes she has herself seen the harm caused by pornography had better pipe down.

Now: imagine we have enough speech. You are on the *Yacht of Plenty*, sailing for China. You are seated peacefully, the wind blowing through your hair, watching the sunset off the Azores. To your right sits Linda Marchiano, aka Linda Lovelace, allegedly raped at gunpoint in the making of *Deep Throat* (her bruises are visible on film), a movie that is said to have inspired an epidemic of throat-rape cases. To her left is the mother of Jennifer Levin, the young woman who was strangled during sex in a park. To your left is Candida Royale, creator of Femme Productions, an ex-porn star who now makes non-violent erotic films aimed at the female audience, and tries to give her actresses better working conditions than those that prevail in the rest of the industry. Next to her is Judy Chicago, the artist who created *The Dinner Party*, a historic event that brought together craftswomen of every kind to decorate a dinner table where great women were represented by stylized vulvas. Near by is the writer Anaïs Nin, who earned money from writing erotica that opened strange and suggestive trapdoors into the female psyche. Next to her is the photographer Cindy Sherman, whose meditations on 'pornographic' imagery illuminate the female inner life, and Annie Sprinkle, the performance artist who invites observers to examine her sex organs. Next to her rests Sappho, who wrote poetry so achingly erotic it would have set the Board of Censors' podiums on fire. No officials or moderators are directing the conversation, threatening, interrupting, shouting 'Pornography!' or 'Censorship!' making lame jokes or cutting to a commercial. It is just all of you, resting, thinking, and talking through an issue that privately and publicly affects your lives. In other words, imagine that women owned a little over half the space in which to think things through, and no one was timing them, poised to turn out the lights.

Wherever you think you fall in the debate as it's framed on narrow land, let me ask: on the *Yacht of Plenty*, wouldn't you ask some new questions? Wouldn't you?

My own sense – for which I have absolutely no evidence except the way I myself have felt after watching some pornographic videos whose provenance was unknown – is that consuming for one's own pleasure a product made out of a stranger's need to exchange his or her sexuality for money – as opposed to enjoying a sexual image made out of someone's free desire to express herself and create communication out of her erotic life – causes an indefinable but palpable abrasion of the soul. If we consume material whose conditions of manufacture are unknown to us, but that might be unsafe or painful for those involved in it, we hurt ourselves; we throw off our ethical equilibrium in some unquantifiable way.

But even if we conclude that some pornography can cause some kinds of harm, that insight should lead not to less representation, but to more. Rather than trying to determine which images 'degrade women' and what to do about them, we must take the responsibility of using art, education, information, the power of speech itself, to change the aura that surrounds scenes of sexual violence.

There is nothing wrong with sexist education that enough anti-sexist education won't cure, or at least inoculate against. A teenager who hears that feminists are boycotting books will run to buy *American Psycho*. The same teenager who has heard stories from real survivors of sexual assault will read *American Psycho* in a more compassionate, and probably less erotic, mood. At one American university, undergraduate men started a discussion group and slide show asking their male colleagues to think about what sort of effect pornography has had on their lives. Many said that being exposed to the *Playboy* ideal since childhood had made them less able to relate to real women. They needed to visualize a photographic image in order to reach orgasm, at the expense of being with the woman who was really there. Many were unclear about what consent looks like, and felt at risk of committing date rape without even knowing it. Setting fire to the *Playboys* on a newsagent's shelf raises more questions than it answers; but discussions like this can build bridges of communication between the sexes.

The women I have heard from don't want to assign blame for the fallout from pornography; they want to be heard and to be safe. Many men I encountered, in spite of initial peer pressure not to admit it, really did want a socially acceptable way to question sexism, to talk about consent. They did not want young women to be frightened of them; they did not want to miss out on love and sexual connection.

More open discussion has the power to change attitudes to images of sexual violence in the media, the way good information campaigns have changed attitudes about cigarettes and second-hand smoke. Sexually violent imagery, like cigarettes, is something that children should not have access to. It is something that puts toxins in the environment, that big business profits from, that can be addictive, that can be damaging to loved ones and hazardous to one's health. It is a substance that demands care in handling and a free exchange of information – even a campaign – about its dangers. Those avenues are better ones to take than the route of the law.

Playboy spends a lot of money trying to counter the work of anti-pornography activists who raise questions about the relationship between such magazines and harmful treatment of women. I would feel safer in a world in which *Playboy* spent its PR money on anti-date-rape films, and on campaigns to show young men what consent looks like and why it's sexy, and what rape looks like and why it hurts, than I would in a world in which *Playboy* was forcibly taken off the shelves.

Images and discussions that resensitize us to violence are the antidote to images that desensitize us. D. E. May, a 23-year-old artist in Oregon, blows up police reports of rape and battery and makes vast, imposing canvases out of them. One image shows a hand grasping a woman's throat and the caption reads, 'Sometimes I want pussy so bad I just take it.' In another work, the following text, taken unchanged from police reports, was printed in white lettering on a black panel six feet by eight feet, a haunting, indistinct swirl of chaotic white in the background. The work is hung at eye level.

VICTIM STATED THAT THE FIRST ARGUMENT STARTED OVER A PACK OF CIGARETTES. VICTIM STATED ACCUSED (HER HUSBAND) HELD HER AGAINST THE BATHROOM WALL BY HER HAIR AND CONTINUED TO BEAT VICTIM WITH HIS RIGHT HAND. VICTIM IS SEVEN MONTHS PREGNANT AT THE TIME. VICTIM STATED ACCUSED KEPT TELLING VICTIM, 'BITCH, YOU ARE GOING TO LOSE THAT BABY' AND THEN ACCUSED WOULD BEAT VICTIM IN THE STOMACH AGAIN AFTER THE ASSAULT IN THE BATHROOM . . .

The most effect protests against offensive speech involve the act of telling true stories. Rapists tell themselves stories about how rape doesn't hurt. Rape activists have found that one of the most effective – and punishing – therapies for convicted rapists is to have victims of rape tell them in person the damage the assault did to them.

Once, children learned social mores from family, school and church, and 'entertainment' was rightly seen as fantasy, as a temporary escape from those mores. That is no longer true. TV and films are the primary socializers about what is 'normal'. Of course, images and words have magical power, especially today. Anti-censorship campaigners are in a preposterous position, and one they should not have to take, when they try to pretend that this is not so. Why should we assume that words and images that make women seem less than human should be more magical than women's own words and images? Women can do better than just uttering the 'no' that good girls have always had at their disposal; women can make better and more magical erotic material than the images that disturb many of us.

For we must not only show what 'no' looks like; we have to start possessing what 'yes' looks like. If we aren't crazy about the way female sexuality is portrayed, let's get out there and seize the means of production: make diaries, novels, plays and painting from our erotic lives; 'come out' unabashedly, every one of us, as sexual beings. We have only begun to map the dark continent of female fantasy and desire. If we think the sexual imagery out there tells lies about what we long for, it's up to us to saturate the airwaves with our millions of erotic truths.

When we dare to call for truly free speech that combines scenes of our real erotic desires with a true accounting of real harm, we will live in both a safer and a sexier world. Metaphor, poetry, testimony, logic, reportage, documentation, persuasion: more room, more speech, more complexity. The master's tools can dismantle the master's house. Only more speech – far more – can begin to reflect the complexity of women's lives and minds.

Chapter Eight

Oxygen Deprivation Leads to 2-D Opinions

Inflexibility of Thought

> Do I contradict myself? Very well then ... I contradict myself.
> I am large ... I contain multitudes.
>
> – Walt Whitman

Once a movement feels it has been pushed out of the great stream of life, it will tend to treasure – and hold on for dear life to – the identity it has. The normal push and pull of mainstream life, which polishes ideas as the ocean polishes glass, feels threatening. The degradation of debate about women's issues has led some aspects of feminism into intellectually destructive habits.

These habits involve either/or thinking. You are either victim or oppressor; you are either for us or you are against us; you are either a non-sexist woman or a sexist man. Either/or thinking is the natural mental reaction to a perception of scarcity. When people feel they have no options, they cling to the assurances of polarized certainties. It is only when people feel rich in confidence and space that they dare to pursue the subtleties of what Gloria Steinem calls both/and thinking. Feminism must embrace this psychology of plenty.

But women do have a uniquely legitimate fear of too-free play with ideas. Since women lack legislative power, words about women too often, and too quickly, become statutes about women.

The legal treatment of women depends not on verifiable facts or on rules of conduct that can be universalized, but on gut feelings and fuzzy impressions about what sort of behaviour towards or by women is appropriate. Attitudes about rape, for instance, and about who 'deserves' it, become the real legal circumstances in which one finds oneself trying to establish the guilt of one's rapist and one's own innocence. If enough voices say that abortion is murder, real abortion rights are at stake. Every gain we have made in the raising of legal consciousness about rape and domestic violence has been the result of years of painstaking persuasion on the part of feminists. In this climate, a research study, an editorial in a major newspaper, even a TV movie about date rape or domestic violence is likely to affect courts and legislatures.

Critics of feminism misunderstand this tendency to retreat into an intellectual huddle about certain contested issues. (This is a trait shared by others who lack space and safety; nuances about Israel's human rights policies are addressed by American Jews when Israel is safe, but we often, understandably, shut down when the country's existence seems threatened.) Often feminists dread not the ideas themselves, but the concrete legislation that may result. When some feminists resist Camille Paglia's opinion that women who go to a man's room are asking for date rape it is because such views can elicit a reversal of women's legal rights. A woman cannot voice anxiety about pornography, for instance, without the cry of censorship being let loose to harry her mental investigation into the ground. But for us to fear dissent and become guarded in our opinions, because legal consequences might follow too closely and uncontrollably behind them, is a price too high to pay.

Consensus Thinking

'We confirm our reality by sharing,' reads a T-shirt produced by a women's group. But today this love of consensus is just the problem. The legacy of the consciousness-raising movement gives great weight to the act of having other women confirm one's own life experiences, thus breaking down isolation and putting individual struggles into a social context. While that 'confirmation of reality by sharing' worked magnificently for Second Wave feminists, it has left a tendency in some feminist subcultures to value consensus thinking in a way that can promote the tyranny of the group perspective over the creation of community from distinct, individual visions.

The American lesbian journalist Donna Minkowitz has seen this fear of dissent cripple her women's group, a lesbian karate school. Though the school emphasized the importance of maintaining one's boundaries, taking up space and defending one's independence, the mindset of the collective smothered dissent: 'Don't disagree with one another, never have an independent opinion, and, above all, *never* have a conflict ... It must be *progressive* to impose decisions by fiat.' Minkowitz astutely proposes that the experience of learning how to fight stirred up a reminder of repressed anger that made dissent even more terrifying to the women involved. She describes how, when a woman presented a divergent view, she was subjected to 'intense hostility'. 'It was sort of fun to cram dogma down the throats of women less politically advanced,' she writes with rare candour, rightly identifying this consensus 'groupthink' as a form, not of community, but of domination: 'Like all unrecognized domination, it was ultimately sterile and life-choking. Both I and the women I was torturing were desperately trying to avoid grappling with something even more painful than our crit/self-crit sessions: our terror of anger and our astonishing fear of conflict.'

The National Lesbian Conference, held in Atlanta in 1992, was a failure, Minkowitz reports, 'precisely because its participants would not tolerate disagreement'. Women who produced flyers making fun of the conference's no-perfume rule had them confiscated so that the women who read them would not be 'hurt'. Lesbian soldiers who risked court-martial or discharge to be at the gathering were prohibited from speaking because their careers conflicted with the anti-militarism of others present; and an official conference bulletin declared that certain erotic preferences were wrong. 'Our fear of conflict,' Minkowitz concludes, 'has destroyed many more lesbian groups' – and, I would add, ravaged the entire women's movement – 'than conflict itself has.'

Recently, I was invited to debate with Susie Bright, a lesbian feminist who is pro-pornography and pro-sadomasochism, and who wrote a column for the lesbian S&M journal called, enragingly, to some, *On Our Backs*. A reader of mine called my office. 'How,' asked this reader, 'can Naomi *speak* to that woman?' 'That woman' – how many Victorian Angels in the House have mouthed those words to one another as a scarlet courtesan passed them on the promenade, showing off her too-bright plumage? I had not yet read Susie Bright's books; I hadn't even been to the debate and heard what she had to say. How can anyone else assume she knows what I think if *I* don't know yet?

Bright's biography presents a set of thorny, tantalizing contradictions; I was eager to experience the rush of clashing perspectives merging into new thought patterns. The 'right-on' reflex of censure and ostracism, of 'not speaking to' someone who has offended us would have pre-empted an energizing discussion.

At the end of her book *Feminism Without Illusions*, Elizabeth Fox-Genovese writes: 'Recognizing the danger that many other feminists, whose views differ from mine, may consider my criticisms disloyal, I can only hope that the scope of the movement permits the acceptance of divergent viewpoints as part of a continuing effort to make sense of what women need.'

I understand Fox-Genovese's caution; I feel her sense of unease myself as I criticize aspects of a movement I champion. But what a depressing sentence to read from the pen of a college professor. If criticism of a movement amounts to disloyalty, that movement has set up the conditions of its own fossilization.

Few will tune into the saga of feminism if they already know how it will end. If we cling to a party line, we bore ourselves and alienate our listeners, who feel that they'll have heard it all before.

Ideological Purity

Feminist discourse is studded with warnings about the dangers of behaving impurely. Money, fame and nasty opinions are the usual culprits. Women risk being 'co-opted', 'assimilated' and 'tokenized'. They have 'sold out' or 'crossed the line'. Victim feminism speaks about ideological corruption in the same language eighteenth-century ballads used to warn virginal milkmaids to beware the wily procuresses who wanted to lure them, with gold and finery, from a life of rural innocence into one of urban sin.

Indeed, we cannot understand victim feminism's fear of corruption without understanding women's age-old relationship to prostitution. All women carry the legacy of our long understanding of the relationship between wives, nuns and virgins, on the one hand, and prostitutes and courtesans, on the other. For centuries, in almost every Western culture, virtually every woman who was not an aristocrat had to uphold an ideology of respectability and chastity to distinguish her from a prostitute. While she was given the benefits of her 'decent' status – protection, shelter, a position in society – this came at a heavy price: sexual self-abnegation and dependency. In contrast to that double-edged respectability, the prostitute's life had a double-edged lack of respectability. Though streetwalkers led the most diseased and unprotected of lives, courtesans lived well, often at the centre of glittering society and intellectual life. By the nineteenth century, everyone knew that even the poorest of prostitutes had the chance to make much more money than the working-class factory girls, shopgirls and domestics who made up the largest category of working women since the start of the Industrial Revolution.

And every 'respectable' woman knew how fine was the line that separated her status from that of the prostitute. Merely by acting on a sexual impulse, getting pregnant outside marriage or losing a husband, a 'nice' woman could be propelled into the whore's life. Such a woman would have to believe in the stigma about 'bad women' and bad behaviour so that she would never give in to her own temptation to 'cross the line'. And since she had forsaken so much pleasure, she had to inflate the value of chastity and perfect a hatred of seduction, or 'selling out', in order to compensate herself.

The conditions that put so much weight on the difference between 'good women' and 'whores' are mostly gone, but the centuries of acculturation, handed down from mother to daughter, remain. This mentality's legacy keeps some feminists firmly on what they perceive to be the 'correct' side of any given issue, even at the expense of a fruitful embrace of intellectual ambiguity or worldly power.

Radical Abdication

The situation at some universities shows how silencing from above results in a climate that permits silencing from below. In a recent article in the *Guardian*, Lisa Jardine, professor of English Literature at the University of London, recalled a series of fellowship competitions in which she had participated: 'The 50 per cent of women applicants had fallen to 30 per cent of the first short list, and to one or at the most two on the final interview list of seven.' The problem, she argues, is the continued bias of appointment committees, where academically brilliant women candidates are turned down because they might not be able to control 'difficult colleagues', they 'looked too fragile to cope', or 'on the grounds of somehow not being exactly what we know we've always had'. The women who, against the odds, are appointed are those challenging the traditional white-maleness of academic power. Their fellow faculty members are, on the whole, more conservative than they were in the late 1960s. The intellectual climate is certainly more conservative and more resistant to change.

Throughout Britain and the United States, directors of women's studies courses and women's centres tell similar tales: funding is cut to the bone, so they can do almost nothing; the courses then fold despite ever-increasing interest on the part of students; and finally, when a new generation of students calls for a women's centre or a women's studies major, the administration rejects the push with the claim that the experiment has been 'tried already – but the programs failed'. Increasingly, women's studies courses have been changed to gender studies, and women-only groups charged with sexual discrimination. Lisa Jardine recently bemoaned the lack of women professors at universities in Britain, especially at Oxford and Cambridge where they remain at just 3 per cent of the total. As she pointed out, it is dangerously wrong to think of the academic world 'as one immune to prejudice – a world of genuine equal opportunity . . . free expression and liberal values'. And Dale Spender, one of the pioneers of women's studies, has described the fierce resistance she met in Australian and British universities when she tried 'to reach a female rate of representation of more than 10 per cent'.

This undermining of women's studies is compounded by distortions of it in popular debate. Anti-women's-studies critics often hoist themselves by their own petard. Critics like Dinesh D'Souza made fun of curriculum additions such as *I, Rigoberta Menchu*, the 'irrelevant' autobiography of a poor Quiché Indian woman from Guatemala, who had worked as a maid. It was probably irritating to D'Souza when the peasant woman's human rights work won her the 1992 Nobel Peace Prize.

Nevertheless, these distortions and silencings take their toll, and lead to an intellectual defensiveness that inhibits the free flow of ideas.

I have heard left-wing professors say that they don't bother to defend the progressive curriculum in the mainstream press because that press would never print their views and, besides, academics are a 'powerless caste'. I've heard middle-class college students scramble to identify downward, thinking they have to pretend to *be* the oppressed in order to *champion* the oppressed; in the process they yield their responsibility for using the power and resources they have. 'Radical' cynicism about the social contract can combine with the insight about some groups' being 'differently situated' in a way that leads to moral incoherencies. Writing the names of alleged date rapists on the women's-room wall is subversive empowerment, but high-school boys' writing the names of girls on the men's-room wall is sexual harassment? Men should take women's studies, but some women students refuse to read texts they deem sexist? Take Back the Night marchers oppose representations of sexual violence against women, but a left-wing campus paper, the *Queen's Journal*, of Queens College in Canada, can fantasize the seduction, torture and death of a 'white boy'? The notion that 'it's different when women do it to men' should not be used as an excuse for having it both ways.

Instead of challenging the unfair rules to make them fair for everyone – a long, hard task – the 'radical' conclusion is sometimes that since the rules are corrupt, no rules need apply at all. The 'differently situated' argument is being used to justify behaviour that may look harmless or symbolic if it comes from a helpless minority, but looks like injustice when it comes from a group that is on the verge of taking power. When 'radicals' deride the authority of the press, the effectiveness of the electoral system, the objectivity of the 'meritocracy' and so on, they do so because those institutions pretend to be fair but are not. That fairness is the myth of liberalism and their critique is necessary and right. But when the criticism leads to the decision to withdraw from community altogether – as when Germaine Greer states that the Oxbridge first-class degree represents a particular style of intellectual achievement to which women should not want to aspire – rather than fighting to make the rules fair, 'radicals' are throwing out a truly radical baby along with the liberal bathwater.

Sure, dead white men formulated the principles of representative democracy and the free press. But the flaws lie not in the ideals themselves, but in the fact that the founders' blindness, in structuring citizenship as white, male and propertied, and the self-interest of those who hold power now, prevents the ideals from unfolding according to their own logic. If 'radicals' take these ideals lightly or turn their backs on them, they defeat themselves. But if we compel these values to open up and work fairly – the goal that is, rightly understood, all that the multicultural and feminist movements seek – then there is no more 'radical' system imaginable than the one we have inherited.

I grew up in a city in which the mayor now marches in the Gay Pride Day parade every year without fail. Was the mayor always pro-gay? Not necessarily. The mayor marches in the parade because the mayor has to. The gay community is organized, vocal and politically involved. I've seen 'radical' values triumph simply because ordinary people took the old-fashioned, even unfashionable ideals of responsible citizenship seriously, and used their clout.

Every successful movement needs an extreme fringe to behave disruptively and make noise, as well as trained insiders to broker the new contract once the disruption has hit home. ACT UP, with its civil-disobedience AIDS activists working in tandem with its task forces on law and medicine, is a good example.

The fact that a situation demands disruptive activism is no reason for a movement to lose sight of the ultimate goal: a working – and fair – social contract. I appreciate 'reverse injustice' as a shock tactic, and there are many times when the 'differently situated' analysis does not apply. But this analysis must be part of a journey to a social contract that includes men and women fairly. I don't want to be part of a movement in which reverse injustice has changed from a challenge to an unfair 'meritocracy' to a policy in itself.

Radicalism is not opting out, staying pure and changing nothing; nor is it a petulant, ill-thought-out demolition of the rules that doesn't bother to work out the implications of the alternatives proposed. Radicalism is understanding the nature of discrimination, arming yourself with as much power as possible, and forcing unjust institutions to learn and legislate and change. A real radical does not stand in the margins, admiring her own purity. She is a warrior to bring outsiders' views into the centre, asking, 'How can my actions spark change for the good in the real lives of as many people as possible?' A true radical is not content just to tear down and turn away; these are the skills of the weak. She assumes the responsibilities of the strong, and builds up. If a system is morally incoherent, she builds it up better, builds it into the light. And if a system of thought is too rigid, she challenges its inflexibility.

I once spoke at a university that was home to the best and some of the worst traits of progressive academic work. Before my lecture, a faculty member warned me ominously that a senior seminar of women's studies majors 'wanted to talk to me'. I found myself ushered into a circle that seemed to have passed some sort of sentence in my absence.

The ring took turns not so much offering criticism of my work – which I would have welcomed – but rather, calling me to account for myself to them. One woman charged that I was too elitist – I had used compound sentences – while another complained that I was insufficiently academically rigorous, since, to make *The Beauty Myth* accessible, I had used endnotes instead of academic footnotes. My critics seemed to see no contradiction between these two positions. How could I have gone on television – didn't I have a problem being co-opted by the corporate media? Why did I publish with a mainstream press? This is not a book I would have written, said one young woman indignantly. (I look forward, I said, to reading your book.) Isn't the act of writing a book, asked a young woman accusingly, in itself exclusionary to women who cannot read?

After my talk, I went out for pizza and beer with some of the same undergraduates. They were affectionate and vulnerable. While they could shoot French feminist theory from the hip in seminars, they lacked the language – or the room – to talk about their real concerns. But safe from the arbitration of peer pressure, they spoke about sexuality, self-esteem, the absence of role models, their young professor's struggle to raise her small child while vying for tenure. They mulled over similar conflicts that loomed ahead in their own lives. Tutored into an arid rhetoric of political self-righteousness, and shaken by the pedagogical mood that turned intellectual inquiry into a grim battle over who would get to make the rules for everyone under the flimsy banner of 'consensus', they seemed to me to have formed a carapace as uncomfortable and unproductive as the intellectual machismo that had been fashionable when I was in college. Rather than granting women's concerns the status of a subject worthy of hard questioning and eager curiosity, the rhetoric of the cadre, despite its 'feminist' label, had reduced the subject of women to an inert set of foregone conclusions. The only difference was that the boxed-in decision about what women should do and think was under *their* control, rather than under the control of men. The undergraduates seemed to have little understanding that true radicalism in education is a woman who is thinking under nobody's control, and reaching no one's conclusions but her own.

The scene in the classroom revealed a gross misunderstanding of what ideas are for. Government must be representative. Panels and anthologies must be representative. Coalitions must be representative. A woman's opinion and voice cannot – must not – be representative. A listener can certainly tell a speaker that she has left out important issues, or that her opinion is disappointing or flawed. But no woman has the right to edit another woman's thought process. We have the right to ask a writer to listen to us. But we must never, ever imagine we have the right to make a feminist thinker tailor her vision to a constituency. I was alarmed by the conversation's atmosphere, in which it was clear that, because we were all feminists, my interlocutors somehow owned my brain and – as if it were a hotel room they'd paid for – were entitled to rearrange the furniture for their greater comfort.

A collective mentality can be just as authoritarian as the 'authority' of Western and Masculine Truth that deconstructionist inquiry has attempted to unseat. The notion that all intellectual endeavours are collective and cannot go forth without the imprimatur of the self-appointed guardians of the imprint of True Feminism will make feminism intellectually self-destruct. There is no feminist version of Casaubon's key to all mythologies. And admit it: you wouldn't want to read it if there were.

Paradoxically, those who think that by coming in groups to trim back the intellectual garden they are helping feminist ideas, are actually hastening the demise of new growth. The ideas that the conventional wisdom of the day calls treacherous weeds can, if left to flourish, cross-pollinate with the future and produce un-dreamed-of new fruit. Feminist literature that lasts is fiercely independent, magnificently wrong in great stretches, and often 'politically incorrect' for its time. *Wuthering Heights*, a great novel of female passion, has a heroine who destroys herself for love; in Virginia Woolf's novel *Orlando*, the heroine/hero is as compelling a character in his male incarnation as she is in her female lives; at the end of *The Female Eunuch*, Germaine Greer runs gloriously into a wildly off-the-mark conclusion – that the capitalist system will wither away when women have their rights. Women whose work lasts allow themselves to make mistakes, take wrong turns, and question their initial assumptions, even if those assumptions have become the orthodoxy of the day. Could these women have written their great works under the eye of a feminist collective?

If we retreat from challenges to our conventional wisdom, we start to die a little inside our own heads. The right to ask questions is the chief jewel in the treasury of rights assumed by men and withheld from women. It is even more precious (though not more urgent) a human right than pay for one's work. Once, laws forbade women from asking questions in the forums in which men gathered. Shall we forbid ourselves to do so now?

Intellectual rigidity betrays the best impetus behind the push to include women's perspectives and concerns in the canon. 'Political correctness' itself is a ghastly phrase and a dangerous concept that was initially coined as ironic and now is too often used sincerely. The consciousness of how race, class and gender affect all of our perceptions provides good questions – indeed, the best questions for our times; but if it is used in order to manufacture certain answers, they cannot be good ones. If we who want to change the canon are sure that our position is solid, we should have nothing to fear from challenges and interrogation.

We do not need to argue on the basis of students' self-esteem, or of cultural politics, or of the need for social change, to make a case for the reorientation of the curriculum. The Western tradition endorses deductive reasoning in which one gathers information as objectively as possible, and then draws from it a hypothesis. To leave out the experiences and history of the majority of people necessarily skews the data and makes one's hypotheses faulty. When a course on Periclean Athens focuses on early democracy and the growing ideal of citizenship, but fails to address the fact that half of the population – women of all ranks – had fewer legal rights than did men, the students' understanding of the lessons of early democracy is compromised. When a course on the US in the nineteenth century talks about industrialization but fails to discuss the religious 'feminization of America', students lack a crucial interpretive tool without which they cannot fully understand transcendentalism and other cultural currents of the day. If a student does not know that 'the woman question' was more frequently debated in Victorian England than was socialism, he or she derives a false picture of the age. When philosophers posit 'man's' existential freedom, meaning 'human' freedom, but do not ask whether pregnancy, for example, reframes that existential freedom, they are reasoning in a faulty, one-sided way.

Just as a student who is ignorant of the history and culture of women is poorly trained, so are the graduates of those very few institutions that offer students a critique of the traditional canon while making the original texts into optional reading. I have met young women who know feminist literary theory inside out but have never had to take a basic English literature class, and cannot defend their views with any more potent weapon than defensive dogmatism. Though they are planning to be the most committed warriors for the cause, they are bound to be the least effective. Young women who want to change the traditional canon – or the world – must be fluent in the tradition that they interrogate. If a student understands *A Vindication of the Rights of Woman* as fully as he or she knows Plato, that student is learned in a way that fulfils the liberal tradition's truest definition of intellectual rigour.

And such a student should never back away from a free exchange of ideas. In 1992, Robert Casey, the governor of Pennsylvania, visited Cooper Union in New York City. He is anti-abortion, and a group of feminists went to his talk. But they prevented him from speaking by shouting and stamping loud enough to drown him out. When asked what motivates them, such women often say, 'Women don't get to speak – women are silenced', and use urgent metaphors: 'Their feet are on our necks.'

Such phrases collapse all women into the identity of the most oppressed. 'Their' feet are indeed on many of 'our' necks, but not equally on the necks of all. Many women in many situations are silenced: women who are forced to act in pornography at the end of a gun are silenced; women who know they will be beaten or lose their livelihoods if they voice their opinions are silenced; teenage girls in Ireland who are unable to obtain abortions are certainly silenced. Illiterate and ill-educated women who cannot fully exercise their rights are silenced, as are women who are so poor that their need to secure food and shelter turns any hope of giving voice to their opinions into an unthinkable luxury.

But it belittles these real sufferers of silencing when those who *do* have education and access to speech use the voicelessness of the genuinely downtrodden as a rationale to cut off debate in universities or public forums. If anyone does have the opportunity – and hence the responsibility – to speak, it is the very women who inhabit these halls: middle-class women who are studying for law degrees; women writers; women who are organizing politically. Do affluent, educated women serve the cause of women who live at the point of a gun or at the feet of a brutal employer by yielding their power to argue on behalf of those who cannot? If we enjoy the luxury (which should be a right) of being able to listen to an anti-abortion speaker we should use the opportunity to try to persuade an entire audience of the need for abortion rights, if that is our view. If we can do that without risking beatings and impoverishment, we have no right to treat the literal silencing of unluckier women as if it were a fashionable new hat, or to put on for effect the straitjacket of their silence, only to shrug it off again when it grows uncomfortable.

Feminism means freedom. And freedom must exist inside our heads before it can exist anywhere else. The nature of freedom is not to freeze, but to flow. Our motto must be that nothing is unthinkable. Let us be Protean, and fluid, and wear down the rocks.

Literalized Theory

This tendency to rigidity led to a too literal translation of influential theories. From the 1970s to the present a number of theories emerged that opened up the way we could think about gender, but that translated poorly into popular conversation. These were then circulated in catchphrases that ranged from the preposterous to the threatening, further alienating many from the movement.

If the average person saw a feminist organization's literature, she or he would probably find very little to object to, and quite a lot to support. But rather than receiving that literature, they are more likely to hear a theorist, quoted out of context, saying something to the effect that 'all sex is rape'. This media sleight-of-hand creates the impression that all feminists want to legalize lesbian separatism or censor nude images, or castrate male domestic pets.

These are some of the theories that came to be perceived as political road maps, rather than as intellectual provocations.

All Men Are Rapists.

Susan Brownmiller's study *Against Our Will: Men, Women and Rape* explained that some men's rape of women keeps all women subjected to all men. She pointed out that rape is institutionalized as part of warfare, and she located men's ability to rape in their biological construction: 'By anatomical fiat ... the human male was a natural predator and the human female served as his natural prey.' Her work trickled down as, 'All men are rapists.' This sentence has helped close down discussion between men and women, clouded feminist thinking about men and sexuality, and done men and women a grave injustice.

All Heterosexual Sex Is Rape.

In her book *Toward a Feminist Theory of the State*, Catharine MacKinnon argued that rape, sexual harassment and pornography are used to enforce female inequality. Her argument was important in changing the way sexual abuse was seen: rather than being an isolated matter between individuals, it became an issue of law. But her insight that sex occurs in a context of social inequality is often misrepresented as: 'All heterosexual sex is rape'.

Andrea Dworkin's troubling and groundbreaking book *Intercourse* also questioned – sometimes too sweepingly – the issue of whether women can really consent to intercourse in an unequal world. 'Intercourse in reality is a use and abuse simultaneously . . . consent in this world of fear is so passive that the woman consenting could be dead and sometimes is.' The book was reviewed widely in the mainstream press. The reviews led readers to believe that this guiding light of feminist thinking was also telling them flatly, 'All heterosexual intercourse is rape', for they did not dwell on Dworkin's theoretical focus, the issue of consent.

All Women Are Lesbians.

The poet Adrienne Rich published an essay, 'Compulsory Heterosexuality and Lesbian Existence', which suggested that since women's and men's first erotic bond is with the mother, lesbianism is in fact the 'natural' state for women. She suggested that those who become heterosexual are forced into that orientation by socialization and by economic dependence. She doubted whether, given 'profound emotional impulses and complementarities drawing women toward women, there is a mystical/biological heterosexual inclination, a "preference" or "choice" that draws women toward men'. And she suggested that all woman-to-woman intimacies, from a mother suckling a child to a dying woman tended by nurses, 'exist on a lesbian continuum'.

While Rich's main theory – that we can't know if our sexuality is chosen until we account for everything coercing us toward it – is perfectly sound, her arguments trickled down into, 'All men get love from women only through coercion'; 'All female closeness is lesbian'; and, not to put too fine a point on it, 'Straight women are deluding themselves.'

As the influence of these theories spread, it became noticeably *démodé* for a feminist to admit out loud to wanting intercourse, let alone to wanting a good steady supply of high-quality intercourse.

Feminists Want Men and Women to Be the Same.
Much feminist writing took apart the assumption that sex differences are 'opposite' and innate; sex differences were called 'the social fiction of gender'. But this idea entered popular conversation as 'Feminists want women to be like men', an idea that many women and men would find unattractive. It even surfaced as the idea that 'Feminists want men and women to be the same.' Phyllis Schlafly and other anti-feminist activists exploited this particular anxiety throughout the 1970s, creating such myths as the feminist dream of 'unisex bathrooms'. This left people with the impression that feminists want to eradicate sex differences, a thought that, understandably, disturbed many. For one does not have to be deluded or sexist to appreciate sexual differentiation, whether it is artificially exaggerated or not, just as one can appreciate racial diversity without being racist.

As journalists transmitted these theories to readers who were unfamiliar with the original sources, mainstream audiences' picture of what one had to believe in order to be a feminist grew ever more bizarre and distorted.

These important theories marked a turning point at which many otherwise supportive women turned their backs in disgust: as one columnist put it, 'By the Seventies an astonishing rhetoric had developed about the wicked penis and the male as rapist ... This is when ordinary feminists started to preface everything by saying, "I'm not a feminist, but ..." and to follow a separate path, or rather many different paths.'

The Academy and Inaccessible Language

These distortions were compounded by the withdrawal of feminist ideas into the academy. In the 1970s the most popular feminist books were written in ways that did not require a course of poststructuralism to understand. Marilyn French wrote *The Women's Room*; Shere Hite published *The Hite Report*; Betty Friedan wrote a monthly column for *McCall's*. Though many feminist authors were academically trained, they also pitched their voices to the mainstream, and the books sold in millions.

But during the backlash years, as the mainstream became more hostile to feminist ideas, the academy became more attractive. The scholarly journal *Signs* began publishing in the late 1970s and early 1980s, as did *Feminist Review* and *Feminist Studies*. Some of the most interesting ideas about women began to be expressed in impenetrable academic language, which locked up these ideas in the ivory tower. The more successfully feminist academic theory developed into an advanced discipline, the less acceptable it became for thinkers to translate their work for a wider audience.

Male academics are often published in the mainstream magazines, which omit academic work on women. But the academy looks down its nose at women's magazines; for an academic to publish in a women's magazine is professional suicide. An academic friend, when urged to write for one, asked, 'Can I do it under a pseudonym?' The barrier between male academics and the mainstream is, thus, more permeable than that between female academics and their potentially larger audience.

In Britain, the feminist retreat into the academy has resulted in the near invisibility of British feminists in the mainstream press and media. The bestselling feminist books of recent years have all been either American or Australian. On International Women's Day in 1993 *Guardian* journalist Catherine Bennett asked, 'Does that include us?' Sally Feldman, joint editor of BBC Radio 4's *Woman's Hour*, said, 'It really does puzzle me that there aren't more women writing about our condition in a way that is entertaining and mainstream.' Author Beatrix Campbell agreed: 'It's absolutely extraordinary that there isn't a feminist of the women's liberation generation, which produced so many intellectuals.

There isn't *one* I can think of who writes regularly in the British press ... and that is an extraordinary achievement.' Women's studies lecturer Victoria Robinson offered an explanation:

'British feminists rest uneasily with so-called success, because it shouldn't be an individualistic endeavour, it should be about collectivity. So by entering public life ... you're saying I've done this, I've achieved this, and at what expense? What other women were involved in this?'

Even those academic feminists who are willing to write for the mainstream are hobbled by their language, which has evolved into something largely incomprehensible to women and men outside the academy. 'It's theory divorced from the practical experience [of our readers]. And often the language is impenetrable,' says *Glamour* editor Judy Coyne, and the evolution of feminist theory explains why.

In the 1980s, the writers Julia Kristeva, Hélène Cixous, and Luce Irigaray, French feminists, were published in English. They drew on the ideas of Freudian psychoanalysis and poststructuralism. The latter is a form of literary criticism that used elaborate wordplay to prove its central premiss: that all language is internally contradictory and has no fixed meaning. As one can imagine, such writing is not easy to follow. Luce Irigaray's prose, from a passage taken at random, reads like this:

> We would still have to ascertain whether 'touching oneself,' that (self) touching, the desire for the proximity rather than for (the) proper(ty), and so on, might not imply a mode of exchange irreducible to any centering, any centrism, given the way the 'self-touching' of female 'self-affection' comes into play as rebounding from one to the other without any possibility of interruption, and given that, in this interplay, proximity confounds any adequation, any appropriation.

One professor of French feminist theory explains these writers' immense popularity among academic feminists as a direct by-product of the anti-feminist hostility of the recent past. 'The men,' she told me in confidence, 'took this presumably decentring set of ideas – Derridean poststructuralism – and used it to recreate an ancient system in which a group of elite priests (tenured male professors) lords it over a bunch of terrified women (untenured female professors). So when the French feminists appeared, the academic feminists jumped on them, as if to say, "Here's something of our own that's just as hard. We'll teach it to our own kids, and no one will know what *we're* talking about, either."'

Brilliant as it may be, feminist theory derived from the French critics is made to be, she points out, 'almost deliberately inapplicable to any engagement with "the real world", at just the time when engaging with the world seemed hopeless'. The prose style of the best feminist academic thinking ensured that the most fashionable and influential ideas would be drained of relevance to the real world of politics and action, and would be couched in what, to the millions of women and men outside the ivory towers who had no incentive to master an exclusive and elaborate professional jargon, amounted to pig-Latin. This development reinforced the perception that feminism was a rarefied subculture, and damaged what should be a foundation stone of feminism: that its core ideas, like the ideas of democracy, are concepts to which everyone is equally entitled, female or male, rich or poor, educated in PhD programmes or by life experience.

Academic feminists cannot be blamed for this development; all professions mutate toward specialization. The crime was that the academy tends to sneer at those who try to translate these ideas for magazines, newspapers, or TV. The end result of this development was that academic feminists, cordoned off from wider debate by the professional constraints of their language, felt, rightly enough, powerless to influence the common culture of ideas. Frustrated, many responded by turning that experience into a theory that overstated women's powerlessness to sway the mainstream and that glamorized the margins. And the national forum continued to distort or omit the very ideas for which women and men were hungry.

Litmus Tests

As all these forces combined, and as the decade wore on, women began to feel that there were certain shibboleths that they had to adhere to rigidly, and codes they needed to use, if they were to be counted in on the subculture of feminism. And they felt that a movement that made them stick to orthodoxies about these issues insulted their intelligence. The fact is that not all women who respect themselves and other women feel the same way about abortion, the military, the environment or housework. If in order to be called a feminist one must be ecologically sound, pro-choice, anti-militarist and left-wing, then feminism has ensured its helpless status as a perpetual minority party. How many women would 'trade jobs for trees'? How many are anti-capitalist? How many supported the Gulf War? If 'feminism' is a specific agenda rather than a conviction of female worth, then we are left with a political movement that has defined itself as of the minority, by the minority.

There is a tendency amongst this minority to see the rest of the world as 'unconverted'. 'How will we get the feminist message out?' I am often asked by university students. 'How do we get other women to *see*?' ('How will the heathens see the light?')

But women have feminist attitudes to spare, whether they label them as such or not. Rather than trying to impose a subculture's very specific language and style on women who are having none of it, the right question to ask is simply how to get more power into women's hands – whoever these women may be, whatever they may do with it. Rather than bringing women to feminism in what writer bell hooks calls 'a conversion process', feminism should go to them. It is not up to feminism to 'teach' the 'unconverted'; it is up to the women's movement to *learn* from the majority of women.

My personal feminism is anti-militarist, pro-socialized-medicine and secular-humanist. It would like women to share housework 50/50, to keep their maiden names, and vote for choice. That feminism feels right for me; I believe it is right in general; but nothing gives me the authority to denigrate the woman who does not share my lifestyle or assumptions.

If her beliefs are based on hatred, I should revile them. On the political level, I must mobilize against her political party. But as a populist, I cannot say that I have a right to a public voice and she has not. In addition, if women are going to tap their power as the majority, they will have to make alliances at times with other women who hold beliefs that make them want to run screaming for cover.

The first principle of power feminism is that every woman has the right to own her self. More radical than any of the left-wing planks I hold so dear is a principle that should overrule them all: that a woman is entitled to define herself, express her beliefs and make her own life. On this level of first principles, any woman who believes in women's right to self-definition and self-respect is a feminist in my book.

An example of a feminist litmus test is the abortion issue. One of the most debilitating legacies of the reproductive-choice battles of the 1980s was that it became a truism that a woman was not a feminist if she was not pro-choice.

Since the law was breathing so heavily over women's shoulders at the time, the pro-choice language of the 1970s and 1980s had to frame abortion in the least ambiguous way possible. It tended to stress the operation as being 'non-anaesthetized surgery', 'like getting your tonsils out'; it balked at inquiries into where life begins, and stressed the term 'embryo' over 'pregnancy'. For feminist discourse about abortion to flatten the sadness and complexity of the issue was entirely necessary at the time, because feminists were caught up in a pitched battle against pro-life language that was even more one-dimensional.

But discussion of the ambiguity of women's real feelings about abortion was one casualty of the urgent battle for choice, and the inescapable need to devote years to securing abortion rights – the bitter circumstances that led feminism to be identified first with the choice to end a pregnancy – wore down the movement's soul. Of all the choices feminism offers women, *that* choice is not a joyful identity to rally round.

For some women, an abortion is nothing but minor surgery and an unmitigated relief. But for others, even for women who are adamantly pro-choice, abortion can mean loss and mourning. We were not able to talk about that too loudly while the Damocles sword of legislation was hanging over our heads.

My own view on abortion is one that I have not been comfortable talking about in public. When I check my feminism against my life, I find the rhetoric of some abortion-rights supporters out of tune with my own experience of trying to avoid pregnancy. My real feelings about contraception are at odds with what I am supposed to say in public as a pro-choice woman.

My friends will tell you that I am sometimes spacy beyond belief. I leave dishes in the sink for a week at a time, forget the names of close friends and even relatives, forget my own birthday, leave passports and wallets on public transport, put shoe polish away in the refrigerator and eggs in the stereo cabinet. To my own regret, I have misplaced money, jobs and friendships by neglecting my responsibilities towards them. But I have never neglected contraception.

When the time comes to use a condom or prepare my diaphragm, I experience an alertness and attention to detail that are completely out of character. This level of focusing feels so mysterious and strong it is almost animal, part of the fight-or-flight mechanism of the autonomous nervous system. It feels as if some dark part of my brain is saying to my body, 'Careful, careful. You have to transcend your blind spots. *This is a matter of life and death.*'

Although my parents and partners would without question have supported me if I needed an abortion, and though many women I knew had had one, the fact remains that I am mortally afraid of needing to have an abortion and desperate to get through my life without having to make that choice.

When I was a teenager, part of the reason I was so careful was that I was determined to have no sense of guilt or punishment for my sexuality. Part was my terror at the possibility of finding myself at the mercy of my reproductive system; that would have undermined my sense of mastery over my destiny, which is vital and fragile in a young woman. But part was that my intuitive grasp of what an abortion would mean to me could not square with the rhetoric current at the time – that the procedure meant little or nothing.

Once at dinner, I found a friend of mine suddenly holding her hands against her face and telling me in a ghostly voice about her second abortion. I tried awkwardly to comfort her. 'I think – it seems to me like – some sort of killing,' said this progressive, independent, pro-choice young woman. 'Can you get comfort,' I asked her, 'from what some pro-choice activists say – that it's a minor operation, like a tonsillectomy?' 'Ah, no, no,' she said with a cynical laugh, and laid her forehead down in the nest made by her arms. 'Why not?' I asked. 'Because,' she replied, 'I've had a tonsillectomy.'

I would never want my subjective views to cast a shadow on another woman; and I will defend with all my strength a woman's right to an abortion. At any earlier point in my life, I would probably have chosen abortion for myself if I became pregnant. But real debate would mean, for me at least, casting abortion as a necessary evil. For the duration of the whole unavoidable struggle for reproductive choice I have felt that I had to stifle some of my deepest convictions. Now that some rights are safe for some women for the moment, I must risk suggesting this:

For me, the other side of having reproductive rights is taking reproductive responsibility. This goes for both men and women. The people I knew who used contraception irregularly, or not at all, were hardly powerless. Educated and middle-class, we had more choices than almost any other women and men on the planet. But almost all of the abortions I know of resulted from careless contraception. In some cases, the men didn't ask, didn't wait, didn't bother to produce a condom. In others, the women didn't want to offer a less-than-ideal sexual moment. In still others, both the men and the women were grazing the edge of destiny almost for the sake of the ride, flirting a little with the idea of parenthood, or forcing a psychodrama in the relationship ('See? It matters. I matter. This – this matters.') In all these cases, the partners were not looking the seriousness of sexual responsibility in the face. As one man said, explaining why he was going to let his girlfriend go to the abortion clinic alone, 'Hey. I'm not into death.'

The legal threat of the 1970s and 1980s meant that, for people of our background and access to resources, abortion had to be weighted almost too lightly. The emergency meant that we took too little room to evaluate abortion except in relation to the law. For us, the demands of defending abortion rights crowded out the individual's need to elucidate an ethical relationship to abortion and to decide how much he or she is willing to give up to avoid an abortion. I think we misunderstood. Our obligation to act publicly on behalf of choice did not preclude the responsibility we had, as people with a myriad of choices, to choose privately to at least try hard to avoid pregnancy.

Contraception is never perfect. Like almost every sexually active woman, I've had scares. When that happened, I did not lie awake praying in fear because I would have trouble obtaining an abortion. As a middle-class urban woman, I would be able to get one easily. Rather, I prayed because I wanted to get through my life without having to make that decision, which I can't help thinking is one of life and death.

But, as Catharine MacKinnon asks, 'Why shouldn't women be entrusted with life-and-death decisions?' Abortion is the miserable, necessary price of heterosexual autonomy. But I would need to be able to talk about an abortion, if I had one, as the death of something, if of no more than a fragment of the self, or the ghost of a human union, or a fingerprint of incarnation. I would have to be allowed to cast it into the realm of the spirit.

The AIDS crisis has taught us that, both physically and metaphysically, when we enter one another we hold each others' lives in our hands. We can save each other by behaving responsibly towards each other, and damn each other by yielding to our own indulgences at the expense of basic carefulness. Heterosexuals can learn a lesson from the gay community, and, whether for a night or for a lifetime, apply that precious understanding of responsibility to our own sexual and reproductive lives. We can demand the luxury of both/and thinking: defend abortion rights, *and* undertake anti-abortion responsibilities. It is time for a new concept of sexual liberation: freedom through caring. The wellbeing of the soul does not, I think, depend on chastity; but it does depend on being certain that we leave an erotic union having left behind as little destruction as possible – no matter how fleeting the connection.

One step beyond heedless hedonism lies the eroticism of care: care for our partners, even if we will never see them again; care for ourselves; and care for the potency of our reproductive capacity, with its power of life, and perhaps even death.

Some of the most thoughtful feminists are beginning to describe abortion as violence against women, pointing out that the abortion mills of China and Romania provide no better guarantee of women's right to control their own reproductive destiny than did the anti-abortion fanatics of the Reagan–Bush administrations.

They point out that in a world in which women's sexuality was really our own, and our destinies truly in our hands, the incidence of abortion would be far more rare.

Ambiguities in issues such as abortion show how damaging to feminism are litmus tests, which ultimately come down to women failing to accord respect to other women. I have met too many women who don't 'look right', in the terms of my own subculture – who are traditionally religious Jews or Christians or Muslims, who are deeply patriotic servicewomen who believe in military solutions, who are free-market, socially conservative businesswomen, but all of whom share commitments to improving women's status and securing their dignity – to believe any longer that my style of feminism, or that of my friends, is the only answer for everyone.

Sometimes, power is letting go. We must reclaim feminism as that which makes women stronger in ways that each woman is entitled to define for herself. Ironically, this 'letting go' of the rigorous litmus tests of feminism will not make us lose the power of consensus that we have, the common feminist fear; it will expand and enrich what we have and draw in millions more women. A feminism worthy of its name will fit every woman comfortably, and every man who cares about women.

Part Three
Victim Feminism versus
Power Feminism

Chapter Nine

Two Traditions

While feminism was having trouble getting its message across, some of the problem had to do with the message itself. Over the last twenty years, the old belief in a tolerant assertiveness, a claim to human participation and human rights – power feminism – was embattled by the rise of a set of beliefs that cast women as beleaguered, fragile, intuitive angels: victim feminism.

Victim feminism is when a woman seeks power through an identity of powerlessness. This feminism takes our reflexes of powerlessness and transposes them into a mirror-image set of 'feminist' conventions.

This feminism has slowed women's progress, impeded their self-knowledge, and been responsible for most of the inconsistent, negative, even chauvinistic spots of regressive thinking that are alienating many women and men. Victim feminism is by no means confined to the women's movement; it is what all of us do whenever we retreat into appealing for status on the basis of feminine specialness instead of human worth, and fight underhandedly rather than honourably.

One of the features of this feminism is its misuse of the reality of women's victimization. Right now, critics of feminism such as Katie Roiphe in *The Morning After* and Camille Paglia just about anywhere are doing something slick and dangerous with the notion of victimization. They are taking the occasional excesses of the rape crisis movement and using them to ridicule the need to raise consciousness about sexual violence. Roiphe, for instance, paints an impressionistic picture of hysterical "date-rape victims" who have made it all up, but she never looks squarely at the epidemic of sex crimes that has been all too indelibly documented by police forces the world over. In her definition, victim feminism includes the acts of fearing rape, and of confronting the real scars that rape inflicts. In her eagerness to do away with the Dworkin/MacKinnon picture of systematic male brutality, she washes away the real differences in power that do exist between men and women – such as physical strength. In her world, of Princeton eating clubs, when a man grabs a woman's breast, the woman dumps a glass of milk on his head. End of story. In real life, where the provosts might not be drinking sherry near by, the spunky lass might find herself dragged into an alley and peremptorily sodomized.

Though these critics' views of how often rape is imaginary belong in another solar system, we do need to talk about the victim problem in current feminism, but we need to define it in a completely different way. There *is* something wrong with the way some feminist attitudes approach the persona of the victim. But documenting or protesting a rape epidemic is not the problem.

There is nothing wrong with identifying one's victimization. The act is critical. There is a lot wrong with moulding it into an identity. Here is a highly subjective comparison of the two different ways by which women can approach power.

Victim feminism:

Urges women to identify with powerlessness even at the expense of taking responsibility for the power they do possess.

Is sexually judgmental, even anti-sexual.

Idealizes women's childrearing capacity as proof that women are better than men.

Depends on influence or persuasion rather than on seeking clout in a straightforward way.

Believes women to be naturally non-competitive, co-operative and peace-loving.

Sees women as closer to nature than men are.

Exalts intuition, 'women's speech', and 'women's ways of knowing', not as complements to, but at the expense of, logic, reason and the public voice.

Denigrates leadership and values anonymity.

Is self-sacrificing, and thus fosters resentment of others' recognition and pleasures.

Sees money as contaminating.

Puts community first and self later; hence tends towards group-think, as well as towards hostility to individual achievement.

Is judgmental of other women's sexuality and appearance.

Believes it it possessed of 'the truth', which must be spread with missionary zeal.

Projects aggression, competitiveness and violence on to 'men' or 'patriarchy', while its devotees are blind to those qualities in themselves.

Is obsessed with purity and perfection; hence is self-righteous.

Casts women *themselves* as good and attacks men *themselves* as wrong.

Has a psychology of scarcity: there is only so much to go round, so one woman's gain is another's loss. If there is inequity, wants women to 'equalize downward' – e.g., to give up 'heterosexual privilege' by not marrying, instead of extending gay rights; to give up beauty, instead of expanding the definition.

Wants all other women to share its opinions.

Thinks dire: believes sensuality cannot coincide with seriousness; fears that to have too much fun poses a threat to the revolution.

Power feminism:

Examines closely the forces arrayed against a woman so she can exert her power more effectively.

Knows that a woman's choices affect many people around her and can change the world.

Encourages a woman to claim her individual voice rather than merging her voice in a collective identity, for only strong individuals can create a just community.

Is unapologetically sexual; understands that good pleasures make good politics.

Seeks power and uses it responsibly, both for women as individuals and to make the world more fair to others.

Knows that poverty is not glamorous; wants women to acquire money, both for their own dreams, independence and security, and for social change.

Acknowledges women's interest in 'signature', recognition and fame, so that women can take credit for themselves and give generously to others.

Asks a woman to give to herself and seek what she needs, so she can give to others freely, without resentment.

Is tolerant of other women's choices about sexuality and appearance; believes that what every woman does with her body and in her bed is her own business.

Acknowledges that aggression, competitiveness, the wish for autonomy and separation, even the danger of selfish and violent behaviour, are as much a part of female identity as is nurturant behaviour; understands that women, like men, must learn to harness these impulses; sees women as moral adults.

Seeks 'bilingualism' – the joining together of what is best about women's traditional knowledge and commitments with traditionally male resources.

Has strong convictions, but is always sceptical and open, and questions all authority, including its own.

Hates sexism without hating men.

Sees that neither women nor men have a monopoly on character flaws; does not attack men as a gender, but sees disproportionate male power, and the social valuation of maleness over femaleness, as being wrong.

Has a psychology of abundance; wants all women to 'equalize upward' and get more; believes women deserve to feel that the qualities of stars and queens, of sensuality and beauty, can be theirs.

Wants all women to express their own opinions.

Knows that making social change does not contradict the principle that girls just want to have fun. Motto: 'If I can't dance, it's not my revolution.'

Power feminism wants more for women. The ideology it upholds is flexible and inclusive. Its core tenets are these:

1. Women matter as much as men do.
2. Women have the right to determine their lives.
3. Women's experiences matter.

4. Women have the right to tell the truth about their experiences.

5. Women deserve more of whatever it is they are not getting enough of because they are women: respect, self-respect, education, safety, health, representation, money.

Those are the basics. No overdetermined agendas, no loyalty oaths, just the commitment to get those unmarked 'power units' – health, education, the vote – to women, for women to use as adult individuals, with conflicting visions and wills. What women do with those units of potential is up to them.

My beliefs about what you should do with that power may contradict yours. Let us claim full representation, and fight our beliefs out in the public arena, as men do who cannot be reduced to a group identity. On this level of the definition of power feminism, the statement 'I am a feminist' means only 'I am a sentient, strong individual who objects to being held back – or having other women held back – on the basis of gender.' It is the very beginning of the conversation about what a given woman believes, not the endpoint.

But doesn't opening up the definition risk making the term meaningless? I think we can lay that fear to rest. When women engage fully in the political process they tend, as we are starting to see, to vote their interests. And we are safer in a country in which women feel empowered to promote a myriad of beliefs than in one in which all women share my views of what is best for the gender, or yours.

On one level all women should be able to own the word 'feminism' as describing a theory of self-worth, and the worth of other women. On this level, saying, 'I am a feminist' should be like saying, 'I am a human being.' It is on this level that we can press for women who believe anything they want to to enter public life; this level wants the world thrown open to all women regardless of their goodness: on this level women should be free to exploit or save, give or take, destroy or build, to exactly the same extent that men are. This is the level of simple realization of women's will, whether we like the result or not. On this level Camille Paglia is certainly a feminist; Indira Gandhi was a feminist; Mother Teresa is a feminist. On this level 'feminist' is a word that belongs to every woman who is operating at her full speed; ideally, it includes wanting other women to operate at their full speed, but it recognizes that women have many opinions about the best ways to empower women, and Mother Teresa's are not going to be mine.

On another level, of course, feminism should be broadly understood as a humanistic movement for social justice. This definition leaves out more people than the former one does, but it draws in far more people than the current popular image of feminism does. On this level, 'I am a feminist' means ' No one should stand in my way because of my gender, and no one should stand in anyone's way because of their race or gender or sexual orientation.' As a humanistic movement its parameters are these: no hate. It is illogical to claim one's rights as a woman yet deny them to others on the basis of their skin colour or sexual preferences. It also sets a narrower focus than does 'humanism': on this level, it is OK to work on behalf of women because female humans are oppressed in ways unique to their gender. But working on behalf of women does not allow one *ever* to deify them as better than, or cosmically separate from, their male counterparts. The 'no hate' plank of the definition includes not hating on the basis of gender, including when it comes to men.

Before we go on to compare power and victim feminism, let us be clear what 'the victim problem' in feminism is *not*. The idea of female victimization is currently very muddled.

Feminists are under siege for allegedly creating a 'cult of the victim'. This wave of 'it's all in your head' theory was inevitable, given the recent success of the victim's-rights movement in drawing attention to the widespread nature of sex crimes. Critics who charge this pursue a scorched-earth policy: if there are some unrepresentative excesses in the fight against sexual violence, demolish the whole, despite the fact of the suffering of millions. I too will be talking about some mistakes feminism has made in framing the theme of female victimization. But my intent is very different. I am calling for a recognition of female victimization that does not leave out autonomy and sexual freedom; I am calling on us to look clearly at the epidemic of crimes against women without building too schematic a worldview upon it.

I will insist that we talk about rape and sexual harassment with greater specificity so that crimes can be prosecuted with the utmost severity while we create more careful demarcations of harm that reflect the complexity of women's real experiences.

The 'victim culture' critics assail even the mere act of analysing real harm done to women. Critics attacked Anita Hill's testimony, the outcry over Tailhook, *Backlash* and *The Beauty Myth*, for having at their centre the image of women as victims. But these critics seem to believe themselves that women have no will or critical intelligence. The act of documenting the way others are trying to victimize women is the very opposite of treating women as natural victims. The premiss of such documentation is that women are not natural victims. The point of exposing the information is that women deserve to decide the case for themselves. Critics condescend to women by suggesting that merely hearing allegations of harm will make women collapse into a jelly of quivering victim-consciousness. I have never heard the argument that informing men of how, say, the Bundesbank controls the economy or investors shape party platforms is bad for men because it makes them feel like 'victims'. Men presumably can handle the information. Indeed, it is assumed that such information makes them better able to make informed choices.

Nor am I joining the chorus that calls women's objections to injustice 'whining'. Women's documentation of rape, child abuse, sexual harassment, educational discrimination and domestic violence is called 'the culture of complaint'; the art women make out of it is called 'a fiesta of whining'. But when white men fret in print about the decline of cricket, that's not whining; that's cultural criticism. Women's desire to be included in the curriculum is called a frothy 'self-esteem' issue; when white men object to reassessed history – as with Christopher Columbus revisionism – this is not a self-esteem problem but a 'battle for tradition'. When middle-class white men refuse to pay high taxes, they are not complaining but engaging in a 'populist uprising', a 'taxpayer revolt'. And when it is real injustice that men object to, they are not producing a 'victim culture' but the Magna Carta, the Declaration of Independence, and the 'Marseillaise.'

The problem that I object to in victim feminism is *not* the act of protesting against harm. There is no way around it: women are not natural victims, but they certainly *are* victimized. In the UK in 1989, 32 per cent of recorded violent offences against women were classed as domestic violence; 46 per cent of violent offences against women took place in the home of the woman and/or perpetrator; increases in domestic violence accounted for a third of the total increase in recorded violent offences between 1985 and 1987; 43 per cent of female murder victims in 1990 were killed by husbands or lovers.

In America 60 per cent of battered women are beaten when pregnant. Women are three times more likely to be victims of violence than men. These are raw facts. And facing them is the first step towards changing them.

But it is not 'blaming the victim' to issue the warning that people worn out with fighting are tempted to redefine victim status itself as a source of strength and identity. When ex-model Marla Hansen, who was slashed across the face by two thugs, underwent treatment to remove the scars, she was asked, 'Will it make a difference in your life not to have a noticeable scar? . . . Is it a psychological adjustment as well?' She replied, 'I've been living with the scar as part of my identity. A lot of people have defined me as a crime victim. My doctor said I should be prepared to lose that. It is a loss, and you have to put up something in its place.' The women's movement as a whole is at exactly such a psychological juncture.

The focus of some feminists, like Andrea Dworkin, Catharine MacKinnon, and Adrienne Rich, on female victimization at the expense of female agency, derives from conditions that once applied more than they do now. During the early 1970s women were indeed overwhelmingly silenced and negated but the genderquake means that the rationale of this kind of feminism is becoming obsolete.

Virtually every women's political organization, and most grassroots groups, seek power-feminist goals. But the language of victim feminism often dominates discussion of the movement in the mass media. Critics of feminism often cast feminists as extremists who are going too far and must temper or dilute their message for the mainstream. I am arguing the opposite – that women in general have gone much further in articulating an embrace of power than has this brand of feminism. But the power-feminist images and icons we have – from Roseanne Arnold to Madonna to Stella Rimington of MI5 – are seldom 'owned' by organized feminism. So women identify intensely with the power feminism that these women represent, but do not identify that vision with the feminist movement.

Chapter Ten

Core Mythology of Victim Feminism

It has sometimes been said that if women were associated with men in their efforts, there would be as much immorality as now exists in Congress, for instance ... But we ought, I think, to claim no more for woman than for man; we ought to put woman on a par with man, not invest her with power, or call for her superiority over her brother. If we do, she is just as likely to become a tyrant as man is, as with Catherine the Second ... [Rather], the elements which belong to woman as such and to man as such, [should] be beautifully and harmoniously blended.

– Lucretia Mott

'Victim' feminism is a composite. It evolved out of the aversion to power of the radical left; the identification of women and nature popularized with the 'cultural feminism' that came of age in the 1970s; old habits of ladylike behaviour that were cloaked in the guise of radicalism; and dollops of the work of such writers as Adrienne Rich, with her belief that language is male; Carol Gilligan, with her view of women's different moral reasoning; and Andrea Dworkin and Catharine MacKinnon, with their vision of overweening male oppression and female lack of choice. All of these writers, profound theorists in themselves, had their work intermingled by some feminist subcultures with all these currents to create a murky brew: this became the belief system of today's victim feminism.

Emmeline Pankhurst or Lucretia Mott, those early champions of power feminism, would be bewildered and even depressed at the state of much feminist thinking today. For victim feminism has developed an elaborate mythology to support its way of seeing the world and seeking power. It harks back to a myth of origin, to a harmonious, non-violent, egalitarian past that predated recorded history, in which women were worshipped, 'female values' predominated, and war was unknown. This mythology, though an inspiring metaphor to give women, stripped of history and country, a sense of original dignity, became a set of beliefs as chauvinist as any other. From it developed a belief system in which all evil – from environmental desecration to meat eating to child abuse – is seen to derive from the will to power, which is confined to men and institutionalized in patriarchy. Men are responsible for hierarchy, and hierarchy is the original sin of all social organization. Women are not hierarchical but egalitarian, inclined to organize in a 'web' rather than a 'ladder'. Men want to dominate and separate; women want to communicate and connect. Men – especially Western men – are individualistic autocrats; women are communitarian healers. Men objectify women while women want commitment. Men kill; women give life. If women ran the world there would be no warfare.

Many insights about the shortcomings of adversarial interaction, Western individualism, and the danger of treating resources and people as if they were discrete rather than interdependent, have made great contributions to the critique of modern life as a whole. The 'ethic of care' is something that more and more philosophers, national leaders and ordinary women and men see as central to the paradigm shift needed for human survival and a contemporary life healed of its loneliness and alienation.

The trouble, though, was that victim feminism cast the two 'ways of knowing' as *gendered* behaviour rather than as two different *human* approaches to structuring society and locating the meaning of human endeavour. This belief system increasingly described men as villains, and women as saints. It sees virtually every institution as intractably *man*-made and, hence, casts the power of these institutions as taboo, untouchable for right-thinking women. It stymied a generation of young activists who inherited a critique of power in which power itself was not morally neutral, usable for good or for evil, but evil in itself. ('Power is bad,' as one feminist professor flatly told me.) It hobbled feminist organizations, setting impossible standards of female harmony and self-sacrifice in groups, and disillusioning support staff who were not treated like the directors. It viewed men as carriers of infection, who transmit 'patriarchal values' to innocent women as the tsetse fly transmits sleeping sickness; women , in contrast, are native members of a chosen race. At its worst, it stoops to create a myth of origin about female superiority that is just as gendercentric as Professor Leonard Jeffries's theory of good, dark-skinned 'sun people' and destructive, light-skinned 'ice people' is ethnocentric. It took rough, generalized distinctions between the sexes – many of those distinctions being clearly cultural or experiential – and constructed from them a falsely perfect feminine principle and a falsely sinister masculine one. And it became ever more self-deceiving, as every hint of female competitiveness, aggression, thirst for recognition, or simply boorishness was explained away as an unfortunate and inauthentic eruption of male behaviour.

In this worldview, it is only men who objectify, never women: 'When [the male pornographer] invents a woman . . . he gives her a body without a spirit,' writes Susan Griffin. Men invented exploitation: 'I think this lie, that one can own another person, must have been invented by men centuries ago before they knew that they were natural fathers,' believes Mab Sagrest. 'There is no respect for the "other" in patriarchal society . . . [in] the simple-minded selfishness of patriarchy,' writes Judith Plant. Men return home to the feminine from 'their ruthless world-making, their bloody battlefields,' asserts Sharon Doubiago.

The castigation of men and exaltation of women can be extreme. In Marion Bromley's words,

> The history of the 'male way' of countering violence with greater violence points directly to the grave. The nonviolent 'female way' of lifegiving, nurturing, protecting the young and cooperative labor has pointed to life, all through human existence . . . We may create the means whereby male aggression will be controlled and women's potential nonviolent power be enhanced.

Since women bear children they are peace-loving: 'I want all the women to scream, *We don't want war* ... Our bodies create and nourish life ... all the world's life-sweet women' (Ellen Bass). And men are death dealing: 'Men's most horrendous invention of all has been war ... The only way I can understand it is in terms of their psychopathic jealousy of us. It's as though they are asserting, "Women may give birth, but we can give death"' (Mab Sagrest). 'Masculinity has made of this world a living hell / A furnace burning away at hope, love, faith, justice / A furnace of My Lais, Hiroshimas, Dachaus' (Joan Cavanagh). 'The patriarchy's answer to everything [is] threat of death ... Violence ... for thousands of years ... has been quite an eccentric quality in half the human population' (Pam McAllister). 'The rulers of patriarchy – males with power – wage an unceasing war against life itself. Since female energy is essentially biophilic [life-loving], the female spirit/body is the primary target in the perpetual war of aggression against life' (Mary Daly). 'Life for women, life for the earth, the very survival of the planet is found only outside the patriarchy ... beyond their wars. . . Women are the bearers of lifeloving energy. Ours is the task of deepening that passion for life and separating from all that threatens life' (Barbara Zanotti).

There is no doubt that history has designated men, in the past, to be the stewards of hierarchy and warfare and assigned women the healing and sustaining arts. And there is no question that the public realm needs to learn 'women's ways' of viewing reality and establishing values. But women also need to learn the use of traditionally male power and face the complexity of their own human struggle between merging and autonomy, self and other, ego and service, peaceableness and aggression. The obligation to rethink power relations and to address social interconnectedness and planetary health is not feminine; it is, urgently, human.

I do not argue that men and women are the same; there seem to be several clear hormonal effects that determine behaviour, though the jury is still out, with all the conflicting evidence. (For example, studies show that men's testosterone and aggression levels fall with time; they become more nurturing as they age. Women's testosterone levels are unmasked with time and they become more assertive in middle life. Research also increasingly suggests that caring responsibilities create caring behaviour in men that mirrors that traditionally attributed to women.) I am certainly willing to admit to a certain melting feeling around chubby babies, as I enter the final third of my reproductive life, which was totally absent from my earlier emotional repertoire.

Nor am I questioning the importance of integrating women's reality into public life; undoubtedly, women's historically dictated tradition of synthesis and healing is the one we need as a species if we are to survive. But the fact that women were relegated by force into creating a tradition of nurturing does not mean that women are themselves naturally better than men, or that they have a monopoly of kindness, holistic thinking or care for others.

I am arguing, rather, that the current split, fashionable in parts of the progressive community, into male-evil-sexually-exploitive-rational-linear-dominating-combative-tyrannical on the one hand, and female-natural-nurturing-consensus-building-healing-intuitive-aggressionless-egoless-spirit-of-the-glades on the other hand, belies the evidence of history and contemporary statistical reality. It denies the full humanity of women and men. And it re-creates a new version of the old female stereotype that discourages women from appropriating the power of the political and financial world to make power at last their own.

For the victim feminist worldview has developed a critique of power that has gone so far as to codify as 'progressive' the traditional female fear of wielding any authority other than that of a woman's right to her own body and private life (and even that can be jeopardized by the needs of the collective). Its rhetoric creates a dualism in which good, post-patriarchal, gynocentric power is 'personal power', to be distinguished from 'the many forms of power-over-others ... [It] is power which arises from an individual's decision to assume control of one or more aspects of her own life.' 'Bad' power is 'centralized' rather than 'personalized': 'Nonviolent empowerment ... also represents a broad-based challenge to the "powers-that-be," the position-holders in the hierarchy of power-over-others.' This dualism effectively establishes that a woman who goes beyond her private life and represents others in a leadership position – whether by standing for parliament, negotiating a deal, whistle-blowing, leading an army, or heading a company – is unacceptably contaminated by having power over others. This whitewashes the fact that any power beyond personal autonomy and self-defence almost inevitably involves power over others, and that one must therefore take great care to wield such power responsibly. It dismantles the possibility of creating a pro-woman vision of leadership, and a new kind of hierarchy based on merit. And it ignores the fact that even when a woman confines herself to that diffuse, private, *feminine*, personal power that stops at her own boundaries and her intimate connections with others, permitted in this worldview, she is still able to be tyrannical, abusive and power-hungry. It has created a generation of young women who find 'the system' so wicked that they have no role models – for all achieving women are by definition wielding 'male' power. They fear engagement with public life, extensive resources, political clout and the public voice, as if all these posed a master seducer's threat to their politically correct virginity. In short, this arch-feminine critique confuses public power, which entails the *ability* to do great harm to others, with the *inevitability* of doing that harm; and it begs the possibility that women could do great good, if they were to grasp that power forcefully and handle it skilfully.

The feminine fear of using power, of course, derives from the fact that in our heart of hearts, we are not at all sure that those aggressive, controlling, dominating and violent impulses are so alien to us after all. That, I believe, is the reason why victim feminism protests women's innocence so much and stigmatizes the female use of power so categorically.

Though the victim-feminist worldview draws on the metaphor of nature to endorse interdependence and Gaia-like harmony, it shies away from the fact that nature too has a dark side, an inbuilt competitiveness: the bloody, matter-of-fact struggle when two adversaries seek the same resources, or when their relation is that of predator and prey. It longs for an Amazonia ruled by Miss Manners. Conflict is depicted as melting away like a dinner guest's tactless remark at the response of a clever hostess: 'Power, in its healthy form, comes from the strength and sensitivity of this holistic understanding and leads *naturally* [italics mine] to the cooperative and nurturing behaviour necessary for harmonious existence ... Competition ... [is] seen as [a form] of domination and aggression.' This worldview uses obfuscating language such as 'always, we work to expand our circles', which drowns in treacle the fact that lobbying, persuasion and, yes, seeking conflicting agendas, are all normal and healthy parts of even the most non-violent egalitarian political life.

Unsurprisingly, contradictions and self-deceptions about women's own will to power erupt with great frequency in these texts. Here are some examples of how the schema is blind to women's own will to power. It sees 'good', feminine power relations as 'a web, with the woman in the center', in contrast to the patriarchal 'ladder', but does not notice that this paradigm mirrors the way women hold power within the family structure. The Fund for the Feminist Majority in America uses the misleading metaphor of 'a web of influence' to describe its clever counter-boycott of the makers of abortion pill RU-486, rather than acknowledging the action for what it is: a brilliantly effective, highly adversarial tactic. In an anthology that promotes healing, sharing and caring, an essay cites with admiration the example of a group of Himalayan women who protested against the opening of a liquor shop: '"We can set fire to the shop." The women spoke firmly and calmly.' This worldview evades the darkness of some inevitable life conflicts: 'Legal abortion is not about killing foetuses. It's about saving women's lives.'

Finally, not unexpectedly to students of racism, anti-Semitism, sexism or cult behaviour, this worldview has produced an essay which proposes a genocidal eradication of men in Orwellian newspeak that keeps the writer blameless.

Asking men to hold themselves accountable for sexism, or analysing the evidence that almost all violence against women comes from men, is not man-bashing, contrary to popular usage. But attempts such as some of these to declare on the basis of that evidence that 'men are' innately this or that negative quality is indeed man-bashing. It is a reflex grossly unworthy of feminism, which should be the ultimate human rights movement.

I have witnessed enough scenes with female audiences in which men were reviled, ridiculed or attacked for no better reason than the fact of their gender, to urge us to consider that, now more than ever, as worldly power shifts into female hands, we root out victim-feminist biases such as these. We are honour bound to look at the dark side, which is as innate to the feminine soul as it is to the masculine, if erstwhile victims are not to become tyrants.

Chapter Eleven

Case Studies

The Rape Crisis Centre and Local 34

When I went to work at a rape crisis centre, I was struck by how my spirits collapsed the instant I walked in the door. At first I thought that the deadening atmosphere was the residue of the thousand acts of violation that had been recounted between those walls. But soon I saw that it was not the traumas themselves that were sucking oxygen out of the rooms, but the way in which we pursued the fight against them.

The physical surroundings were like a stage set for the evocation of grief. You walked up a flight of damp concrete steps sticky with rubbish. Once inside, you were met by the sight of sofas with their stuffing spilling out, rickety folding chairs flung on their sides, and bare light bulbs that made skin look dead white or liverish grey-brown. One wall held nothing – not a cheap reproduction from a passing art exhibition, not a fruit or a flower, only a pockmarking of gouges from drawing pins. The other wall held only a relentless battery of bulletins from the war: '*Jamais encore!* Women say NO to the shame of rape!' These were our only decorations.

In the 'crying room' where women told their stories, light could not filter through the dusty black curtains. There was nothing on the table but a box of Kleenex. All the rooms had been painted in odd colours – jarring reds, disturbing murky greens – because someone's cousin had some paint left over. The office had a battery of telephones that were always ringing. The cupboard in the kitchenette contained dried milk, jars of instant coffee, and chipped, caffeine-stained mugs.

The result of poverty, you would imagine; of under-staffing. But no; there was money enough for a softer light bulb, a reproduction of Cézanne's apples, a carton of milk or two. The shabbiness was an integral part of the culture. For the rape crisis centre was staffed by a core collective with its own ingrained ways of doing things; the insufficiency, the misery were almost beloved, for they underlined how much we had suffered, how pitiful were our resources in the face of the mighty opposition, and how good we were to volunteer our time in such conditions. Any attempt to lessen the physical sadness of the place was met with strong resistance as being somehow unfeminist, unworthy.

And yet — the faces of the survivors as they walked in, when they saw that after the bitter thing that had been done to them they would have to do time in *this* place because of it! Surely if anyone deserves a warm colour on a wall, a gentle light, good hot coffee in an undamaged cup, a clean soft sofa to sit on, and a welcoming plant in the window, it is a woman who is brave enough to begin healing the wounds of sexual assault. Even more importantly, rape had made its survivors feel like they were worth nothing. Flowers on a table or a picture that served no function but to be beautiful would have told the visitor that she was worth at least the respect intended when something is chosen for beauty rather than function. But the shabbiness of the centre reinforced the 'moral' of the rape: you were made to feel like nothing by the crime; now come and try to recover in a place where we treat ourselves like nothing, too.

Even worse than the décor was the political culture of the place. Meetings were conducted via the 'collective process'. This is a time-honoured feminist ideal of group organization, which came out of the early feminist criticism of men's meetings as domineering, ego driven and rigidly hierarchical events at which men shouted down or interrupted less aggressive men and virtually all women. In the collective process, everyone must speak about every decision, there are no leaders or elections, consensus must be obtained before any decision can be carried out, and long accounts of personal feelings about a given policy are welcome.

There was no crisp way to set priorities, since everything was equally important. And speakers produced many minutes of softening language – 'I really don't want anyone to feel under-appreciated, and I feel funny about raising this at all, but ... ' – before saying something as basic as 'The rally was disorganized.' So meetings, unsurprisingly, took three or four hours. This quickly weeded out many newcomers, who had family or work commitments. That indirect selection process made the remaining group members highly unrepresentative of the community: there were almost no mothers or wives, and few working-class women or women of colour. Most of those who remained were ideolog-ically self-selected, educated, middle-class feminists, who shared the personal style of that subculture, sported its haircuts, listened to its music, and read its books.

Inevitably, the women who were natural leaders took over more responsibility. One woman, for instance, took notes, mod-erated often, and dealt with the media. Though no one else wanted to absorb the fairly heavy commitments and the drudgery this entailed, and though there was little grumbling to her face, she was viciously criticized behind her back – not for the quality of her leadership, but for the very act of the leadership itself, of 'putting herself forward' and assuming responsibility. This resent-ment reached a peak whenever her name appeared as spokeswoman for the group in the press.

Since consensus involved hearing from everyone, our level of irritation with one another rose exponentially as we all inflicted increasingly acute boredom on one another. Impatience would flare at someone whose speech was meandering or irrelevant. But this would immediately be followed by a wave of guilt at how in-adequate we were in comparison with the ideal of the perfect collective member, who would genuinely want to hear from everyone equally. Finally, when consensus was reached – usually because we couldn't bear the thought of spending one more minute arguing fruitlessly, *nicely*, back and forth – the majority felt tyrannized by the minority, the minority felt overruled by the majority, and the happy face of complete agreement in public was betrayed by a frenzy of backstabbing in tiny Machiavellian groups as soon as we were out of the room. These 'alliances', of course, were unreliable, as you always knew you could be vivisected in turn.

I began to dread the weekly meetings. After a gruelling evening, I treated myself to a nice long drink of self-righteousness to compensate myself for the ordeal. That dose of self-righteousness seemed tastier in direct proportion to how miserably the meetings proceeded. And after many gatherings, I would unconsciously be prompted to pick a fight with my perfectly friendly, non-abusive, housework-sharing boyfriend – a symbolic target for all the undirected, hopeless anger I had taken in.

The emotional culture of the place seemed to cling to pain in a way that made us ever more ineffectual. Day after day we witnessed the inferno of sexual violence that normal consciousness cannot bear to behold. We saw five-year-old girls who had been sold by their fathers to drunken friends in bars; women whose exboyfriends, having been diagnosed with AIDS, came back to rape them so as not to die alone; a retarded young woman whose father had raped everyone in her family, male and female. The law was at best indifferent, at worst downright punitive, and our conviction rate was laughably low.

Faced with these situations, we had three choices. One: we could protect ourselves and just do our jobs, thus delivering professional warmth to the survivor, but undergoing the internal detachment that so many medical workers describe. Though that option would have been efficient, it would have wreaked havoc with our self-image as compassionate, selfless fellow sufferers. Two: we could make a great leap of the heart and stretch of the imagination, seeing the hellfire clearly and yet admiring the strength of the survivors, so violated, yet so intent on healing. We could praise ourselves for fighting the good fight, and take pride in the inch-by-inch legal changes that we were bringing about. But that option would have required us to think very highly of ourselves and of other women, two achievements that do not yet come easily to women. Three: as the conventionally feminine culture of the centre led us to do, we could make female victim status into our main source of identity, and even of prestige. Thus, we could see our 'enemies' as eternally evil, all men as potential rapists ('potential' meaning not 'physically capable' but 'emotionally capable'), sexual violence as our unchangeable lot, and the painful nature of our work as proof that we were better than everyone else. This third option prevailed.

Behaviour at the rape crisis centre was based on the unwritten rules that followed from that view of ourselves. If we had been a tribe, an anthropologist would have said that our grieving rituals were highly differentiated, but that we had no concept of victory. You were not allowed to laugh too much – even though rape survivors, when they begin to heal, often laugh achingly, from a sense of existential comedy at the fact that the assault could be so devastating and yet that they themselves are still alive. You were never supposed to talk affectionately about your boyfriend (though you could talk with grim solidarity about your girlfriend), even though survivors said that slowly resuming contact with men they trusted was instrumental to their healing. You could cry with others after a courtroom loss – in fact, the etiquette of holding one another, weeping and commiserating was complex – but you never threw a party after a triumph, and the etiquette of triumph was totally undeveloped. Suffering a collapse because you had worked at the switchboard without relief (though it was available) for days at a time was admired, but going out to educate police officers and hospital workers, who were actually eager to be trained, conferred little status. It even bore a disreputable whiff of self-promotion. Self-prostration was our theme song.

We sat around a lot talking about details of physical torture and legal injustice, and how inadequate we were in numbers and resources for the task at hand. We had confessional sessions in which we shared with others how emotionally drained we were by the struggle. We even turned down funding for a full-time employee because the 'special' quality of an all-volunteer office would be tainted. We never, ever, in my memory of two years' work there, sat around rehashing a win, or congratulating one another heartily for helping a woman reclaim her life. In short, we never let ourselves enjoy feeling strong.

Rape, of course, must never be thought of as fun. But should it be heresy to suggest that changing attitudes about rape should sometimes be fun? This must not be taken out of context, but there is no other way to say it: the rape crisis centre starved for lack of fun. We must be able to keep the two concepts in mind at once:

Rape *is* hell, rape *is* trauma, rape *is* pain; *and*, the power we have to change the world is a source of joy.

For in time, looking *only* at our weaknesses, and never at our strengths, wore us down. It was not the survivors who drained us; their resilience was energizing. It was the volunteers themselves whose culture of hopelessness was so different from the quality with which survivors brought themselves back into life. Forbidden as we were to compete or to do battle in public, overt ways – through elections, or with conflicting points of view – our little group turned those repressed impulses inward and evolved a hierarchy of miserable saintliness. Members competed for the most exhausting tasks, the most stressful time slots on the phone.

Worn to the bone, we took out our stress on one another, with scandals, hurt feelings and accusations. Trust broke down. After an amateur inquisition took place that left scars on us all, the brave and committed little band, suffering the hangover of an obsolete femininity, dispersed. And when women in crisis called the lifeline telephone number, a crackling recording was all they heard: 'We regret that the centre is closed . . . until further notice.'

In contrast to the victim feminism story of the rape crisis centre, this is the power feminism tale of the Clerical and Technical Workers' Local 34 strike in America in 1989.

There was once a great institution renowned throughout the world. But like so many other great institutions, its entire economy depended on the low-paid, ill-respected, invisible labour of an army of female clerical workers. At Yale University, the institution in question, those women had long laboured in the warrens of the library, washed the test tubes in the labs, and filed the famous professors' index cards, all without organized complaint, for it was supposed to be a privilege to work for such an important institution for an average salary of $15,000 a year.

Sometimes, even in such places, workers get tired of not being able to get their children's teeth fixed; in 1981 the clerical and technical workers of Yale University began to lay the groundwork for a union. They took a community-based approach, holding open forums about anti-union perceptions, using networks of friends and family to build a rank-and-file committee, and training workers to run their own organization. It turned out that in discussions about what they most needed, the clerical and technical workers (84 per cent of whom were female) raised the issue of respect as much as they did more concrete concerns like wages and benefits. The workers saw low wages and benefits as a result of the university's general failure to recognize and value the 'feminized' work they did. Other manifestations of this lack of respect included 'inconsistent and arbitrary hiring and promotion practices, lack of voice on the job, and patronizing treatment by managers'.

The Local 34 organizers built their efforts around this theme of respect, and encouraged workers to document and testify to the many ways that the university avoided respecting their work's value and their needs. When Yale seemed unwilling to compromise with the union, the organizers took their case to the public, and astutely tied in the economic issue – a salary structure that, they argued, discriminated against women and minorities – with women's underpayment nationwide. The union held a one-day strike to call press attention to the connection between Yale's fee structure and the 59 cents that American women were paid for every male dollar.

More than 75 per cent of Yale's clerical and technical workers went on strike on 26 September 1984. These women, 16 per cent of them African-American and Latina, were telephone operators, librarians, lab technicians, hospital aides and secretaries.

The 'C&Ts' engaged in extremely disruptive, clever publicity tactics. They set up pickets at critical university sites like the administration building, the library and the gym, and asked the Yale community not to cross the lines. Their protests were strengthened by growing community support: student groups helped the union and educated other students about why the picket lines should not be crossed. The students even withheld their tuition fees to protest about the loss of services that the strike caused, and they threatened to withhold more the following term. Past and current presidents of NOW appeared with the strikers in support; news coverage was nationwide and thorough, sparking a debate about the issue of comparable worth.

Indeed, the organizers knew they had to raise the workers' inner sense of self-worth before they could ask them to hold out for more. The meetings turned into breakthrough therapy sessions, where the women's sense of the value of who they were and what they did rose from meeting to meeting. The more they stepped out of their roles as invisible female worker bees who made the Yale hive buzz so others could consume its nectar without distraction, the more inner strength they found, and the greater grew their certainty that they were not, in fact, 'lucky' to work for Yale at a wage that could not feed a family. They discovered that they deserved more.

Two acts of civil disobedience were staged, by a group made up overwhelmingly of women who had rarely been confrontational before. One woman described sitting by her children's bedside the night before the action, explaining to them why she needed to violate the law and possibly be arrested in the morning. One hundred and ninety-two union members, along with more than 1,000 supporters, blocked the entrance to the president's mansion; all the union members were arrested, hauled off in police buses. Two weeks later, 434 members, again supported by a crowd of thousands, formed rows before the administration building while the Yale Corporation held a meeting. Again, the union members were arrested.

Still Yale would not make substantive offers. The strikers played their last card: a complete boycott of Yale events. Though Yale resumed negotiations, it did not raise its final offer; talks broke down, and all hell broke loose.

Management felt it had 'lost control', as one union member put it, and 'started overreacting'. Campus freedoms began to disappear; deans of Yale College threatened professors and graduate teachers with unspecified retributions if they observed the moratorium; department chairs forbade teaching assistants to talk about the issue in class; the head of the philosophy department warned that faculty who honoured the faction 'should expect a loss of pay' and perhaps 'other penalties' as well. Students were even compelled to get rid of bed-sheets bearing pro-strike messages, which they had flung from their windows. Finally, the violations of free speech were so severe that the Connecticut Civil Liberties Union had to censure the university for 'an unwarranted and highly unfortunate chilling of the speech of members of the Yale community'.

But the moratorium was as effective as it was disruptive. The pressing task of selecting and admitting the following year's students was at a standstill. Documentation of the disruption showed that it had adversely affected teaching, research, conferences, fund-raising, maintenance, career counselling, recruitment, labs, museums, libraries and student groups – in short, everything that made the university function as an institution for which parents were willing to cough up $18,000 a year.

On 18 January 1985, Local 34 got its contract: a 20–25 per cent pay raise over three years; a new pay scale that redressed discrimination; better pensions and job security; a new dental plan; and a joint union–management committee formed to address comparable-worth complaints. Since then the union has stayed strong, transforming labour relations at the institution. It kept its commitment to grassroots leadership, grooming from its ranks female leaders. Since the strike, union members have won more than two-thirds of the disputes that went to arbitration.

As important as the material benefits and victories won was the change in the way the women began to see themselves. The questions: 'What are you worth?' and 'Aren't you worth more?' led women to re-evaluate not just their jobs but also themselves. The grassroots source of their leadership gave them the knowledge that leadership qualities do not have to descend from the top, but can be aspired to by all. Rather than eschewing leadership altogether, the women practised it as fairly as possible. They focused not on their common victimization, but on their common goal. There was no ideology except 'more for women'. Rather than enforcing a 'collective' in which personal financial goals are disdained and no one may get more than anyone else, Local 34's first premiss was '*I* am worth more', and its second, 'We are *all* worth more.'

Chapter Twelve

How the Traditions Clash Today

During the backlash years, the following events occurred under the banner of feminism. They were really examples of victim feminism:

Feminists urged a boycott of the publishers of Bret Easton Ellis's *American Psycho*.

Feminists criticized Hillary Rodham Clinton for submitting to what they saw as a campaign 'makeover'.

A young woman stood up in a bookshop discussion to declare that until pornography and rape were eradicated, she vowed to have no sex of any kind.

Zoë Baird, a corporate lawyer with a $500,000 annual income who was chosen by President Clinton to be the first female Attorney-General, defended herself against charges that she illegally employed a Peruvian nanny, thus avoiding paying Social Security taxes, with the explanation that she was thinking more as a mother than as a potential Attorney-General.

Take Back the Night rallies in various communities forbade men to march in support – even at the back of the procession.

Undergraduates at Brown University, Rhode Island, wrote alleged rapists' names on walls in the ladies' toilets.

Women academics at Oxford University tried to block the creation of fifteen new professorships in favour of readerships which, they argued, women would have more chance of winning; they would also run the risk of being ghettoized in readership posts with a permanent glass ceiling above them.

The London Women's Centre, a meeting place for various feminist groups, although, in the words of one regular user, 'no one could call it a joyful place', was criticized for trying to create a new, more professional and polished image and for building a health spa and Jacuzzi.

Body Shop founder and millionaire Anita Roddick complained that 'success means that you're not viewed as a sexual, warm woman. Success has diminished my sexuality.'

Eve Pollard, currently one of the two women editors of national newspapers in the UK, declared: 'I have no grand plan for editing anything special ... And anyway, there is that funny feeling that, in a way, as a woman you could give it all up in a way that a man can't.'

Candia McWilliam, one of six women to be included on the list of 20 Best Young British Novelists in 1993, complained that 'with the birth of each child you lose two novels'.

These responses reflect outdated Victorian assumptions that:

Since women can never hope to out-argue, out-persuade, or out-publish objectionable speech, the best hope they have is to cut it short.

It's better to be perfect and powerless than to make compromises in order to use power for social change.

'Disreputable' sex, even if it is consensual, degrades women, and that virgins and ladies are better than whores.

You can only hope to whisper about sexual assault in the most feminine of spaces, the ladies' room, where no one gets a fair hearing, rather than shouting to make the investigation of sex crimes really work.

Even the most powerful women, especially if they are mothers, are really powerless over their circumstances.

We are wholly defined by our sexual, racial or class 'identities', rather than being unique human beings who are influenced by them.

Women never choose to act aggressively.

Power imbalances between the sexes are innate, even in situations where there is no economic disparity.

In contrast, here are some recent examples of power feminism:

Emily's List in the United States supported fifty-five candidates, and twenty-five won.

Barbara Follett and women Labour MPs launched Emily's List UK and raised £50,000 in the first three months.

The Women's Action Coalition, understanding that overlooked groups have to make news to be news, took over Grand Central Station in New York City and passed out witty Mother's Day cards with poems about mothers being overworked and under-supported.

A pressure group of women artists publicized the fact that 83 per cent of solo shows are men's and only 19 per cent of reviews cover the work of women artists; they sent greetings cards to over 1,000 curators, art dealers and editors in Britain, saying 'Fanny Adams invites you to reconsider' and 'Fanny Adams puts you in the picture.'

The Guerrilla Girls donned gorilla masks and miniskirts to call attention to the absence of women artists at the Guggenheim Museum in New York.

FemFM, an all-woman radio station based in Bristol, went on the air for eight days to mark International Women's Day.

The number of women running their own businesses in the UK has trebled since the early 1980s. In the US, the number of woman-owned small businesses leaped from 4.6 per cent to 30 per cent of the total, and the federal government projected that by the year 2000, the number would be 50 per cent.

Feminist writer bell hooks warned undergraduate women against the practice of objecting to sexist books by not reading them.

Canadian women's groups ran a TV ad that showed a date rape in progress and explained how both sexes can take steps to avoid a similar situation.

In the wake of Anita Hill's testimony, Los Angeles rock promoters Nicole Panter and Excence Cervenka raised $54,000 at a benefit concert for Barbara Boxer, then campaigning for a seat in the Senate.

Gold-record country singer Mary Chapin Carpenter gave her voice to Rock for Choice.

A young woman asked by her interviewer what he would do if she left the job to have a baby, replied, 'Exactly what you would do if a man left to join another bank.'

Labour MP Betty Boothroyd urged MPs to 'elect me for what I am and not for what I was born', and became the first woman Speaker in the 700-year history of the British parliament.

Finland was run by women throughout July 1992 because all 11 men of the cabinet were on holiday.

Teenage girls in America, fed up with fluffy and condescending teen magazines, published their own magazines about 'Girl Revolution'.

A mother in Chicago, annoyed at how images of female perfection undermine girls' self-esteem, created and marketed the 'Happy to Be Me Doll', with more realistic proportions.

The American working-women organization 9 to 5 offered representation and legal advice to 14,000 clerical workers.

Guardian journalist Maggie O'Kane broke the news about Bosnian rape camps and won the 1993 Journalist of the Year award. *Ms.* magazine ran the exclusive, first-person testimony of Bosnian rape survivors, and women's groups and feminist lawyers then compelled the UN to define sex crimes against women as human rights abuses and to bring the rapists to trial. *Newsweek* put the atrocities on its cover, and Katie Couric of the *Today* show relentlessly questioned a Serbian leader about the rapes.

Two hundred British women, including MPs, actors, writers and prominent businesswomen, demanded 'Let the Women's Voice be Heard' and put their names to an advertisement which appeared in all the national newspapers calling for an immediate end to the atrocities in Bosnia.

The American Association of University Women protested when Mattel produced a Barbie that said 'Math class is hard'; the company withdrew the doll and sent a spokeswoman to *Oprah* to explain that Barbie is fully employed.

A group of African-American models met to protest at the way the fashion industry makes room for only one African-American at the top; they demanded better representation of African-American women in the media. Model Cindy Crawford used her MTV slot *House of Style* to campaign against breast implants, counsel girls about bulimia, and discuss why she supports a woman's right to have an abortion.

In its annual 'Give Something Back' campaign, *Mirabella* magazine ran a drive for more research into breast cancer.

A London women's centre installed a pool, gym and Jacuzzi and still met its activist commitments.

Designer Liz Claiborne underwrote public-service announcements against domestic violence, saying: 'I wanted to give something back to the women who made us what we are.'

US Attorney-General Janet Reno used her office to prosecute deadbeat dads and domestic violence.

A UK Labour working party headed by Clare Short MP decided that women must represent the party at the next general election in half its target seats. Women MPs and women's organizations protested at John Major's first all-male cabinet until he appointed two women. In the US women's organizations pushed the President-elect to put more women in his cabinet, so much so that he snapped at them as 'bean counters' – and then appointed another woman.

Historically, power feminism is Harriet Tubman taking the liberation of African-American slaves into her own hands by running an underground railway. Power feminism sparked consumer boycotts in England on behalf of votes for women; they were so effective that London department stores competed with each other to demonstrate their support for women's suffrage. Harrods declared 'Votes for Women Day' and decorated its displays with the purple bunting of the suffrage movement. Fashion and furniture manufacturers rushed to support feminist magazines with glossy advertisements in order to lure the suffrage purse. Power feminism was responsible for the 'daring guerrilla tactics and uncompromisingly tough line' that finally won the seventy-year suffrage struggle.

Victoria Woodhull and Madame C. J. Walker are two early

power-feminist heroines. Woodhull was a beautiful, sensual, charismatic, scandalous and very eccentric New York stockbroker who, with her sister, produced her own newspaper, in which she championed sexual autonomy and the right for women to vote. In 1872, before women could vote, she declared her candidacy for the presidency of the United States. Contrast the meek voice of nineteenth-century victim feminism with Woodhull's unapologetic words:

> I hold that the so-called morality of society is a complicated mass of sheer impertinence and a scandal on the civilization of this advanced century, that the system of social espionage under which we live is damnable, and that the very first axiom of a true morality is for people to mind their own business, and learn to respect, religiously, the social freedom, and the sacred social privacy, of all others ... [Evil] lies in the belief that society has the right to prohibit, to prescribe and regulate, or in any manner interfere with the private love manifestations of its members, any more than it has a right to prescribe their food and drink.

Sarah Breedlove, Madame C. J. Walker, the poor daughter of former slaves, was born on a cotton plantation in Delta, Louisiana. She spent her early adulthood as a washerwoman, and later as a cook. When she was 37 she had a dream, she said, in which the formula for a hair preparation to nourish black hair was revealed to her. She manufactured the mixture for her friends, and soon was marketing her products in the community, providing free demonstrations. Her sales swelled and she discovered a talent for marketing and distribution; soon she was training more than a thousand black women to start their own franchises. At the beginning of the twentieth century, few black women earned more than $1.50 per week. But her agents, said Breedlove, could find the independence and upward mobility that the few occupations open to African-American women denied them: 'I have made it possible ... for many colored women to abandon the washtub for more pleasant and profitable occupation.'

By the time she reached middle age, she was one of the wealthiest women, Black or white, in the country. And she was committed to advancing opportunities for other women. In 1900, when invited to attend Booker T. Washington's National Negro Business League, the businessmen on stage deliberately overlooked her. She stood up and spoke. 'Surely,' she said, 'you are not going to shut the door in my face. I am a woman who came from the cotton fields of the South ... I was promoted from there to the washtub. Then I was promoted to the cook kitchen. Then *I promoted myself* into the business of manufacturing hair goods and preparations. I have built my own factory on my own ground.' The men gave the speaker their attention.

As Walker grew ever more successful, she used her power increasingly to return power to the women she employed. She encouraged her agents to become community leaders, and then taught them to become lobbyists. She formed a national organization for her agents and in her speech to it, 'Women's Duty to Women', praised them and urged them to remember their responsibility to use their success for other women's advancement: 'I want to show that Walker agents are doing more than making money for themselves.' She compared selling to a battle: 'Hit often and hit hard,' she said. 'Strike with all your might.'

She urged her agents to tithe their profits to charity: 'We are anxious to help all humanity, the poor as well as the rich, especially those of our race.' Though she built herself a palatial home, she also, whenever possible, invested her money in the Black community. 'By giving my work to colored men,' she said of a group of houses she built for Indianapolis's Black citizens, 'they are thus able to employ others and, if not directly, indirectly I am contributing more jobs for our boys and girls.' At the height of her power, Walker travelled to the White House to urge President Woodrow Wilson to make lynching a federal crime. When she died, thousands of dollars of her fortune went to support antilynching work.

Power feminists such as these two start with the assumption that women can marshal their power and win. They assume that women need not be better or worse than men, and certainly need not be the same, but deserve rights simply because they are human beings. They assert that where the system works unfairly, women should use their resources to force it to change, rather than pleading for kinder treatment on the basis of victim status.

The Historical Origins of the Two Traditions

When critics claim that feminism is puritanical, or attack feminism as reimposing a sexual double standard, they strike a chord for many. This is because women are not informed about their own history, and most don't fully realize that two distinct traditions have always coexisted tensely in feminism. One tradition is severe, morally superior and self-denying; the other is free-thinking, pleasure-loving and self-assertive. How did these two traditions originate?

The degree to which women are kept from public life has fluctuated over time. In the West before the Industrial Revolution, both women and men produced food and clothing for the household; the goods and services that women sold were a vital part of a town's economic life. *A Midwife's Tale*, for instance, shows that in a typical Colonial-era New England town women were in charge of a complex economy, exchanging wool, renting out looms, and bartering household help for profit. The diarist, Martha Ballard, an elderly midwife well respected in her community, ran her own practice, travelled alone throughout the region at all hours to reach her patients, kept her own books, collected her own debts, and supported her jailed husband. No one looked askance at this. Women were independent and capable in public life as well as being nurturing in private; there was no contradiction between these qualities.

All of that changed, at least for middle-class women, in the nineteenth century. While working-class and immigrant women were forced to keep the tradition of powerful women moving competently between family, community authority and working life, middle-class white women had to give up participation in the world outside the home. With the rise of industrialization, paid work was taken out of the home and into the office or factory, where it was redefined as belonging only to men, who were then expected to support their now unproductive wives on a 'family wage'. Industrialization combined with the rise of the middle class in such a way that a class of full-time consumers was desirable to the economy; affluent women were assigned this role. An ideological push began to drive these women out of public life and into the sex-segregated home.

This entailed the creation of an elaborate belief system that cast the middle-class woman as the 'Angel in the House', who was to be cordoned off in a plush, safe, 'separate sphere'. The separate sphere ideology succeeded in driving bourgeois women into lives of enforced domesticity, sexual repression, economic dependency and unpaid 'good works'. Women, it was said, lost their 'feminine grace' if they sought education, training or meddled in public affairs or, worse still, they risked their health. In 1874 eminent Victorian physician Henry Maudsley wrote of the dangers facing a scholarly teenage girl:

> For a time all seems to go well ... she triumphs over male and female competitors ... But in the long run nature asserts its power ... health fails ... [she] leaves college a good scholar but a delicate and ailing woman ... the special functions which have relation to her future offices as a woman, and the full and perfect accomplishment of which is essential to sexual completeness, have been deranged at a critical time.'

An elaborate propaganda of flattery gave these women a sense of pride in their imprisonment: their maternal qualities were lauded, their spiritual activities heaped with praise. Commentators urged them to embrace their suffocating condition, for it was proof that they were too special to work, struggle and play alongside men. They were told that the now wholly male public sphere of competition, fame, politics and money was evil, and that their exclusion from it was proof of their higher nature. 'I would not,' wrote Senator George G. Vest in 1887, 'degrade woman by giving her the right of suffrage ... It would take her down from that pedestal where she is today, influencing by her gentle and kindly caress the action of her husband toward the good and pure.'

When feminist organization began in earnest in the middle of the nineteenth century, it developed into two strands. While one stressed women's humanity, individuality and need for self-determination, the other drew on the Angel in the House stereotype.

The basic tenets of the Angel in the House ideal included self-effacement and uncomplaining martyrdom; an obsession with rigid norms of 'respectability', which include the task of policing other women's behaviour; the belief that women are sexless, and men sexually bestial; the belief that money and fame corrupt women; the elimination of aggression; and the belief that women's 'maternal nature' makes them fundamentally different from and better than men. These tenets, of course, sound familiar because they are the foundations of modern victim feminism.

How could a woman hemmed in by such a set of conventions possibly ask for power or lay claim to her rights? Not by fighting, yelling, marching or dragging her petticoat through the bad, muddy outdoors. No, such a woman's tools for exerting power are necessarily indirect. Her dominion is the world of social relations. With her children, she can withhold herself emotionally. With her husband, she can withhold herself sexually. And with her female peers, she can use censure or disapproval. Since her primary weapon is the guest list, her primary power is to include or exclude others. Her most familiar retaliation against a world that displeases her is to stop speaking to it.

As John Stuart Mill put it, 'An active and energetic mind, if denied liberty, will seek for power; refused the command of itself, it will assert its personality by attempting to control others ... Those to whom others will not leave the undisturbed management of their own affairs, will compensate themselves, if they can, by meddling in the affairs of others.'

In terms of public debate, the most comfortable way for the Angel to protest injustice is to stress her status as a victim. In a world that, for its own purposes, is reluctant to see her as a human being with the same combination of good and bad as everyone else, she must persuade the public that harm done to her is wrong not because she is a person, but because, as a woman, she is good. Since the women's movement began, this 'familial', 'domestic', 'maternal' or 'cultural' feminism, as it has been called at various times, has highlighted women's traditional virtues to justify their inclusion in public life. Josephine Butler, who led the fight against the Contagious Diseases Acts during the 1860s and 1870s in Britain, spoke of the home as the 'nursery of all virtue', and of the need to re-establish a moral order both by improving the position of women as wives and mothers and by extending the ideal of 'family values' beyond the home. Both suffrage campaigner Millicent Garrett Fawcett and feminist author Frances Power Cobbe argued that 'women's virtue, tenderness and eye for detail – in short the special qualities they developed as wives and mothers – were necessary to complete man-made legislation'. Theresa Billington-Greig was virtually the only feminist of her generation to criticize the suffragettes for regarding the home 'as an exemplar of what ought to be in the political world'.

In America, the same pattern was emerging. Frances Willard, head of the Women's Christian Temperance Union, 'described how the sanctity of the home could be preserved and the moral purity of the nation uplifted if the spiritual influence of women could be exercised through the vote'. She urged not self-determination, but 'useful womanhood'. Sarah Josepha Hale attacked suffragists for placing 'the true dignity of woman in her ability to do man's work, and to become more and more like him. What a degrading idea; as though the worth of porcelain should be estimated by its resemblance to iron! Does she not perceive that, in estimating physical and mental ability above moral excellence, she sacrifices her own sex?'

From the mid-nineteenth to the early twentieth century, these feminists campaigned against vice. Springing out of early nineteenth-century charitable groups, they saw feminism primarily as a movement for moral reform. They held prayer meetings outside public houses, organized around the issue of 'Social Hygiene', and devoted themselves to the rescue of prostitutes, the regulation of men's excessive sexual claims upon their baby-weary wives, and the eradication of the sex trade.

This feminism, originating as it did in the feminization of nineteenth-century church life, is devotional, emotive and idealistic. One of the earliest documents calling for a 'Union of Women for Association' – that is, a feminist movement – is an 1847 letter to a Boston newspaper, the *Harbinger*:

> The religious element must be at the foundation of such an organization. There must be a moral and religious consecration of ourselves ... Baptised anew in the spirit of love, let us go forth in our mission, prepared 'to die daily' if need be; content to be poor, outcast, and despised, to cheerfully meet contumely and reproach, and to pour back on those who condemn us floods of all-subduing love, of generous, hearty forgiveness.

While this 'domestic' or 'maternal' feminism left many lasting achievements, it also evolved a rhetoric of women's sexual innocence and men's sexual brutality. It was easily shocked; in 1869 American doctor and activist Mary Livermore clucked over the 'loose utterances' of other feminists on 'marriage and dress questions'. This strain of feminism has the virtue of keeping a steady eye on the real injustices and sufferings of women and children; its concerns for victims is built in and cannot be forgotten, since all are asked to identify themselves with and as victims. But its vice is related; since no one really likes identifying as a victim unless everyone else does too, it can be judgmental towards other womens' pleasures.

The second strand of feminism asserted women's rights as people, and it was closer to most women's needs and sensibilities 130 years ago than is the 'victim' strain of feminism today. Of what rights is woman deprived? asked Lucretia Mott at the Seneca Falls Convention in 1848: 'She wants to be acknowledged a moral, responsible being.' 'The proper sphere [of women],' wrote Harriet Taylor, 'is the largest and highest which they are able to attain to.'

This feminism celebrates female sexuality: eighteenth-century polemicist Mary Wollstonecraft attacked the notion that women lack 'the common passions and appetites of their nature'. She was self-supporting, lived with a man before marriage, and had a child out of wedlock. A century later Annie Besant began to champion a woman's right to birth control, and to practise and promote 'free love', while across the Atlantic Ocean, Margaret Sanger explicitly stated that 'no woman can call herself free who does not own and control her body'. Victoria Woodhull believed that sexual self-determination for women was an 'inalienable right'. Edith Ellis called upon women to 'realize passion as the flame of love'. Olive Schreiner proposed that 'the sexual passion' was as powerful a force in women as in men. Vera Brittain claimed that enlightened monogamy was to be brought about by 'the detailed technique of intercourse . . . the abolition of censorship, toleration of experimental unions', sex education, and general openness; Marie Stopes stressed the importance of men acquiring sexual skills for women's pleasure. The tradition represented by these women has nothing to do with the repressive 'hangdog dowdies' of Camille Paglia's invective.

This feminism is anti-dogma: that women require intellectual freedom is a tenet it passionately held. Frances Wright, a feminist who in 1829 began to publish her own newspaper, believed in the 'broadest possible range of freedom for everyone and in everything' and wanted her readers to take nothing on faith: 'Examine, inquire . . . Know *why* you believe, understand *what* you believe.' Lucretia Mott believed that men and women must act, not according to fixed creeds, but according to their own inner sense of truth. The approach of this feminism is based on the belief that women can connect authentically with others only after they have found and taken possession of a separate identity.

This strand of feminism values reason, seeing it not as the enemy, but as the counterpart of emotion: clear thinking and the public voice are not 'masculine'. In a century when American President Grover Cleveland could say that 'it is one of the chief charms of women that they are not especially amenable to argument', Margaret Fuller wanted to teach young women 'to systematize thought and give a precision and clearness in which our sex are so deficient, chiefly, I think, because they have so few inducements to test and classify what they receive'. Fuller was intent, too, on training girls to express ideas effectively so they could speak in public. Suffragist Angelina Grimké bemoaned women's separate education: 'Our minds are crushed, and our reasoning powers wholly uncultivated.' Feminism such as this values teaching girls to express and defend their opinions even at the risk of not being liked by the group. Lucy Stone and Antoinette Brown formed a secret debating society at Oberlin College, where girls were permitted to listen to boys' debates but not to participate. Early feminists found that women were incapacitated for public life because, unused to large groups, they spoke in the same soft, hesitant tones that they would use in a drawing room, and people could scarcely catch a word. This led Susan B. Anthony to vow that she would spend her life ensuring that women could stand up and say anything at any public gathering.

Power feminism honours the wish for recognition: one charge in the 'Declaration of Sentiments' of the Seneca Falls Convention is that '[man] closes against [woman] all the avenues to wealth and distinction which he considers most honorable to himself'. Margaret Fuller said of a book of hers that 'should I go away now, the measure of my footprint would be left upon the earth'. Lucy Stone wrote an essay that was chosen for the commencement speech of her university; when told that a male professor would have to present it because 'it is improper for women to participate in public exercises with men', she refused to complete it, even at risk of being forbidden to graduate. She also insisted, scandalously, on keeping her own name after marriage. Sojourner Truth spoke blazingly before audiences, making famous the refrain 'Ain't I a woman?'

These women were daring individualists, and they showed their commitment to social justice by their own political actions. Many of them lectured widely at a time when for women to speak in public was considered immoral.

This feminism claims full moral choice for women. Men and women are not the same, but 'they are both moral and accountable beings, and whatever is right for a man to do, is right for a woman to do,' according to Grimké. This feminism does not plead female superiority: 'I ask no favors for my sex,' said Grimké. She completely rejected the 'doctrine of masculine and feminine virtues'. Lucy Stone wrote: 'We ask to be regarded, respected and treated as human beings, of full age and natural abilities, as equal fellow sinners, not as infants or beautiful angels, to whom the laws of civil and social justice do not apply.' And Frances Power Cobbe asked, in a provocatively entitled magazine article, 'Criminals, Idiots, Women and Minors: Is This Classification Sound?'

This belief system uses the master's own definitions of civil rights and democracy to open up his house. Suffrage protestors outside the White House bore nothing upon their banner except President Wilson's own remark about democracy: 'the rights of those who submit to authority to have a voice in their own government'. Rather than rejecting democracy, power feminism pushes it to live up to its own self-definition. It uses the master's tools to bring female experience into the master's house. The organizers of the Seneca Falls Convention drew on the Declaration of Independence for the wording of their manifesto; Elizabeth Cady Stanton later wrote The Woman's Bible. One tenet of these feminists was that, as long as women were without rights, they should refuse to pay taxes. The protest against taxation without representation, a rallying point for the Revolutionary War, was theirs too. These women understood that money is crucial to independence: said Susan B. Anthony, 'Woman must have a purse of her own.' When they are economically dependent, she wrote, 'there is no true freedom for women'.

Power feminism does not wait around for others to find their way towards treating women justly. Margaret Fuller ended her *Woman in the Nineteenth Century* (1845) with a challenge to female self-esteem and self-help: women, she said, must develop 'self-reliance and self-impulse' and take responsibility for raising their own status.

This feminism never thought of men as separate from its struggle; men were not enemies but partners in the fight for social equality.

Like 'domestic' feminism, this strain too left monuments to its success. Its virtue is that it treats women like adults and men like human beings. Its vice is that its stress on rights and female individualism may lead the luckier or more successful to overlook those who are less so. Many people of both sexes share the fear that a woman who is self-determining risks becoming selfish.

Which feminism should we choose today? I submit that we choose the one that works. In the last stretch of the fight for the vote, history proved the lesson that the genderquake proved again in 1992: power feminism moves mountains with astonishing ease, even as victim feminism spins its wheels over the same manicured ground.

Between 1867 and 1919 feminists like Lydia Becker and Millicent Garrett Fawcett, the president of the National Union of Women's Suffrage Societies, clung to a feminine 'influence' over the political parties in the hope of winning the vote. Millicent Garrett Fawcett pressed for women's suffrage on the grounds that she 'wished to strengthen the womanliness in women, and because I want to see the womanly and domestic side of things weigh more and count for more in all public concerns'. Meanwhile, the men continued to play political football with women's suffrage.

But the more militant Women's Social and Political Union, founded in 1903 by Emmeline Pankhurst, was getting impatient.

The fight for suffrage had lasted for half a century. Emmeline Pankhurst, together with her daughters Christabel and Sylvia, led a campaign of militancy in 1913 in which thousands of women broke windows, destroyed letterboxes and burned slogans into public monuments. Arrested and in jail, many women went on hunger strike to prove their determination to win the vote. The extensive newspaper coverage of their activities attracted public sympathy and outrage, the membership of the WSPU grew and politicians were forced to take 'the woman question' seriously. As unladylike as it was, this tactic succeeded. In four years, it accomplished more than sixty-five years of victim feminism's exemplary behaviour and gentle entreaties.

Why Victim Feminism Now?

We have arrived again at just such a moment. But old expectations about how women must approach power, though proven useless, still threaten to hold us back.

In the 1980s victim feminism became a popular way to phrase women's will to self-assertion for some very good reasons.

The first reason is historical: the backlash came down hard on a feminism of rights. The idea that women were entitled to equal choices because they were people became unpopular; so the claim was refashioned into the supplication that women should have equal choices because they were, well, superior.

As the Western world grew more conservative, it was safer and easier to set up a 'better', but totally unthreatening, feminist separate sphere than to fight for more power to restructure the system as women saw fit. It became safer to say that power was male than to say that men had too much of it.

From the mid-1970s onwards, a number of books emerged that focused on women's separate speech, separate organizational styles and separate value systems. These include Deborah Tannen's *You Just Don't Understand*, Carol Gilligan's *In a Different Voice* and Jean Baker Miller's *Toward a New Psychology of Women*. These disparate but thematically related ideas became lumped together as what Katha Pollitt calls 'difference feminism'.

The basic idea behind difference feminism is sound. The opposition calls traditionally feminine qualities – nurturing, intuition, emotionality, a focus on attachment rather than autonomy and on listening rather than speaking – weakness, and values them less highly than the traditionally male values of assertiveness, reason and 'blind' impartiality. Difference feminism provided a way of looking at 'feminine' qualities that turned them into a separate, coherent system that is not inferior to men's.

'Difference' ideas became enormously popular. One reason for this popularity was that 1970s feminism had upheld an ideal of androgyny that felt sterile to many women. The opposition had been using women's difference – particularly their role as mothers – to keep them out of positions of power. Seventies feminism, which struggled to prove that women could be 'just like men' in the workplace, had to play down those differences.

But the more contact women had with the 'male' world, the more rightly critical of its shortcomings they became. They saw that the workplace was structured to cut workers off from the demands of family, and that the most fortunate careerists traded money and status for quality of life. The 'superwoman ideal', promoted by advertisers, alienated many women who felt that traditionally female values – nurturance, co-operation, caring – were being given short shrift.

But the theories of difference feminists, great contributions in themselves, were interpreted not as *descriptions* of women's behaviour, but as *prescriptions* for it, and were used to justify women's withdrawal from public life. Instead of using the insights to demand that male power make room for female values, the ideas' interpreters further built up the barrier between 'women's values' and public life.

The hostility of the backlash years deprived women of cultural permission to feel good about gaining prestige through success, achievement or the overt use of clout. So the impulse to set up a separate sphere, in which everything that the opposition despised about women was revered, proved seductive. Women might not have been standing for parliament but they were *nicer*.

The elaboration of separate sphere ideas was a function of feeling powerless and hating it. Ironically, an ideology that castigated power and celebrated lack of status became popular because it was one of the few venues that gave women the experience of power and prestige.

The second reason for the attraction to difference feminism was psychological: women are socialized to fear touching 'male' power. Feminists often ridicule the fear in many men that if they acknowledge 'female' qualities or do 'female' work like parenting, they will become 'like women'. But we overlook our own parallel irrational fear – that if women use traditionally masculine power, they risk becoming 'like men'. Rapid change is unnerving: psychiatrists studying stress, for example, find that happy events like marriage and promotion are as stressful as divorce and death. Women's lives are changing at the speed of light compared with the lives of their mothers and grandmothers. The embrace of power is behaviour that would have had women burnt at the stake in the past. The psychology of the separate sphere feels like home. So at a time when many women are actually learning to use power, a threat is posed to our psychological comfort. In response, victim feminism took the better-worn path backwards, rather than forging ahead.

We are all struggling against impulses that draw us backwards, and compensate psychologically for the strangeness of a great leap forward. The backlash wasn't generated just by men; part of the stasis women experience derives from their own ambivalence about entering the alien land of equality. We must admit that many women – perhaps, in isolated moments, all women – want both to abandon their passivity and revel in it too. We resist giving up the sweetness of dependency, the moral lightness of being infantilized, the simplicity of having limited choices, the sense of specialness that comes from being treated as a frail exotic flower. If women were familiar with the delights of men's privilege and power, they would fight against giving them up just as many men do; but if men were familiar with the less material, but no less seductive, delights of dependency, they would become as attached to those experiences as many women are today.

I call this ambivalence the 'trousseau reflex'. When white settler women first set out across America, some of them were so unnerved by the newness, rawness and freedom of the lands they were seeking that they brought the heavy artefacts of their respectable, cloistered pasts with them in their wagons. Bustles and corsets swaddled them in the Nevada heat; painted china dragged their wagons' back wheels into shifting sands; wooden trousseau chests filled with handmade broderie anglaise, upholstery doilies, and six-implement silver place settings slowed their thirsty horses and, when the horses died, their staggering oxen.

'Women started out the journey,' reads one account of the migration, 'wearing the popular long dresses of linsey-woolsey, fashioned with tight long sleeves, sloping shoulders and layers of petticoats over their bloomers. As the trip progressed, many women tossed modesty aside and discarded their skirts.'

And some women did not. Their identities were inseparable from their respectability, which became ever more important to them as they faced the wildness of their new terrain and the absence of social convention. These women would insist that their party jettison tackle, tools and seed before they would leave behind their whatnots and player pianos. Faced with a terrifying need to reinvent themselves, to be open to a new status that could bring everything or nothing, they clung all the more fiercely to the certain status of the old, cramped past. But sadly, this attach-ment to the symbols of the trousseau slowed their adaptation to the new environment, and led some wagons to founder in the high passes before their passengers glimpsed the promised land. We, too, need to learn to breathe new air and move with new freedom.

Another part of the psychological appeal of victim feminism is that even before women are kept from power they are raised to disavow even admitting they want it.

A girl's pull toward normal aggression and competitiveness, her dreams of personal glory, her childhood egocentricity, are knocked into an exaggerated self-effacement. What surfaces then? Like people who hate homosexuality because they fear it in them-selves, such a woman will express an exaggerated abhorrence of the will to power. With others who have suffered and renounced in the same way, she will develop a formal system in which those qualities are 'other', totally alien. In victim feminism's taboos on ego, money, aggression and power, we can see the projection of a blocked set of wishes.

A related appeal derives from the widespread female experience of child sexual abuse. This trauma can elicit a rage so terrifying, especially to women, that they need to put as much distance as possible, no matter how artificial, between themselves and those feelings. As Donna Minkowitz points out, 'Survivors of violence have two choices: to repeat the violence themselves, or to march down Andrea Dworkin's Via Negativa in a vain attempt to wipe our brains clean of rage and the desire to hurt . . . so desperate to see ourselves as innocent that we repress any identification with the tormentor.' In survivors of male violence or abuse, the projection of all badness on to 'male models of behaviour' masks an unacknowledged terror of normal violent retaliatory impulses.

Another consequence of sexual abuse in childhood is a crippling sense of guilt. 'I felt,' said one survivor, 'that if it rained, it was my fault.' An ideology in which women are not only victims of abuse, but innocent victims, serves to absolve survivors of that sense of blame.

The impulse to claim that one is an innocent victim also derives from bias in the courts. The judicial system unofficially maintains a spectrum of female guilt that determines whose hurt matters and whose does not. The rape of a prostitute is fairly meaningless; the rape of a divorced working mother who drinks is slightly more serious; the rape of a churchgoing housewife, more serious still; and the rape of a nun may even matter. A recent Home Office study revealed that reported rape cases in the UK have only a one in four chance of resulting in a conviction, and that 'if the woman was married or cohabiting, not physically injured and met her alleged attacker in a social setting, it was far less likely that the incident would have resulted in a conviction.' In 1982 Judge Melford Stevenson released the rapist of a 17-year-old girl saying that, because she was hitch-hiking, she was 'asking for it'; over a decade later, Australian Judge John Ewen Bland told the rapist of a 15-year-old girl that '"no" often subsequently means "yes"'; Judge Derek Bollen, of the South Australia Supreme Court, said their was nothing wrong with a husband using 'rougher than usual treatment' to persuade his wife to have sex; and, most recently, Judge Sinclair said in the District Court of New South Wales that one of the reasons why he could not accept that a woman raped by a stranger had suffered 'any substantial psychological effects' was 'the fact that she continued to live with her boyfriend . . . and . . . to have intercourse with him'.

Women are blamed for getting raped if they drink or wear short skirts; they are told they provoke beatings. In the mid-1980s the American Psychiatric Association proposed a new disease, 'self-defeating personality disorder'. This 'disorder' labels a person sick if they experience sex discrimination, for the afflicted person is 'drawn into situations and relationships in which he or she will suffer'. Dr Margaret Jenvold, an American researcher, was said to have this personality disorder after she filed a sex-discrimination complaint. Given this bias, it is not at all surprising that many women should focus on establishing their blamelessness.

Finally, modern feminism has been disproportionately articulated by middle-class white women. And upward mobility for women who are not of Anglo-Saxon descent often involves leaving behind other female traditions (Latina, African-American, immigrant Italian and Jewish) that often have less ambivalence about women's use of power, personal forcefulness and money, even as some of the traditions assign women less room, at least overtly, in which to use them. A great irony arose from this situation: many women aspiring to power had to do so within an atmosphere that rewarded an Angel in the House mentality that was not even part of their heritage.

All of these influences led victim feminism into the centre of debate in the 1980s, and brought women to a series of 'feminist' impasses.

Chapter Thirteen

Victim Feminism's Recent Impasses

Sex: Are Men Naughty by Nature?

The 'male vice/female virtue' view of the world that dominated the nineteenth century resurfaced in victim feminism's treatment of sexuality in our own time. Though Andrea Dworkin and Catharine MacKinnon's theories of how deeply embedded is male superiority in all social relations are fundamental reading, ripples from their analysis led others to perceive sexual coercion or force where they should not have.

The trousseau reflex of being sexually judgmental, which fostered these readers' attitude, dates from the nineteenth century, when feminists were rescuing prostitutes and speaking on behalf of married women exhausted and endangered by the births resulting from their husbands' sexual greed. The language these feminists developed, about men's bestiality and women's sexlessness, echoed that of conservative men, who called women 'so pure-hearted as to be utterly ignorant of and averse to any sensual indulgence'.

In 1987 Gary Hart, the Democratic frontrunner, was brought down by the revelation of his affair with Donna Rice, a Georgetown-educated ex-model. The young woman was photographed sitting on the politician's lap on a yacht disastrously named *Monkey Business*. He was not the first, nor the last, male politician to be brought down by the untimely revelation of an extramarital affair. In Britain, Cecil Parkinson's affair with his then secretary Sara Keays, which came to light only when she refused to terminate her pregnancy, led to his resignation – even though his role as chairman of the Conservative party in the run-up to the general election was widely believed to have helped Margaret Thatcher secure her second term of office. Cecil Parkinson had to go, just as he was about to be made Foreign Secretary, as David Mellor more recently had to resign a cabinet post, because their sexual infidelity was seen by fellow Tories to be making a mockery of the 'traditional family values' promoted by the Conservative party. But Gary Hart was different. He was a Democrat, a potential torch-bearer for a more liberal America and a means of escape from the conservative morality of the Reagan years.

In the depth of the retrenchment years, feminist fury about being nearly invisible to the electoral process found expression in the trousseau reflex of sexual moralizing. Suzannah Lessard, a *New Yorker* writer, declared in a *Newsweek* article that 'a feminist sensibility has seeped into the public consciousness sufficiently to make philandering appear to many at best unattractive, maybe unacceptable and possibly even alarming where the candidate's emotions and psychology are concerned'. This alarm is not, she claimed, '"moralism" in the sense of old-fashioned rectitude. Rather it is awareness of the dignity and equality of women.' She went on to compare Hart's philandering with the death of Mary Jo Kopechne at Chappaquiddick in the presence of Edward Kennedy. She noted that when he ran for office in 1980, 'a number of feminists were concerned about Kennedy's behavior. It meant to them that Kennedy did not respect women and would not put them in high posts and would respond to feminist causes only as an expedient.'

Concluding that Hart's adultery is a feminist issue, Lessard wrote: 'We found out that many people now believe that if a man abuses his wife by womanizing there could be something abusive in his nature.'

These victim feminist conclusions are based on Angel in the House assumptions that can only rebound destructively on women. A consensual sexual encounter between two adults, one of whom has no direct power over the other, is not tantamount to a fatal accident that involved alcohol and reckless driving. We do not know how Hart treated Rice, how he treated his wife, what their problems or agreements were. We know that Rice joined him of her own volition. However little Lessard may like it, consensual sex with a married man is not the moral equivalent of a drunken car crash that leads to a death by drowning.

Again, in 1992 Robin Morgan condemned Democratic presidential nominee Bill Clinton for the Gennifer Flowers scandal, in which intimate conversation with a blonde nightclub singer taped by a tabloid paper suggested an affair. Morgan's objection implies that by having consensual sex with Flowers, Clinton disrespects either the singer, his wife, or his constituents.

Personally, I was persuaded to vote for Clinton by the transcripts of the tapes. They convinced me that Clinton respects women more than do most male politicians. Whatever the relationship between them, the man, a state governor, listened to the woman, a small-time singer, as much as he spoke to her; he asked her about the details of her life; and when, so far as he knew, no one important was listening, he said to an obscure woman who could not possibly help him win office, '[George Bush] doesn't have a clue what's going on, what ordinary people's lives are like. He has no idea how awful it is for them.' Morgan evidently presumed a martyred wife at home who needed 'support' from a sisterhood. But, as Hillary Rodham Clinton declared with power feminist defiance, it was nobody's business but their own.

What sexual behaviour in politicians is relevant to power feminists? Buying or hitting women, certainly; harassing women who are professional colleagues or underlings; having sex with underage women who cannot freely consent. But consensual sex outside marriage? No. So long as the encounters are consensual, infidelity is not a power-feminist issue.

When Lessard presumes that a politician who treats monogamy lightly is likely to treat women voters' issues lightly, she is making a leap of reasoning that reveals another reason why victim feminism flourished in the 1980s: transference. There was not enough cultural support for women to say to politicians, 'You are treating female voters like one-night stands, you are unfaithful to us, you are seducing us in the campaigning but betraying us in the morning-after legislation, you are not leaving your number, you are not calling, you are not making a commitment.' In the Gary Hart case, that 'shrewish' set of legitimate political demands was repressed, and those feelings were projected as outrage at sexual behaviour. Hart was merely a repository for women voters' feelings of having been politically betrayed. The fact is that when women voters get enough political clout and use it, politicians will have to do their bidding, whether sincerely or not. As women begin to use their political power, fewer will care at all what their politicians do in bed. Those acts will have lost the symbolic weight they carry when women are powerless.

The 'feminist' mythology of female chastity has grown ever more baroque in the recent past. In 1993 Sally Cline published a book called *Women, Passion and Celibacy* that repackaged Angel in the House sexuality in the guise of feminism. Cline argues that celibacy is a route to female liberation. She casts sex as a power struggle with what she calls the 'Genital Elite' – men – and identifies female orgasm as part of the media-maintained package of what women have to do in order to please them. Women's orgasms 'were a form of manipulated emotional labour which women worked at in order to reflect men and maintain male values': 'Like militarism today, fur coats the day before, sexual intercourse and general genital thrashing about are things a woman is expected to purchase.' Cline sees 'the genital myth' as having 'increasing domination over women's lives' and reinforcing the imbalance of power between the sexes. The notion that 'genital thrashing about' implicitly subordinates women and is imposed on them by their brutal masters is an offence to women who feel that sexual choice – including the choice to take a man's body inside one's own – is the wellspring of one's inmost sense of worth, 'the passion of life'.

In 1992, female students in Berkeley, California, forcibly clothed a nude man in the name of feminism. A 22-year-old student who calls himself the Naked Guy had taken to walking around the University of California campus wearing nothing but a sun hat and sandals. He strolled around the dining halls nude, he studied nude, he sat peacefully in classes and in the library nude. He was nude under the sparkling jacaranda trees and in the cafés on Telegraph Avenue, nude in the post office, nude as he queued to get into the cinema, nude as he sat his exams. His clothing-free existence was a statement: anti-materialist, anti-conventional, pro-nature and pro-freedom.

Several women students tried, unsuccessfully, to get him to cover up. Finally, they told the administration that he made them feel 'sexually harassed' by his nudity. The administration acted, and the Naked Guy sorrowfully wrapped up his genitals in a sporty red bandana.

The Naked Guy was probably the least threatening man in the greater Berkeley area, and the women near him, the safest. He was nude and the women around him were fully clothed; he was visibly unarmed, utterly exposed. He had laid down his power and status along with his clothes, for his nakedness made him a subject of constant scrutiny. He had even defined his nudity as an alliance with nature, a rejection of a world that turns people into commodities. He had offered himself up naked to the female gaze, and in doing this taught himself about female experience, for he had made himself more vulnerable to the eye than women were. What could be more tender, more honest? Isn't this just what we say we hope men will do, metaphorically – become naked to us, come to us freely in the responsive skin of their humanity, show us who they are, potent and gentle, costumes and armature discarded? How could women repudiate a gesture like that in the name of 'feminist' delicacy?

There are not many scenes one can draw upon in trying to envisage peace and harmony between the sexes. When I need to invoke the memory of how women and men can be the best of friends, I remember afternoons sunbathing half naked in casual mixed-sex groups under the swaying eucalyptus leaves on the pleasantly weedy lawns of the Berkeley campus. I recall those moments with absolute gratitude. The sun on our companionable bodies covered the scene with a sense of truce. Who was the lamb and who the lion? It did not matter. We were friends, neither prey nor predator, at ease together in the sun's equable shining.

If, fifteen years later, the nude male body offering itself in its loveliness and power to the eyes of all the women on a college campus makes women feel not affection and amusement, not even pleasure in a gift (for the Naked Guy was beautiful) but fear, then we have fallen hideously backwards to be trapped in a gilded cage now marked 'feminism'.

Victim-feminist anxiety over robust female heterosexuality has led to a situation in which there is an elaborate vocabulary with which to describe sexual harm done by men, but almost no vocabulary in which a woman can celebrate sex with men. Indeed, there is little feminist culture in which I can recognize my own sexual life.

There is a highly sophisticated lesbian erotic culture, boasting writers like Jeanette Winterson and Pat Califia, and venues like the Clit Club; there is a highly proscriptive PC straight culture, in which any notions of power, darkness or fantasy are taboo; there is a New Age straight erotic culture, which is big on flavoured massage oils, feathers, books in which all the men are bearded, appliances with baroque attachments, and a lot of material from the Kama Sutra (if it's Eastern, it's OK). There is the fluffy, formulaic erotic culture of Mills and Boon romances, and the bouncy, aerobicized erotic culture of women's magazines, where sexual variety is displayed with the subtlety of a Haagen-Dazs ice-cream menu. And the one truly witty, irreverent subculture for straight women is, unnervingly enough, the S&M enclave where people do things with fishhooks that beggar description and daze the ethical compass. Not a very comprehensive set of carnal options for the developing heterosexual woman. Where are most girls to go for a feminist vision of their erotic life?

The next phase of feminism must be about saying a sexual yes as well as a sexual no, and women are going to have to start telling their truths about their sexual lives. I'll come clean with my subjective truth.

I am sick of people trying to make me choose between being sexual and serious; and I am sick of being split the same way by victim feminism. I want to be a serious thinker and not have to hide the fact that I have breasts; I want female sexuality to accompany, rather than undermine, female political power. I want to be able to talk, without fear of political repercussions, about things that are among the most important in my life. I know that the experiences of degradation that millions of women undergo are all too real; and I know I may be a statistical anomaly but the

Dworkinite description of coercion, invasion, and one-sided objectification as the *norm* of male sexuality just does not match my own experience. I have unquestionably felt sexual threat and hatred from men on the street, seen it often in the mass media, and witnessed the terrible evidence in my work with rape survivors. But that tragic side of women's experience of some men's sexual violence is not the whole truth, nor should it stand in for the whole truth. Millions of men rape and sexually abuse; many, many more millions do not. Instead of looking solely at the damage done and defining all men and all male sexuality by those violent acts, we must also begin to study and celebrate whatever choices and conditions lead so many more men to be unable to include rape, coercion or abuse within the scope of their actions.

Why should the sentence 'I want to make love', when spoken to a man, subordinate a woman? Or even 'I want to go down on you'? or 'Fuck me'? Why shouldn't I talk about the absolute delight that male sexual response instils in me? When I hear an unqualified narrative of global male sexual destructiveness, and do not interrupt it, I feel that I betray my body's deepest friendships. Where is the story that I recognize? The story of how male sexuality has comforted me when I was sad, energized me when I was listless, grounded me when I was feeling tentative, and been to me the source of creativity?

The armoured monsters attacked by critics of masculinity and sexual violence certainly exist. But I have had the good luck not to have slept with them. I do not recognize them in my knowledge of how the male body needs kindness as well as tension. I've seen men delirious with affection; I have seen the word 'love' trigger an erection. Give me room for my knowledge too; it is no less important than that of a woman who has experienced nothing but abuse. Don't tell me that the best friends of my body and heart are undifferentiated predators, who think of their genitals as if they were guns. My joyful life experiences with men are neither politically invalid nor so aberrant. Let us give the love of men, too, its legitimate feminist weight.

I want men, male care, male sexual attention. This desire doesn't necessarily make a woman a slave or an addict; I am a human organism with a dominant orientation: what can be intrinsically wrong with that? Male sexual attention is the sun in which I bloom. The male body is ground and shelter to me, my lifelong destination. When it is maligned categorically, I feel as if my homeland is maligned.

There has got to be room in feminism for these loyalties too; for a radical heterosexuality, an eros between men and women that does not diminish female power, but affirms it.

Straight sex poses a conundrum for feminists. It is understandable that one might be tempted, if one is trying to live as a free woman, to let others shroud the activity in rigid critical proscriptions.

First, there is the physical fact of it, which challenges one's orientation as 'free' and 'independent': one wants to be opened, possessed. I know there was some feminist effort at popularizing the notion of 'engulfment', and sure, sometimes it can feel vaguely that way. But most often one feels discovered, reconfigured – whatever it is, the sensation of being entered does not lend itself easily to the active voice. Then there is the enjoyment, perhaps, of the weight of the man's body; there is even perhaps enjoyment, of the man's being larger than oneself; there is the pleasure in contrast. And if he is larger, what is the woman but smaller? And must it not be suspect to *like* that?

Then there is the fact of what straight sex does to a woman: it basically makes her need men. On a purely physical level; then perhaps, on an emotional level; you need the man, what he can give you that no one else can. One longs; one feels lost, incomplete; one does foolish, embarrassing, unspeakable things for love. One is, if not a slave, then surely less than free.

Then there is liking the maleness of the man, uncritically. One might like a swagger; or a kind of virile demeanour of responsibility; or a worn leather jacket; or the way he looks in a tie. One might love his nurturing side (I fall in love with men who feed me). Whatever it is, it is something about his being 'masculine'; and if it is about his being a man, then it is open to theorizing and questions. Is it OK to like that steadying voice? Or is that a throwback to the little-girl state? Am I a free agent, or a robot of my erotic conditioning?

But must all this to be so heavily weighted with categorical evaluations? Some of this longing might be acculturation; but some of it is the roll-on-your-back abasement of any animal in love. I have done abject deeds for sexual passion. So, I am sure, have presidents and prime ministers. It is the human condition to need another; to want to give the self over as well as to take in the self of another. How much of this yearning should be the stuff of political proscription, and how much is it the natural pull and sway of the organism in the unstoppable dance of its mating?

We should be kinder to ourselves. It is frightening for a feminist woman to acknowledge that she is also an animal, because it is just our animal nature that a sexist society wants to use to constrain us. But women and men are beasts of the field, with all of those impulses. Let's be less afraid of our animal nature – even when it leads those of us who are heterosexual to feel the greater knowledge of self in the arms of a man.

Feminist critics of heterosexuality point out how deeply imbued our fantasies are with dominance and submission. That is true: any of us could probably have an easier time imagining ourselves as a French maid or a Roman slave than as a female roué or as Cleopatra. And the reason for that is purely cultural. Sexist culture does make submission sexy for women. But if you look at those fantasies with a clear eye, you find that as you come to know yourself, the more superficial scenes fall away; they look less compelling, more obviously about an inequality that isn't that sexy.

According to a critic like Andrea Dworkin, the goal of eros is mutuality. But what do we do when we find that even after all of that heightened consciousness there is a desire – not for violence – but still for the play of pursued and pursuer, possessor and possessed? What do we do with the need to take and to yield?

Some feminist critics call this objectification. I am not so sure. Beneath our acculturation there is, I think, a primal place that leads back to infancy. And there, these longings to have the other and to give oneself are not political, not imprints of the evil patriarchy contaminating even our most secret dreams. On this level, the infant does not want to 'affirm' the love object; she wants to possess the breast. She does not want to be 'respected as an autonomous individual'; she wants to be cared for.

We can reclaim that primal and animal nature with its voluptuous ebbing and flowing of who does what to whom; this does not make us traitors to consciousness. At times, the critical mind has got to shut down; we have to become simply breasts, simply mouths, simply sex, even as men are known sometimes to want to be just sex. Let us make room for that need without being made to feel that we are abdicating evolution – or revolution. When a woman sleeps with a man, she is not 'collaborating' by taking the 'enemy' within; she is saying yes to one of many ways of being female in three dimensions – mind, spirit and hungry flesh.

We must do a better job of separating hating male violence and sexism from hating men. Editors at *Ms.* once entitled an essay of mine on how men are not the enemy, 'Sleeping with the Enemy'. When I went with a pro-feminist boyfriend to hear Andrea Dworkin speak, he was almost dismembered by a mob that began to mutter, 'We don't want men here.' The partner of Helena Kennedy, QC, was verbally abused at a Women in Publishing conference in London when he discreetly, and without interrupting the speakers, brought her newborn baby on to the stage for her to breastfeed. Men who take women's studies classes are sometimes told, 'You'll never understand – you are the oppressor.' When theologian Mary Daly lectures, she refuses to take questions from men.

The Fund for the Feminist Majority in America sells badges that read 'Adam Was a Rough Draft' and 'A Woman Must Be Twice as Good as a Man to Be Considered Half as Competent. Fortunately, This Is Not Too Difficult'.

Ms. magazine ran a cartoon of a shivering, slippered woman hurrying to a bed in which a man waits; the caption was: 'Why Women Mate'. A postcard shows a girl asking her mother, 'Is it true that sex is all men have on their minds?' The mother answers, 'Men don't have minds, dear.' These sentiments might have been cute and subversive once, but no longer. If a man wants to be a feminist, he should not have to lay down his basic self-respect. If the women's movement is becoming increasingly aware that prejudices against gay people, people of colour and people with disabilities are all interconnected, how can we exempt, even encourage, any prejudices that make generalizations about men? Coming from powerless people, such comments are good jokes. Coming from those who are beginning to win power, they are sexism. And it is the job of a feminist, male or female, to fight sexism, female or male.

Women surely need separate spaces and groups of their own. But when separatism becomes a policy, rather than a personal choice this institutionalizes a mood no more enlightened than racism or homophobia. Why shouldn't most meetings of a group be all female, and some mixed? Why should we assume that if men talk too much and try to dominate the agenda, we can't tell them to let others get a word in? How is it that men can be environmentalists, and men can be anti-racists, but somehow, magically, men cannot, equally legitimately, be feminists?

Those who say men cannot be feminists are ignorant of their own history. American reformer William Lloyd Garrison insisted on women's rights. Emmeline Pankhurst's husband, Richard, father of Christabel and Sylvia, spoke eloquently in favour of women's suffrage, as did American abolitionist Henry Stanton. Liberal politician Henry Fawcett championed women's rights. Lucretia Mott's father believed in educating girls, and promoted his daughter's early talents, as did Elizabeth Cady's father, who taught her law. Susan B. Anthony's father believed girls to be as precious as boys; he helped subsidize his daughter's fight for the vote. The African-American writer and orator Frederick Douglass believed strongly that women's rights were inextricably connected to the enfranchisement of all people; he helped organize the first Seneca Falls Convention. In 1869 John Stuart Mill published his classic attack on women's inequality, *The Subjection of Women*. At his wedding to Harriet Taylor, Mill protested against the current marriage laws' inequity to women. Theodore Weld was to do the same when he married Angelina Grimké, as would Henry Blackwell upon his marriage to Lucy Stone.

In our own time, Phil Donahue regularly beats the drum on behalf of women. Harvard law professor Derrick Bell renounced his post, at considerable economic sacrifice, to protest about the lack of a full-time African-American woman on the faculty. Dr David Gunn, a gynaecologist who devoted his life to ensuring that rural women in Florida could exercise their abortion rights, lost his life to a man, fanatical in his opposition to abortion, who shot him in the back. A co-worker said of Dr Gunn: 'He was never too busy for the women. He was a sweet, caring man who was very much devoted to seeing that women kept all their rights.'

Everywhere, men listen to their girlfriends' nightmares as they recover from rape; they wake them up carefully and hold on to them. Fathers show daughters how to turn a lathe; husbands shoo children away from a closed door behind which a wife studies for her exams. It is offensive that in 1993 one should have to spell out the ABCs of male humanity to clear the name of feminism.

Fathers, brothers, sons, lovers, husbands, friends: all the men who care about the women in their lives are, whether they know it or not, male feminists. And they deserve better than caricature and dismissal. They deserve their place alongside women in the discussion of how to heal the gender divide and make public life fairer for their daughters, and home life more compelling for their sons.

Harassment and Date Rape: Collapsing the Spectrum?

Many critics are claiming that the feminist campaign against sexual assault, harassment and date rape is collapsing the spectrum of assault. These critics argue that the 'grey area' should be left alone. The enormous sensational attention the issues have received, and the absence of serious debate around them to set clear, agreed-upon guidelines, is, in fact, leading to a fuzziness in definition that conflates grave and lesser harms in a way that is of no lasting good to women.

The answer is not to avert our eyes from the 'grey areas', or to see the excesses as an excuse to be sceptical of the overwhelming seriousness of the problems. The answer is to be *more* specific in our definitions, and to make sure that advocates of the issues make room for the fact that women are powerless in some situations and far less so in others. We must be wary of new definitions of harassment that leave no mental space to imagine girls and women as sexual explorers and renegades.

The opposition's trivialization of date rape set the stage. Cover-ups of assaults on campus are routine. *New York* magazine's 1993 coverage of date-rape activism is typical of journalistic bad faith. One article 'Crying Rape', suggested that the definition of the crime used to compile date-rape statistics was problematic because many victims did not call the event 'rape' – but omitted the fact that the definition used was legal in several states. The *New York Times Magazine* repeated the charge (Katie Roiphe: 'Rape Hype Betrays Feminism') and let the author claim, despite Justice Department numbers to the contrary, that there was no 'rape crisis' outside feminists' imaginations.

It is not surprising that this atmosphere, which turns down the volume on enormous harms to women, should sometimes foster a tendency for some women activists to turn up the volume on less drastic violations. Activists often felt they needed to shout in order to be heard at all, and were reluctant to insist on nuance in thinking about sex crimes and abuses. In a few rare but definite moments, this aversion to acknowledging different levels of female victimization did indeed weaken the evolving argument. My intent in the next few pages is *not* to undermine the victim's-rights movement or the movement against sexual assault and harassment. These people save lives. My intent is to chart a path through the controversy that will let a woman simultaneously embrace sex and fight rape. I will argue that the *right* to be free from sexual assault, and to expect men to be clear about our sexual boundaries and wishes, brings with it the *responsibility* to be clear about them to ourselves and to others; and that the other side of insisting that others cannot possess our sexuality without our consent is that we ourselves must possess our sexuality more fully.

The dismissive notion that women should just sleep around, and if rape happens, too bad, is a call for women to yield their self-respect in the name of a bogus liberation; it also reinstates the retrogressive 'swept away' scenario, in which the decision about what happens sexually is yielded wholesale to men. This view also presumes that men are instinctive rapists. I will argue, reframing the same subject from another point of view, that we should not have to present ourselves as sexless or will-less in order to assert that sexual harm done to us is a despicable wrong.

At a 'speakout' a couple of years ago, I heard story after story of appalling rape, rape at gunpoint, rape by 'friends', rape by trusted acquaintances. Clusters of the kind of students who often ridicule the issue when it is presented in the abstract stood silent at the corners of the lawn, heads bent, struck into respect by the details of life after life torn apart.

But – only once or twice throughout the hours that I listened – I was struck by a false note and felt a creeping unease. An anxiety began to waver under my thoughts. I tried to overlook it or banish it altogether, but I couldn't; there were one or two stories – out of hundreds – that were not quite right.

In one of these moments, a grieving woman took the microphone and recounted an episode that brought her shame, embarrassment, humiliation or sorrow, an episode during which she was unable to say 'No.'

My heart went out to her because the event had felt like rape. There had, doubtless, been many sad ways in which that woman's sense of self, of her right to her own boundaries, had been transgressed long ago. But I kept thinking that, as terrible as it is to be unable to speak one's claim to one's body, what the sobbing woman described was not rape. I also thought of how appalled I would be if I had had sex with someone whose consent I was certain of, only to find myself later accused of criminal behaviour. Susan Brownmiller made the point in *Against Our Will* that men cannot hear women's 'no'. But the other side of that truth is that some women, for whatever unfortunate reason, cannot yet say no so that it can be heard.

Critics who dismiss the urgency of the campaign to teach men to secure consent, are living in a fantasy world without viruses. They are also mystifying female sexual passivity.

For, after all, what is so innately un-erotic about consent? 'Do you want to make love?' 'Can I fuck you?' 'I'd really like to ――― you. Would that feel good?' 'Can I come inside you?' There are plenty of erotic ways to make sure someone wants it. It is imperative that the man involved be sure he has a woman's consent. But it is not enough to stop there. The other side of the feminist demand for men to learn to listen should be feminist responsibility for women to learn to speak.

Courts, press and family often will not believe women when they say they are raped, so it is common for therapeutic reasons for activists to go by the premiss that 'it's rape if she thinks it's rape'. This was the credo at the rape crisis centre where I worked, and it is necessary in a counselling context. But guidelines for those who are comforting become dangerous when they are translated without modification into the public realm. A sensibility that is harmless – even healing – when expressed by a powerless person becomes a wild card when that person begins to have power. Good crisis therapy is different from good social and criminal policy.

It is absolutely true that all sexual harassment lies on a spectrum; but let us not take the opportunity granted by the new attention given these issues to narrow that spectrum. Taking harassment and date rape seriously means demarcating the inappropriate from the criminal. A 49-year-old teacher in America committed suicide because he was accused of sexual harassment. The circumstances were these: a student poked his chest and commented upon it, and he replied jokingly that she herself was flat-chested. Inappropriate? Definitely. Sexual? Yes. Harassment? In a manner of speaking. Should the teacher have been discouraged from talking about his students' breasts? Sure. Is this lapse the *same as* the egregious violations that are routine? Absolutely not.

A woman had a sexual relationship with a married priest. The affair continued over the course of many 'pastoral visits', long phone calls and intimate lunches. When the priest called off the relationship, the parishioner accused him of sexual abuse. An abuse of his authority? Without question. But the woman was an adult and the man was not her employer. 'Systematic oppression' feminists might say that he coerced her because he represented God. But he was not God.

A waitress describing the customers' habitual rudeness to food-service workers, said that when a group of men came late to the restaurant and, after closing time, ordered dessert, she felt like it was 'emotional rape'. In a college newspaper, a student described finding a computer exchange in which men had talked obscenely about her body; she remarked, 'I suppose that's how it feels to be raped.'

These episodes *are* sexual; they *do* involve power imbalances, they *do* create hostile climates in which women must struggle to work or study with dignity. But they are not sexual harassment in the way that a quid pro quo – sex for employment – is sexual harassment. And they are not rape; nor should we have to pretend that they 'feel like rape' in order to show that such episodes are offensive or humiliating.

An American survey on sexual harassment in school found that 39 per cent of girls were daily harassed at school and another 29 per cent were harassed at least weekly. Disturbingly, 83 per cent of the girls reported being 'touched or grabbed'.

This is appalling. And the everyday violence the girls report is heart-wrenching. But the survey raises troubling questions about where such researchers put teenage girls' sexual agency. Four per cent of the incidents involved teachers, administrators or other school staff. So most of the harassment was by students who had no institutional power over the girls. The study also defined *sexual comments or gestures* from fellow students as 'sexual harassment'. Eighty-nine per cent of the girls reported such behaviour from their peers. Unwanted touching or threatening is completely inexcusable and should be met with expulsion. But sexual comments and gestures? We made sexual comments to boys; they made them to us. It can be vile; it can be sweet. If the school is free of direct menace and the girls are entitled to be sexual too, these gestures lie within the realm of growing up.

In Minnesota, school guidelines against sexual harassment – which cover grades from kindergarten – list 'students "rating" other students', 'sexually descriptive notes and letters', 'dirty jokes', 'spreading sexual rumors about other students', 'boys grabbing girls or girls grabbing boys', 'teasing students about their sexual activities or lack of sexual activity', 'students giving other students the finger', and 'displays of affection between students (i.e., "making out") in the hallway (may offend others and is heterosexist)'. These acts can lead to expulsion. Sexual contact, rumours, joking, teasing – if these are innately abusive even in an environment free of economic coercion, we have done a poor job of making girls sexually strong. The assumption is that even when both the boy and girl involved are students and he has no power to fire her, demote her or derail her career, he still has more power than she does.

I would rather my daughter learned to talk back or yell back or tease back than that she try to grow up in an environment in which a new code of conduct based upon her powerlessness and delicacy hamper her and 'protect' her like invisible stays and petticoats.

A *Glamour* interviewer, writing a story about street harassment, once pressed me hard to say that I objected categorically to being looked at in a sexual way on the street. That interview was one of the first moments when I realized that there was a gap between what I really experience and what popular feminist debate makes room for. My own belief is that the reaches of the harassment spectrum – even blatantly sexual 'looking' – are *always* inappropriate when there is a power imbalance in the workplace and the recipient objects to the behaviour. But on the street or in the school playground the power imbalance is not built in as overtly as it is in the workplace. In my experience, the impact of 'looking' depends on the context. Who is looking? Where am I? Am I in danger? Do I feel menaced? Is the look directed at a thing that is being denigrated or a person who is being admired? The same look can be delivered in an objectifying or a respectful way. And while nearly all comments range from the unpleasant to the unspeakable, the rare remark treats you like a person rather than a thing. 'Bless your eyes' from a kindly looking, enfeebled old man seated in the sun on a park bench feels different from a 'Sit on my face' emanating from a six-foot-two salivating thug.

I must confess: I look. I look, indeed, at every opportunity, and so do all the women whom I know with any affection. I'll bet *you* look. And in my own life, that look of pure appreciation, that male joy in the female presence, has lit up the eyes of an attractive stranger passing me on a suburban path in a way that releases elation for the rest of the day. I have remembered some of those faces for years, and I wish them well. Those moments are a gift between men and women: the gift of 'What if . . . ?' That carnal recognition is a sweet secret between the sexes, the acknowledgement of how easily mating and coupling can be imagined, just body to body, when freed by the imagination from class, identity, circumstance and culture. Looking can be invasive and belittling. But if there is no power imbalance framing the encounter, a sexual gaze has no place on a spectrum of sexual assault.

We are not well served by generalizing all inappropriate behaviour as harassment, and we are actively hampered by the current critics who trivialize the genuine sex crimes of 'date rape', crimes whose repercussions in the age of AIDS can be fatal, with contemptuous admonitions to women to get over it. We are well served by creating a new vocabulary for the relative nature of harm, a vocabulary that makes room for the fact that a woman's choice and vulnerability, a man's authority and power, are not always constants. The opposition is reluctant to demarcate levels of harm, treating rape like a bad evening. A very, very few individuals have responded to that by treating a bad evening like rape. People in power, as women can begin to be now, should claim the luxury of drawing careful distinctions. It is because we must renegotiate the sexual contract from a 'reasonable woman's' point of view that it is so important that all women make themselves heard by the judiciary and the media, so that that new line may evolve through popular debate, rather than be imposed by ideologues at either end of the spectrum.

Aggressors as Victims: Jean Harris

Victim feminism cannot process evidence of female aggression.

Jean S. Harris, headmistress of the exclusive Madeira School for Girls in Virginia, was no one's idea of a murderess, with her grey-blonde hair always impeccably coiffed, her white cardigans and her pearls.

For years she had carried on an affair with the famous Scarsdale Diet doctor, Herman Tarnower. One night in 1980 Mrs Harris drove to the doctor's palatial Westchester house with a gun and a bouquet of flowers in her car, hoping, as she claimed later, to kill herself by her lover's pond. Instead, Mrs Harris shot him four times and left him dead.

Some women embraced her cause. Tarnower had insulted Harris, left cufflinks given to him by other women in full view, had given her prescriptions for sedatives, and, most painful, was easing her out of her long-held social status as his hostess and consort, to replace her with a younger woman. Because Tarnower had begun to date a 38-year-old woman, supporters depicted Harris's plight as a consequence of the social vulnerability of older women. Mrs

Harris was portrayed as the 'archetypal female victim, the woman who loved a creep too much'. Her supporters, the mainstream press, and Harris herself collaborated perfectly in enshrining the killer as a victim.

Harris's lawyer made the case that Harris would not have killed Tarnower intentionally because she was too emotionally fragile. Lawyer Joel Aurnou's approach was to advise potential jurors that 'men can respond to something [i.e., the love triangle] because they feel strong ... but a woman would not be considered to respond that way because she feels weak'. Female observers echoed that sentiment: Bernice Berman, a Scarsdale criminal lawyer, said, 'He destroyed her ego ... I see her in terms of being the victim, and I can imagine what went through her mind. If I was on that jury, she would be a free woman.'

Judge Vito Titone echoed these sentiments when he commented, 'If you ever saw a psychological manslaughter, I think this was [it] ... She was a battered woman. The guy went for a younger woman and scorned her.' The press, too, stressed her fragility and his boorishness. CAD AND MOUSE read a piece in the *New Republic*. Other headlines like THE THINGS SHE DID FOR LOVE and MURDER WITH INTENT TO LOVE made the crime sound like self-sacrifice, or like a mishap, as when a child squeezes a beloved kitten to death. Such headlines implied that the cause of the 'tragedy' was an excess of feminine affection. Some headlines strained to turn Harris from a 'mistress' into a schoolgirl, and indeed into a good little schoolgirl – for example, SCHOOLMISTRESS JEAN HARRIS GETS AN 'A' FOR EFFORT IN PRISON. Others – I ONLY WANT TO DIE – stressed her masochistic tendencies; these echoed Harris's defence – that she had shot Tarnower four times in a struggle over her suicide attempt. The aggression involved in driving from Virginia to New York State to commit suicide in the home of a wandering lover went unremarked, since that was nice, feminine, self-annihilating aggression. Other headlines stressed Harris's good breeding. Shana Alexander's account was entitled VERY MUCH A LADY; *Time* called a story on Harris's sentencing NO WAY TO TREAT A LADY; *Newsweek* contributed THE LADY AND THE DIET DOCTOR; and, in case readers had missed the point, Harris called her own book about women in prison *They Always Call Us 'Ladies'*.

Whence the notion that Harris was not aggressor but victim? There was a suggestion that Dr Tarnower had hit Harris, though she did not use that allegation as part of her defence. Harris was also suffering from drug withdrawal on the night of the murder. But the real reason was that Harris was seen as helplessly in love, trapped, in her words, in a 'magnificent obsession'. Obsessive love and drugs or alcohol are the two most common reasons abusive men offer for murdering their wives or girlfriends.

Jean Harris's character or culpability is not my subject. The way the popular mind turned somersaults to see her as an innocent victim, is. Jean Harris's emotional, if not criminal, exoneration says a lot about how women are asked to redirect aggression.

In the age-old struggle between respectable 'wives' and vile 'whores', Mrs Harris was the archetypal wife, and her rival, the threatening courtesan. (As Mrs Harris revealingly said on the witness stand, 'A whore is a whore is a whore.') In contrast to her curvaceous rival, the matronly Mrs Harris was seen as sexless.

Once imprisoned in Bedford Hills Correctional Facility, she behaved like a perfect Lady Bountiful, in the style of do-good upper-middle-class women embroidering tea cosies for charity jumble sales and venturing into slums to elevate the morals of their female social inferiors. She taught prisoners a two-hour class in mothering skills, gave away the $100,000 from her first book to educate the prisoners' children, and knitted sweaters for them in the best nineteenth-century tradition.

Men and women both cheered Harris on. A review in a feminist journal was glad that 'murdering her "diet doctor" did not ultimately define Harris'. And when New York governor Mario Cuomo set Harris free before she had completed her sentence, 'There was cheer among many that came from knowing that something glaringly wrong, at least in their minds, had finally been put right.'

The unconscious factor underlying that cheer is our unwillingness to absorb the fact that a woman accomplished in supremely feminine skills can really shoot her lover four times at short range. Even if she did the deed, such defensive reasoning goes, her 'goodness' makes her 'really' a victim and not an aggressor, and

she must be considered outside the normal workings of moral culpability and retribution. Even Governor Cuomo's announcement
sounded like a Mother's Day card: 'There are no rules,' he said,
referring to his decision to grant Harris clemency. 'There are no
criteria. Everyone will apply their own. And there's no way to
define justice. You define it for yourself. You define it in your
heart.'

You do? As governor of the State of New York? Sweet as this
sounds, it is very dangerous to women's pursuit of justice. If
'good' women are not really responsible for their crimes, the flip
side is that 'bad' women should be penalized disproportionately.
So the courts stay in the business of dictating, rewarding and
punishing women's non-criminal social behaviour, rather than
being required to provide 'Equal Justice Under Law'.

The murder of the diet doctor struck a chord in women because
women, just like men, sometimes harbour feelings of aggression
and vengeance toward the opposite sex. Women were interested in
the case because they were angry that middle-aged men often
dump women their own age in favour of younger companions. (It
did not hurt that the dead man had urged millions of women on
to diets that 'allowed' them four ounces of liver and two carrots in
a typical dinner.) This anger got a vicarious catharsis when Jean
Harris killed her lover, perhaps for no more elevated reason than
that she wanted him to die.

But victim feminism refuses to acknowledge those feelings of
aggression and then take responsibility for keeping them safely in
the realm of fantasy. So instead of seeing Mrs Harris as a woman
who had a wealth of options compared with other women who
kill, victim feminism turns her into a hapless perfect lady to whom
bad things happened. Her rehabilitation is not tied to the facts of
the case; it is the result of an unconscious imperative. When Mrs
Harris was released from prison she was made a contributing
editor of *Lear's*, a magazine for upper-middle-class older women.

The way victim feminism turns towards 'ladies' and away from
'whores', even if the crimes of the former are worse, is clear in
contrast with the lack of broad feminist support shown to another
famous aggressor, Amy Fisher. (Fisher's distraught mother, long a
supporter of feminism, was surprised and hurt when feminists
steered clear of her daughter's plight.)

The 18-year-old Long Island girl, who wore short shorts and cherry-red lipstick and let her long, thick, dark hair fall over her almond eyes, drove one afternoon to her married lover's house and shot his wife in the face, paralysing her facial muscles and lodging a bullet in her skull. Fisher was a bad girl, not a lady; she engaged in prostitution, used a beeper to take calls from clients, drove wildly in her sports car, made a sexy video for a lover, and lost the sympathy of the court by being taped saying, 'I'm wild ... I love sex.' (In prison, according to tabloids, the young woman allegedly likes to dance topless with her bra on her head.)

Both women's actions were violent and destructive. But Harris, with her self-effacing femininity, became almost a victim-heroine and was granted clemency, while Fisher, with her assertive sexuality and her badness, found her bail set at $2 million and went off to an eighteen-year sentence. If she wants to cut her jail time, she'd better start crocheting. Her bad-girl reputation fascinated women – her story was made into three top-rated TV movies and a bestselling book – but she remains, to date, insufficiently chaste or pathetic, unredeemable and unredeemed.

This 'feminist' reluctance to assign women responsibility for their actions, evil as well as good, mirrors the opposition's traditional claim that women are children, incapable of signing a contract, managing their own affairs, bearing witness in court, or voting. One of the injuries on the list of injustices set forth by power feminists in the Seneca Falls Convention's 'Declaration of Sentiments' was that men withhold from women the right to be held accountable for crime: 'He has made her, morally, an irresponsible being, as she can commit many crimes with impunity, provided they be done in the presence of her husband.' Accountability for crime sounds, from a victim-feminist point of view, an odd 'right' to demand. But the moral adulthood of power feminism knows that real justice is not a sentimental pardon, but a contract or covenant, and that the sword of justice has two sides.

Azalea Cooley and Susan Soen: Prestige Through Victimization

One of women's most deeply ingrained trousseau reflexes is that though they are willing to honour other women's suffering, they resent it when women are honoured for their success. In 1992 Azalea Althea Cooley, a wheelchair-bound African-American lesbian, and her white partner, Susan Soen, appeared to be the targets of the longest string of hate crimes ever to take place in Portland, Oregon. In late spring, a swastika and the word 'nigger' were painted on the women's door. In the aftermath of this crime, the two women were bathed in support from a broad coalition of groups.

The initial crime was followed by sadistic notes. Acid was spattered on the hood of Soen's car. Finally, a cross was burned on the couple's lawn. Weeks later, another burning cross appeared. The activist community rushed to the couple's aid, offering round-the-clock vigils, a therapist to help Cooley exorcize her fears, a rally, security cameras and a reward. 'For two months,' said an activist, 'these women were our whole lives.'

Finally, police officers moved into the house and posed as the couple in an effort to capture the stalker. Nothing happened; the crimes stopped altogether.

On 1 November Cooley kicked off an anti-hate rally with a speech. Women gathered around her and pressed her in a communal hug, which they called a 'spiritual wombing'. Banging a drum, Cooley led a parade of 500 to Portland's central square. Simultaneously, the police found matches, lamp oil and two handguns in the couple's home.

Confronted, Cooley confessed to having committed twenty-one hate crimes herself, apparently with Soen's complicity. The activist community was stunned. Activists had willed themselves to suspect nothing, because of the attraction of a situation that had produced 'the perfect victim'. As one activist rightly said, 'Why did we believe it so readily? Because it all could have been true. The racism, the homophobia, the fear of those who are different – it's all out there, all terribly real.'

But why did Cooley's mental illness unfold in this particular way? It is easy to see, in retrospect, how the identity of 'perfect victim' provided more support and recognition than might an identity of successful coping. When Cooley brought tapes of a death threat to her women's group, the facilitator said, 'Suddenly our whole focus shifted to Azalea.' Cooley then told her best friends in the women's community that she had brain cancer and was facing imminent death. She even shaved her head and eyebrows to maintain the illusion. One woman friend saw Cooley suffering two (staged) heart attacks. As the hate crimes unfolded, Cooley confined herself to a wheelchair, claiming that the brain tumour had metastasized to affect her spine. The worse her afflictions, the greater, she found, was her prestige.

But we must ask: would she have been rewarded the same way if she had displayed to the community, not a string of injuries, but a string of sparkling achievements? The fashionable lapse in logic among the left right now is that you can't identify *with* victims of oppression unless you identify *as* a victim. There is a search for a spurious authenticity – the most harmed woman is the *real* woman. Azalea Cooley's tragic hoax took place in a location that had seen hundreds of real hate crimes, many of them brutal, even fatal. But it also took place in a dangerous intersection. A dominant culture that does not 'see' the strength and achievement of 'invisible' women met with an activist subculture that has many heroic qualities, but also a weakness for glamorizing the status of she who is harmed at the expense of honouring she who can cope – and even triumph.

Liz Holtzman and Geraldine Ferraro: Nice Girls Don't Campaign

In 1992 a bitter four-way primary race for one of New York's Senate seats pitted activist candidate Elizabeth Holtzman against Geraldine Ferraro, the *éminence grise* who had become a national icon as the 1984 Democratic vice-presidential nominee. Holtzman was seen by critics as a harsh, prosecutorial outsider, and by her supporters as a staunch women's rights advocate of long standing. Ferraro was an at least equally respected insider, who was also a strong women's rights supporter and had a track record worth betting on. Many well-known feminists rallied to her flag; her national recognition made the race winnable by a woman, while Holtzman was a long shot at best.

As the race heated up and Holtzman saw that she was trailing Ferraro three to one in the polls, she began to hit Ferraro with increasingly biting – many said vicious – charges. Holtzman called into question Ferraro's husband's connections and real estate dealings, and accused the couple of renting space to a pornographer.

Many feminists reacted with horror. Ferraro's supporters decried the 'unsisterliness' of the attacks, and the press headlined them as a setback for feminism. 'It is sadly ironic that in the otherwise inspiring Year of the Woman, Holtzman's slash and burn tactics are not directed at any of her Democratic primary opponents but [at] Ferraro, the only other woman in the race,' said Letty Cottin Pogrebin, a *Ms.* magazine founder; 'The public' she said, 'is being asked to see women candidates as a metaphor for change . . . Women are promising to do it differently and do it better. With her sleazy campaign, Liz Holtzman has betrayed that promise.' 'The women's movement,' said former representative Bella S. Abzug, 'has tried for a considerable time to make the point that we need women in political power in order to change things. It's very sad to see antifeminist standards being used, and I believe they are, in trashing Geraldine Ferraro.' To a reporter (who noted that her own political style was 'to take no prisoners') Abzug commented: 'I've always taken the position that women will change the nature of power rather than power change the nature of women.'

Others saw the matter very differently. Ethics was already an issue in the campaign. Questions had been raised about Al D'Amato, the Republican in office, and, as Manhattan borough president Ruth Messinger said in the *New York Times*, 'There are complicated questions being raised about all the candidates in this race, and they'll be raised by Senator D'Amato . . . [in return]. Everything about you as a person is game in a political race . . . the good things and the bad. That's life.' Still others saw the attacks as standard strategy for someone trailing in the polls. 'Liz's gambit was to take Gerry out,' said an anonymous political aide. 'When it didn't succeed, there was this perception that this was some kind of horror. But she tried to deliver a death blow and that is an option that any politician has at their disposal, though many people have taken it as some kind of betrayal of feminist ideology.' Still others pointed out that if Holtzman's opponent had been a man, her feminist critics would probably be saying 'Go, Liz!'

Holtzman herself observed that 'it's dangerous to sentimental-ize gender. There are differences between women ... You can't consign women candidates to the kitchen and say they can't ask tough questions ... Campaigns aren't necessarily polite debates.' She added, 'To be accused of not being a feminist – that's just a joke; you just have to laugh ... No one's had more bruises, and taken more lumps – and never bowed out – than I, in the name of feminism.'

Holtzman lost badly, ending up with a low number of votes; Ferraro lost, barely; Bob Abrams, the Democratic primary win-ner, then lost to the Republican D'Amato. In the aftermath, many women were furious with Holtzman: 'If she couldn't have it, she didn't want Gerry to have it,' concluded Pogrebin. Marie Wilson, director of the Ms. Foundation, said that if Holtzman had dropped out of the race, she would have been a 'feminist hero'. Instead, 'she ended up, I think, being the tool of a Republican man'. Post-mortem articles took Holtzman to task for refusing to say publicly that she had made a serious error: 'If the defeat has led the 20-year veteran of New York City politics to search her soul, question her judgment or soften her prosecutorial demeanor, she has not told anyone.'

I was sorry that neither of these women won the seat. How easy to feel frustrated, even resentful, about a woman who used 'slashing' attacks against another woman. How tempting to ex-press revulsion that women should behave like that when they seek power. And yet those reflexes need to be reconsidered. America did not lose by having missed the chance to get a woman in the Senate; America, and all its women, won a lot by the example of that fight – by having the chance to see two strong, committed feminist candidates fight it out. The short-term setback is a small price to pay.

Perhaps Holtzman's questions about her rival's finances were gutter politics; perhaps they were simply politics as usual. (Abrams also levelled various charges at Ferraro, and was not lam-basted.) Nevertheless, we are stopping short of power feminism when we let feminism appoint one woman to be the favourite daughter and call another woman a traitor to the movement for fighting like a true underdog for herself, even to the point of poli-tical death. And we linger squarely within victim feminism when we let the opposition dictate a permissible ladylike style of campaigning. That style may be 'better', but it also perpetuates a double standard by which men can fight harder than women, even against women. Perhaps Holtzman believed she was the better candidate, and that she owed it to New York State to fight with everything at hand in order to serve the public better. Who are we to say? Isn't feminism the right of every woman to run her race as hard as she legitimately can? How can feminism ever have reached the point where we call those who give up their dreams and quit the race true 'feminist heroines', while we disdain those who, with track records of sterling activism, bruise and are bruised, but never give up? How dare any woman tell another to drop out of her race because she is behind, and how dare she call that 'feminism'? Holtzman's behaviour may be denounced as mud-slinging or as self-destructive, but it cannot fairly be denounced as anti-feminist.

The more women we have fighting for their own visions, even fighting for them against one another, the better for all, and the more women will be inspired to enter the fray. But if we show women a face of feminism that is one political machine instead of a million individual conflicting political dreams, we may have short-term gains for the very few, but the majority will rightly turn away in disillusion.

Applying a double standard to women in politics will hang us. The equation 'Women equal a change for the better' should mean 'Women, because they represent the other half of America's interest, are a change for the better' or, 'Getting the women who are the best for the job is a change for the better', or even, 'Women equal a change for the better because we have enough men.' But never, ever, should 'Women equal a change for the better' mean 'Women *are* better.'

Why should women have to be perfect to use power? Political power is fire from the gods; women must steal it and learn to use it for no more reason than that they are entitled to it. Once they get it, let us pray, as we do for male leaders, that they use it *for* justice and *with* compassion. But whether used to scar or to illuminate, whether used by men or by women, fire is fire. Women should have political clout because it belongs to them, for better or worse, not because they promise to play safely.

Victim feminism evades the fact that, just as girls (before they are broken) have healthily aggressive impulses towards the world at large, they also have competitive and territorial impulses toward other girls and women. But since we lack rituals to contain open conflict, we remain reluctant to explore this minefield in sisterhood's garden. As Rosalind Coward has argued in *Our Treacherous Hearts*, 'Feminism is partly responsible for having peddled an ideal of female solidarity and friendship that would transcend hostile competitiveness, which was seen as a largely male characteristic. What was stressed was the common bond between women, rather than the rivalry.' The recognition that women often have feelings of competitiveness towards one another does not make it impossible for women to co-operate; it makes it possible for them to do so more soundly. It does not make them 'like men'; it makes them honest women.

Both the patriarchalists and victim feminists denigrate women's competitiveness towards other women. To the former, women are catty backstabbers. This idea is useful to those who realize that women had better *not* ally with each other, for an alliance would blow the master's house down.

In reaction, victim feminism painted a view of female alliance that was benign. Women must shower each other with positive reinforcement and sheathe any stray claws. When bad feelings erupt between women, they are met with guilt and shame. Since their training in alliance is personal, conflict between women tears them up in a special way. They fear ostracism, a childhood sting that never healed. If alliance is seen as intimate friendship, conflict is seen as 'betrayal'. And, indeed, disputes within feminism are phrased in terms of betrayal in a way that disputes among men are not. (Rape hype *betrays* feminism.) We have no model of conflict that is not all or nothing; no scenario of respectful disagreement.

But there are going to be times when woman-to-woman aggression is a healthy, even energizing, corollary of our having reached full participation in society. Women competing for a job or prize are going to feel aggression towards one another, and a sense of conquest when they triumph. Women are managing, criticizing and firing other women, and their employees sometimes, understandably, hate their guts. Women on opposite sides of the abortion debate do not always harbour tender feelings for each other's 'life'. Rather than repressing these feelings, let us understand and honour them, and keep them reined in but under direction, like the energy of a racehorse.

These feelings don't unwoman us; they heal us. We are starting to share in one of the oldest and most beautiful archetypes in the world, the image of the *agon*. '*Agon*', a Greek word with the same root as 'agony', means 'struggle'; the struggle between two evenly matched antagonists is at the centre of male mythology, from Jacob and the angel in the Old Testament to the two cyborgs in *Terminator 2*. But that does not make the *agon* male.

There are many ancient archetypes of the woman warrior, from Zenobia the Palmyran queen to Boadicea. But today, the few images of 'the fight' available to women lack that bracing sense of a self, with all its values, pitted in total commitment against an opponent. The rare images of women fighting each other are either comic or pornographic, and mock the notion that a fair public fight could ever be female: in female mud-wrestling, the combatants are literally smeared with filth so as to symbolically 'smear' the notion that women might be principled warriors.

We are maturing into the understanding that women of different classes, races and sexualities have different, and often competing, agendas. Those conflicts should not be a source of guilt to us. They do not represent the breakdown of sisterhood. In the fullness of diversity, they represent its triumph.

A Zombie for Love: Hedda Nussbaum and the Battered-Woman Syndrome

In 1984 a six-year-old girl, Lisa Steinberg, was found comatose in a squalid apartment in New York's exclusive Greenwich Village. She died in the hospital. Her adoptive father, Joel Steinberg, a lawyer, had severely abused her for years. Her adoptive mother, Hedda Nussbaum, a crack addict, also severely beaten and traumatized by Steinberg, stood by while her child slipped into unconsciousness, and did not call for help. When Nussbaum was arrested, she had a fractured jaw, fractured ribs, a broken nose, and cuts and bruises all over her body. Charged with second-degree murder and two counts of endangering the welfare of a child, she was never indicted.

But her arrest sparked off a storm of controversy. Nussbaum was understood to have been battered so brutally that she was in no condition to rescue the child. The psychological underpinnings of the deterioration of her will also became clear: According to a friend, Nussbaum, a middle-class white woman who had been an editor at the Random House publishing company, had a 'gentle nature' and 'sensitive soul', as well as self-doubts. These traits allowed her lover to overwhelm her psychologically and convince her that she was worthless to everyone but him, so that winning his approval became all-important. 'She was afraid not to see things from his point of view,' said a friend. Steinberg also became a source of confidence. 'I didn't have much confidence in myself, and I didn't think that I should ask for raises and promotions,' Nussbaum said, but Steinberg urged her to. She always got what she asked for, and she attributed these achievements to his power. 'She was a slave,' said her doctor, 'totally submissive to this man, with no ability or will to save her own daughter.'

Her lawyers stressed that Steinberg's domination left Nussbaum physically and psychologically incapable of committing any crime. The man had attained 'Svengali-like control' over her. She described the months after he ruptured her spleen as 'the best of the relationship and of my whole life'. As for the night their daughter died, Nussbaum explained, she didn't call for help because she believed that Steinberg would supernaturally heal the child, and 'I didn't want to show disloyalty or distrust for him.' She was alone with the child for several hours. Seeing that the girl was unresponsive, Nussbaum spent the time rearranging Steinberg's files. She admitted lying to police to cover up for Steinberg when they came to investigate the bruises on Lisa's body.

In the hospital after her arrest, Nussbaum was inundated with support from women. Accompanying a large bouquet of red roses was a card reading, 'You are an inspiration to battered women.' Many women saw themselves in Nussbaum. The *New York Times* suggested that Nussbaum fascinated people because they 'recognize a part of themselves in her tale of submission'. Gloria Steinem observed that 'we are fascinated by what we recognize' and said that women saw their own vulnerabilities in the case. Ellen Goodman also noted that 'Hedda's Hurt Is Too Close for Our Comfort'. Mary Cantwell acknowledged that many women, including herself, are 'a little bit like Hedda'.

As in the Jean Harris case, commentators remarked sympathetically that the man 'had been her God'. Like Harris, Nussbaum was seen doing craftwork: she passed the time in the courthouse waiting room doing embroidery or macramé.

Feminists were divided on the matter of her culpability. Ann Jones, author of *When Battered Women Kill*, said: 'I am firmly in the camp of those who believe she is not culpable.' Jones cited the psychological effects of battering, which are, she said, as much like brainwashing as what terrorists do to hostages. Susan Brownmiller disagreed:

> The feminist movement says, 'If you are equal, then you must take equal responsibility' ... Hedda Nussbaum collaborated in her own destruction and then became incapable of acting to save her child ... There are those who feel that once she was battered, she became so demoralized that she lost all willpower, but that is not good enough for me. Women do get out. They have chosen terrible means to get out – they have killed batterers. So few women have been so unable to extricate themselves as Hedda Nussbaum. I think it is wrong to focus on her victimization and say that Lisa's death is a separate matter. I hold her responsible for destroying her own life and, in the process, that of an innocent child, though she did not kill that child.

Compassion is one thing, Brownmiller wrote in the *New York Times*; identification under the guise of feminism is another. 'Calling Ms. Nussbaum a heroine, as the battered women's advocacy movement has done, for testifying at the trial of her lover, is not only a serious misreading of the facts, it does a disservice to women and, ultimately, to men.' But to Marilyn French, Nussbaum was 'as completely the subject of bondage (to a man who exercised no restraint) as if she *had* been sold into slavery or marriage, as if laws granted Joel the rights he took, as if she had lived in Assyria in the third century BC.'

The Hedda Nussbaum conundrum is at the heart of our

dilemma now: what is choice; what is coercion? Where does volition begin? Where must we see that a woman is denied options? My own growing conviction is that it is crucial to understand how low self-esteem, drug addiction, lack of institutional support, the pressures of destructive ideals of romantic love, the unwillingness to go outside with a battered face, and the psychological effects of battering all conspire to erode the choices of a woman like Nussbaum. But when we say that these overwhelming obstacles effectively suspended her capacity for moral judgement, then we endorse the forces that wore away her self-determination to begin with. Nussbaum had what other women do not have: access to some money; some credibility; her educated middle-class status. For many women, most of the time, battering is exactly like enslavement; but not for all women, all the time. We can never waive a woman's moral responsibility for another life entirely, just as we can never entirely waive a man's. We need not convict, but we should be wary of a moral exoneration that seals the tomb on a woman's will in the name of compassion.

For perhaps what lay behind the chorus of voices saying 'Nussbaum is like us' is the dark side that women dare not own. Mothers are not perfect, and women are often torn between the wellbeing of their children and their own psychosexual allegiances, which formed at least the basis for Nussbaum's attraction to her batterer. The thought of a child's being sacrificed to this seduction is a woman's conscious nightmare; and perhaps the wish to see Nussbaum as will-less, and hence blameless, comes of women's need to ward off the knowledge that sometimes they might be tempted to *choose* themselves and their lovers over their children.

A legacy of the trial was the acceptance of the notion of a 'battered-woman syndrome', a condition in which the battering becomes so severe that a woman's normal thought processes are suspended. This syndrome, defined on the basis of very compelling evidence, has been used to explain why battered women don't leave even when their lives or those of their children are in danger, and to defend battered women who have killed their partners. Ann Jones, writing in *Lear's*, believes it should also be used to defend women who did not intervene when their husbands or partners beat their children to death. While the victim's-rights movement sees the acceptance of this syndrome by the judicial system as a victory, others are starting to demur.

Elizabeth Schneider, the Brooklyn College Law School professor who helped promote the argument that abused women who killed their husbands were not aggressors but victims, has had a change of heart. 'Courts and society have glommed on to the victim image,' she told the *New York Times*. 'But it's a two-edged sword. Many battered women lose custody of their children because judges see them as helpless, paralyzed victims who can't manage daily life. And if a woman seems too capable, too much in charge of her daily life, she may not be believed.' Nan Hunter, another professor at the college, agrees: 'Woman-as-victim is a cultural script that evokes sympathy without changing the hierarchical structure. It's a kind of melodrama that doesn't lead to any change in the conditions that cause the victimization.' Charlotte Taft, founder of a Dallas abortion clinic, says that feminism 'has been afflicted with the hallmarks of victim status: whiny denials of responsibility, and attempts to blame someone else. We've been whining for some white-guy legislators to pass laws taking care of us ... I don't want to blame the victim, like Jesse Helms and the conservatives, but instead of trying to change people who don't want to change, we need to be changing ourselves'.

The plea of not guilty that is based on the battered-woman syndrome creates a situation in which a woman must prove that she is traumatized, even destroyed; this leads to 'confessionals' in court, in which women must demonstrate the degradation of their psyches and be seen to be falling apart. If they are not sufficiently cowed or weak, they lose their case, as Sara Thornton discovered. When she stood trial in 1990, charged with murdering her husband with a knife as he lay drunk on the sofa, the Crown accepted that Malcolm Thornton was an alcoholic who was violent towards his wife but maintained that the murder was cold and calculated: Sara Thornton had sharpened the knife beforehand. Moreover, a period of time had elapsed between Malcolm's last bout of violence and her action. In the Crown's view, no quarrel or abuse had provoked the final scene. Sara Thornton was convicted of murder, appealed and was reconvicted. But as Helena Kennedy argues in her study of women and the British justice system, *Eve Was Framed*, it was accumulated abuse which drove Sara Thornton to violence – a fact which, incidentally, would have been recognized in an Australian court. In Britain, however, she was, as Julie Bindle of Justice for Women said, 'not just on trial for killing her husband but also for failing to conform to society's notion of a good woman'. Throughout the trial, the prosecution argued that Sara Thornton was a bad wife and mother. Birmingham academic Sue Bindali later observed, 'Sara Thornton was tried, not as a defendant but as a woman, and as a woman she was found wanting.' ITN's Home Affairs correspondent, Jennifer Nadel, argues that the questions raised by this case, and those of every other battered woman accused of murdering her violent partner, 'go to the heart of how the legal system and how society treats women; and they beg the question whether women ... are allowed to be real, flawed, three-dimensional beings or whether, if they want understanding and justice, they must still obey the rules society has prescribed for their sex'.

This is why the battered-woman syndrome plea is fundamentally so unsatisfactory. American law theorist, Susan Levitt advocates, instead, an interpretation of women's violent reaction to violence that establishes not that a woman's reason and will have been demolished, but rather that she acted according to them. If she stays and kills her batterer it is not because she is demented but because she is like a hostage, doing what a reasonable person in such a situation would do in order to survive.

The law is increasingly torn between victim and power feminism. In 1986 the Supreme Court in America ruled nine to zero that the law prohibits not only demands for sexual favours in exchange for jobs or promotion, but also behaviour that creates a 'hostile or abusive work environment'. (Sexual harassment was made illegal in Britain under the Sex Discrimination Act of 1975 and is defined as 'behaviour of a sexual nature which is unwelcome, unwanted and unreciprocated, and which might threaten job security or create a stressful or intimidating working environment. It can come in many forms – comments, looks, jokes, suggestions, pin-ups or physical contact.') Subsequently, federal courts were split over whether sexual harassment is present when there is serious offence that 'a reasonable person' would find objectionable, or whether there must be 'psychological harm'. Three federal courts require a showing of psychological injury; three others have ruled that the standard should be behaviour that a 'reasonable person' would find offensive.

Victim psychology is bad for women. Many people are reaching this conclusion in arenas outside feminism too. *No Pity*, a book about the disability-rights movement, proclaims the motto 'Pity oppresses'. Activists in this burgeoning movement detest the 'poster child' image of disability, and people with disabilities are claiming words like 'crips', 'gimps' and 'blinks' the way the gay and lesbian movement claimed 'queer' – to ward off victim status, to offer the world, as one 'crippled' performance artist put it, 'a raised, gnarled fist'. The movement rejects stereotypes of 'courage' as absolutely as it rejects stereotypes of people with disabilities as being dependent, innocent children, defined by their 'affliction'.

A growing body of research about the development of the self is proving that defining oneself as a victim results in a 'debilitating primary identification'; that is, a lousy self-image. A person who identifies chiefly as a victim will do less well than someone who sees herself chiefly as powerful and effective. If a woman sees herself as a victim she becomes less competent, less happy, and even more likely to be victimized.

The consequences of identifying yourself by the harm that has been done to you extend to emotional health and sickness. Dr Diane Tice, a research psychologist at Case Western University, studied 400 men and women, and her results suggest that the types of behaviour that victim feminism encourages are the ones most likely to entrench people in apathy and despair. The most effective ways of alleviating depression are (1) bolstering self-esteem by reminding yourself of your successes; (2) rewarding yourself with a treat, such as a special evening or a meal out; and (3) making a downward comparison – that is, reminding yourself that you are not as badly off as someone else.

One of the hallmarks of the differences between victim feminism and women's culture has to do with optimism versus pessimism. Much feminist discourse is unrelievedly grim; waking up to feminism includes a certain pride in being able to stare un-flinchingly at 'the horror, the horror' of it all. Horrifying the world of sexism truly is, but this sometimes monolithic focus on the dire leads straight to burnout.

Feminists often disdain the self-help movement and the indivi-dualizing, unrealistically optimistic tone of women's magazines that urge readers to 'Cheer Up!' or 'Banish the Blues!' without re-ferring women's moods and life choices to a larger analysis of sexism and discrimination. But pursuing the hope that one can have some control over one's life is a better long-term perspective from a psychological point of view. The most effective option to offer women would bring the strengths of the two cultures to-gether: combining women's magazines' hopeful tone, and the self-help groups' faith in transformation, with the clear political analysis and the organizing potential of the feminist movement. We should be able to look squarely at just how bad things can be for women without turning that ability into a kind of *machisma*, or ridiculing faith in potential change as being hopelessly naïve.

Chapter Fourteen

The Turning Point

The final problem with victim feminism is that it is based on assumptions about women that are, increasingly, untrue. As women gain more power, some behave in ways that victim feminism consigns to men alone.

Are Women in Fact Helpless Victims?

The premiss that women are helpless victims, unable to defend themselves, was entirely ignored by 12 million American women who have done something highly unvictimlike. They have bought guns. As violence against women reached epidemic proportions women were not just sitting around. Quietly, with thorough training and in unprecedented numbers, while they looked after their families and tended their marriages, they were also teaching themselves to shoot potential assailants. By 1992, women had become the fastest-growing segment of the US firearms-buying public. One woman in nine had legally acquired a handgun.

The female director of Gun Owners of New Hampshire claims that, according to the US Justice Department, only 3 per cent of 2,000 rape attempts succeeded when the woman defended herself with a knife or a firearm. The *Washington Post* reported that 'the most compelling arguments for [gun ownership] come from women themselves who say they are tired of being easy prey'. The monthly publication, *Women & Guns* found that 81 per cent of its readers cite self-defence as the reason for gun ownership; 30 per cent say they have been a victim of serious crime; and 93 per cent agree that, even if doing so was illegal, they would carry a handgun if they felt threatened.

America's newly armed women are neither rich eccentrics nor impoverished prey in an urban wasteland. Sixty-two per cent are middle class, on annual incomes of between $25,000 and $50,000. Nor are they delinquent young girls: 71 per cent are aged between 26 and 49. The evidence suggests that, for many women, *Thelma & Louise* is no longer a fantasy.

This trend created a subculture that uses feminist language to talk about the realities of gun ownership. *Women & Guns* started as a newsletter, but quickly became so popular, going from word-of-mouth circulation of 18,000 to a news-stand circulation of several hundred thousand, that it was bought up by the Second Amendment Foundation. While we should keep in mind that the gun lobby wants to use the magazine to attract new female members, its popularity makes it a credible reflection of one shift in women's thinking.

The magazine is far from a feminist circular. It appears to address the unlabelled power feminism of women in America; working-class, lower-middle, and middle-class women, married housewives and single mothers. The politics seem to be those of Ross Perot and the fashion sense is country and western.

The publication uses the words 'independence', 'autonomy' and 'self-respect' to describe female gun possession, and even features an engraving of a suffragist to encourage women to vote against gun control. The women's letters to the magazine reflect a pioneer feminism of women who know that no one will take care of them but themselves. One writes, 'I still see the violence that bad elements in society are doing to women and children . . . I believe that nobody will take care of me but me. The concept that the female only takes care of the baby and home and the male takes care of both is passé because we are no longer at a time when home is safe and the male is around to protect the family. Now he goes to work, and she goes to work, but she does the housework, takes the kids to school, and runs errands in between. Where is the male? Nowhere near, so we are on our own. We must be able to protect ourselves and the home and the children. We don't have built-in protective mechanisms like the porcupine or the skunk, so we must acquire something from the outside – guns.'

Another writes, 'I made my choice: I will not be a victim', and says that she is encouraging her women friends to become gun owners: 'I dearly hope that none of us will ever be forced to use our weapons in self-defense. But if any of us [is] threatened with deadly force, I know I'll be glad to have presented my friends with an alternative to becoming a helpless victim.'

The magazine takes the clichés of feminist language, but uses them in the service of such an unfamiliar goal that reading them can be downright disorientating. Women are called upon to consider 'joining the armed sisterhood': 'A mechanical tool called a handgun,' one editorial declares, 'offers them the potential to truly take back the night.' Standing in their way are 'unjust laws ... and an obsolete, residual cultural prejudice against women possessing power that could threaten men who are otherwise blithely secure in their ability to inflict abuse'. The magazine's stated purpose is 'empowerment of women through self-defense choices', and a monthly legal column provides information on restraining orders for battered wives and victims of stalkers. One such column concludes a description of a woman's death at the hands of her estranged husband with the suggestive words: 'the courts did all they could, but it was not enough'.

In a piece entitled 'Perpetuating the Victim Status of Women', Karen MacNutt complains about a typical neighbourhood crime seminar in which police officers talk down to women by urging them to put locks on their doors, bars on their windows, and carry only 'the ultimate defense for women', as MacNutt puts it sarcastically, 'the rape whistle'. She describes what happens when a woman asked, 'What about a gun?' 'Now little lady,' replied the officer, 'you wouldn't want to kill someone, would you?' Another officer says, 'Guns aren't very good defense ... An attacker is more likely to take it away from you and use it against you than you are to defend yourself.' At which another woman responded, 'If they aren't much good, why do you carry one?'

MacNutt concludes with a rhetorical flourish that connects gun ownership with female emancipation. 'There is a lot of talk about "women's liberation",' she writes impatiently, 'but women will not be truly liberated as long as they are perceived as victims or are dependent upon others for safety.' MacNutt draws a connection between the nineteenth-century manufacture of 'muff' pistols and Lady Derringers and 'a growing independent female population'. She even manages to suggest that gun control is a form of sex discrimination since it keeps women from being able to advance professionally in urban areas that have the most opportunities, but are also the most crime ridden. 'What is truly amazing,' she writes, 'is the large number of otherwise intelligent, so-called "liberated" women who blandly accept and even promote the idea that women are incapable of defending themselves with these devices ... As single parents, [women] must be able to protect their families. If they are to compete successfully in the business world, they must be free to travel without fear ... For too long women have accepted the roll [sic] of natural victim. This must stop.'

Using a format similar to that of *Cosmopolitan*, *Women & Guns* treats gun ownership as another sexy accomplishment, like Tantric yoga or gourmet cooking. *W&G* runs a regular feature on women who have used guns to repulse attackers. One, headlined 'Survivor Kills Rapist During Second Attack', features 44-year-old Barbara Angeli, who killed a man who had raped her and had subsequently been following her. Despite a restraining order, the man followed Angeli, blocked her path with his car, and displayed a gun. At this point, Angeli 'drew her own weapon and fired five times at the windshield'. The feature's tone makes it read like a staple item of women's magazines, the resourceful-woman-overcomes-the-odds story. There is no mention of any trauma, regret or lasting psychological damage on Angeli's part. Indeed, the story concludes on a virtually upbeat ending: 'The shooting was ruled justifiable homicide: "He kept hounding her," said the police inspector.'

The magazine stresses fun, fashion and the word 'femininity'. It highlights elegant leather handbags with easy-access gun compartments ('Be Safe, Feminine and Stylish!'), a 'Holiday Gift Ideas' section where one can buy personal speed-loaders for $7–$12, and it even includes a version of the classic *Cosmo* feature, the humorous personality test questionnaire. Entitled 'The Armed Women's Aptitude Test', it asks:

For rape assault and prevention, a whistle is:
A) All you'll ever need.

B) Next to useless with nothing to back it up.
C) The signal to 'Fire!'

What is your reaction to a bra holster?
A) Yeech! It would be an obscene juxtaposition of the icon of death with the symbol of nurturing!
B) Uncomfortable and impractical, designed by males for females.
C) Not a bad idea, so long as it doesn't get in the way when you reach for the MC-10 submachinegun in your shoulder sling.

For this audience, victim feminism's worldview is far from accurate, and less than useless. The fact is that women are psychologically burning the clothing of victimization. Women's relationship to violence is changing. Ordinary women are at a turning point. The fury generated by sexual abuse, which has traditionally been turned inward, is beginning to be directed outward. This should begin to challenge our assumptions about female gentleness and forgivingness.

Sarajevo is a test case for how the enfranchisement of women can also release their capacity for aggression. In the Balkans, women have begun to take part in the violence that has engulfed the region, and to reject their submissive roles in the traditionally patriarchal culture. 'Women have changed since the beginning of the war,' Sarajevan Jasna Delalic said. 'Women have banded together . . . I will never slave for anybody any more.'

Balkan women are reacting to their victimization with a matter-of-fact military vengefulness. 'We have three times more men patients than women,' said a Sarajevan doctor, 'and the women have recovered from traumatic stress syndrome faster than the men . . . I've treated eighteen raped women between twelve to forty-seven years old. About a third waited to have their gynaecological problem resolved and then went out and picked up a gun.'

Izudina Sisic, aged 30, said: 'I joined [in the fighting] because of the mistreatment, the killing, and the rape. It is revenge . . . When I'm on the front line, I don't think about being a woman . . . I was on the front line on October tenth when the special forces attacked ... I shot at them. I don't know whether I hit anyone because it was night. But I wanted to hit someone.'

Women are expressing vengeful wishes in everyday terms. Of the five men who raped her when she was unconscious, a New York victim said, 'They should be lined up and hanged for what they did to me.' Richard Ellis of the *Sunday Times* described South African women who have graduated from a course on urban survival taught by a former soldier. A white woman, Lynne Carson, recently broke the leg of a male mugger armed with a knife; 'I felt great,' she said. 'Before, I would have been too frightened to do anything.' Themba Kuluse, a Black South African businesswoman, said that 'if anyone so much as touches me, I'll blow them away'. In the US, between 32 per cent and 41 per cent of women in prison are doing time for violent crime.

Does Motherhood Make One a Nurturer?

Victim feminism assumes that women's higher nature comes from their maternal capacities. But the statistics on child abuse and neglect show how vulnerable the flow of maternal kindness can be to other stresses. In the United States, women are responsible for 49.5 per cent of all physical abuse of children, including 56.8 per cent of major physical abuse, 48.5 per cent of minor physical abuse, 17.6 per cent of sexual abuse or exploitation, 69.7 per cent of abuse by neglect, 52.2 per cent of 'emotional maltreatment', and 65.5 per cent of 'other maltreatment'. It seems that many mothers are as capable of harming their children as are fathers. To note that childbearing capacity does not automatically make women better than men is not to denigrate the amazing skills of compassion that parents tap in themselves and learn from their children's needs. But, as Carol Tavris demonstrates in *The Mismeasure of Women*, evidence shows that single fathers, or men looking after aged parents, develop and exhibit those same traits just as highly as women.

Victim feminism cites 'nature' as the origin of women's maternal goodness. But what actually happens in nature? Women, of course, are not apes, but primatologist Jane Goodall's classic account of her life with chimpanzees makes it clear that in the 'natural' state of the African wilderness, not every chimpanzee mother is a paragon of loving kindness.

Goodall tells the story of Pom, nature's own abusive mother, and her hapless daughter Passion. Pom laid the baby on the ground the very day she was born, showing little concern for her welfare. When only two months old, far too young to grip properly, the baby chimp was flung on to her mother's back. The infant clung there frantically as her mother gallivanted about with a group of adult males, 'seemingly quite without concern for her infant,' writes Goodall. Passion whimpered to squeeze under her mother's protective body to get out of the rain; Pom would have none of it, and shoved the child repeatedly back into the wet and out of her way. When Passion learned to walk, Pom became 'positively callous' and did not bother to attend to the toddler when she cried. At length it became routine to see Pom walking briskly, ignoring her whimpering daughter who was struggling desperately to catch up.

The understanding that mothering and self-sacrifice are not mystically paired would be a healthy change for society as well as for women. We have a vital lesson to learn from the dark failures of a bond often portrayed as transcendent. I am not saying that 'feminism has caused the breakdown of the family'. I am urging that we begin to see not only men's parenting but also women's as a daily,* difficult, sometimes counter-instinctive effort, which should be placed at the apex of human endeavour rather than at the bottom. To see the element of choice in maternal behaviour will not lower motherhood's status, in the long term, but raise it.

'Maternal instinct' has long been the margin of error that a sexist society has taken for granted. Society has assumed that it could leave women and children at the bottom of the heap; that some profound mammalian force would manage to overcome lack of income, health care and childcare, and somehow nurture and socialize the next generation. This evidence of the vulnerability of the maternal connection should lead us to realize that if we want civilization to continue, we cannot take women's nurturing behaviour as a given and expect it somehow to transcend the burdens placed upon it by the rest of society. Men as well as women will have to confront the fact that it takes not mere instinct, but also a lot of steady effort, to wipe away children's tears year after year.

Are Only Men Capable of Sexual Sadism?

Some of the female retaliation fantasies that erupted along with the genderquake involved sexual mayhem. In 1989 Helen Zahavi published her novel *Dirty Weekend*, in which the protagonist gets fed up one day – a voyeur is following her and peering through her blinds – and systematically sets out to seduce and physically destroy every man who treats her abusively. (*The Sunday Times* felt compelled to call on a panel of psychiatrists who claimed that to imagine such a plot line, the author must be insane.) Also in 1989, Andrea Dworkin's *Mercy* had a victim of multiple rapes declare, 'It is important for women to kill men.'

The ceremonial burning of the clothing of victimhood took place in a tremendous proliferation of images of violent femmes on film. The sequence began in the 1980s as simple self-defence: in an American TV movie *The Burning Bed* Farrah Fawcett starred as a battered wife who sets her husband on fire as he lies sleeping. Later, Fawcett reappeared in *Extremities*, a film in which a rape victim traps, ties up and torments her rapist.

By the 1990s, female vengeance fantasies had really begun to explode: *Sleeping with the Enemy, Single White Female, The Silence of the Lambs, Body of Evidence*. The industry that had been putting violent rapes in one movie out of eight because 'it's good box office' now discovered that it was good box office to turn the gender tables as well.

Feminist critics generally interpreted such films as having been conjured up by the backlash. But to see women simply as passive victims of culture ignores the enormous control they exert over much of Hollywood's fantasy factory, which manufactured anti-victim images for women at the same time that it was churning out anti-feminist images for sexist men.

Hollywood issues movies like paper money, hoping that audiences will give them monetary value by using them as a means of exchanging current ideas. They become significant only when people give the currency value. These female revenge fantasy films were hits because women saw them and wanted men to see them. They sent out the message that women were tired of being humiliated, underpaid, abused, and having their reproductive lives treated carelessly. Women were sick of being the only ones whose dismemberment was turned into popular entertainment. Women called the films into being.

Underground magazines – the self-published 'zines' – reveal the furthest limits where the female psyche travels, and the view down there is of precisely the kind of cruel fantasy violence against male aggressors that feminists have long abhorred when the roles were reversed. The American cartoon character Lesbian Terrorist Hothead Paisan, drawn by Diane DiMassa and published by Stacy Sheehan, is a beloved cult figure:

> Ever had some idiot yell something about your tits as he drove by and wish you had an AK-47 hiding right there under your jacket? Ever want to storm into a gynecological ward full of overpaid white male doctors and do some of your own 'pesterectomies'? Hothead is a raging city dyke with scary hair and a fetish for guns, grenades, mallets and sharp objects.

In one strip, a white man in a suit chains himself to a statue of Christopher Columbus ('I found it, it's mine, kill those people' is engraved on it) and declares, 'Women will have the right to choose over my dead body!' Hothead cries, 'Now that's an engraved invitation!' and beats him into the ground with a mallet.

Frighten the Horses, an American underground magazine, ran features on Aileen Wuornos, the Texan female serial killer, as well as on Hothead Paisan. In 'Penis Envy II' a man reads violent pornography until he becomes a giant penis that devours the lonely women he picks up in bars. After his rampage ('More Girls Disappear! Almost 200 Reported Missing,' announce the headlines) the penis man meets a woman who becomes an enormous vagina dentata and devours and destroys him ('I'll quit tomorrow,' she says. 'I swear!'). In 'Dirty Plotte' by Julie Doucet, a male monster figure degrades a woman character sexually in an alley. When the character Charlotte comes upon the scene, she yells, 'Leave my girl alone, you pig! I dare you to touch my baby again, scumbag!'

She kicks him in the groin, beats him into a stupor, and then castrates him.

Nancy Friday's *Women on Top* details fantasy after fantasy of female sadism and sexual violence against men. In a chilling chapter, Friday reports that there is a new group of women who report fantasies of sexual violence against men that would have been unheard of just twenty years before: 'Woman as rapist had never turned up in my research on women's fantasies until now,' she writes. Many of these fantasizers are survivors of child sexual abuse, and 'the people the women attack in fantasy are always men . . . [They] tie men up, starve them, infantilize them, gangbang them, treat them as "sex objects", and then, finally, to show men what they really think of them, turn their backs on them . . . This is real revenge, the final devaluation/elimination of the male.' Friday rightly asks if there is not a moral dimension to such fantasies that women must begin to examine.

Do Only Men Objectify the Opposite Sex?

Victim feminism accuses men of objectifying women, but claims that women do not objectify men. Men are assumed to be polygamous and visual; women, monogamous and emotional. Men selfishly trade in older women for younger ones; women would never be tempted. Men are faithless; women faithful.

But the more often women have the power and opportunity to treat men as sexual objects, the more likely it is that some will do so. A *Glamour* survey found that women wanted more male full frontal nudity in their movies. A spate of Hollywood actresses, from Cher to Michelle Pfeiffer, have taken up with younger, pretty men.

Though this is still by far the exception, Sabino Guiterrez, a handsome, married 33-year-old who worked at a California hot-tub manufacturing company, was awarded $1 million in compensation for a six-year campaign of sexual harassment by his 39-year-old female supervisor, Maria Martinez. Guiterrez claimed that, for example, Martinez brought him into her office, closed the door, took the token gift he had brought back from his vacation, said 'I want to give you my thanks this way,' and went for him. 'The kiss,' the employee recounted, 'was coming straight to the mouth.' After that episode, the woman's advances included 'unwanted caresses, kissing, fondling of genitals and demands for sex'. When Guiterrez became engaged, Martinez stripped him of his management responsibilities. 'She was treating me like a sweeper,' he said.

Penthouse's editors decided to feature more male nudity to draw female readers. Beefcake is appearing in women's magazines. Glossy new porn magazines aired at a female audience, like *For Women* and *Women Only*, are selling briskly in Britain; readers write in urging the editors to show erections. *Australian Women's Forum*, a new pro-feminist, gay-and-lesbian-positive, body-image-inclusive female-oriented porn monthly that offers full frontal male nudity, is outselling *Playboy*. The *Tailhook Report* details a number of cases of women grabbing and pinching men's buttocks and seizing their testicles with the shout 'Package check'! At the thriving Chippendale's nightclubs, gorgeous male dancers gyrate for screaming female audiences, who clamour to stuff money into the men's G-strings. In Holland, there are rumours that wealthy northern European businesswomen on holiday in Morocco pick up young boys to use as sexual playthings, only to discard them, without winter clothing, in the streets of the cold cities when they tire of them. In Rio de Janeiro ten nightclubs for women offering male strippers have opened within the space of a few months. The clubs offer 'sexy boys – a show of beauty and seduction exclusively for women', and specialize in staging elaborate erotic fantasies of 'Roman centurions, New York leather bikers, army troopers, beach boys and a Greek God type ... sailors, pirates, cowboys' as well as 'a James Dean look-alike'. 'I have gotten scratched,' stripper Alexandre Hakan told the *New York Times*. 'The women always try to rip off my underwear.' A Brazilian soap opera raised its ratings with a male strip-club sub-plot, and magazines have devoted photo essays to the phenomenon.

An athletic young male stripper performed at my sister's-in-law hen night. The women, a mix of Midwestern students and hair-stylists, certainly watched him perform in a different way than men would have watched a woman: there were lots of offers of orange juice and chit-chat about his 'real' life; there was no full nudity or body contact. But when the lights went down and the music went up, the group watched. And the sense in the room that such performances give – that the viewers are being flattered or worshipped by the performer – was probably very similar to the ego boost that men feel in similar situations, even though we knew that it was economics, and not adoration, that had brought the young man into our midst.

I know from my own experience that women can objectify men. I now understand a little better that I wrote *The Beauty Myth* not only because I knew the harm that comes from being treated like an object, but also because of my own struggles to try to resist my temptation to treat men like beautiful objects. When I was younger, my friends and I chose men on the basis of their personal beauty, style, and ability to make us laugh and feel good. We had difficulty being faithful; we were compelled by novelty. We talked about men's bodies and performance and physical endowments as greedily as men talk about women. We told each other how you could tell what their penises were like by the shape of their hands.

We looked, we chose, we fantasized, we pursued and were pursued, we told story after story about our conquests. Sex with beautiful men, exotic men, new men, taboo men, was the glittering prize. It was a ritual for which we applauded and adorned one another as we set out into the night, for which we bestowed on one another birthday gifts of French lace G-string panties, for which we stocked the cabinets with spermicide and massage oil and bath beads. In the process, we more than occasionally overlooked our partners' feelings, attachments and vulnerabilities. Partly because victim feminism made it hard for us to account for our own power and men's own full humanity, we did not always treat our partners with respect. Our relationships to them were I–It rather than I–Thou.

This was not 'masculine' behaviour on our part. It was human immaturity. Like men, we had to learn to see the person inside the sex object; like men, we struggled between selfish sensory gratification and the deeper commitments that a long-term relationship requires. We were not trying to be macho; we were healthy young women lucky to have been born in the first generation when women could have sex on their own terms. And that led us into patterns of behaviour that were remarkably similar to the ones that were traditionally considered male. Though all of us eventually learned, with effort, how to be committed to one partner and see beyond the immediate pleasure he could give, we found that effort transcended gender. We experienced it as a difficult human journey. And I know that in my weaker moments I am perfectly capable of wanting to be surrounded by adoring nubile 17-year-old soccer players, or to escape to the Bahamas with a surfer who is beautiful rather than bright, or to displace my sorrow about how time will mark me, with mourning about how it will mark my mate. All of the sillier fantasies that some feminists, including myself, have castigated men for having about women are fantasies that inhere in all of us when we are tired of being grown-up. We don't have to make social policy out of them; but we can look at them again with a compassion and fellow feeling that can help to heal the sexual divide.

Integrating the Bad Girl

This thing of darkness I acknowledge mine
Prospero, *The Tempest*

Victim feminism has had good reason to turn away from both the image and the fact of evil women. The stories at the heart of our Western and Judaeo-Christian tradition identify women as the source of all evil – from the Greek Pandora, whose curiosity let disease and suffering out of a sealed casket, to Eve, whose curiosity led her to bite the apple, bringing sin into the human heart. Other misogynist images of evil women have proliferated, from the wicked stepmother of fairy tales, who sends children to their deaths, to the man-devouring *femmes fatales* who proliferated at the end of the nineteenth century. Second Wave feminism explained that many of these images came from men's fear of women.

But that has changed. Today, many of the images and episodes of feminine aggression and retaliation derive from women's own choices.

We do not have to celebrate violence to value what can be healing about acknowledging the 'dark side' of women that is now emerging.

There is currently a trend towards integration in the feminine psyche. The theme that is springing up throughout women's culture – of the 'perfect' good girl metamorphosing into a seductive, compelling, violent, even demonic 'bad girl' – must not be understood as a sign of moral degeneracy or an indication that women are becoming 'like men'. The creation of these images is simply a way for the female mind to complete itself.

Male culture, and, more recently, victim feminism, have split women apart. Both declared that women could not be both good and evil, selfish and selfless, mother and lover, nurturer and aggressor.

Social conditions finally eased just enough for female dreamwork to begin to declare a great truth that has never yet been granted room: 'I am good and evil, nurturer and aggressor, creator and destroyer. I am no victim, no saint, but a potent human being: loving to friends, dangerous to those who endanger me.'

There is a tremendous new interest in female badness. Singer Sinead O'Connor fascinated fans and critics alike when she tore up the Pope's picture on stage – an act she later explained was intended 'to draw attention to the issue of child abuse the Vatican ignores'. The Bohemian Women's Political Alliance declare that they are 'the weird girls who didn't fit in ... the little girls your parents wouldn't let you play with ... the teenagers who dressed in black'. Huggy Bear, Britain's leading Riot Grrls group, were ejected from The Word after noisily accusing presenter Terry Christian of sexism. 'Huggy Bear are the most badly behaved guests we've ever had and they're a crap band and we are never having them back,' a spokesman for the increasingly popular show reported.

The shamelessness of cult zines about turning women's status as victims on its head, and reclaiming the most degraded imagery of femaleness as a source of defiance, is clear in their titles: 'Dangerous Pussy', On Our Butts; Brat Attacks (The Zine for Leatherdykes and Other Bad Girls); 'Dirty Plotte' and 'Meat Cake'.

The bad girl is sexual. And images of the genderquake did what victim feminism could not do: they established a clear distinction between sex and rape. The sex icons of this awakening are in charge of their own sexuality and enjoy it shamelessly, but can fight to the death against rape.

Catwoman became the archetype of bad-girl sexuality, the sexuality of the anti-victim. In the film *Batman Returns*, Michele Pfeiffer plays a clerical-worker Everywoman trapped in the pink-collar limbo familiar to millions of working women. At first she is a bumbling, miserable underling whose tyrannical male boss throws her from a window. Near death, she is brought back to a new life by an army of cats – those prowling, mysterious familiars of transgressive women since the two were burned together for witchcraft in Europe in the Middle Ages.

Pfeiffer's new incarnation is as the masked avenger of the slights and humiliations of clerical work. She uses a stereotypically feminine skill – sewing – to craft a very atypically feminine warrior garb: a second skin of black latex, half dominatrix suit and half superhero costume. It is the perfect outfit for Catwoman's new role as the dream warrior of the new female psyche: it is seductive, for it shows every curve; it conceals weapons – retractable claws – so that her willing embraces of men are always under her control. It is a second skin that cannot be raped, a manifestation of women's longing to be absolutely sexual but absolutely inviolable. Indeed, Catwoman's role as power-feminist avenger is clear in a scene when she saves a woman from rape, but as the woman meekly showers her rescuer with thanks, Catwoman looks her up and down with a mixture of pity and contempt and sneers, 'You make it so easy.'

The mythology of Catwoman was elaborated further in a 1991 American comic, *Catwoman: Her Sister's Keeper*. Though Catwoman had existed in comic-land since 1940, beginning life as 'a thrill-seeking jewel thief', she eventually developed into her current incarnation, the 'good' bad woman with an attraction to her partner/antagonist, Batman. In the myth-of-origin edition, timed to coincide with the release of the film, a victim metamorphoses into a masked avenger of abuse against women. The theme throughout is of a woman, split into virgin and whore, seeking to draw back together the bright and dark sides of herself.

At the comic's opening, Selina Kyle, a prostitute, lies in an alley, her clothes ripped and her eyes blackened. She has been left for dead. Patched together at a hospital, she returns to her life of torment under the abusive rule of Stan, her pimp. But a policeman directs the miserable woman to a mysterious trainer, Ted, a kind, tough and respectful father figure who puts Selina through extensive and rigorous street-fighting instruction. (The initiation into 'male' self-defence skills by a good man echoes similar initiations in the films *Nikita* and *The Silence of the Lambs*. The archetypes suggest that women do not want to 'fight men', but long for the good father/lover to aid them in fighting bad men.)

Transformed by her new power, Selina cuts off her hair and dons a sexy black-leather, lace-up Catwoman costume. In this guise she rescues a fellow prostitute, who is little more than a child, from being beaten by a sadistic john.

Selina's sister, a nun who looks just like her, comes to find her. The nun is captured by Stan as a lure to attract her sister. In a scene in which Stan torments the nun, we can feel the passive victim being exorcized.

Catwoman leaps down on to the scene, whip and switchblade in hand, and rescues her sister. Stan falls to his death.

In the penultimate scene, the two sisters confront one another, one in her nun's habit, the other in her dominatrix costume. 'Do you really feel so much safer in there?' asks the nun. 'Do you?' retorts the ex-prostitute Catwoman. In the final scene order is restored, the child prostitute cared for by the nun, who urges her to brush her teeth and go to bed. But both look out the window, missing something. 'I know, Holly. I miss her too. But she'll never come back ... Never.' The parting shot shows Catwoman poised above the church, outside their lighted window; the bad girl, the powerful dark side, is ready to return, invincible in moments of bliss, danger or fear.

This allegory reveals in full the dreamwork of women who are rejecting the victim persona, seeking to reclaim their fierce dark side and reunite the 'virgin' and the 'whore' – who are, after all, split-apart elements of one identity.

Why Own the Dark Side?

It's time to claim that natural interest in female badness for our own, for we too are involved in a lifelong struggle between Plato's white and black horses, good and wicked inclinations.

Many women suffer from feelings of imperfection; if we see how much destruction women are capable of, then the ability to be a 'good enough' mother or wife or friend is an achievement, rather than a burden of inadequacy. If evil and violence are not innately gender-specific, then neither is the social labour of kindness and love. Our understanding that the ability to do harm is not male, not 'other', but innate to women too can ease the rage between the sexes while doing nothing to slow the fight against injustice. And it can lead us to tap the power of that darkness, while being morally alert about it lest it needlessly damage others.

Aristotle believed you could not teach philosophy to women and slaves. A sexist society would love it if women continued to see themselves as either saints or slaves, victims guilty of nothing or demons guilty of everything, for none of these roles demands inclusion in the human contract of responsibility and justice.

In reassigning women the status of saints or martyrs, victim feminism recreates the old trap that women have to be better in order to be equal. If we suppress the truth that sometimes women do have choices and consciously choose to do wrong, then we have fallen short of what should be our fundamental feminist goal: laying claim to our humanity, all of it, not just the scenic parts. We must dare to assume full responsibility as well as ask for full rights, because human status brings with it the ineradicable moral weight of making choices – including the most wicked ones. Feminism should not mean being a saint. It should mean owning one's own demonic, angelic soul.

Part Four
Towards a New Psychology
of Female Power

Chapter Fifteen

Are We Ready to Embrace Equality?

Beware your dreams: They might come true.

– Yiddish Proverb

Here at the crossroads of power we see our majority status, and understand that much of our fate is ours to choose. But before we can act on that knowledge, we must look at the very last obstacles in our path: feminine fears about using power.

Analysing the backlash of the immediate past is the vital first half of the story, but there is a second half. While it is urgent to account for what the opposition has done to women, we must also have the courage to ask, 'What do we do to each other, and to ourselves?' For while women certainly suffer from a lack of power, women also suffer from a fear of power.

Are women psychologically willing to enter into power? It is not only women's cynicism and uncertainty about their own power that keeps them from using it; the problem is also that the realization that women are not at the mercy of historical events but can determine them strips women of many of the identities of femininity that feel right and comfortable. The female psyche still harbours great ambivalence about claiming power. Often women's fears are legitimate: they come from seeing power used harmfully. But often, too, they are like phantoms in the path. Women must understand what leads them to view power, whether in their own hands or in those of other women, as a taboo, unfeminine substance. We are almost certain to suffer the inertia and backsliding that have followed every previous leap for women's rights if we retain a psychology of femininity that forbids us to fully consider the implications of the genderquake.

Many critics, including some feminists, attacked Gloria Steinem's *Revolution from Within* for focusing, as they saw it, upon 'soft' issues of self-esteem at the expense of 'hard' politics. But we in the Western world have reached the point at which that distinction between inner and outer life is obsolete. Women can't change their world until they feel at ease with using power, and with understanding how powerful they already are. Self-esteem is not limited to feeling confident about oneself. The step past that is feeling confident about one's right and ability to change the world.

Developmental-psychology researchers are finding that people with high self-esteem who do well at an important task 'are likely to attribute their success to [their own] skill and effort. Those with low self-esteem who succeed may often say that the task was easy or that they were just lucky.' Applying this insight to the events of 1991–2, we must see that women's self-esteem determines not just their mood, but also how they will interpret the events of the genderquake: whether they just happened to women, or whether women made them happen.

Dragons of Niceness

The male psyche has produced a host of fairy tales about the quest for full manhood. In these tales, men's fears appear in the form of monsters to be tricked or slain. Though its struggles have gone mostly unilluminated, the developing female psyche also follows a quest toward full womanhood. One passage involves learning how to steal one's own female power from under the gaze of the monsters of femininity. We can call these, half-ironically, the Dragons of Niceness.

Unlike the more direct, fire-breathing monsters of men's tales, these behemoths are soft-spoken and passive-aggressive. As they manicure their sharp claws and groom their glittering scales, they breathe, *sotto voce*, an ongoing commentary at the woman who tries to journey past them to reach the treasure stores of her authority. 'Pushing hard, aren't we? Maybe a little too hard? Not nice,' they mutter. 'No one will like you.'

'Don't ask for the moon.'

'Treasure? You want *your* treasure?'

'All that treasure?'

'She says it's hers.'

'She should offer it around to others first.'

'How selfish!'

'How rude!'

'Thinks she's awfully *special* doesn't she?'

Evidence that women put limits upon themselves is everywhere. Author Rosalind Coward found that 'many women feel extremely uncomfortable about personal wealth – money above and beyond their immediate needs – unless they can justify it as bringing their own family particular advantages'. Silver Moon women's bookshop in London's Charing Cross Road not only survived the recession but expanded its premises at a time when many other businesses were closing down. Sue Butterworth, joint owner with Jane Cholmeley, is convinced that had they been men, they would have expanded years earlier. 'However strong we seem,' she added, 'many of us still impose limits on ourselves . . . Quite a lot of us are frightened by success.' Another woman who feels she has imposed limits on herself is Jill Tweedie. Despite a prestigious career as a *Guardian* columnist, novelist and writer, she still maintains: 'I am absolutely certain that if I'd been a boy, I would have done much more. I would have wanted to be powerful.'

The notion that fears about using power stand in women's way just as concretely as do external obstacles was brought home to me by my own experience. To my amazement, I discovered that in spite of my sound feminist upbringing, when it came right down to it, I was averse to power.

To tell the story of how getting what I had hoped for shook me to the core, I will have to push aside two taboos concerning appropriate feminine behaviour. Women are never supposed to mention that they have access either to power or to money. These strong admonitions work exactly like the taboos on women expressing the ownership of their own beauty, appetite or sexuality: they keep those potent resources mystified, to be manipulated by others' hands.

When some of my girlhood hopes for a public voice became

realities, I found that I had somehow absorbed enough of the weakened defences of traditional girlishness to be psychologically ill-prepared.

When I was 26, my first book, *The Beauty Myth*, was published. Soon after, I was set upon by my own dragons. The ones that dragged me down are familiar to many women: the dragon of the Fear of Criticism and the dragon of the Fear of Having Too Much. Witnessing my own ambivalence about attaining a measure of power led me to look around and realize, firstly, that I was in good company; and secondly, that no legal or professional victory will bring women full equality – or happiness – if they fail to develop for themselves a new psychology of power.

As often happens in the public arena, the book generated controversy. My job involved appearing on TV and radio programmes with people who represented the industries I was criticizing. Many of them were, understandably, angry and defensive. Hosts sometimes fanned the flames. Even sympathetic interviewers prefaced their questions in an adversarial way: 'Aren't you ...' 'Don't you ...' Though my task was to argue my views as forcefully as I could, and I did my best to hold to it because of my conviction that the issues were really important, I was acutely uncomfortable.

The normal give-and-take of media debate involved me in a style of discourse that was, in traditional terms, very unfeminine. I was having one long, gruelling moment: part of what I wanted to be was a warrior for justice, and part of what I wanted from the world was connection and love. The two drives were at odds. Though I had 'started it' by writing a polemic my need for approval left me shaken by the clash of voices coming back at me. The tension generated by the two conflicting impulses felt like a coat of fire.

I had few role models for enjoying the fight, for feeling good about rocking the boat on behalf of an important cause. Like most of my friends, I had only a hazy idea of what public scrutiny would be like. The only role models I had of younger women engaged in public behaviour were of entertainers, and people rarely got angry with them. My young woman's eager approval receptors were in a state of deprivation; and, like most young women, I had not yet developed receptors for those reactions that are closer to respect than they are to love.

It was not that I regretted holding the views I did; my parents had raised me to know that my inner convictions were far more important than my outer discomfort. But I began to hate the strong emotions that my own words had unleashed.

My self-image was shattered. I had always thought of myself as warm, friendly and feminine, for that was the reaction I had generally been able to count upon in close personal relationships. I did not recognize the person who was being reacted to as a critic, an antagonist, a threat to comfortable ideas – even though a critic was precisely what I had set out to be. I could not help taking personally the impersonal clash of opinions.

Like most women, I felt that words of support rolled right off me, while criticism sank in deeply. When I thought I'd done poorly, I felt I was letting down others as well as myself. And when I did well, I was unable to derive more than a fleeting boost from the encouragement of others. While I knew in my heart of hearts that I did not want to retreat, I felt that being where I was, let alone going forward, just wasn't worth it.

Then a lesser dragon, the Fear of Having Too Much, appeared in my life, bearing in its mouth the first substantial cheque I had ever earned. Since I grew up in a household that was culturally middle-class but perpetually broke, I started out in life with a healthy attitude to money: I wanted it, without apology. As a girl I did paper rounds and baby-sitting, and I stashed away money with gusto. But in college I was exposed to the deadly combination of upper-middle-class feminine gentility about money and left-wing victim-feminist guilt. Money was shameful, according to many of my peers, for Daddy was a capitalist pig. By the time I earned that cheque – which was not even that much compared to what my male peers were earning – I was paralysed by the fear of money.

Those funds also shook my sense of self. If I was no longer so actively deprived, I was no longer virtuous. The cheque was a phantom presence disrupting my sense of where I stood in the world. It felt defeminizing, like a mark of maleness stigmatizing me.

I reacted like many women, with a dizzy inability to discuss my income. I was embarrassed talking to the woman who helped with my taxes. I thought it was inappropriate for me to learn about handling my money.

My general discomfort was reinforced by my sense that whatever visibility I did have might be hurtful, in some way, to people I was close to. I, who had once babbled away about every detail of my life, became quieter and quieter about trips, lectures, all the ways in which my life was changing as it became more public. Whenever something I said appeared in print I felt vaguely uneasy around my friends, particularly my women friends; I felt that I had been somehow selfish or rude to them by 'going public'. The more often 'good news' came my way, the more silent I would be with them, for I feared that what looked like 'too much' would threaten our intimacy. As I withdrew, the good news that came my way felt less good, because I was not able to share it.

Finally, I was in such a state of anxiety that I went to look for answers from those modern-day wise men and women, psychotherapists.

One, a woman, said: this discomfort is what you signed on for. Lump it: it goes with the territory. But no, I thought, I had no idea it would feel like this. If you don't like it, she said, disappear; leave the public arena, go away, be quiet. It's easy.

The other, a man, concurred. Stop writing, then, he said. I can't do that, I replied. Well, then write under a pseudonym. I can't do that, I answered. Well, write under your own name, but just don't say controversial things; tone your work down. I nearly howled with frustration. Even in my shaken state I knew that telling my truth and signing my own name to it were fundamental to what I felt to be my job. There would be less than no point to writing that truth in a diluted form; that would be a perversion.

In my confusion, I even paid glancing attention to counsel from another dimension. My mother knew someone who read Tarot cards. 'Tell Naomi,' the woman said, apropos of not much, 'that she has to get over the little-girl aspect that sidesteps power and wants approval.' Thanks a lot, I thought with irritation. I knew what I had to do, but I had no earthly idea how to go about it.

What did I want from these authority figures? I didn't want to be told how to withdraw from power. I wanted to be told that it was all right to move forward. I did not want the clash of voices to abate because I was politely refraining from annoying them. I just wanted permission not to care so much what they had to say. I wanted permission to be a bad girl in the interest of serving my voice. I wanted someone in a respected position to say, 'It's OK to make people angry. Change causes friction, and that is good. Tell your truth and fuck 'em.' Though my family and close friends were saying that to me loud and clear, I had few female cultural role models to whom I could relate and whose examples could confirm that the advice was sound.

Then one day I read something that began to ease the coat of flame off my shoulders. It was an essay by Audre Lorde, from her book *Sister Outsider*. Upon being diagnosed with breast cancer, she wrote: 'I was going to die, if not sooner then later, whether or not I had ever spoken myself. My silences had not protected me. Your silence will not protect you . . .'

These sentences put my worst anxieties in perspective. And I realized that indeed, my silences would not protect me. What was absolutely the worst thing that would happen if I continued to claim the space available to me and tell my truth? I didn't live in a Fascist country; I was not poor or battered. Unlike women in less free countries, I was unlikely to suffer much real harm for expressing my views. I would probably not be gang-raped in a prison cell as a political dissident, or run off the road at night. The very worst torment that I was facing was in my head. Lorde's essay let me begin finally to learn a lesson I'll doubtless have to keep working on for the rest of my life: how to claim ownership of the power that is mine.

Soon the moments that guided me out of my anxiety came more often. A teenage student visited me. Almost in passing, she said matter-of-factly, 'You have power, and – '

My reflex was to say cynically, 'Hah!' and point out all the ways in which it was not true. But as I began that ultrafeminine, deeply conditioned, even courteous deflection, it dawned on me that from her vantage point, what she'd said was true. By evading, in however socially sanctioned a way, the responsibility she was handing me, I was welching on my obligation to her – and to myself. I had a dizzying flash of memory: how powerful, how masterful older women had seemed to me when I was in my teens. I had wanted them to share with me, show me, use their power on my behalf. There were indeed things that I could give to this student, just as almost every older woman has access to power-full things that she can give younger women. I stopped in mid-sentence, and began to rethink my power-shy reflexes.

Another such moment came when I employed someone to help me run my business. Whether I was ready for this or not, and in spite of my hopes for an office that was as low in hierarchy and as high in mutual respect as possible, the fact that I paid her gave me a measure of power over her. Her wellbeing depended upon my taking responsibility for that power, looking straight at it and not abusing it. If I evaded the power I had, and the responsibility to use it well, I would now hurt not only myself; I could harm someone else.

Soon thereafter, a writer whom I met by chance told me that one Native American tribe has a ceremony in which members make a circle with a rope, and then cut the rope into pieces. The concept is that there is a rope connected to everyone's soul, and the opinions of others can literally 'jerk them around'. The ceremony, particularly important to women, anchors the rope within, so that women cannot be jerked off-centre by the expectations and criticism of others. That metaphor helped me see what I had to learn.

Finally, I have Anita Hill to thank for starting to get me over the fear of money. The day after the Hill–Thomas hearings, I was so furious that I sent a large cheque to a women's organization. I was determined to do everything I could to show that, like so many other women, I was angry.

Sending that cheque made me euphoric; it made me feel powerful in a way that felt right. I began to tithe my income. Paradoxically, the more steadily I did this, the greater the sense of possession and entitlement I felt about my own potential earning power. And, of course, the more comfortable I then felt learning about money, trying to make money yield money, and even trying to negotiate for more. Money was not just a selfish, dirty indulgence that made me part of an oppressive system. It was an agent of change.

These moments began to add up. I started to enjoy the fight. I felt happy when silicone implants were banned; along with many others, I had opposed their use. I felt buoyed when someone told me that something I'd written had been helpful. It felt good to be a mentor to younger women, and to pass on the resources I have access to. My sense of self returned; my friendships stabilized.

I began to tell young women something that I had never, ever heard from a woman when I was growing up: it is really fun to use power, to use money to further positive goals. Achieving whatever power they sought would probably not turn them into masculine monsters or lonely misfits. Not only was it permissible to learn to ask for more, always more, but it was a political act. It was imperative.

Power Literacy

As I came to see how power-shy I had been, I saw the same kind of aversion or 'power illiteracy' in many of the women I knew, including the most affluent.

These fragments and images stayed with me: a young female TV producer, who had just been given a rise that would add a third to her salary, sat in a restaurant, practically trembling with anxiety, and talking about how to ask the independent production company she loves to reduce her rise 'so it won't take too much out of the pot'. A well-known biographer, popular across the country for her books on women's lives and their value, called her literary agent in the midst of a bidding war to beg him not to let the offers go much higher. A secretary I know bought office supplies and couldn't bring herself to turn in all her receipts, since that would be 'ungenerous'. A florist spent twenty minutes on a long-distance phone call explaining to a client who did not require an explanation why she needed a deposit in advance. An employment agency admitted off the record that when employers want to weed women applicants out, they do so simply by readvertising the same job at a higher salary.

Generations of female college students opt for humanities studies that guarantee them the lowest professional salaries of all while 80–90 per cent of undergraduates in the high-paid hard science, engineering and maths fields are male. When working-class schoolgirls are asked to choose professions, most opt for low-paid service and support fields; less than 4 per cent choose the higher-paid trades.

I began to listen more attentively to what an acceptable female voice discussing money sounds like. 'Oh, pay me whatever you want.' 'I told him I would take any job in his office.' 'I won't charge my clients much now, so I can build up my practice.' 'The cost is two hundred ... is that OK? I can bring it down.'

The lack of confidence about power and money is shared by women the world over. Amongst my women friends, almost none of us – though we came from many backgrounds, including the most privileged – knew how to read the financial pages, make an investment, hold a press conference, read a contract, negotiate a salary or use our basic consumer rights. It looked as though men and women of the same social class were taught two different languages about money, one that enabled and one that disabled. I found that all my men friends understood that, at a professional level, a salary offer was an opening bid for negotiation; they were supposed to come back with a counter-offer. In contrast, almost all my women friends, though of the same age, class and educational background as the men, understood the same offer to be, quite simply, what the job paid.

My friends and I discussed our power illiteracy and decided to try to bolster one another in the nerve-wracking effort to raise rates for our work. To our surprise and astonishment, these women, whose work ranged from filing to teaching to freelance writing, began to get more as they asked for more. While they did not always get everything they requested, they virtually always got more than they had been willing to settle for before. 'At first,' said one, 'you're inclined, as a woman, to blurt it out or shout or something to get it over with, when you ask for more money. Then you think, "Oh, that went badly." But with repetition, you become more relaxed about it. Soon it seems normal.' The injunction to press for more is certainly most useful to women who are not without safety nets; but the importance of seeing our work as being worth more goes up and down the class spectrum.

As I watched women and men express the value of their work, it seemed as if the two genders saw themselves as inhabiting separate economies. Many men, especially upper-class men, view themselves as luxury items in an expansive economy. They think of themselves as rare – indeed, as unique and irreplaceable; so they try to command the highest price the market will bear. Women, regardless of class, tend to see themselves as cheap raw materials in a depressed economy. Told they are worth little and that their skills are interchangeable, they tend to assume that they will do best by pricing themselves so low as to undercut all competitors – and throwing in the best service, to boot. I have seen women of various classes express almost a sense of relief at being offered a low salary, because they assume that means their job will be secure; and I have seen middle-class women practically break out in a sweat when they are offered a high salary, because they are convinced on a visceral level that the money is 'too much' and they will be cut out like any overpriced luxury if the going gets tough. On top of these assumptions, of course, is the curse of women's tendency to feel grateful.

Gradually, a pillar of women's oppression came into view that I had never wanted to believe in before. In many ways the insight is far truer of women above a certain income and educational level than it is of poorer women. But it can fairly be said of almost all women in comparison with almost all men.

Men get more not just because they rigged the system, but also simply because they ask for more. Certainly, women are kept down directly, but they are also counted upon not to ask for enough in the first place. There is a margin of 'more', for those who are not at the bottom of the economic heap, that women fail to ask for.

Spencer Stuart, one of Britain's leading head-hunting companies, carried out their own study of women in management to find out why there were so few women at the top. Women represent roughly half the new entrants to most professions and to management trainee programmes, they claim, and yet somewhere along the line these highly educated, expensively trained women disappear. Currently only 20 per cent of all managers in the UK are women, women occupy less than 2 per cent of all senior executive positions and only 7.5 per cent of the Institute of Directors' members are women. In Australia 17 per cent of companies have one or more women on the Board of Directors but there are no women on the boards of the top ten companies and only 3 per cent of company directors are women. Again and again, Spencer Stuart found that, together with the continuing prejudice and discrimination of too many company directors, women managers appeared to collude with those who would ignore their skills and talents. One company director recalled: 'We advertised internally for a new senior position. Not one woman applied. And I know of at least three women who were twice as well qualified as the men who applied.' Another commented: 'There is a big problem of women coming forward for big jobs. They are meeker, know their capabilities and don't push it. There are a lot of men like that too, but they don't get very far either.'

The route to the top of corporate Britain is via headhunters like Spencer Stuart, who are commissioned by companies to help with appointments at board and senior executive levels. Yet women comprise a meagre 5 per cent of those who write in to such firms – and women cannot be appointed or promoted if they do not apply for the job.

When the BBC World Service was criticized in 1992 for making slow progress towards the equal employment targets agreed by its Board of Management two years earlier, equal opportunities officer Laurence Benson said that a major problem was the 'missed opportunities' because so few women were applying for senior positions. Even the Lord Chancellor, Lord Mackay, advised women solicitors to be more ambitious and aim to be judges. Eager to defend the notoriously secretive judicial appointments system, he told the Association of Women Solicitors in London, 'I do want you to feel it is accessible to you.'

The Women's Adviser's Unit of the South Australian Department of Labor recently set up What's in a Word? (WIAW) in an attempt to show women how they tend to enshrine their low status, and to persuade them not to minimize their skills. WIAW found that many women 'invisibilized' their work by describing it in the broadest terms, like 'word-processor operator', implying that the machine did the real work. They also regularly represented their skills in personality terms, for example 'you have to be a friendly person'. Women pay dearly, in terms of pay and status, for such deprecatory descriptions.

I began to see how a measure of financial autonomy had helped to burn away the invisible veil of economic fear that had shrouded me ever since I could remember. I saw how cripplingly that fear had affected my entire life. Powerful men who had adversarial attitudes to women now seemed less intimidating, and I felt how much of their inhibiting aura, their assumption of superiority, depended upon their supposition that they made far more money than did the women whom they encountered. I felt in a new way that the easing of financial fear was more fundamental to female liberation than were any of the other, more ideological and social issues that often take priority in feminism.

This is no new insight: Virginia Woolf expressed it long ago when she wrote that women need £500 a year in order to be free. But this realization will not take us far – indeed, has not taken us far enough in the seventy years since Woolf wrote *A Room of One's Own* – as long as women's relationship to money remains distorted.

Women's relationship to money is often distorted in the same way as are their relationships to food and sexual pleasure. This makes sense, since all these riches lie on the same spectrum of forbidden abundance, forbidden self-regard. The disorders relating to money are symptoms of women's 'early power deprivation', and the effect of that deprivation on appetite. The means of 'self-indulgence' – food, sex and money – are weighted with taboos because they are seen as the addictive titbits that will entice women down the slippery slope of selfishness. Many women accept those taboos because they know, if only unconsciously, that they must restrain their natural appetites. Many women say they are afraid that if they give themselves permission to eat, they will never stop eating: hence the binge-and-starve cycles. Many women are 'financially bulimic': they will spend compulsively, orgasmically, and then hate themselves and welcome the discipline required by the debt they've incurred. Such women commonly describe the spending phase as giving them a feeling of power, and the deprivation phase as putting them back under control.

Women are not just ambivalent about their own money. They are ambivalent about other women's. The image of a woman's having money makes both genders reflexively want to overwhelm that money with conditions. 'Loose' female money is as threatening to the status quo as 'loose' female sexuality. Men are often threatened by a financially independent woman; but women themselves often feel a mixture of admiration and acute resentment for her. Anita Roddick, multi-millionaire businesswoman and entrepreneur, understands this ambivalence, with the success of her Body Shop empire: 'Wealth is corroding . . . That's why I spend so much time thinking up obstacles and challenges. So that I don't become a rich bitch.'

Why should this urge to put strings on women's money, as on women's sexuality, be so strong and irrational? Like the conditions that women tend to apply to other women's intake of food or sexual pleasure, it is a hangover from infancy. Men are not the only ones who long to control women's money, appetite and sexuality. On a deep level, many women too wish to be able to control the power choices of other women.

Most of us were cared for by mothers. Since we are taught to see women as those who should perform the nurturing functions of the world, our anxiety about women being truly financially independent derives from the infant's need to control the caretaker and to stave off abandonment. If Mother has money, sex and caviare she might go away and dance all night at the Ritz. If she is not dependent on someone or something, we fear we cannot depend on her.

This wish to impose conditions also reveals how self-deceiving is the premiss of victim feminism: if women are so nurturing by nature, why should everyone feel such a need to make sure they will use their money for others' wellbeing and not their own? What are we so afraid women will *do* with that money? Power feminism means letting go by overcoming the visceral impulse to dictate to women what they will do with their money, their sex, their power.

But women still lack a culture, feminist or otherwise, that casts the pursuit of money as a legitimate feminine drive. While women are beginning to list 'more money' as one of their main concerns, feminist culture often seems hostile to precisely the kind of capitalist skills that would empower women most. Marxist academic feminists use their economic analytical skills to excoriate capitalism, but not, generally, to find ways for women to use it to their own advantage. It seems archaic that after the fall of communism in Eastern Europe, some of the last reflexive anti-capitalists remaining can be found among middle-class academic feminists.

Capitalism *is* innately exploitative. It *does* oppress the many for the benefit of the few; its excesses *must* be tempered by compassionate policies. But the collapse of communism in Europe suggests that the left in Britain or the United States should not hold its breath waiting for the socialist revolution. The progressive community serves its values better by engaging with capitalism to fund social change than it does by professing an aversion to it that ends up keeping benefits out of the hands of those who need them most.

Feminism often seems to be more comfortable with the important tasks of pointing out economic discrimination against women, or with legislating for more money for women, than it is with the 'masculine', potent act of putting the means to generate profits in women's own hands. In its hostility to capitalism, feminism has not yet made the jump from asking to taking.

There has always been feminist entrepreneurship – businesses like the Women's Bank. Some groups, like the Ms. Foundation, run programmes teaching wealthy women to take charge of their resources and poor women to start small businesses; the Fund for the Feminist Majority runs an economic empowerment programme.

These efforts survive despite their harsh environment: the women's culture as a whole has qualms about using big money for big change. The Ms. Foundation is struggling to raise a $10 million endowment in spite of board members' fear that financial stability will cost the organization its grassroots soul. Members regularly complain about the foundation holding its awards ceremony for their poor and working-class community activists at the elegant Rainbow Room and sending them on a retreat where they are comfortably housed and deliciously fed. Gloria Steinem, when she described the crafts collectives of the Ms. Foundation to me, was careful to note that 'these groups are not profit-making'. Before my own conversion about the use of money, I was guilty of warning a graduating class of women, 'Never do anything for the money alone.' The introduction to *Sisterhood Is Powerful* bears this disclaimer: 'The monies from the book's sales, by the way, will go to the women's movement for day-care and abortion projects, bail and defense funds, etc.'

Those aims are noble; of course feminism should teach women to give their money for the good of all. But it should also teach them that it's OK – even 'correct' – to acquire and invest it. This feminine/feminist anxiety about money reflects the strand of Victorian feminism originating in middle-class women's church groups that saw money as 'filthy lucre'. It also reveals how strongly the vows of poverty taken by female religious communities have affected women's political organizations.

Compare those qualms with the voice of Amy Haydn-Rod, a 19-year-old student who works full time in a bookshop and has to dance at stag parties to pay for her education at a community college:

> When my mother divorced my father, she had no job skills, no education. She'd been sitting at home for fifteen years, she had to go on welfare, she had to go into Section 8 housing – she worked in a grocery store. She still only makes $14,000-$15,000 a year, and raises my siser on that. The effect on me? I think capitalism is ideally a good thing. By ideally, I mean open to everyone, without artificial barriers of class, race, gender. I now have a lot of friends who are upper middle class. And now I have a better idea of what needs to be done. You have to dive right into that society of power, the men's clubs, the money, and open it up from within.

Our old reflexes about money are increasingly out of step. Black activists are turning with significant success to economic empowerment zones, private–public partnerships, small-business training, and 'Buy Black' campaigns. African-American leaders in Los Angeles, who are seeking to invest in their communities, are articulating the fight against racism in economic terms: 'It's not enough to sit at the front of the bus. We won't be able to fight racism effectively until we own the bus company.'

Why should women be wary of doing things for profit? Why

should self-sacrifice be women's ideological standard even when it comes to business dealings? Given the chance, many women should be just as creative at making and using the raw material of money as they are at making and using the more 'feminine' raw materials of pastry dough or macramé threads. But as recently as 1991 a British survey found that six out of ten women felt that banks, building societies and insurance firms treated them like idiots. The following year *Business Age Magazine* published a list of Britain's richest women. The list consisted mainly of heiresses with only two or three self-made women coming close to the 'serious wealth' mark. 'It shows,' said Keven Cahill, who compiled the list, 'how little women have advanced in the last fifty years, how far they are from a proper role in the economy or public life, how dependent they remain on men for their wealth.'

Financial literacy is a goal as basic to women's empowerment as reproductive literacy. Is there not something unseemly going on when rich and middle-class women of a certain ideological bent are more comfortable with giving their own money away than with putting in the hands of middle-class, working-class and poor women the number-one resource they expressly ask for: the means to make money of their own? Is this really feminist progressive politics – or is it, persisting unconsciously, the class-based condescension of the Angel in the House, whose dainty baskets for the 'deserving poor' always had strings attached? Many women identify organized feminism with self-denial rather than enrichment. Would not millions more women feel warmly about a movement that they could identify with the tool they need more than any other, apart from reproductive rights: more money, from which flow more real power, autonomy and choice?

The ambivalence about money in some feminist ideology serves women poorly. With more money, more women could buy for themselves many of the items on the feminist wish list that languishes at the mercy of legislators' whims and the winds of public opinion. Women tend to see sex oppression and poverty as eternally linked. But enough money buys a woman out of a great deal of sex oppression. Misogyny would still exist if women were no poorer than men; but much of its impact would be neutralized, whether misogynists liked it or not. Imagine a world in which those who wanted to keep women down might still have those desires – but could not afford to act upon them.

Voice of Powerlessness, Memory of Power

I began to ask women to tell me about their feelings about power, authority and leadership. Many women's ambivalence about taking power, I discovered, mirrored many men's fears of women's taking power – and was in some ways even more categorical and extreme.

When women spoke about the issues, their body language changed in one of two ways. When I asked women to talk about being leaders or being powerful, they almost invariably recoiled, as I had done with my student friend. They would shrug, as if wanting to shake off a burden. They would also lower their heads, cross their arms and legs, even push back from the table at which they were seated, and hunch their bodies over. It was almost as if they had to make a physical effort to demonstrate that they rejected taking power.

But when they were encouraged to take credit for showing leadership, and when they were given 'permission' to take credit by other women's confessions of such experiences (for in woman-to-woman language, it is a confession), the body language went just as dramatically in the opposite direction. They sat up straight. They lifted their chins. They looked directly at the questioner. Their voices grew noticeably stronger and more resonant.

And something else unexpected almost always happened: a response that was flirtatious, even sexual. The women's skin would flush, and they would laugh – a sensuous, rich laugh. The reddening surge, the breathlessness and the laughter took place regardless of class, race or circumstances. In women, powerlessness has been sexy for a very long time. But these reactions suggest that power, long understood as being erotic in men, is beginning to be experienced as erotic in women too.

I am not a social scientist, but seeing this dynamic so often suggested three things to me. (1) Obviously, there is a taboo that makes it virtually impossible in 'women's language' directly to claim power or achievement. But women's willingness – indeed, their eagerness – to do so when it seems 'safe' suggests that this reluctance is not due to women's aversion to asserting their strengths and successes; it is due to women's sense that they are not allowed to assert them. (2) Women's claim to power is not held in check only by men; standards set by other women create a strong force that can either inhibit female self-assertion or let it flourish. Women are deeply conditioned to fear visibly 'rising above' other women, and their claiming of power is largely determined by how much latitude other women permit them. If the female subculture lets women act like winners, they will; if it punishes that behaviour, most will have a much harder time producing it. (3) This nearly universal erotic reaction to being given social permission to claim and communicate power suggests that women's might is not the grim, masculinizing force that victim feminism and the opposition portray it to be. These responses may suggest that writers such as Deborah Tannen, Jean Baker Miller and Carol Gilligan (in her first book, *In a Different Voice*) are premature in assuming that women's interest in connection so greatly outweighs their interest in recognition, status and individuation. The responses indicate that in spite of taboos and inhibitions, women on some level recognize their own use of power for what it is at best: acutely pleasant, profoundly feminine and magnetically erotic.

Young Women: Virgins to Power

In my experiences discussing these matters, younger women were the most hesitant about touching power. Carol Gilligan and Lyn Mikel Brown write, in *Meeting at the Crossroads*, about the inner voice going 'underground' and putting young girls in a state of conflict. I saw this when young women discussed worldly power: the inner voice was not still, buried, but was tearing at them from within. Whether the 'voice' was a set of convictions, certainty about their own excellence, or a vision of something they wished, to build, the young women I heard from dread letting it emerge for fear of the punishment they are certain will follow, swiftly and harshly.

Talented young men feel themselves to be destined to do the

great thing of their lives. Talented young women feel doomed to it.

What I heard confirmed my own experience: the greatest barriers to women's will to power and leadership were the fear of criticism and the fear of having too much. The women I spoke with described being on the receiving end of criticism as feeling almost physically painful, like a series of blows that left them virtually incapacitated. Many expressed what I too had learned: the punishment they saw as an inevitable consequence of taking power made the pursuit of leadership or success seem 'not worth it'. Many saw becoming a leader as dangerous. Paradoxically, they said that the more visibility, recognition and power they had, the less they felt in control.

Many respondents had cautionary tales to tell. These stories had made the rounds of their communities as a kind of inhibiting folklore. They told of other women who had spoken out or taken charge and been socially ostracized or publicly ridiculed – even, in some cases, threatened or attacked.

The folklore was already having an impact on their hopes for success. Career counsellors tell me in frustration that young men win all the scholarships because young women, who are just as deserving, adopt a powerless voice: 'I want to go to graduate school?' they ask in interviews. 'To study economics?'

Almost all the young women I heard from raised the issue of how women are treated in the media. They saw the omission of powerful women as a form of psychic deprivation, denying them what they needed in order to imagine themselves in new roles. And they describe the coverage of women as being like a humiliating, agonizing gauntlet that they had to walk in order to get to power. They characterized these news stories as object lessons warning them away from overt success, dissuading them at all costs from standing out and placing themselves in the glare of public life. The image of female achievement was that it was far more painful than pleasurable. While they could imagine that actresses and fashion models enjoyed their power and recognition, the young women had strikingly little sense that using power in other positions could be enjoyable enough to outweigh the pain of scrutiny. Indeed, my question 'Have you never been given the message that using power can be fun for women?' was often met with bewilderment, so alien was the concept. The absence of real-life (rather than fantasy) images that portrayed female power as being pleasurable made ambitious young women feel that their ambition was really a form of masochism.

Metaphors of high altitude and flying appeared consistently in the young women's descriptions of their ambivalence about power. They described a combined lust for and fear of heights. Boys express their desires to be 'high flyers' by drawing pictures of invulnerable rockets and combat planes. Girls' flight dreams cast them as light, vulnerable birds – always at risk of sniper fire if they draw too much attention to their trajectory. Girls' longing to 'fly' was often expressed alongside a conviction that they would be 'shot down', a phrase that came up again and again. As if warned by the story of Icarus, the yearning to try their wings at the highest altitude was matched by the sense that the air of power is too rarefied for them to ride without hazard.

The following typical conversation took place in a late-night café on the main sreet of Geneseo, New York, a small town that supports a relatively inexpensive state university. The speakers are members of the campus women's group. All are bright, articulate, committed and ambitious; almost all are white, working-class or lower-middle-class. These young women should be among the leaders of the next generation; their male counterparts will go on to climb the socio-economic ladder, add new energy to the political scene, and influence the media. But their conversation reveals how miserably little support for their development as leaders is available to them from the culture at large. And it reveals how unhelpful one kind of victim feminism has been to their search for power.

NAOMI (NW): What will you all do when you graduate? How will you go about taking on your roles as leaders?
NICOLE: [As a leader], you feel you need to be justified all the time. Success by yourself is like, oh God, people are going to be judging me. Standing on your own – I don't want hierarchy. I want people around me. Somehow I feel that to shine your light you need to step on people.

NW: Imagine that you are President, and tell me how that makes you feel.

NOËL: When it comes time for questioning and responding, Clinton stands alone.

COREY: He gets all the blame.

NW: What is it about blame that's scary?

COREY: It's negative. Criticism and attention are focused on you, it hurts.

NW: What is the worst thing about standing out?

NICOLE: Being shot down. What you have to go through [in an election] is so wrenching. Women are socialized to please people. In elected office, you can't please everyone.

JESSICA: Being not liked.

LAURA: I decided to run for office. Winning it was the most important thing – failure is the scariest.

NW: What's scary about failure?

COREY: That stigma. Of being a woman and failing. It's not like me, Corey, is failing. You're bringing everyone down.

NOËL: I always have really high standards for myself. It's like proving to myself and everyone else every time that I'm a woman and I can do it.

NW: Does anyone else feel that running for office means standing alone in an uncomfortable way?

JENNA: It's that I need people around me giving me ideas.

NW: The President has people around him.

JENNA: Yeah, but it's still him always at the mike.

NW: Why is that so disturbing?

JENNA: Like you tonight. What if you couldn't answer one of those questions? When I can't answer a question about my feminism, it shoots down my credibility.

NW: But presidents often don't have the answer. So it's a fear of losing credibility?

JENNA: Yes. Not only for me, but for the causes I'm working for.

NW: Has there ever been a woman who used real power in a way you respected?

JENNA: Only in my family. Not on the national level ... If I were a leader, I'd want to have my own ideas. And in having them heard, I'd have to step on other people.

KIRSTEN: I went through my history book and there were hardly any women. They're not there. The examples are not there. If you don't show women role models – that women can get in positions of power – then why should you even try?

JENNA: I can't look at a President as a man, and think, I can do that. Women in my family conquer little things and are really good at them. I know I can do big things, but I don't have role models to show me I can carry it out. Young women aren't shown how to do big things. When women are in power, they're so highly criticized. Hillary Clinton –

JENNA: You mean Zoë Baird.

TAMI: You mean Geraldine Ferraro –

COREY: Just because she cried, and that was supposed to be bad for the country.

SERENA: That was Pat Schroeder.

MOIRA: There's a split. If you speak, you fear dominating. But if you get power, you fear losing your voice – being dominated.

COREY: Even at the top, you're still dominated. By judgements.

NW: You seem to be saying you are less dominated if you have less power.

JENNA: Yes.

NW: I want to take you to the presidential podium. You are there. Are you comfortable?

JENNA: *No.*

NW: Why?

JENNA: I want to be somewhere with less power.

NW: Why?

JENNA: Because with less power, I'm in control. I would be afraid of losing the emotional side.

KIRSTEN: [Striving for leadership] is like a vision of constant fighting, with nothing for you. Not any fulfilment. Criticism kills you and makes it not worth it.

NW: No one tells you that using power and making change is possible and fun?

KIRSTEN (emphatically): I've never heard anyone say it's fun. [Seven other women agree.]

SERENA: The concept of power as fun is completely foreign.

NOËL: No one ever weighted these things together and said that the goal outweighs the shit [you go through].

SERENA: It doesn't end. We don't see the victories.

NW: What about that young woman who just went into space?

JILL: That kind of achievement is seen as patriarchal and there is a move away from that.

ANNA: She should go out and do something for women.

NW: But she did! She just announced that she is teaching so she can be a role model for young women in science and engineering.

ANNA: We never hear about it. We're not force-fed our own victories the way we are theirs.

JILL: Do you think people are turning to radical separatism because they have no mentors?

NW: What do you think?

JILL: We have no one to teach us how to take the next step. This is why we turn away from power. No one is teaching us how to get access to it or use it. They just teach us that it's not worth it.

The rising generations of potential female leaders need much more than equality legislation. They need mentoring. They need role models. They need basic power skills. They need an old-girls' network. They need to be led from victim feminism to power feminism. And most of all, they need overt permission to kill the Dragons of Niceness that make success and achievement seem truly 'not worth it'.

Not Just a Personal Problem

Women have been a demographic majority for as long as they have had the vote, but it was not until 1992 that they really began to use their political power. Why is this so?

Historians present us with somewhat unsatisfying explanations for why feminism fell apart once women won the vote. Shulamith Firestone in *The Dialectic of Sex* glosses over the way feminism collapsed on attainment of the right to vote; she ascribes it to exhaustion and 'ridicule'. Susan Kingsley Kent writes that feminism fell apart after the vote was won in Britain because of three things: the Depression and the rise of Fascism; 'the rise of anti-feminism'; and division in the ranks of the movement. As the press and government turned against feminists after 1918 in 'an ideological backlash', women backed down.

But isn't this somewhat odd? If Black South Africans gained the vote and then used it for seventy years to vote for white politicians with little interest in Black African concerns, we would ask why. Some maladaptive psychology would have to be at work.

'Why,' Kent cites Winifred Holtby writing in the 1930s, ' . . . are women themselves often the first to repudiate the movements of the past hundred and fifty years, which have gained for them at least the foundations of political, economic, educational and moral equality? . . . Modern young women,' Holtby asserted, prefiguring the situation today, 'know amazingly little of what life was like before the War . . . and show a strong hostility to the word "feminism" and all that they imagine it to connote.' In the 1930s, Holtby wrote, magazine articles told women it was their job to yield the workplace to men. This 'persuasion' was 'all too effective'. Women 'made little protest,' she wrote, 'and let their gains slip from them, allowing the old rigid exclusions to be reimposed because they thought it was their duty'.

Women's poverty, racial discrimination, their lack of access to education or the media, politicians' disdain, all conspired to keep women from using the vote in the way that is becoming possible today. But there is also a psychological factor at work.

In other words, following a gain, women were frightened away from political power by all these concrete obstacles, but also *by criticism*. This foreshadows the 1980s, when, following gains, many women backed away from political power because of real enemies, but also because of *criticism*. Certainly, women in both eras faced genuine structural impediments, including in our time the ones Susan Faludi documents in *Backlash*; but many also lost the psychic energy to stand up in defence of their gains; though many devoted organizers stayed the course, the will of many of those whom they tried to organize was shaken.

So we must ask: why should women be energized by oppression and deflated by success, with its attendant criticism? Why did the women's movement collapse in the decade after the one in which women got the vote, and again in the 1980s, a decade after seeing a wave of pro-women legislation? Is it *only* the backlash –

or the backlash in combination with something less palpable, less external?

Psychologists have identified a syndrome: 'negative therapeutic reaction'. This means, according to psychologist Jean Baker Miller that people 'make a major gain and then seem to get worse after it'. Negative therapeutic reactions are understood as depressions that 'occur when a person has made a major step toward taking on responsibility and direction in her/his own life. The person has seen that she/he can move out of a position of inability and can exert effective action in her/his own behalf, but then becomes frightened by the implications of that new vision ... She/he then pulls back and refuses to follow through on the new course.'

What Miller describes as often true of individual women (and men) in therapy is true as well of the great international tides of women's history. We must understand that two things happen when women start to win. The first, of course, is that there is a counter-reaction – a backlash – from the opposition. The second is that women – not as individuals, but on the level of the mass unconscious – experience a disorientation that leads, as it did in my case and in the lives of the young women I spoke with, to ambivalence about making further progress, and even to with- drawal. Like waves advancing much and retreating a little less under the direction of an inexorable flow tide, women yield ground to the backlashes that they encounter by encompassing them within the temporary ebb tides of their own psychic ex- haustion.

As women have long been a majority, it is just possible that this faintness of heart follows upon women's political gains because to see ourselves as the determining force in the fate of nations, rather than as those who are externally determined by others, is a trauma great enough to shake up feminine identity and reverse the direc- tion of feminine political desire.

Chapter Sixteen

The Feminine Fear of Power

How can the achievement of power have come to feel so traumatic? We start our life with little respect for the muttering dragons at the gates. We are at first unsocialized little power feminists, almost every squalling one of us, but the peer-group socialization that begins at the age of about six and reaches a peak at adolescence includes the fear of power along with the rest of our girlhood training.

Deborah Tannen, Carol Gilligan and Jean Baker Miller have produced insightful work that describes a 'women's consciousness' as focused on connection and intimacy and averse to competitiveness, achievement or 'masculine' forms of power. I am persuaded that their view overlooks a submerged, forbidden half of the feminine psyche. In my opinion, some of their theories account *psychologically* for behaviour that is determined by politics and that is changing rapidly as women's access to power changes. Tannen's and Miller's conclusions, along with those Gilligan arrived at in her first book, must be tempered by the fact that girls and women are happy to report the wish for intimacy and connection, but are not happy reporting, say, fantasies of rage, competition, victory, fame, wealth, control, conquest and dominion, no matter how real those fantasies are. Finally, it seems that when these writers offer scenes of girls behaving in collaborative, supportive ways, they tend to leave out the scenes of girls behaving in ways that are competitive, aggressive and exultant in conquest. (Gilligan's second book, with Lyn Mikel Brown, addresses conflict far more directly). Tannen, for instance, tends to take girls' groups' collaborativeness largely at face value, whereas I believe that the apparently effortless harmony and 'niceness' are purchased at the price of great control, cruelty and vigilance. These groups are the training grounds where girls are taught to do something that goes against the grain: to give up power and subvert the will.

Gilligan's second book, *Meeting at the Crossroads*, written in collaboration with Lyn Mikel Brown, describes girls' struggles against the imperative to 'be nice'. But the authors still present the personality of relatively healthy, untrammelled girls in pretty unobjectionable terms: girls are not afraid of 'speaking out about what feels bad or wrong'; they can be, at worst, 'disruptive and resistant'; they are 'candid, confident, sure of [their] perceptions and judgements, stubborn, determined'. Gilligan and Mikel Brown still see girls' primary drive as 'relational'. They eloquently recognize the girls' clarity of will, but interpret it as having to do not with a will to power but merely with a wish for more 'authentic' relationships.

Little girls certainly want intimacy and connection. But these theories don't account for the other deep drive: little girls also want to rule the world. I honour what these writers see, but their observations stop far short of my own memory of the girlhood will to power, autonomy and mastery, which coexists with the desire for connection. Nor do these writers' theories account for the fascination with using power that girlhood and adult female fantasies reveal.

When I asked women to tell me if they had had girlhood fantasies of power, a treasure trove opened (or a Pandora's box, depending on your point of view). And it looked nowhere near as presentable as Brown's and Gilligan's descriptions of pleasantly self-assertive girls intent on 'authentic connection'. My question elicited from women of all backgrounds fantasies of being rulers, queens, empresses; memories of harbouring grudges and wishes for retaliation that had elements of cruelty and domination; scenarios in which the girl was lauded on the front pages, worshipped by adoring fans, surrounded by attentive courtiers, awarded the Nobel Prize, carried on the shoulders of fans; in which she conducted symphonies, made life-or-death judicial decisions, discovered buried treasure, shamed her rivals, put her enemies in torture chambers, ruled her own colonies, fought alligators and was knighted by the queen. These fantasies were nowhere inhibited by the fear that if the girl triumphed, someone would get hurt or left out. They were not about deriving an identity from others' feelings (except perhaps for their feelings of awe). They did not suggest that the classic definition of ego is inapplicable to authentic female development – only that it is driven into hiding.

The women I spoke to confirmed my own memory: in contrast to the theories of difference feminists – that girls never need to separate and claim autonomy the way boys do, that they embrace egalitarianism and eschew hierarchy, and that they cannot disengage their own identities from the feelings of those around them – it seemed clear to me that healthy girls fantasize separation, recognition, achievement, mastery and conflict too – in lush detail. And that then they learn to conceal and deny those will-to-power fantasies, which become unspeakable, obscene.

Here is one woman's memory. She is college educated, 31 years old and of half-Indian, half-Moroccan descent:

When we had conflicts, I remember having revenge fantasies against my mother. I would be proven right; she would be proven wrong. She would be completely humbled.

Also, there were revenge fantasies about enemies you had at school. Dungeons. These fantasies were really common among a lot of my friends who were considered different or outsiders at school.

I remember lots and lots of dreams of grandeur. Everything had to be World Famous. World Famous Surgeon, World Famous – I'd be an actress-singer-model. An explorer. Definitely recognition, applause – that people would feel humbled – there was a lot of humbling. Everyone would be jealous and be sorry they were mean.

The idea was to be gritty, tough, courageous – stopping trains, saving people – being a spy and smuggling state secrets.

It was the feeling of power. I would have these secrets that no one else knew or was clever enough to work out. And then they would be presented with a flourish to *someone* – what a snotty little kid – people would be *awed* by my brilliance.

This World Famous thing was a fantasy about being different. I wanted recognition that I would go further than
anyone else. Or at least be different from everyone else.

We would play with dolls. One of us would be queen. The
others were servants. We were incredibly mean to the servants.
But everyone swapped. I had a friend who always wanted to be
queen. But forget it, you know? No one wanted to be the servants. You want to be queen.

This memory suggests another interpretation of girlhood psychology to those offered by some feminist theorists. Tannen sees
girls' interest in secrets as being about intimacy. But to this
woman, secrets were clearly about power. I believe that the 'egalitarian', connection-centred, collaborative girl group pulls into its
system, against their will, girls who are wrestling with the com-
pulsion to relinquish their strong attachments to ego, power,
separateness, even the unseemly wish to dominate and punish.

The idea that girls want connection more than they do independence is based on work by Nancy Chodorow (*The Reproduction
of Mothering*), which claims that since girls are cared for by their
mothers, their identity depends upon intimacy rather than the
autonomy that underpins that of boys. Chodorow writes that
since 'women, universally, are largely responsible for early child
care', therefore, 'in any given society, feminine personality comes
to define itself in relation and connection to other people more
than masculine personality does'. She also writes: 'Girls come to
experience themselves as less differentiated than boys, as more
continuous with and related to their external object world', and
that 'Girls emerge from this period with a basis for "empathy"
built into their primary definition of self in a way that boys do
not.'

But changes – however minimal – in childrearing arrangements
are already beginning to make these theories outdated; the thread
shared by the women who were most readily able to admit to
these common girlhood fantasies was that their mothers had held
jobs and that their fathers, if they were around, were intimately
involved in at least some aspects of their care. Since this was my
own situation, I never learned at home that achievement and nurturing were at odds, or that female separation was dangerous: the

father who changed my nappies also taught classes; the mother who fed me also wrote her thesis behind closed doors; and I still got plenty of love. My sense that the two modes conflicted was learned later – outside the home.

I believe that all healthy little girls begin with a will to power that is at least as strong (depending, of course, on individual temperament) as their desire for intimacy; that it aids the survival of the will to power if the girl child is tended by her father as well as by her mother, and if the mother values her own authority as well as her caring skills; that leadership, creativity, genius, original thinking and integrity in the face of adversity derive as surely from this will to power as do the darker impulses of aggression and cruelty; that girls are socialized to repress this side by same-sex playgroups, as well as by mimicking the women they see; that because they have repressed the will to power, many adult women are ambivalent about using power, the natural longing to do so having been so distorted that women secretly fear they will become monsters given the chance; that this blind spot in the self creates ideologies that cling to the idea that women are innocent of the will to power; and that when women describe or act out, to social scientists or to the world at large, their allegiance to connection and collaboration and their rejection of solitude, competition and conquest, they are telling a socially sanctioned story that represents only half the truth. Given permission, women would come out with the other half, which exists, in those who have not been utterly victimized, not too far below the surface.

Each of us born healthy and given half a chance in earliest life, was once an unbridled megalomaniac. Before little girls are playing with the petite interiors of their dolls' houses, they are having fantasies of absolute dominion.

One example of how little girls' will to power is not seen is in the conventional wisdom about what architecture means. Men and boys build big, the wisdom goes; women and girls make homes. The psychologist Erik H. Erikson noticed that little girls build safe, small enclosures – tiny houses – with blocks. He did not consider that to the little family of dolls they were moving about, the girls were gargantuan forces of nature.

Many feminists agree that women do not wish to transform the environment or master their surroundings; Evelyn Fox Keller, a feminist theorist of the sciences, argues, for example, that the scientific wish to expose nature's secrets is masculine.

Many other feminists have ridiculed men's phallic look-at-me architecture as somehow indicative of a masculine pathology. In this view, women are closer to nature than to culture; they sort of wash about like tides, or root, swell and grow, like tubers. If women were by some fluke to build, presumably they would build low, communal, ecofriendly huts – round ones. But I am not convinced that the desire to shape, transform, even dominate the environment arises from a defective male gene. It is a human impulse. And if women assume, even in their dreams, that they would not build big, it is because they are seldom encouraged to fantasize about having that kind of power.

When I was a little girl, I built grandiose, ostentatious, vulgar, Trump-style palaces. I built big. At least in my imagination, blocks and Tonka toys became soaring bastions, flagpoles, crenellations, lookout points, projectiles, flying buttresses, cupolas, archers' walks, towering turrets. I surrounded my castles with that unnurturing feature, a moat with a drawbridge that I could raise and lower at will.

Gilligan, in *In a Different Voice*, asserts that 'individual achievement rivets the male imagination', as do 'great ideas or distinctive activity', versus the female imagination's wish for 'fusion of identity'. But the women whose interviews she reproduces have already had to forget the early will to power. When I built cathedrals, was I suffering from patriarchal confusion about my true nature? Was I showing odd masculine tendencies towards dominance and separation rather than collaboration and union? Did I want a penis? Heavens, no. I wanted to be a girl. But I wanted to be a *big* girl.

The truth about women's most profound desires is not to be found in their behaviour or their self-description to an interviewer, but in their culture of escapism: in the stories they choose. My girlhood wishes for power are echoed in other girls' and women's fantasies.

Harlequin Romances, the American equivalent of Mills and Boon, recently initiated a series focusing on the new female fantasies, not of yielding the self, but of acquiring 'Wealth. Power.

Privilege. Acclaim.' The heroines are 'Ambitious women ... who want it all and who are driven to turn their dreams into reality'. The fact is that the books girls love best are not about egalitarian merging or harmonious fair play. They do not 'illuminate life as a web' or 'portray autonomy ... as the illusory and dangerous quest', as Gilligan claims women will do. They are fantasies of autonomy, separation, adulation and dominion. Here are some of the most popular girlhood fantasies of power.

The Princess Fantasy

It is no coincidence that beauty contests are structured under the metaphor of crowning new royalty, or that girls' competitive and egoistic impulses are redirected safely into this harmless *agon*. The fantasy of being royalty is widespread.

Many women remember being convinced in girlhood that they were secretly descended from royalty, and would soon be revealed in all their aristocratic splendour to abash those who had humiliated them. Echoes of the princess fantasy, particularly the aspect of it in which the little girl rules supreme over her father and other grown men, survive in phrases like 'Daddy's little princess'.

Consider Frances Hodgson Burnett's *A Little Princess*, a seemingly benign tale about Sara, a little rich girl attending a posh London girl's school. At the death of Sara's doting father, the schoolmistress demotes her to the level of scullery maid and she is forced to wait on cruel girls who were once jealous of her and who now abuse her. But at the nadir of her poverty and humiliation Sara still has an adoring maid, even more pathetic than she is, who decides spontaneously to serve her.

When her father's wealthy friend discovers her circumstances, she is mysteriously provided with an attendant, an obedient (dark-skinned: this is colonial England) adult male, who does her bidding. Finally her anonymous patron reveals himself, exposes the injustice of the cruel schoolmistresses and classmates, and spirits Sara off to even greater wealth than before in a blaze of Electral glory so dramatic as to strike envy in the heart of every schoolgirl who had done Sara wrong.

In this story, mid-Victorian bourgeois attitudes about colonials, class and wealth combine to produce a more overreaching fantasy of power than a modern tale can offer. The 'natural' aristocracy of an eleven-year-old English girl allows her to exert a benevolent dictatorship over another child lower than herself in the social hierarchy, as well as over a full-grown manservant.

This amount of power, along with the story's description of life at the top of a schoolgirl hierarchy, of owning wealth and exacting revenge, are all highly seductive to a little girl. The book has been in print for decades.

The one situation in which women who are not beauty queens can revel in their queenliness is in the traditional wedding ceremony which, despite an ever-rising divorce rate, is as popular as ever. When they are 'given away', women's repressed regal nature is allowed to emerge in the image of the 'Princess Bride', with her sparkling tiara, sweeping train, and attendants; with the great 'aura' cast by the veil; with the pageboys and bridesmaids, the suitor offering gems while on bended knee, and the great moment when her entire court turns to watch her make her awe-inspiring entrance to the sound of processionals. All this gives women back for a day, though in safely circumscribed form, the buried psychological dimension in which they knew they were rulers by nature.

Many women love the paraphernalia of bridehood for that very reason, whether the appreciation of regaining their 'court' is conscious or not.

The All-Powerful Eccentric

Girls' favourite heroines are not engaged in showing 'a much greater and more refined ability to encompass others' needs', as Miller describes women's psyche. Nor are they willing to curtail their originality or skill for the good of the group. No, they are wildly independent little girls who show superhuman courage and deliberately, gleefully break all the rules of being a 'good girl'.

The adored heroine of French children's books, Madeline, lives in a convent school where good girls move in 'two straight lines'. They say their prayers, break their bread, brush their teeth, and go to bed. But not our Madeline: though she is the littlest of all, she faces down a tiger, falls into the Seine, and is generally disruptive before the timid and cowering eyes of the regimented good girls (who are all drawn mechanically alike): 'Nobody knew so well/How to frighten Miss Clavel.' 'To the tiger in the zoo/ Madeline just said, "Pooh-pooh".' Unlike the other little girls, who 'cried, boo-boo!', Madeline is 'not afraid'. She is not collaborating or conciliatory. She is the original tiny warrior-girl hidden in quiet ranks of schoolgirls everywhere.

Eloise, an American children's book heroine, is similarly eccentric. Omnipotent mistress of her own luxurious universe, she lives without parents in the Plaza Hotel, plays in the elevator, orders room service, and has numerous adult men at her beck and call. She also has unchecked control over money, saying with every purchase, 'Charge it, please.'

Pippi Longstocking, the Swedish children's book heroine, is the most unusual and solitary of all. She lives by herself and is supernaturally strong and completely self-sufficient. She does everything a little girl must not do. Like Madeline and Eloise, Pippi makes journeys that are decidedly vertical. Eloise rides elevators; Madeline climbs on bridges; Pippi Longstocking walks on the ceiling and climbs high up in the trees. She, too, has mysteriously unlimited access to money – magic gold coins.

She has, as her avatar of power, a talking horse, Mr Nillson, who lives with her indoors (thus bringing little girls' wildness into the interior). Pippi is capable of stealth, conflict and vengeance: when she catches robbers, she forces them to dance until they are exhausted; she puts abusive policemen away in treetops to punish them. She embodies the integration of two principles that are split apart by late girlhood: her mother is an angel, and her father a cannibal king.

The Horsewoman

By the time girls are between about nine and fifteen, they understand that the will to mastery and power has almost no acceptable outlet. It is then that they often become preoccupied with horses. The adolescent Elizabeth Taylor rode to fame in *National Velvet* because of young girls' libidos.

Observers who watch middle-class young girls obsessively curry-comb and feed the mighty animals have assumed that the relationship expressed pre-sexual female worship of male sexuality and aggression. This is nonsense: the girls are worshipping their *own* sexuality and aggression, which in their lives outside the stables are in the process of being split off from their acceptable identities.

When a pre-teen or teenage girl mounts a horse (or when the vast majority who cannot afford to do so in real life fantasize having a horse) she is exerting total control over a quarter-ton beast that could crush her under one hoof. She absorbs its speed and its fierceness, and in becoming one with it she reclaims the force of will that in other contexts is receding from her so definitively. She makes it leap, stop, circle, a being larger than any man. One flick of her wrist and the creature has no choice but to resist his own impulses and obey her. When a girl rides a horse she is able simultaneously to release and control her larger-than-life runaway will to power, which is straining at the bit.

When we are conscious of the wildness and will to power in little girls, even the most banal, 'nice' activities show another dimension. One toy that is enormously popular with little girls between the ages of five and ten is My Little Pony. It is, or seems, so frivolous that I have heard feminist mothers express alarm about it. Coloured in pastel shades, painted with hearts and flowers, it can even be bought in a baby version that wears nappies. Its synthetic mane is rainbow-hued, long, silky and elaborately curled. Little girls cannot get enough of it.

But the pretty tints are a light overlay to reassure the adult world. If the beast were My Little Bunny, it would not enjoy a fraction of the sales. Girls love ponies because they already know how big and powerful horses are. Owning, combing, stroking their plastic horses, they enter imaginatively into a world in which they are bigger than any adult and can run faster and jump higher.

The Keeper of Big Secrets

Another common fantasy is that the little girl is privy to a secret dominion, or possesses secret knowledge that gives her power over other people's lives. In Frances Hodgson Burnett's classic, *The Secret Garden*, the heroine, orphaned Mary Lennox, has the key to a walled garden where adventures unfold hidden from the eyes of the adult world. Mary has power over her dominion; everything is dead, and she can make it grow again. Mary's sense of entitlement to the garden is free of the self–other vacillations of Gilligan's interviewees in *In a Different Voice*: '"I've stolen a garden ... It isn't mine" ... [Mary] began to feel as hot and contrary as she ever had in her life. "I don't care, I don't care! Nobody has any right to take it from me when I care about it and they don't."' In Louise Fitzhugh's *Harriet the Spy*, 11-year-old Harriet keeps information about everything she sees in a spy notebook. Her ego is large. She loves her name, adding an apocryphal middle initial, and she declares, 'I am going to be a writer. And when I say that's a mountain, that's a mountain.' Her power with words and secrets gives her power over the rest of her class. Her friend Jamie is a mad scientist who has turned her room into a laboratory. 'They may take it *all* away,' she tells Harriet. 'What would you do?' 'Leave. Of course,' says Jamie. At the mention of the dreaded dancing school, Jamie says, 'They will *never get me*. These two are not in agony about the conflicts of self-versus-others.

Harriet also fantasizes revenge against the classmates who form a club against her. '*I would like to hurt each one of them in a special way that would hurt only them.*'

The Long Secret, by the same author, and the hugely popular Nancy Drew books are based on similar premises. The catch is often that the bad guy miscalculates because the young girl looks so harmless. The subtext is the feeling that roils in the hearts of all little girls who feel themselves to be the most explosively potent but least visible and respected of human beings: 'If they only knew!' The secret garden or secret world fantasy is a way to play out feelings of control while sparing the girl the consequences of being caught exerting the will to power overtly.

The Guardian of Treasure

In keeping with their will to power, little girls go through a phase of acute interest in earning and saving money. Popular girls' books go into detail about the workings of small-girl-owned businesses and about the drama of turning girls' hard work into income for the family. Stories about getting money for themselves give girls a sense of autonomy and successful separation while stories about contributing to the family income give them a sense of self-esteem and importance. The first sentence of Louisa May Alcott's *Little Women* is 'Christmas won't be Christmas without any presents.' The climax of the book is when Jo publishes her first short story, 'The Rival Painters'. 'Meg wouldn't believe it till she saw the words "Miss Josephine March" actually printed in the paper ... "I shall write more, and he's going to get the next paid for and I am *so* happy, for in time I may be able to support myself and help the girls,"' says Jo. The Laura Ingalls Wilder *Little House* books also detail the romance little girls have with work and money. The series gives modern girl children, who are generally barred from any role in productive labour, the vicarious satisfaction of seeing little Laura's livestock-feeding and vegetable-growing turn into family resources. The *Babysitters' Club* series describes the small-business efforts of five pre-teens who form a baby-sitting concern. When girls go through a phase of collecting money, it represents their wish to separate from childhood and survive in the world, just as it does in boys. It represents the autonomy that difference feminists have such qualms about.

Models

In adolescence, girls become fascinated with models and modelling, but it is not the models' beauty that is of primary interest. It is that models represent, if in degraded form, a semblance of absolute female power.

When a model is prepared for a shoot, she is surrounded by professionals focused only upon her. Men as well as women groom and attend to her. A photographer gazes at her steadily and 'frames' her. She appears on the covers of magazines, where male heads of state appear. Though she is young, she earns buckets of money. Every detail of her life matters to others: what she eats, how late she sleeps, how much she drinks. She has a retinue; she walks up and down above the heads of an audience. Girls don't want to be models to be pleasing to others; they want to be models in order to have power themselves. The model image is the closest thing to a vision of unpunished female recognition and dominion that most girls are ever permitted to see.

Hidden behind all these images and stories is the greedy, passionate, self-assured wild child, the little girl's good dark side. As women move into power, their socialization will often be at odds with the wisdom of their will. We do better to reclaim that little-girl's secret darkness and potency than to create belief systems based on denial.

If we face up to our dark, potent past, the implications may be profound. Some feminists suggest that the will to power is male and that women are doing themselves violence in the public sphere by trying to be 'like men'. But if the will to power is also innately female, the problem with women's experience of power is that it has been cast in the male mould, not that the use of power is alien to their libido. Women have been uncomfortable in the 'male' workplace largely because they have not had enough power to remake the workplace in a way that is more congenial to them. When women have enough power, they will probably reconfigure it somewhat differently or use it to serve agendas different to those of men. But we should not characterize the 'different voice' of women as including an aversion to power; it is an evolving re-imaging of a force that is just as attractive to women – if secretly – as it has always been openly for men.

We begin life with an inner tigerishness. But what happens to it? Other little girls are taught to be the instruments to tame us. The very first wounds we feel of being excluded, made invisible, are not inflicted directly by male institutions – that comes later – but by other little girls. So we seek, in vain, to soothe those wounds in adult female social organization, not by seeking a world in which women win – for we cannot truly, from our hearts' memory, imagine that – but one in which no one feels left out.

Girls' groups teach many wonderful things. As Tannen has pointed out, they are testing grounds for the skills of intimacy, sensitivity, compassion and communication for which women are so renowned. But this socialization comes at a cost.

Gilligan and Mikel Brown, in *Meeting at the Crossroads*, movingly detail girls' loss of 'authenticity' as they grow. But girls lose even more, even sooner; the spunky, assertive girls, like the 8–9-year-olds whom the authors interview, have *already* learned to repress the will to power. Their fantasies of aggression, fame and ego worship, so much less socially acceptable than the mere vitality that they lose as teenagers, have already been driven underground.

I am by no means contradicting these writers' insights, but hope to add to the picture a shade of girlhood that is less culturally condoned but no less deeply felt. Nor am I saying that the distortions of men's socialization are preferable to those that women undergo. Nor am I denigrating women's traditional skills. As Gilligan, Miller and Tannen all point out, both genders' socialization leaves people off balance and less than fully capable of integrating their impulses of forcefulness and nurturing. I am, however, cautioning against a picture of femininity that leaves out the female will to power and that can keep women from using worldly might. Every item on the list of 'patriarchal' attributes – aggression, competitiveness, territoriality, logic, libido, the desire for signature, and the will to shape the environment – inheres in the very core of female consciousness from the cradle on, only to be redirected. These elements do not make women 'like men'; they make women, in combination with the softer qualities lauded by some feminists, more like real women.

Emerging from women, the 'power qualities' may have their own distillation, flavour, perhaps even essence of femaleness. But the musk of animality and the sulphur of destructiveness are as much a part of the female scent as are the delicate florals of kindness and nurturing. These undertones are organic, not some testosterone-poisoned rogue pheromone. And we do not come any closer to self-knowledge by refusing to recognize them.

In girls' socialization within same-sex groups, we see how each of the seven cardinal feminine fears of power are passed on: the Fears of Leadership, of Egotism, of Ridicule, of Standing Alone, of Having Too Much, of Seeing Other Women Have Too Much, and of Conflict.

The Fears of Leadership and Egotism.

American authors Carol J. Eagle and Carol Colman describe girl groups in their study *All That She Can Be: Helping Your Daughter Achieve Her Full Potential and Maintain Her Self-esteem during the Critical Years of Adolescence.* Their account inadvertently reveals how girls learn that female leadership is neither fair nor admirable, and that diva or star-quality behaviour will make them pay dearly by the sacrifice of intimacy.

The fear of leadership comes from girls' alliance on the basis of intimacy rather than of goals: 'Female adolescent friendships,' Eagle and Colman write, 'are not based on going somewhere and doing something so much as they are on sharing thoughts and feelings. Through these friendships, girls learn about what goes on between two people in a fairly intimate setting and how to care about somebody else.' Instead of the impersonal, impartial and, to some extent, interchangeable experience of teamwork that sports provide to boys, little girls are led to direct their competitive and organizational energies toward social cliques.

Feminist theorists like Deborah Tannen have cast the world of men as relentless one-to-one competition, and the world of women as an egalitarian and mostly nurturing matrix. But men's team sports can actually be very collaborative and supportive; and women's cliques can be rife with veiled aggression and competitiveness.

Boys learn, through sports, that you can win; they learn what winning feels like. The leaders of sports teams may be resented at first for being picked for the position, but if they lead their team to victory the whole team shares in the triumph. This experience teaches boys to root for leaders who can bring benefits to the whole group, and to identify with the strengths of those who lead wisely. Even when boys are inadequate athletes in real life, they can adopt a sports team and, through passionate identification, 'win' again and again.

Girls who do not play team sports learn that 'alliance' is not teamwork, but closeness; that 'leadership' is not skill put popularity. Girls do not learn from their societies what fairness or victory feel like. Instead, they learn what love feels like. The goal of their social organization is not a trophy; it is inclusion.

In contrast to the methods of boys' sports teams, girls' social organization is profoundly subjective and undemocratic. The 'system of government' girls learn in the playground ranges from a 'popularity oligarchy' to an Evita-type personality cult that is, at best, a benign dictatorship.

Unlike boys' athletic leaders, whose achievement can be measured objectively and whose prominence can be grudgingly accepted by less athletic boys as being 'just' physical, leaders of girls' groups rein on the unmerited basis of charisma, looks, clothes, popularity: that is, on the basis of a rudimentary celebrity. Girls learn that leadership is subjective, shaky, undeserved and personal. They have little sense that a good leader can bring the whole group triumph and cohesiveness. The aura of celebrity cannot be abstracted into a workable rule of social organization that applies fairly to everyone. Indeed, resentment of leadership and of others' excelling is built into girls' social structure.

This early organizational experience gives women a lot of practice in feeling that female leaders of women are 'getting too much'. It gives women little practice in accepting the notion that someone has legitimately won a leadership position through her own merits and that the prize is open to all. In this situation, the led are well prepared to do what now comes almost naturally: look for an authority to whom they can yield their power and whom they can then resent.

Playground lessons mean that women lack a working model of female meritocracy. Until recently it was marriage, rather than achievement, that determined a woman's rise in the world; women saw other women getting ahead on the basis of their beauty or sexuality. This old corruption of female meritocracy is compounded by the way the media today attribute women achievers' status to their looks or to a husband, male relative or male mentor.

All of these factors strip women of the belief that their own leadership qualities will be met with due admiration, or that other women are entitled to admiration for their achievements. The economy of kudos that fuels the male desire for achievement is stagnant in the case of women, making it difficult for women to band together behind a female leader or to affiliate to build on successes.

Competition and conflict between girls is subverted into social or verbal power plays, and women grow up without a straightforward vocabulary with which to claim those natural feelings. When women do play sports and their aggression and competitiveness are safely framed, those 'unfeminine' feelings surface again effortlessly. It is no accident that the burgeoning culture of female athleticism set the stage for the current renewal of a language of female empowerment.

Cindy Watters's mother is an elementary school teacher; her father is a sales rep. At 22, she is the student body president at an American University, having won the election against three men. A basketball player, she believes that her sports activities taught her how to claim her power:

Athletics gave me opportunities to learn how to be a leader. It was just girls I was competing with. You could test new ideas. It gave you confidence because it was a skill you knew you could do. Athletics is one of the best things to happen to women. You learn it's OK to win, to compete. You're competing against yourself. You see results when you work for it. You develop a new enthusiasm for challenges because you overcome so much. Humans innately are competitive. You don't like to lose. Women may compete differently – but it doesn't turn you into a man; it turns you into a whole person who can be part of any society.

I definitely think athletics prepared me for leadership. When I coach I say, 'You're not just doing this to be good at a sport. This helps you be a woman in society.' Let's face it: You'll never make money as a woman in this society from being an athlete. But you can make money from what you learn in athletics: how to compete, be a leader, be part of a team. You learn to lose and bounce back, to be an underdog and work hard. You develop a definite work ethic and that's because it's fair. The playing field is levelled by talent and hard work. That makes winning OK. It's OK to win because you've said, 'I worked hard and, damn it, I earned it!' People can't take [the victory] away from you.

But few young girls have Cindy Watters's experience, and victim feminism's discomfort with 'patriarchal' qualities leaves little room for girls' own aggression and autonomous 'quest' narratives. This ambivalence about competitiveness and separation – which has heavily influenced progressive educational theory – risks creating an educational environment in which girls get only half of what they need – the nurturing half. It can also undermine the self-esteem that comes to girls from achieving a hard (hierarchical) goal, like winning a game or a debate. Some kinds of hierarchy – such as hierarchies based on experience, wisdom and skill – are OK; some kinds of leadership – like leadership that absorbs and focuses others' light for their own benefit – are fine; some kinds of struggle – like the struggle for justice – can demand an adversarial mood. Victim feminism has thrown out some potent, potentially constructive tools of power, instead of redefining them.

The Fears of Ridicule, of Conflict, and of Standing Alone.
Since girls' social organization is based on cliques, a girls' originality of spirit, which implies dissent from the norms of the group, can put her at risk of social death. Colman and Eagle put it like this:

> Typically, there are one or two 'in crowds' consisting of the very popular girls or the trend setters ... Popular girls constitute a small minority, but nevertheless, most of the excluded girls wish they were members of this exclusive club and feel bad that they're not.
>
> The popular girls are not necessarily the nicest or even the most well liked. Although they're looked up to, the girls on the outside know that their values are not necessarily good ones ... The majority of girls are in the 'other crowds'. Although these groups are not the 'best' or the most popular, from the girls' point of view, they are better than no crowd. A sizeable minority of girls fall on the fringe; for some reason, they don't connect to any crowd, although they may desperately want to.
>
> Girls of this age can be extremely cruel in the way in which they exclude others whom they feel to be 'social liabilities.' As they search for their own self-identity, they believe in 'guilt by association,' that is, if they are even seen hanging out with less

'worthy' girls, they will lose their superior status. Girls may be excluded for being 'immature,' for making socially inappropriate remarks or for wearing the 'wrong' clothes. Smart girls may be labelled nerds, the kiss of death ... The world of the adolescent girl is a Byzantine one, and parents may never be able to fully grasp why some girls are 'in' and others are 'out' ... Adolescent girls are very fickle. The girl who is 'in' one day may be 'out' the next.

Deborah Tannen cites a study by sociologist Marjorie Harness Goodwin which showed that when a girls' behaviour was strongly disapproved of she was ostracized for a month and a half – 'the ultimate means of social control'.

Since originality can be penalized in this way, girls learn that they must seek safety in consensus; they get little reinforcement from other girls – unless they are very lucky and have found a clique of rebels – for taking an unpopular view, challenging the status quo, or sticking to a conviction in the face of general condemnation. Women learn in girlhood to fear that people will not back them up simply because they are right; they will back them up only if they are nice.

The Fear of Having Too Much and Seeing Other Women Have Too Much.

Colman and Eagle describe a teenage girl power struggle:

The Aggressive Girl may become very threatened when another girl tries to usurp her authority or if other girls in the group find someone else to admire and follow. In some cases, she may try to maintain her upper hand by becoming even more dominating and 'pushy.' This kind of behaviour will usually alienate the other girls, and The Aggressive Girl will eventually be forced to back down. Sometimes in order to fit in The Aggressive Girl may submerge her own feelings and become very passive.

In this world, status is always an unstable commodity; it depends not on skill or respect, but on the shifting winds of allegiance. Another popular girl can be a threat to the constellation –

whereas another good fielder is an asset to the whole team. Any overt fighting to maintain position is inappropriate, so the popular girl must repress her instincts. But when someone has repressed her own will, she is unlikely to want to see other girls or women express *their* wills and get away with it; hence the fear of other women having too much.

What all of this conspires to teach women is that they must go along to get along, and the affiliation is always intense and romantic rather than being sometimes romantic and sometimes pragmatic. According to Eagle and Colman:

> Girls often prefer relationships with a few, select friends over casual relationships with many friends. For this reason, these relationships appear to be impenetrable to outsiders. In reality, the girls may simply not be ready to welcome another friend into their circle until they know her better. Or they may be afraid the newcomer will 'steal' their friends away, or change alliances in a way that makes them uncomfortable.

This training makes female friendships marvellous, passionate, ever-changing; but it also makes the impersonal attachment that creates large political coalitions infinitely harder to visualize or achieve.

Looking at girl societies through this lens suggests that it is a fallacy to believe that girls are less aggressive or status-conscious than boys. Rather, boys express aggression through dominance, and often express intimacy through competition; whereas girls express intimacy through inclusion – and aggression through exclusion.

Tannen, Gilligan and Miller speak important truths about the need for all people to move towards connection and away from competition, but they often idealize the feminine psyche. In their understandable wish not to put a negative value on women's traditional qualities they sometimes applaud not only the authentic but also the inauthentic and inhibited aspects of female dependence on others. And they, along with many other feminist theorists, stop short of making a case for the real-life use of power.

Women, writes Tannen, focus on intimacy and men focus on

independence: 'It is as if their lifeblood ran in different directions.' Girls prefer activities that 'do not have winners or losers'.
'They don't grab center stage – *they don't want it* [italics mine] –
so they don't challenge each other directly.' Girls in one of Tannen's examples 'mitigated the conflict and preserved harmony by
compromise and evasion'. In another, they played in an 'egalitarian' way that 'would increase the power of the community, not
the individual power' of the child playing. In contrast, she
describes boys engaged in 'ritual combat', saying: 'I'll punch him
right in the eye.' 'I'll punch you right in the nose.' She contrasts
two girls who sit very still and talk intimately with two boys who
wriggle, play-fight and tumble about.

I believe that Tannen saw that behaviour predominate because
good girls who play nicely still outnumber more emancipated
ones; but in my experience the kind of behaviour she describes
depends on how traditionally socialized the little girls are. *Pace*
Tannen, I give you my transcript of the play of two little girls,
sisters aged four and 'six and three-quarters'. Raised by a loving
father as well as a strong mother in the wilds of rural Virginia,
they are granted the freedom of the farm, they are surrounded by
artists, and they never watch television. I will call the elder Ann
and her little sister Sara.

NAOMI (NW): What would you do if you had a magic wand?
ANN: Turn people who are mean into frogs.
NW: Anything else?
ANN: Make them feel better.

(As Ann speaks, she and her little sister are leaning against a
wall, their limbs intertwined and grappling. The physical movement is perpetual. The wrestling, twisting, pulling and patting
seems to be so familiar and longstanding a form of interaction
that it is like a dance step they could do in their sleep. They are
very close playmates and good friends.

While Ann is speaking, Sara tries pounding rapidly four or
five times on the top of Ann's head. Getting no reaction, she
digs her two forefingers in above her sister's hipbones and says
to herself, 'Poke. Poke.')

ANN: Do you know what an Indian burn is?
NW: No. (Ann seizes her sister's arm just above the wrist,

places both palms on it, and twists the skin hard in opposite directions.)

SARA: Ow! (She wriggles away.) Let me do that. (She grabs her older sister's arm and twists as hard as he can. Her features contort with the effort. Her face turns red. She is practically hanging with all her weight from her sister's arm. Ann, unhurt, looks theatrically bored.)

NW: She might hurt you. (Ann makes a face of elaborate scepticism at the suggestion. Sara, frustrated, squeezes, if possible, even harder. Suddenly her face changes. It lights up gleefully as she remembers something.)

SARA (growling): Wait till I'm *seven*. Then it'll *hurt*.

(I follow them into the living room. Ann jumps around the floor like a frog; Sara jumps just behind her, pounding Ann's back with open palms. Then Ann lies down languorously under the piano, opening her arms out to Sara. Sara, on her knees, leans in for the kiss, and just when her lips get close to Ann she say 'Pooh!' loudly in her face. Ann seizes Sara's nose and twists it smartly between her fingers. Seamlessly, the two then tumble back out from under the piano. A new game has emerged in which Sara is a cat. Sara pretends to kiss Ann, but licks her cheek instead, provoking Ann to pummel her. They do this five or six times.)

ANN: If you lick me again, I'll turn into a bigger cat and I'll eat you – and a lot of your friends.

(Sara laughs, and places her hands around Ann's neck, throttling her back and forth. Then she hugs Ann and licks her cheek again.)

ANN (now, apparently, the forewarned-against bigger cat): Mrweaow! (Ann makes her hands into claws and tears repeatedly at her sister's ribcage. The clawings become quick slaps. The two fall into a grapple. Ann whacks her little sister's rear.)

SARA (hugs her; then speaks quietly and intently): Ready. Set. Go. (Somehow, the two know just what this means. By silent, simultaneous consent, they rain blows on each other's chests, pounding and slapping. They push and twist each other by both arms.)

ANN: I'll turn into a bigger cat . . . and bigger . . .

(Sara, undeterred, leans in again and gives a big provocative lick. Ann jumps, screeches, yowls, and lunges at her sister. In a frenzy, she evidently tears her apart with her claws. Then she gets up, dusts off her knees, and walks casually away from the little heap of sister on the floor.)

ANN (calmly, over her shoulder): I ate you.

This scene of girlhood aggression should not alarm us; girls who behave like this won't become chainsaw murderers, or 'like men'. It should remind us that those of us who were most intact played that way before groups of 'better-behaved' girls socialized such impulses out of us. The interaction between Ann and Sara was an easy flow of intimacy and aggression, a harmonious switching of roles back and forth, as each tested, provoked, dominated, made incursions into the other's territory and defended her own (It is also like the play of kittens or puppies, which includes licking and snapping.) The line of intimate connection was never severed – indeed, the aggression was part of that intimate connection – as, Tannen points out, it often is with boys. Each girl took pleasure in her own strength and, by challenging it, in the strength of her sister.

The feminine socialization against aggression was already evident, for when Ann was talking to an adult she was quick to temper the magic wand that punishes 'people who are mean to me' by making people 'feel better'. That socialization process is even ritualized: the violent Indian burn and the peaceable butterfly kiss are two sides of girlhood lore that are transmitted as part of one package. I remember the same double-sided rituals from my own girlhood. But when the girls were away from the gaze of adults and immersed in the realm of fantasy, the alternating waves of aggression and bonding were wild and free flowing, like the play fighting that is routine in the friendships of young boys. Ann and Sara's bouts of aggression and passionate, even sensual, closeness were both far more extreme and uninhibited – and far more overtly intertwined – than will be permissible in the socialization into proper girlhood that awaits them.

While each girl was playing out sisterly competitiveness and affection, the wish to obliterate the other and the wish to affiliate in a union, each was also playing out the struggles of the little

Darwinian animal that some feminists are more ready to recognize in boys' aggressive and territorial play.

'Difference' feminism raises other questions about power. Jean Baker Miller see that 'an important aspect of women's psychology is their greater recognition of the essential cooperative nature of human existence': 'Serving others is a basic principle around which women's lives are organized,' she writes. Thus, 'women's reality *is* rooted in the encouragement to "form" themselves into the person who will be of benefit to others ... Out of [this experience], women develop a psychic structuring for which the term ego, as ordinarily used, may not apply.' She attributes to male psychic development 'war games ... conquest and destruction'.

Miller cites the fact that 'for many women, the threat of disruption of connections is perceived not just as a loss of relationship but as something closer to a total loss of self'. She concedes that this can lead to problems, such as depression, but believes that if society were restructured to value affiliation over self-enhancement, this quality would make women more advanced in their psyches than men. Miller rejects the use of 'a word like *autonomy*' as being derived from men's rather than women's development, and says that the idea is threatening to women because it suggests that a self-directed individual must 'pay the price of giving up affiliations'.

Miller and Gilligan are careful to disagree with male psychologists who cast women's 'dependence' as a weakness. Their point that all of us are interdependent, and that being able to work within that framework can be a form of strength, is well taken. While the writers are careful to say that the differences are not innate, and to say that extremes can be self-destructive, they do tend to describe all the feminine qualities as being positive; but to my mind, though some are authentic and healthy, others are externally imposed – and disastrous to women's political and mental strength.

In her first book, Gilligan attacks the 'distortion' in the 'developmental litany [that] intones the celebration of separation, autonomy, individuation, and natural rights'. She asserts that 'narcissism leads to death'. This view has been influential when women on a campus had protested about sexism in an anonymous group letter and I expressed regret that they felt they could not sign their names, their teachers accused me of falling into the 'male trap' of valuing individual identity. But it is almost impossible to encourage an ego in a girl that is *too* robust. The stories girls read and love are delighted with signature, individuation and mastery.

'Excelling, being different, and fighting are threats to rapport' for women, Tannen points out. But surely that perception keeps women from taking what they need from the world in addition to what they need from relationships. Women's 'feelings that they should not boast' can keep them from negotiating for a higher salary or position. If 'the majority of women who reported acting alone portrayed themselves as suffering as a result', those women will have trouble fighting peer pressure, or assuming what can sometimes be the solitary weight of even the most responsive leadership. If women's stories about violating social norms end in fright or embarrassment, while men tell stories of contests in which they use their skills to overcome obstacles, the women will lack a vocabulary with which to present themselves in heroic guise, and will be subject to the psychic erosion of self-deprecation. If what Tannen calls 'troubles talk' is an accepted way for women to bond, that's not so bad; but if 'victory talk' is taboo, women have no familiar framework for presenting their resources or skills to one another in a way that leads to consolidating political or economic power. Is it so terrific for women's groups to find 'creative ways of keeping the girls equal in status' if that egalitarian impulse is directed at equality of outcome rather than equality of opportunity? Is it really empowering for women to value equalizing each other *downward*?

Tannen cites research in which a Ms M. 'held back what she knew, appearing uninformed and uninterested' in her writing and speaking, 'because she feared offending her classmates'. Mr H., in contrast, 'spoke and wrote with authority and apparent confidence because he was eager to persuade his peers. She did not worry about persuading; he did not worry about offending.' Tannen warns against value judgements: 'Calling Ms M.'s sense of self "dependent" suggests a negative view of her way of being in the world – and, I think, a view more typical of men.'

But wait a minute: as a woman and a human being, I think it is absolutely all right to have a 'negative view' of the fact that a woman censors her own authority because she fears that merely speaking persuasively will offend her peers. That censorship is not a sign of compassion or sensitivity; it's a sign of self-annihilation. As a writer, I see that as a tragedy.

Some of the differences these writers see are a result of politics and not psychology. In her first book, Gilligan looks at a boy, Jake, and a girl, Amy, engaged in moral reasoning about whether a man should steal a drug from a pharmacy to save the life of his wife. Jake came up with a logical abstraction that is 'rationally derived'. Amy considered neither property nor law but rather the effect that theft could have on the relationship between the man and his wife. She also asserted that the pharmacist 'should just give it to the wife and then have the husband pay back the money later'. Gilligan concludes that Jake reasoned impersonally through systems of law and logic; Amy personally, through communications in relationship. Gilligan builds a much larger theory of difference about men's and women's moral reasoning out of examples like these.

But the difference in moral reasoning this case shows may be due merely to what kind and amount of power these two expect to have in their lives. Abstract reasoning is necessary when someone expects to be a lawyer, a judge, or in other ways a participant in crafting broad social decisions that must be applied to many; immediate, contextual, 'connection'-based reasoning is appropriate to those who make decisions about personal relationships alone. Just as too-abstract decisions make for disastrous parenting, decisions based only on personal considerations make for disastrous public policy. The boy and girl may have been reasoning differently not because there is any deep difference in their moral development, but because *he* was encouraged to imagine himself as someone who will some day make 'law' and own 'property' while *she* is prepared to think in ways appropriate to those whose power to affect others' lives does not extend beyond making friends.

Deborah Tannen describes men's interest in the world of 'politics, news and sports' as having to do with their concern with status, and women's lack of interest in such talk – in contrast to their interest in 'gossip' about relationships – as having to do with their orientation towards connection. I think this is a misreading: the difference has to do with the fact that women are bored by a public world that is all male, just as men are bored by a private world that is all female. As their fascination with the Year of the Woman in the United States made clear, when women are included in 'politics, news and sports' they are *extremely* interested in such 'status' talk; the same shifting of interest is being noted in men with respect to the details of childrearing. People are concerned with what is presented to them as being legitimately their world. Finally, as Ann Hornaday points out, on some level *all* gossip is about status.

Jean Baker Miller is generally right to insist that 'the pull toward connection that women feel in themselves is not wrong or backward'. But not all dependence on connection is equally valid or helpful to women. As women move into power, they must begin to separate some connections from others. The young women I interviewed agreed that our problem was not that we were connected to those whom we loved, but that we were wary of upsetting people whom we didn't even *respect*. Women must begin to distinguish between those with whom they should maintain their connection at almost all costs, and those whom it is perfectly all right to infuriate, contradict – or even conquer.

Here is an example of the feminine need for affiliation being manipulated at the expense of the good fight. The scholarship programme that paid for my graduate school education shows a consistent bias against women. For many years women have won far fewer than half of the awards. When this happened yet again, I called the chairman who runs the programme and pointed out the bias, as many other female recipients had done. He chatted in a friendly way about the problem, but gave many reasons why nothing could be done about it. I raised other options. We met for breakfast. Everything was perfectly pleasant, but we were still getting nowhere, and the issue was clearly being given the brush-off. Finally I told him that, if the bias remained, I planned to write about it publicly.

At this, the cordial – if tedious – mood froze. The man became tense and said harshly, 'You don't have to turn a friendly situation into a threat.'

In that instant, I knew a number of things simultaneously: that the situation was 'friendly' primarily to keep me spinning my wheels; that I was justified in having politely informed him of my intentions; and that it was an appropriate use of the power I had to enter public debate. And also that I felt miserable, chided, rude, infantile and wrong. For he was making clear that my demand, no matter how legitimate, was disruptive to the 'connection' – made of a half-eaten bagel and commonplace pleasantries – that he had sensibly sought to establish between us.

I suggest that many of those who would like to keep women's demands in check are highly aware of women's fear of disrupting connection and their fear of criticism, and that they manipulate those fears shamelessly. I got through the moment because by that time I had learned that this man was someone I could risk making angry. One of the hardest things for the female psyche to bear about the use of power – even in the interest of the most legitimate, non-violent, egalitarian of goals, as this was – is that it can contain in itself the seed of others' fear. And even if women can bear being respected, we can scarcely tolerate being feared.

Jean Baker Miller addresses how important it is for women to learn how to have conflicts, as do Gilligan and Mikel Brown in *Meeting at the Crossroads*. But they all confine their discussion of conflict to the realm of intimate relationships, in which their view of conflict *in* connection is appropriate. In real-world public life, though – even in utopian public life – some conflicts don't unfold under the warm blanket of connection, 'in which,' in Gilligan's words, 'responsibility ... includes both self and other, viewed as different and connected rather than as separate and opposed'. We must develop a psychology for women that acknowledges this.

In Miller's book, the language turns in circles to skirt round real descriptions of win/lose conflict. Miller sees women as being better at 'simultaneous self-development and service to others' than men are, and proffers the hope that occasions that provide the opportunity to do both at once will expand. She urges women towards 'fully valued effectiveness', asking, 'how do we get the power to do this, even if we do not want or need the power to control or submerge others?' She argues that 'there is an important distinction between the ability to influence others and the power to control or restrict them'. Women, she writes, 'need the power to advance their own development, but they do not "need" the power to limit the development of others'.

Now, I too long for a world in which power is not domination, and in which no one takes pleasure in restricting or controlling anyone else. But the way these theorists frame conflict within 'connection' has the unintended effect of setting conditions around how women dare approach power, and stops short of preparing women adequately to take up the management of mighty resources.

If you are a warrior for your rights, you must accept that some interests and people *should* lose. It's OK to harm a rapist in order to escape; it's OK to embarrass a discriminatory employer.

When women take up their share of power, war may not be so reflexive, or sadism so rampant. Then again, they may. But if you are a judge fighting the sexual abuse of children you will need to be able to 'limit' the abusers' 'development'. If you are standing for parliament, it is OK to want to win – even, of course, to want your rival to lose; in a fair, free election, you will still need to 'submerge', to an extent, your opponent. I confess that when I was campaigning against breast implants, I was uninterested in 'encompassing' the manufacturer's 'needs' inside my own. When women pass laws and run governments, the society they make may perhaps be fairer than this one; but every decision they make will 'control' or 'limit' some groups' options, whether the farmers' or the long-eared owls'.

Gilligan, Mikel Brown and Miller may well focus on the skills of listening, connection and care at the expense of other attributes because they are *psychologists*; it is those attributes that make practitioners in their field most effective (and lead, incidentally, to greater status and respect). Valuing those qualities creates a paradigm in which a female psychologist is automatically better at her job than is a male one – a tempting worldview to promote in any work situation! As a writer, I highlight qualities of inner-directedness, mastery and quest because they are essential to my field. A group of women lawyers or female builders would probably see 'women's ways' of interacting with the world in less schematically 'feminine' terms than do these writers.

Miller or Gilligan (in *In a Different Voice*) do not intend to evade the kind of conflict that power entails. But those who extrapolate from their theories to a general view of female virtues are being evasive. Euphemisms for the great truths about power ultimately do not serve women. And until women are encouraged to step inside the psychic dimension in which they know perfectly well that those truths about power are inescapable, they will never cross the threshold into ownership of their clout, whether for good or for ill.

Part Five

What Do We Do Now?
Power Feminism in Action

Chapter Seventeen

New Psychological Strategies

If women are to take their rightful power, there will have to be a vast surge in organizational activities among us. The opposition says derisively that women can't work together; we react to this with terrific defensiveness but know there is a grain of truth in the charge. Something unique to women often leads woman-to-woman organizations into failure.

The girlhood 'web' vision of social organization makes women's organizational bonds tenuous. Such an intimate view of alliance leads women to think of other women's dissent as betrayal, rather than as a difference of opinion. This reading of female affiliation also sets women up to feel resentful of feminism and feminist leaders.

Since girls base connection on affiliation, women have a harder time identifying with a women's movement than men do with men's groups. We often feel bitterness towards visible feminists, either resenting them if they are like us but we feel ourselves to be on the outside, or resenting them if they are not like us and we do not identify with them personally. When women speak of their disaffection with feminism, they often describe factions of women who are different from them, whom they perceive as 'the radical feminists': 'the lesbians'; 'the straight women'; 'the establishment'; 'the professional women'; 'mothers'; 'single women'; 'middle-class women'; 'working-class women'; 'yuppies'. Feminism is hampered by women's sense that whichever 'clique' is visible at that moment *is not their clique*.

Since girls organize around relationships rather than activities, the personalities of other women involved loom larger in their eyes than does the political goal in question. It is harder for women to see the struggle for female equality as if they were part of a sports team whose players may be different, but whose goals are often shared.

Sisterhood Is Problematic

Since its first stirrings in the nineteenth century, feminism has drawn on a utopian vision of 'sisterhood' that would hold women together. Remember the 1847 'Letter from the Union of Women for Association': 'Nay, we are in truth, sisters the world around – if one suffers, all suffer, no matter [if] she tends her husband's dogs amidst the Polar snows . . .'

Notice that the writer went to the very limit of human habitation – the pole – for her example. Had she written, 'whether she tends my drawing-room fire with coals she has dragged from the scullery of my house', the metaphor of sisterhood would immediately pose problems.

The notion of sisterhood was revived in the last wave of feminism, and remains the prevailing metaphor for feminist organization. But this ultra-intimate model of female connection is wrong for the task at hand and can no longer be trusted to help women bring themselves to power. This model is intended to hold women together with the honey of personal love, intermingled with the gall of shared personal pain. But both those materials are highly 'feminine', and both are far too weak. Happily, we are too diverse, our numbers too great, and our relationships with one another, properly, too complex and impersonal now for this model to do its job.

Where did the intimate ideal of political affiliation come from? Second Wave feminist consciousness-raising groups were structured like therapy sessions. The strategy worked well, in that it allowed the women involved to view their private lives in political terms and to forge intimate bonds despite the isolation experienced by many. The consciousness-raising group still offers riches to women who need the affirmation that others' similar experiences bring. But we need other, less intimate models of affiliation too.

Female political problems that arise out of girls' understanding of affiliation as intimacy, and out of the legacy of the conscious-ness-raising group, can be seen in the crisis around the issue of diversity. This is a typical scene on college campuses: several white women sit in a circle on the floor, feeling miserable because they are all white. 'We want to be diverse in our group, but the women of colour refuse to join us.' Several women of colour sit in another building, feeling irritated: 'They want us to come and in-tegrate with them; they want us to teach them. But we're tired of having to explain ourselves all the time. We need a place of our own.'

The assumption is that everyone must join in a big circle and 'have it out', 'talk things through', and 'clear things up' before the groups can join together for specific actions.

To anti-racist white women, the impasse is a devastating re-jection, like a lover's. 'Aren't we listening?' they ask. 'Aren't we trying to address the issues?' To Black women that very artic-ulation of the problem is often annoying, for it sounds as if white women believe that their good intentions will make racism dis-appear overnight, at which point everything will be fine. White women's wish for intimacy and love from Black women often carries the implicit hope that they will be magically absolved; the 'egalitarian' assumptions of feminine intimacy seem to whitewash the inequities of race.

If we learned to substitute respect for intimacy and teamwork for sisterhood, these tensions would not paralyse women's organizational efforts to such an extent. Remembering play-ground scars, feminism is trying to be one single circle only one woman deep. It seeks to stretch itself further and further, thinner and thinner, determined to maintain personal, hand-to-hand con-tact, even among people who are not especially interested in being personal friends. With this model of the ever-expanding clique, the movement's flexibility diminishes as the circle grows ever more taut and vulnerable to any casual incursion.

A New Relation Between Women: The Power Group

The women's groups that self-destruct today do so because they are structured for consensus; because they encourage a style of speech that places at its centre the question 'What hurts?' rather than 'What can be done?'; because women think they have to like each other personally and work *through* their differences instead of working *with* them; and because women are unused to the idea that they can gather to share power and pleasure. Women tend to assume that a group must do some self-sacrificing chore rather than create resources for its own members and open up opportunities for others in a way that feels good. In its new phase, feminism must begin to utilize the only substance strong enough to forge coalitions from the diverse agendas of those who constitute the majority of the human population: mutual self-interest bolstered by impersonal respect.

A new form of social organization for women should complement the grassroots activist group and the CR group: the 'power group'. Or if that is too threatening a term, call it the 'resource group'. Women's affiliation groups have a long history; the world of white women's clubs fostered the actions that won women the vote, and Black women's clubs were active in fighting racism. Women are often nervous about the idea of consolidating power in affiliation groups because such groups suggest elitism or exclusiveness. But the fact is that women do have different agendas, backgrounds and interests. And the resource group is a way to have a comfortable community – and at the same time to develop a new psychology of power and consolidate female clout. Before I describe the power group for women it is important to recognize the way powerful men consolidate their might.

Feminists portray men's power games as fiercely competitive and individualistic. When men work together, according to these critics, their bonds are cynical and hollow because they are based on the exchange of power: 'At certain times, [men] form alliances based on well-calculated estimates of the power each has to trade. Many know and anticipate these ways of behaving and have been well trained in playing these games. Women typically are not allowed into such games. More important, many women do not desire to engage in them,' writes Jean Baker Miller.

But at the top of the social hierarchy the world of male power is remarkably collegial rather than atomistic. It is a series of clubs, both formal and informal, through which the most powerful men create a collective, closed economy of power. Places at elite universities are sought after not only because of the quality of the education, but because they informally teach the skills of creating these 'clubs' and pooling power.

At the age of 30, I can already see the men and women of my acquaintance, both sexes of whom had equal educational training and have identical professional goals, separate into two different paths that provide the men with better jobs, more money and more access to power than the women. Partly this is, of course, due to discrimination; partly it is due to the fact that the men are mentored by an old-boys' network and the women are not; but the biggest reason is that the men are pooling their power, and the women do not yet have those skills.

It is not men with power who behave, generally, in individualistic, defensively competitive ways; it is the few women with power who tend to do so, misunderstanding what is really going on in the subterranean dynamics of the culture in which they find themselves. How do men at the top behave with their power? They pass it around to their friends.

First, of course, they make connections in the 'right' schools, but then the semblance of meritocracy ends. In the world of work, men at the top of the professional hierarchy basically spend the rest of their professional lives investing power in the guys in their Filofax. They set about publishing, interviewing, photographing, hiring and recommending their friends. To the outer world – and to themselves – they then define the results as 'achievement'.

They do not hoard power; they select a group of men whom they get along with and take every possible opportunity to do them favours. (Indeed, their behaviour looks 'nurturing', 'collaborative' and 'caring' in its own weird way.) Sooner or later, the favours come home to roost. In the meantime, network members meet for lunch on their expense accounts, play squash and gossip. Much of their gossip revolves around other people in their professions, and it determines who is taken up with them and who gets left behind.

The gossip is deeply, unconsciously imbued with the view that other men are potential members of the power club, while other women are not. 'He's sound; he's good,' they'll say about a man who is 'like them'. Or: 'His stuff may be sloppy at first, but he's worth the investment of time.' But: 'She's preoccupied with her new baby.' 'She needs a lot of encouragement.' In ways so coded that they are doubtless totally invisible to the not-consciously-sexist men from whom these quotes are taken, powerful men tell each other stories about selected other men's competence and other women's inadequacy. Years of this storytelling enable them to justify to themselves the fact that when they reach the top they find themselves distributing the spoils among their closest male friends.

When women have tried to form versions of old-boys' networks, they have often felt very uncomfortable. It is alien to women to see others as a means to an end rather than an end in themselves. They feel they are using people, being insincere. They tend not to perceive how much genuine emotion men deploy in their power affiliations, how much love male mentors invest in their protégés, and what a sense of emotional fulfilment it gives powerful men to cultivate their power garden and see other men in whom they recognize aspects of themselves pool their resources as well as compete for more.

As my friend and I discussed women's difficulties with power, we decided to try a kind of feminist organization that was new to us. This became the power group. We structured it to try to avoid the psychological pitfalls women face when dealing with power and to give women a way to consolidate power that suits their psychic makeup.

A group of twenty or thirty women meets every month. These women can be from any walk of life, but they will probably have a trade, profession, religious affiliation or other major interest in common. The gathering is structured around that most frivolous of events, in victim-feminist terms: a party. The women are well fed; there is wine and music. They meet, talk, drift through the room, happy to see the women they like personally but not forced to pretend intimacy with the 'collective'. Then, at some point in the gathering, each women announces to the group what she is doing and what resources, contacts or information she has access to. She also tells the group what resources, contacts or information she needs. Every woman gets a list of the other women's numbers; anyone can contact anyone else to make a request, propose a project, exchange information or suggest a deal. Anyone can decline. Every woman can take what she needs without being compelled to follow the agenda of the almighty group.

There is currently a resurgence of women meeting in small groups. The hunger that the renewed wave of feminism has unleashed in women is being fed by book clubs, cooking clubs, salons, trade and professional groups, playgroups and church and synagogue women's groups. Any of these can easily turn into a power group as well.

The group can be opened up to new members on a circulating basis, so that other women are perpetually being entered in the 'resource Filofax', the circle always has fresh resources coming in, and access moving out to others. The group asks its members to tell them when they have had a victory, or gained something from the affiliation. This news bolsters everyone's sense of effectiveness, and gives women practice in recounting their own triumphs and sharing in other women's. The group should see as part of its mission providing psychological support to women as they ask for more money. It can – and must, I believe, for the sake of its psychological health – mentor younger women, distributing their job applications or CVs. It can take united action about issues in the trade or profession in which the women work (including the professions of childrearing and homemaking). It can invite speakers. It can collect dues and send them to a larger women's political organization. For its own sense of effectiveness and to bolster women's status overall, the group should 'give back' some money or services to the larger movement for women's rights.

It should be made clear to everyone that dissent and differences of opinion are welcome, and that it is a pleasure to disagree as well as to agree. For economic health, and to get women used to discussing money, forming an investment club, even if the amount of stock is minuscule, is a good idea. Since such groups are obviously going to pool more resources among women of higher socio-economic classes, groups of women who are middle class and above should mentor talented young women who lack the resources they have, and give back a portion of the resources the group generates to organizations that support economic empowerment.

This sounds simple – too simple, perhaps. But in our own limited, mostly middle-class experience, such a group has generated power in ways unimaginable to us if we were all acting alone.

Most people have access to goods, services or information that are not useful to us at the moment, but may be of critical importance to someone else. Women in our resource group have found jobs, houses and freelance work; swapped services, compared salaries, or informed each other of the going salary for a certain position; sought investors, assigned stories, held a benefit, and started a programme in which women go to schools to talk to girls about their jobs. Much of the new access we generated was a result of the fact that the group was disproportionately middle class and even more privileged. But such a group can enlarge its members' access at many points on the socio-economic scale.

For women usually lack money, but they often have access to one thing that is increasingly valuable in today's economy: information. Men swap information like football cards and men can discriminate against women in part because they are able to assume that women are bereft of either contacts or steady sources of information outside the domestic hearth. But when women join together in power groups, no man who might wish to discriminate will know exactly what information or which connections the woman he is dealing with may have at her fingertips.

While it is still in infancy, the power group solves many of the psychological problems women have about getting and using power. It makes feminism fun. It makes feminism lucrative. The structure of the gathering itself forces women to claim their power, recount their skills and resources, and focus on what is possible rather than what is oppressive. 'Troubles talk' is not forbidden, but it is not the main point. 'Possibility talk' is; and the shift in discourse actually seems to change the way women behave in groups. At first, even the most powerful women in our group had trouble with sentences describing 'This is what I do; this is what I have.' Soon that recounting of one's power became matter-of-fact and even enjoyable, as did listening to other women present their access, resources and skills.

The power group expands every woman's network (to use a term I detest) by a factor of thirty or more. It creates community, so that women do not feel they are using one another heartlessly and avariciously. It creates new friendships for their own sake. It eases women's anxieties about seeking power, because members are also able to contribute to the community. It makes women happy about other women's achievements: other women's increased access goes right on to the table. It makes women feel far more powerful because of the way it directs their gaze. At every point in the economic ladder, women can feel insecure because there is a man above them whose power over them is often total. But when women join laterally with the power of other women, and look downwards at young women just struggling to begin their journey, they recognize considerably more strength in their position. Finally, the power group changes women's view of other women, who now become resources and repositories of power, just as men are, and who are not threatening competitors (or sentimentalized 'sisters') so much as comrades in strategy.

If women form such groups up and down the spectrum, this will create fairly effortlessly an alternative power structure that can match the traditional male one, if not in resources then in numbers. And it will allow young women to forge ahead knowing that they will not necessarily have to hide their voices to gain access.

We must replace the sentimentalized model of sisterhood with a pragmatic model of affiliation. Immigrants in all countries affiliate because it is in the individual's own best interests to do so as well as the community's. The element of altruism in immigrant associations comes from a sense of honour and responsibility for one's cultural and social heritage, rather than being dependent solely upon some 'natural' maternal bond, or burdensome bond of victimization.

Such a model would heal some of the rifts in feminism that have opened along class lines. Immigrants do not believe that all must be at the same economic level in order to work together; they pool and pass on resources because all seek to raise their status and multiply their access. They do not expect to believe the same things; they merely expect each other to honour the basic social contract of giving back to community organizations. And they are not separatist, but intent on raising the status of the group *within* the life of the larger society.

In the immigrant model of the power group, feminism is not self-sacrifice; it incorporates self-interest too. Women's needs for connection and independence are served equally. Women forge allegiances because they get more money and better choices and because they are paying dues to earlier women whose work made their lives possible, and levelling the field for younger women. Like any immigrant group, they can take pride in their own qualities and heritage; this group feeds the hunger for community without smothering women in consensus. Historically, this model has proven to be the strongest, up and down the socio-economic scale and across racial and ethnic divisions.

The less intimate immigrant model of feminism – based on pragmatism, mutual self-interest, idealism and respect, rather than on 'troubles talk', love and shared victimization – lets us avoid the sense of total personal betrayal that is built into the CR group 'sisterhood' model. If you have a clear social contract with another woman or group of women, you have only one area in which to feel let down if they disagree with you or don't live up to the commitment in question. The connection of respect, which honours conflict, is more flexible than the connection of supportive love alone.

By reinventing the tried-and-tested club system, and adding money-making and access-pooling to political action, the heavenly, treacherous playground circle of sisterhood can become a mesh of fluid, distinctive, interlocking circles. Each circle of women of diverse or shared backgrounds, professions, ethnicities and interests can strengthen the others, forming a network of female power that can cover the world.

Chapter Eighteen

What We Can Do Now

You are not responsible for being down.
You are responsible for getting up.
— Reverend Jesse Jackson

Obviously, it's going to take a lot more than building an alternative female power structure to turn the corner into female equality. But we have seen what works and what is not working for women, and we can see ahead to ways in which women's power can be built up to transform the twenty-first century. What works best for most women is heavy on results and flexible in its ideology.

Visions of Power Feminism: Success Stories

It's ironic that as Marxist feminists scorn using capitalism at home, Third World women are rushing, when they can, into small business enterprises. A majority of the world's poor women are 'farmers, producers and traders and when development organizations seed their small businesses, they welcome investment over direct aid. We must start to make business more directly the business of feminism.

When women use money to invest in other women's independence, power feminism takes root. Women's World Banking (WWB) is an international group of women bankers who realized, after the 1975 UN conference on the status of women, that discrimination against women worldwide was perpetuated by their exclusion from the economic mainstream. WWB raised almost

$6 million to help female entrepreneurs get low-interest loans, 25 per cent of which the organization guarantees; it developed a management training institute to teach women how to establish small businesses, conduct international trade and raise funds.

WWB made almost 45,000 loans in ten years, and 99 per cent were repaid, a better rate than that of most high street banks who are conducting their business in developing countries. The local affiliates who make the loans are women from the same culture, with the skills to train the fledgling businesswomen in everything from bookkeeping to marketing. The programme has become a training ground for poor women to control their own economic life and has provided a global network for women entrepreneurs.

Even given all of capitalism's injustices, pending 'the revolution', women are better off with the means of production in their own hands. We need to bring those international lessons home. Women's businesses can be the power cells of the twenty-first century. In the UK, three out of ten firms are started by a woman and the growth of women entering self-employment is as fast: women now account for one in four of all self-employed. In Australia 24 per cent of small-business managers are women and, on average, women who start their own businesses are five years younger than their male counterparts. There are 600 women's business organizations in America, according to Wendy Reid Crisp, director of the National Association for Female Executives (NAFE). These range from women in film to women in construction. In a 1989 interview Hillary Rodham Clinton pointed out the distinction between NAFE and 'the organized women's movement'. The association's focus is on practical solutions, not rhetoric, she emphasized, and men are often included in gatherings. 'Who wants to walk around,' Hillary Rodham Clinton asked, 'with clenched fists all the time?'

Just as Emily's List's success should be only a harbinger of the future might of women's political action committees, so a business association's current membership should be seen as a tiny fraction of what it will be – as a pointer to the future.

When women have money, the opposition has no choice but to listen. When they have equity, they have influence – as sponsors, shareholders and alumnae. The status quo is not subtle. The only language it understands is that of money, votes and public embarrassment.

We Need More Flexible Actions

The left-wing insight that *everything* is ideologically driven is true. But power feminism keeps autonomy in women's own hands by focusing on winning those 'power units' that are as unmarked by stringent ideology as possible. Basic 'power units' are, of course, money, health, opportunity, education, representation and safety. On the populist level, power feminism tries to steer clear of dictating what women must do with that opportunity, that money, that representation in government. A great populist success story of the genderquake in the United States was seen in the Breast Cancer Drive of 1992, in which the National Breast Cancer Coalition (NBCC) used a broad-based appeal, with the theme of 'Better Health Care for Women', to win all of its 1992 legislative objectives. In October 1991 it launched a massive 'Do the Write Thing' letter-writing campaign to Congress. It aimed for 175,000 letters to be sent from fifty states, or one letter for each breast cancer diagnosis. The grassroots appeal of an issue that transcends 'right on' feminist ideology was proven by the 600,000 letters that were delivered to the Hill, exceeding all expectations.

In February 1992 the NBCC Research Task Force held hearings, open to the public and the media. In March 1992 NBCC told Congress that it would take $300 million to jump-start the search for a cure. To raise awareness, in May 1992 NBCC coordinated thirty-eight Mother's-Day-related events in thirty-one states; the events were covered in more than thirty national publications and broadcasts, on national TV, and by many local news outlets. When President Bush vetoed the bill authorizing the National Institute of Health to spend the money, NBCC demanded in response 1 per cent of the research and development portion of the defence budget. Angry women came to Washington in busloads, used the NBCC hotline, and faxed and phoned their representatives. When it looked as if the goals would be overturned at the last minute, NBCC maintained a round-the-clock vigil outside the committee room.

These methods paid off. The NBCC won more funding: more than double its $132 million 1991 appropriation and more than triple the $90 million appropriation of the year before. It won the Cancer Registries Act of 1992 and the Mammography Quality Assurance Bill that provide better research and treatment methods. It won, in short, everything it had asked for. Women flexed their political muscles and could not be denied.

Another success story was also totally inclusive. In April 1993 the Ms. Foundation sponsored Take Our Daughters to Work Day. The idea was to instil strong ambitions in girls and to raise their self-esteem by taking them into their parents' workplaces. The day was a runaway success, attracting more positive media attention than any feminist project since the Second Wave began. A million parents and childminders participated.

The day is a perfect example of flexible power feminism. It positioned no one as a victim. It appealed to Republicans and Democrats, the religious and the secular, men and women, urban and rural. Self-confidence is a unit of potential power for each woman to translate into her own goals, and young girls are, themselves, units of potential power. The appeal to adults was that the day let them stress their own strength and competence to inspire young girls; it cast mothers as role models rather than as the downtrodden; it cast fathers as respected participants in childrearing. Everyone loved it.

The lesson? On the populist level, focus on generating for women units of potential, rather than ideologically rigid agendas; focus on more space in the media, more confidence, more time, with few ideological strings attached. All these translate into more independence for women, and greater feminist clout across the board.

What Women Have and How We Can Use It

Anna Quindlen once wrote about women's status as a glass that is either half full or half empty. Let us look at the resources women have already to see why half full is enough to begin to get us all the way.

Women Have Electoral Power.

While few women have money, all women have a vote. In America the number of women in state legislatures has risen from 424 in 1973 to 1,516 in 1993; 16.9 per cent of state senators are female, as are 21.7 per cent of state representatives. In 1992, 2,373 women ran for state legislatures and 1,373 won. If large numbers of women contribute even small sums of money to organizations like Emily's List or the 300 Group, they will vastly magnify their voice.

Despite the fact that American women earn an average of 68 cents for every male dollar, British women earn 74p for every male pound and Australian women earn only 85 per cent of a man's salary, a stratum of women are not quite so poor any longer. According to the 1991 census, there are now 2.339 million women in America with personal incomes above $50,000 a year. That is a vast change.

According to US census data, there has been, in upper echelons of the job market, 'rapid progress for women of all races'. More women now work as managers and professionals than as clerks or administrators. Seven per cent of Hispanic women, 7.4 per cent of Black women, and 11.9 per cent of white women are now executives or managers (this last figure is up 7.7 per cent since 1980). The membership of the National Association of Black Women Attorneys has risen from fewer than 1,000 in 1972 to 17,000 today. The shift of women into higher-paid fields helped narrow the gender wage gap.

But having wealth has not yet led women to use their wealth. American women with household incomes of less than $10,000 gave away an average of 5.4 per cent of their income in 1989, compared with the 1 per cent donated by women with incomes between $40,000 and $49,000.

To make political contributions a normal part of life for every woman who can afford it, a new view of money is critical. Fundraisers have found that men and women given money for different reasons: men give to see their name on a plaque, or to compete with other men; women want to know the context in which the money is spent.

Emily's List brings their larger donors together and gives a list of the women to each participant. Campaigns, women's organizations and alumnae funds can recreate the psychic comfort of the power group by holding gatherings at which local donors, of whatever amounts, not only meet the candidates (or whoever benefits from their contributions), but are also encouraged to approach one another to exchange resources and information. This way, the organizations make money; a power base for women is consolidated with each drive; and when women give – an act that elicits in many fears of poverty and insecurity – they get something tangible in return. Giving becomes a good investment. Some will say that my interest here in women with money is elitist. But why should battered women not have first-rate legal counsel? If a shabby rape crisis centre is good, isn't a multitude of palatial ones even better?

Women Have the Power of Cross-Targeting.
There is a story about heaven told in Christian retreats. A group of people who cannot bend their arms are sitting at a table heaped with bounty. They cannot feed themselves; this constitutes hell. In the second scene, similar people sit at a similar table with a similar inability to bend their arms; but they are feeding one another. This, of course, is heaven.

The allegory has a lesson: women often have trouble fighting on their own behalf, but are fearless warriors on behalf of children, communities, spouses or the environment. They also can be punished economically for fighting for their own rights.

One approach to this problem, suggested by the scene above, is what I call cross-targeting. In cross-targeting, women or groups of women make deals to do for each other whatever it is that would get them sacked – or terrify them – if they had to do it for themselves. Are women in the police force unable to make a noise about the lack of protection against sexual harassment? Their power group can tip off a power group of secretarial staff who can yell and scream about it. Then the police women owe the secretaries some use of their own access or courage. Do women nurses at a given hospital need childcare? Women patients' groups can agitate on their behalf. Are women professors being denied tenure? Women students' power groups can lobby university chancellors to force action. Does one airline have unfair weight restrictions for flight attendants? Power groups from another airline can tip off the press.

These cross-targeted 'favours' enable women to engage in activism that is far less frightening than anything they have to do on their own turf. And they indicate to the opposition that one cannot treat a woman too lightly, since one never knows who she might have fighting on her behalf.

Women Have Power as Consumers.
British women spend 70 per cent of the consumer pound; American women spend 85 per cent of the consumer dollar. Reader pressure can force advertisers of fashions, cosmetics and other goods whose sales depend on women's goodwill to give something back to women's political empowerment and to the image of feminism itself.

Advertisers are currently courting women's goodwill with programmes to fight breast cancer, or to subsidize measures against violence. We don't have to pretend their motives are pure in order to use this trend to our advantage. If women realize their true consumer power and see that the advertiser–consumer relationship, like the media–consumer relationship, is actually dictated by the mobilized consumer, they can treat these efforts as a drop in the ocean.

There are dozens of untapped ways for women to use that consumer clout to advance their political and economic interests. One way is for readers to compel advertisers and women's media to improve the image of feminism. (*Cosmo*, ahead of the pack, is already pursuing this aim in its own way. In June 1993, That Cosmo Girl finally stood up and declared, 'Am I a feminist? Yes.')

Women's organizations are the only large lobbying groups that lack a sustained media effort; even the Catholic Church has its PR people. A third wave of power feminism must base itself on the premiss that, at the end of the twentieth century – at least in the First World – populations are not controlled mainly by laws and militias, but by images and attitudes.

The gay and lesbian movement has just committed half a

million dollars to a year-long effort to educate the public and change prejudiced attitudes about homosexuality. Feminism needs a similar all-out PR effort. Since other manufacturers have run effective ad campaigns by using feminism, why not run an effective campaign for feminism by using feminism?

Readers of women's magazines can be mobilized to claim the women's press. Readers can ask for an expensive, beautifully produced, colourful series of advertisements in which all kinds of women – housewives and students, models and teachers, celebrities and scientists – 'come out' as feminists. They can press women's magazines to 'give back' by running the ads that they think best suit their readers. The campaign can feature a 'What Feminism Means to Me' theme, designed to present the idea that feminism includes any woman or man standing up in any way for women's rights. If readers press for this, they will find that they have sympathizers at the top. Though they can't say it directly, many of the women who run the women's magazines are feminists, eager for their readers to demand more serious coverage of women's issues and more direct advocacy than their advertisers now allow them to offer.

The images should show people of all races and backgrounds: a housewife, perhaps, saying: 'The right to cash a cheque. Drive a car. Vote for my MP. That's what feminism is to me.' A grandmother: 'My granddaughter's degree in dentistry. That's what feminism means to me.' A single working mother: 'The right to take out a loan in my own name. That's what feminism means to me.' A teenager wearing street fashions: 'The right to wear what I want without asking for it.' A lesbian couple: 'The right to love whom I want.' An attorney: 'Custody laws that are fair.' A factory worker: 'The right not to have to choose between my kids and my job.' A clerical worker: 'Decent research on breast cancer that improves my prognosis.' A college student: 'Doing something about date rape.' A mother with a little girl: 'Making certain she can stay as sure of herself when she's a teenager as she is now.' Individual prominent women could contribute their images to the campaign. Jodie Foster: 'The director's chair instead of the casting couch.' Then, beneath the image, a text something like this: 'The rights to vote, drive a car, get an education, have a job, plan a family, get decent health care, have a say: you weren't born with them. All of these were brought to you by the Feminist Movement. Feminism is real democracy. If you value those things, pass them on. Call yourself a feminist, speak up when you are put down, vote for rights for women, and give to women's organizations.'

This ad campaign – an idea that I can already hear some feminists ridicule because it is simple, direct and, to them, obvious – will help break the stalemate. *It must establish that feminism is anti-sexist and not anti-male*. It will redefine the word to encompass the many feminisms which most women already cherish in their own lives. A standard of beauty is set when enough images of a particular kind are presented as beautiful and seen by enough people to become instantly recognizable. That's why offering many different images of beauty opens up one's chances to iden tify oneself as beautiful. By the same token, a barrage of positive, *diverse* images of feminism will allow women not only to recognize themselves, in one if not in all, but will reassure them that if they can say, 'I'm a feminist', enough people will have seen the series to guarantee that the word's connotations have become more inclusive.

Women Have Power as Readers and Viewers.
When I claim that the advertisers and media that appear to dictate so authoritatively to women are actually their servants, and significantly under their control, the numbers bear me out. Advertisers want 25–40-year-old women's good opinion more than they do that of any other demographic group. Women have such tremendous power as consumers that when a woman writes a letter to a magazine – objecting, for example, to an advertisement, or a sexist feature – that letter is counted as representing thousands of readers, according to the editor of one woman's magazine. And a disproportionate number of the readers whom the media are trying to woo are women.

The reclamation of the women's press is important, but a campaign to take proportionate space in the media generally is crucial to women's turning the corner into power. A readers' rights movement can take many actions to force general coverage of the world of women.

Such a movement can erect a neon-lit noticeboard in Piccadilly Circus or over Times Square, so that major newspapers' and magazines' 'scores' in coverage of women and inclusion of women's bylines can be broadcast for all to see.

It can also organize an electronic 'zap' system. Readers can log on – for a monthly fee – to add their names to inundate media outlets. Callers can dial a number to respond to specific portrayals of women in the news or treatments of women's issues. A weekly breakdown of their comments can be released to the media in question. At the same price per minute as recorded horoscopes, the system would soon pay for itself. And women would have a satisfying way to talk back effectively to the TV and newspapers – something they do often now anyway, in private, to little effect.

When a national newspaper persists in relegating women to a tiny minority of those quoted, the readers' rights campaign can inundate it with cards and faxes, not a tiny minority asking for a certain view, but for more space for debate. The newspaper or magazine should be told that an outraged letter is going to its advertisers, explaining that the reader will not purchase their products if the gender bias – resulting in censorship – persists.

Women Have the Power to Create Awards, Recognition and History.

The toxic relationship to power that comes from being deprived of recognition is healed when women take the creation of kudos into their own hands. *Time* magazine overlooks a Woman of the Year? *Glamour* has created a popular award to honour many. In the UK, Women in Publishing present an annual award to women achievers in the industry; the Fawcett Society, named after the suffrage campaigner Millicent Garrett Fawcett, annually hosts the only women's book award in Britain; Women in Film held their first awards ceremony in 1991, awarding prizes to writer Lynda La Plante and producer Verity Lambert, amongst others; the biennial television award, the Prix Niki, rewards producers of programmes that provide new insight into the position of women in Europe. If the opposition will not let women into the economy of acclaim, we must make one ourselves.

Awards breed recognition, and recognition inspires achievement. In Portland, Oregon, the friends of a woman artist who was killed in a mountain-climbing accident endowed a prize to recognize young artists, particularly but not exclusively women, in her name. The $2,000 award is less valuable than the courage and renewed energy that the recognition bestows.

I asked the first recipient of the award, Christine Bourdette, what it meant to her to win the prize. 'It does a lot for your self-esteem. The money you spend, but the recognition you keep in here,' she said, hitting her heart lightly. 'The fact that it's going to go on and benefit other people – it's being part of a continuum. A curator had asked me, "How do you think history will treat you?" And I thought, "What a male thing to be worrying about!" But now I think' – and she laughed gleefully – 'maybe not.'

Did Bourdette think that making and giving recognition was important to the female psyche? The award, she replied, 'is a very ennobling thing – feeling like you've been singled out for honour and respect. This will be kind of like a torch passing . . . but it's like an inclusion. The community saying, "We embrace you, we take you to heart, and don't you forget it."' Recognition – prizes, awards, honours – costs nothing to generate. Women without a lot of money can give formalized public credit to those they honour, in a way that inspires the givers as well.

Women Have the Power of Their Charity Donations.
Women give to charity more than men do. According to the Charities Aid Foundation, women give a little over half of the charity pound, though they make proportionately less than men. Though American women also give more of their income than men, women's and girls' programmes get less than 5 per cent of the total kitty.

In 1990, according to the Fund for the Feminist Majority report, the United Way charities organization gave the YMCA $39 million more than it gave the YWCA. The Boy Scouts got $32 million more than the Girl Scouts. Of $3.25 billion in a sample of 1990 foundation grants, only 5 per cent went to programmes specifically aimed at girls and women. Of grants to women, only 4 per cent went to women of colour, who are three times more likely to be poor than white women are. Even organizations that are funded as gender-neutral give the lion's share of the money to benefit boys: in the Big Brother/Big Sister programme, 75 per cent of the children served were boys; 70 per cent of the young people served by the Boys and Girls' Clubs are boys. Though domestic violence is the number-one crime in America, the United Way earmarks only 0.5 per cent of its budget for shelters. In America, as in Britain, there are five times more shelters for abused animals than there are for women.

Since it is unquestioned that women give, the best we can do is specify what our giving is to be used for – even though we know that, if we earmark our pathetic little £20 it is a drop in the ocean and we never see the result of what we've done.

But turn the problem on its head. What happens when you dare to withhold the giving until you get something back? When women never think of withholding, society takes their giving for granted.

Giving separately makes every woman a fraction as potent and visible as her gift could make her if united with others'. What if we put all our charitable donations in a savings account for a year? Women could specify that organizations could get the money when they prove parity in giving. This arrangement gives women total control of their giving, and a part in an exhilarating demonstration of great force – their own – used for good ends. All donors could be kept posted via a special telephone number, with information updated daily, to add momentum and excitement.

With half their revenue potentially taken away from them, charities would have to adapt within the year, or else collapse. In one year, without having to win one more election or company position, without costing themselves a penny more than they already spend, women would multiply the resources available to them – shelters, health-care research, antenatal care, training programmes.

Women Have the Power to Make Scenes.
Public embarrassment is a mighty motivator. Most women, regardless of their income, can reveal the abusive behaviour of those who do not have physical or financial control over them. The

more we 'tell' – within the limits of honesty and fairness – the safer we are. And the power of 'telling' turns liabilities – secrets we were forced to keep – into assets – secrets we can expose.

Women Have the Power of Technology.
Women have not yet begun to tap the power of information systems to serve their political ends. A sexual-harassment computer link can be set up to record when a number of separately entered cases at a given institution all involve the same offender. The system could alert an independent watchdog.

Another cheap and easy use of technology would be to link up a national computerized mentor–protégée database, where women can enter their C.V.s in their respective fields. The price for using the database is that if you move up the career or trade ladder, you in turn have to mentor a younger woman.

Women Have the Power to Publicize Their Self-defence Skills.
Every woman is left to walk the front line of violence alone. Feminism's best efforts have centred on recovery – rape crisis centres, education of the judiciary and police. Being the nurturers of the injured is a familiar role.

But why not be proactive? What is keeping us from selecting a hundred women from every county, taking them on a two-week course in effective self-defence, and then publicizing the fact widely? Our cities and towns can be plastered with announcements that read, 'A hundred women in this town are trained in combat. They may be nurses, students, housewives, prostitutes, mothers. The next woman to be assaulted might be one of these.' Indeed, what keeps us from putting up those posters *without* doing the training?

Women Have the Power of Existing Networks.
Instead of trying to bring women to feminist culture, feminism should go to women's culture. Girl Guides, PTAs, religious organizations – even diet centres, health clubs and freelance cosmetics-sales companies – are places where women congregate and organize. Women's centres have started to offer anti-date-rape education, and health clubs have sponsored anti-breast-cancer

drives. This can be just the beginning. All of these organizations can be pressed by their members to add pro-girl and pro-woman political and economic projects to their list of activities. This lets feminism arise naturally out of the beliefs or interests of an organization already in place, rather than trying to build an organization out of an ideology to which everyone must be converted.

Women Students Have the Power to Control Their Tuition Payments.

Financial activism would be instantly effective in American universities and increasingly effective in British universities where fee-based courses are more and more common. Universities do not pursue women's issues with much concern because they are making a calculated guess that women will be less affluent graduate donors than men throughout their lives. But if graduates put their contributions in a bank account, promising that the money will be released when the college grants women professors tenure at the same rate as men, achieves parity in admissions for women students and installs a decent sexual-assault grievance procedure, the administration would jump. I have seen more than one college president turn pale at the mere suggestion of such a tactic.

Between 1975 and 1988 the proportion of women studying in British universities increased from 35 to 42 per cent, and yet in 1993 only 21 per cent of the faculty was female. There are even fewer women professors: 5 per cent nationwide and 3 per cent at Oxford and Cambridge. Most of the women, nearly a third of all academics, are on the basic lecturing grade. Moreover, the effect of opening former men's and women's colleges at Oxford and Cambridge to both sexes has meant that men have been appointed to tenured posts in the former women's colleges while hardly any women have gained tenured posts in former men's colleges. And in traditionally 'male' subjects, the men reign supreme: across a range of scientific and technological subjects in the UK in 1990, 99 per cent of professors, 97 per cent of senior lecturers and 92 per cent of lecturers were men. In Australia, women make up 12 per cent of the Royal Australian College of Obstetricians and Gynaecologists but 41 per cent of medical students.

When the issue of promotion arises the figures are equally insidious: in the fields of medicine and dentistry in 1990, women received 18 per cent of the promotions but comprised 37 per cent of lecturers; in language and literature studies women made up 27 per cent of lecturers but received only 16 per cent of promotions. 1993 figures released from an AUT study of eleven British universities showed that women professors were paid at least £1,500 per year less than men. The salaries of nearly half of all women professors fell into the lowest band, whereas this was the level for only 20 per cent of men. Over 25 per cent of male professors earned more than £38,000, compared with just 7 per cent of women.

By March 1991, 10.707 million American women had completed four years of college. That year, there were 7.752 million female full-time and part-time undergraduates, which is a whopping 1.347 million more than the 6.405 million male undergraduates. But though female undergraduates outnumber male, women get less financial aid at both undergraduate and graduate levels, according to the Association of American Colleges. And according to a US Department of Education study, women students receive 73 cents in grants, to every grant dollar men receive; and 84 cents in loans, to every loan dollar.

Such financial activism by female students should shake up the status quo and get undergraduate women and women faculty members the respect they deserve. If there is a rape cover-up on campus, mobilize parents to threaten to withhold contributions in the future. It is an easy threat to make, and an impossible one to ignore. Parents are paying sums far beyond their means to get their daughters educated; if they are shown a campus without mentors, leadership training or safety for girls, they will realize that their daughters are not getting their money's worth and their consumer outrage will move hidebound trustees.

These are only a few suggestions to show just how much clout women have when we approach change through power feminism rather than through victim feminism. This approach is not new, and the examples are just a beginning; but they demonstrate how women will win their rightful place when they change their image of themselves and focus not on being good, or being hurt, or begging for justice, but on consolidating the clout that lets them dictate the terms of their lives.

Psychological Strategies

As we put power feminism into action, we must revise our day-to-day dealings with one another. Power feminism cannot work until we try to make changes in the way we treat ourselves and others. Let us:

- Avoid generalizations about men that imply that their maleness is the unchangeable source of the problem;
- Avoid generalizations about men that do not admit to exceptions;
- Never choose to widen the rift between the sexes when we can narrow it without censoring the truth;
- Never unreflectingly judge men in a way that we would consider sexist if men applied it to women; let us be able to explain why inequality makes the situation different, if it does;
- Distinguish between the men we love, who are on our side, and the male system of power, which we must resist. It is not 'hating men' to fight sexism. But the fight against sexism must not lead to hating men;
- Resist the idea that sexual orientation is fixed and categorical, or that any one woman's sexual choices are more legitimate than any other's;
- Resist the notion that there are any fixed truths or right answers about feminism, or that any one woman's way of sticking up for women is divinely better than any other woman's;
- Practise evaluating our participation in a pro-woman effort on the basis of the goal in question rather than on the basis of whether we like the people involved and 'identify' with them personally;
- Distinguish between the right to have an opinion about a woman's choices and the right to judge her;
- Challenge ourselves when we engage in 'women's talk' that

involves putting ourselves down or joining on the basis of inadequacies;

- Make it socially acceptable for women to discuss their skills and achievements;
- Urge women to 'come out' about the financial details of their lives and make it socially acceptable to discuss money;
- Remember and take possession of the girlhood will to power and fantasies of grandeur;
- Challenge the impulse to shy away from acknowledging the power, or admitting to the leadership skills, that we possess;
- Practise asking for more money, and urge our friends to do so;
- Examine our financial behaviour, and question the sense women often have that money is polluting or masculinizing;
- Institute courses in schools so that girls of all backgrounds know how to debate, fund-raise, call a press conference, run a campaign, read contracts, negotiate leases and salaries and manage a share portfolio;
- If we are older, investigate our fear of younger women 'taking too much' or 'having it too easy'; if we are younger, pay due respect to the women who paved our way;
- Challenge our reflexive unease at the sight of another woman with 'too much'; question the ritual in which we join with other women in putting down achievers or leaders;
- Claim our dark side and take responsibility for it. Acknowledge that impulses towards aggression, retaliation, dominance and cruelty are innate to women as they are to men;
- Abandon the double standard that women as well as men impose on female political leaders;
- Give our daughters room for the 'bad girl' to survive;
- Welcome dissent and differences of opinion among women; foster debate; create rituals – the equivalent of men's handshakes – in which women in conflict with one another express not conciliation but mutual respect;
- Visualize having the power we seek; then imagine the very worst thing that will happen if we attain it. Does it destroy us? Or do we survive, and even have a good time?

- Distinguish personal emotional connections that must be preserved from situations in which business, politics or simple justice means that a connection may be disrupted or renegotiated;
- Create private pantheons – in our minds or even in a scrapbook or on a notice board – of women, real or mythical, who braved dissent, created controversy, showed leadership and wielded power. History books and biographies are helpful because they show that our demands for power are not so unheard-of, or even so pioneering;
- Abandon the notion that the fight for equality has to be gloomy; take every opportunity to make it playful, witty, sexy and fun.

The Bad Girl's Route to Equality

In most women the original power feminist, with her brazen will intact, is not lost, but only lightly sleeping. She exists in almost every woman, no matter how ambivalent that woman is consciously about the use of power.

Current theories that encourage adults to remember and nurture their 'inner child' see the inner child as a helpful therapeutic presence for survivors of abuse. The inner child is good and does not deserve the abuse she has suffered. The adult's relationship to the inner child is one of compassion.

But this 'innocent victim' inner child must be joined by her mischievous, boisterous, unregenerate twin, the inner *bad girl* lurking in the female psyche, who has a very different set of qualities.

Think back, back before you were hanging out in groups of girls saying 'Let's play mummies and daddies!' and taking turns playing skipping games. Just behind that leaping, verbal creature so practised at weaving in and out of others in a pattern is an anterior being whose energy could never have been fitted into civilized play without a struggle.

She is between eighteen months and five years old. Sparks come off her; she cannot keep still. She turns objects upside down, she revels in the mess, her hair is electric. When she eats, she is dissolved in the pleasure, she wants her appetite to go on for ever; when she sees a sparkling surface, she grabs at it and pulls. When she does not want to move forwards, she digs her heels into the floor and crouches down, instinctively using her centre of gravity to achieve her will. When she is tired, she lies face down on the cool floor. When those who should not do so try to pick her up in their arms, she wriggles like a snake and screams like a banshee, and uses her feet and hands to break their hold. When an older child tries to take away something that belongs to her, she clutches the toy tighter and hunches over it, or howls or runs. She can gaze at her hands or feet or little body in the mirror for a long time, since the miracle of her being herself and not anything else is so new and complete. Every time she waves her hands, or slaps her palms against the surface of water, she gets the thrill of that self being separate, not-mother, not-father. When a parent tries to spoon up food for her she snatches the utensil away, for she would rather do something poorly all by herself than have someone else do it well.

As soon as she can talk, she can talk back. 'Mine' is part of being two. 'You can't make me' begins at about three. By five, she is telling authority figures, 'You can't tell me what to do.' When she piles up sand she is queen of the mountain, because she has moved a mountain.

Every molecule of the child seeks every pleasure. She is sensuous, grasping, self-absorbed, fierce, greedy, megalomaniacal, and utterly certain that she is entitled to have her ego, her power and her way. For the few years between her first consciousness and the curtailment of all her badness, her dreams are more vivid and her world more saturated with passion, apparitions and ecstasy than it will ever be again. She has no manners. She is a very naughty girl.

And she in all her badness is the other, unacknowledged side of female consciousness. At her worst she is narcissistic and destructive; at her best, she is the force of creativity, rebellion against injustice, and primal self-respect. If we are trying to grow strong at all, we will spend the rest of our lives trying to find her again, even as we think we spend our lives trying to bury her. Whenever there is a moment in sex or danger or fantasy when we are swung too high and pushed up through the lace nets of our niceness, we almost reach her, almost place a sliding foot on home – a savage, unrecognizable, familiar place we did not know we had lost, even as we lose it again on the downswing.

Now imagine that you can reach her when you need to. Imagine that you can lay claim to the force of her desire, to her sky-high self-regard, when you are fighting for your rights, negotiating about sex or housework, or putting a price on your work. Amplify her wishes to adult scope: the respect she wanted on the playground, and in her fantasies of recognition, you want from government. Do not call it 'masculine', that will to power in yourself, that desire to transform the world and be *seen*. That drive is *in* us. It always was. Use it to cross over this historic threshold.

Historians agree that just after the American War of Independence, the Civil War and World War I women failed to take advantage of what they called 'the open moment'. This is another open moment.

Whatever feminism is to you, to me it is at heart the logical extension of democracy. Power feminism's use of *realpolitik* and capitalism for the next stage of women's empowerment is not selfish, not 'selling out', not imitating men, not settling for a less radical position. Nothing is more radical than going to the roots of power.

If we continue to distrust the power of our imaginations, our money and our words, we hand over victory to those who want the majority to remain silent. By dint of sheer numbers and a handful of change, women have already begun to win. Are we psychologically prepared to see this potential for victory in our lifetime? Will we take up the responsibility to contribute the hidden perspectives of women to the policies of the twenty-first century, which will sorely need them in order to ensure the wellbeing of everyone, male as well as female?

We have reached a moment at which sexual inequality, which we think of as the texture and taste of femininity itself, can begin to become a quaint memory of the old country – if we are not too attached to it to let it go.

A hundred and forty years ago Charlotte Woodward, a factory worker, wrote of her time: 'I do not believe that there was any community anywhere in which the souls of women were not beating their wings in rebellion.' Those words are true once more. Yes, we can wait another 140 years for the next open moment to come and go.

Or we can ask: if not now, then truly, when?

Notes

Introduction

PAGE

xv   **Sexual harassment:** *Guardian*, 12 February 1993.

xv   **'Policewomen had experienced sexual harassment':** Duncan Campbell, 'Nine in 10 Policewomen harassed', *Guardian*, 12 February 1993.

xv   **Prejudice against women:** *Sydney Morning Herald*. 4, 14 and 19 May 1993.

Part 1: The Decline of the Masculine Empire: Anita Hill and the Genderquake

4   **'Credentials or credibility':** Timothy M. Phelps and Helen Winternitz, *Capitol Games: The Inside Story of Clarence Thomas, Anita Hill and a Supreme Court Nomination* (New York: HarperCollins, 1992), p. 221.

5   **'Right on':** ibid., p. 264.

6   **'Than the women candidates':** ibid., p. 422.

6   **The explanation:** transcript of the *Today* show, 14 July 1992, p. 35.

9   **46 per cent to 41 per cent:** 'National Election Final' The Gallup Organization, National Election Study and CNN/*USA Today* Gallup poll, 30 October, New York, p.6.

9   **Women were 54 per cent of the voting public:** The Fund for the Feminist Majority Report, "Women Crack Political Glass Ceiling". Vol. 4, No. 4 (Arlington, VA: December 1992), p. 1.

9   **Abortion, Social Issues:** David G. Broder, 'Lasting Effects of Perot, Religious Right Debated, *Washington Post*, 6 September 1993, p. 6. Citing Susan E. Howell of the University of New Orleans, who found that "the [abortion] issue jumped in importance and became attached to the definition of both conservatism and Republicanism – to the detriment of the GOP, at least in 1992". According to David C. Leege of the University of Notre Dame and Lyman A. Kellstedt of Wheaton College, John C. Green of the University of Akron, and Corwin E. Schmidt of Calvin College, 'The Emergence of abortion and other "family values" issues [i.e. Genderquake themes] could presage a realignment of Democratic and Republican coalitions.'

10   **Packing their women MPs:** Madeleine Bunting. 'Why Labour went a'wooing but tumbled disastrously into the gender gap', *Guardian*, 17 July 1992; Michael White 'Tories to campaign for more women MPs,' *Guardian*, 1 September 1992; Candy Atherton, 'Politics, power and the purse', *Guardian*, 27 January 1993;

Madeleine Bunting, 'Men's club or one for the ladies?' *Guardian*, 16 November 1992.

10 **Childcare concerns alone:** Nikki Barrowclough, 'Keating Goes A-Wooing', *Good Weekend*, 6 June 1993.

10 **'Women of Australia':** quoted in *The Australian*, 15 March 1993.

10 **'He won':** *Sydney Morning Herald*, 16 March 1993.

11 **'Rocked the system':** Melanie Phillips, 'The miracle of President Mary', *Guardian*, 27 February 1991, p. 23.

11 **Priorities were irrelevant':** Beatrix Campbell, *Guardian*. 28 May 1992.

11 **Made it easier to convict rapists:** John F. Burns, 'Canada Moves to Strengthen Sexual Assault Law', *New York Times*, 2 February, 1992, p. A18.

11 **'Fatally branded':** Clyde H. Farnsworth, 'Canada's Tories Name A Woman as New Premiere', *New York Times*, 14 June 1993, p. A1.

11 **'Childless woman':** Charles Truehart, 'Woman Set to Succeed Mulroney', *Washington Press*, 14 June 1993, p. A1; Jeff Sallot and Ross Howard, 'Campbell Calls for Unity as Tories Elect Her Leader', *Globe and Mail*, 14 June 1993, p. A1.

12 **In Turkey:** 'Woman Tipped to Become Turkey's Next Prime Minister', *Washington Post*, 14 June 1993, p. A15.

12 **Promote women's rights:** John Murray Brown, 'Woman Gets Call to Lead in Turkey', *Washington Post*, 15 June 1993, p. A15.

12 **'In lieu of jobs':** *Guardian*, 20 April 1993.

12 **Front page news:** Louisa Saunders, 'Pulling Their Stockings Up', *Guardian*, 9 June 1993.

12 **Domestic violence:** *Guardian*, 5 May 1993.

12 **Bias in rape cases:** *Sydney Morning Herald*, 14 May 1993.

12 **Right to have abortions:** *Ms Magazine*, March/April 1993.

12 **Danish women:** *Guardian*, 23 May 1993.

13 **Husbands' pension benefits:** *Observer*, 23 May 1993.

14 **'Women have not hurt':** Jean Baker Miller, *Toward a New Psychology of Women* (Boston: Beacon Press, 1986), p. xvi.

15 **'The plan did not work':** David Brock, *The Real Anita Hill: The Untold Story* (New York: The Free Press, 1993), p. 285.

15 **'Deeply hidden operatives':** ibid., p. 40.

15 **'Basis of no evidence':** ibid., p. 375.

15 **'Feminist frenzy':** ibid., p. 136.

16 **A fifth to a third more income:** See the category of 'Engineers', 'Physicians' or 'Textile Sewing Machine Operator's, in Table 7.4 'Median Weekly Earnings of Full-Time Wage and Salary Workers in Selected Detailed Occupations by Sex, 1990', Paula Ries and Anne J Stone (eds), *The American Woman, 1992–3: A Status Report* (New York: W. W. Norton, 1992) pp. 264–5: women engineers earn 89.5 per cent of their male peers' salaries, women physicians 82 per cent, and sewing machine operators 82.7 per cent.

16 **A third more income than women across the board:** Table 7–1 'Median Weekly Earnings of Full-Time Female Workers Compared to Full-Time Male Workers by Age and Race, 1980, 1989 and 1990', in ibid., p. 355, citing US Bureau of Labor Statistics, *Handbook of Labor Statistics*, August 1989 and unpublished data, 1990. In America women of all races earned in 1990 71.8 cents for every male dollar.

16 **Representation in state government:** Center for the American Woman in Politics, cited in 'Women Crack Political Glass Ceiling', The Fund for the Feminist Majority Report (Arlington, VA: December 1992), p. 1.

16 **'Twice its natural size':** Virginia Woolf, *A Room of One's Own* (London: The Hogarth Press, 1929), p. 53.

16 **Getting to the top:** Women represent 6.6 per cent of executive management. 'A Report on the Glass Ceiling', US Department of Labor, Washington, DC, 1991.

17 **True figures for parity:** UK and European figures: OECD, *Economic Outlook*, December 1991, table R.1.

17 **51–49 per cent in the USA/7 million more:** 'In 1990, there were about seven million more women than men in the United States'. US Bureau of the Census, *U.S. Population Estimates by Age, Sex, Race and Hispanic Origin, March 1990, Table 1*, cited in Ries and Stone op. cit., p. 213.

17 **Gender gap:** The Fund for the Feminist Majority Report, 'Women's Voices: A Joint Project', Vol. 4, No. 4, December 1992, p. 30.

18 **342 years:** 'The Feminization of Power', pamphlet, The Fund for the Feminist Majority, p. 2; Sources: The National Information Bank on Women in Public Office, Center for American Women in Politics, Rutgers University, fact sheets; and National Women's Political Caucus, Washington, D.C., National Directory of Women Elected Officials.

18 **Sidney Blumenthal:** quoted in Women, Men and Media's conference, 'Sex, Lies and Politics', December 1991, at New York University. Reported in Mary Anne Rower, 'Women's Concerns: Is Anyone Listening?' *Professional Communicator*, April/May 1992, pp. 15–18.

18 **By 1996:** British Film Institute figures, March 1993.

18 **Average has risen to 5 per cent:** *Guardian*, 12 May 1993.

18 **A third of those selected:** *Women at the Top*, Report of the Hansard Society Commission, January 1990.

19 **'A woman vice-president':** The Feminization of Power', op. cit., p. 31.

20 **Pre-industrial societies:** Margaret Mead, *Male and Female: A Study of the Sexes in a Changing World* (New York: Dell, 1967), pp. 167–9: 'In every known society, the males' need for achievement can be recognized. . . In a great number of human societies men's sureness of their sex role is tied up with their right, or ability, to practice some activity that women are not allowed to practice. . . .'

21 **Lamp at her husband:** see Jacob Weisberg, *Vanity Fair*, September 1993, pp. 73–81.

22 **Chung:** Tom Shales, 'Connie Chung's Eager Eye', *Washington Post*, 17 June 1993, p. C2; 'The decline and fall of virtually everything', Tom Shales, 'Connie and Dan: Meeting Cute; Miss Perk Joins Mr. Serious on "The CBS Evening News"' *Washington Post*, 2 June 1993, p. B1.

23 **'The sins of all men':** Lynn Darling, 'Sex and the Single Guy', *Esquire*, June 1993, pp. 97 and 99.

25 **'So what if . . .' :** Peter H. Engels. 'Letters to the Editor', *Vanity Fair*, June 1993.

27 **To bar women:** 'Garrick-goers Close Ranks and Doors', *Guardian*, 7 July 1992.

28 **38 per cent, were more likely:** Norman Ornstein, Andrew Kohut and Larry McCarthy, *The People, The Press and Politics* (New York: Addison-Wesley, 1988), p. 38.

29 **40 per cent of news and editorial workers:** 'Trend in Female Employment by Newspaper Departments', ANPA Survey or Employment of Women and Minorities in US Daily Papers, Belden Associates, 1992, p. 13.

31 **Cluelessness and malice:** George Lardner, Jr, 'Justice System Lax in Cases of Rape, Senate Report Says', *Washington Post*, 28 May 1993, p. 1.

31 **Packwood:** Florence Graves, 'Feminists See Packwood Case as Pivotal Test of Strength; Groups Cite Opportunity to Build Base for Wider Hill Reform', *Washington Post*, 30 January 1993, p. A4.

31 **Deborah Tannen:** John Cushman, 'Senators Shaken by Thomas Debate Get a Lesson in Gender Dynamics', *New York Times*, 7 March 1992, p. A8.

31 **Guilt denied at trial:** Linda Greenhouse, 'Legality of Therapy Requirements to Be Addressed', *New York Times*, 3 March 1993, p. A15.

31 **Model for feminist lawyers:** Guy Gugliotta and Eleanor Randolph, 'A Mentor, Role Model and Heroine for Feminist Lawyers', *Washington Post*, 15 June 1993.

32 **Combat positions:** 'New Milestone for Women in Combat', *USA Today*, 17 June 1993'. 'May 22 1991, The House of Representatives passes a bill allowing the assignment of female Air Force and Navy Pilots to Combat Missions', Ries and Stone op. cit., p. 75.

32   **More sympathetic to women:** Tamra Henry', 'Civil Rights Crusader Begins New Mission', *New York Times*, 15 June 1993, p. 4D.

32   **Sexual harassment ... at BATF:** Stephen Labaton, 'Agency Checking Sexual Harassment', *New York Times*, 12 January 1993, p. A16.

32   **Manon Rhéame:** 'A Net Victory', *Time*, 5 October 1992, p. 24.

32   **'God and Women':** Richard N. Oftling, 'God and Women: A Second Reformation Sweeps Christianity', *Time*, 23 November 1992, pp. 53–8.

32   **'A woman with a gun':** 'The Insider', *People*, 7 June 1993, p. 37.

34   **Car sales to women:** Lynn Hanna, 'The Body Beautiful', *Guardian*, 26 October, 1992; 'Revenge of the Bonnet Bimbos', *Observer*, 4 April 1993, p. 37; Tom Shone, 'Catwalk Divas Torque up a Storm', *Sunday Times*, 4 April 1993, p. 6.

34   **Special features for the female driver:** *Guardian Weekend*, 22 May 1993.

36   **'Women who get the job done':** 'Garzarelli's Latest No-Nonsense Move', *USA Today*. 26 March 1993.

36   **'Cosmo':** Stuart Elliot, 'That Cosmopolitan Girl Won't Be A Girl Anymore', *New York Times*, 4 January 1993; says Seth E. Hoyt, *Cosmo*'s vice president, '*Cosmo* as a magazine, as a big sister, if you will, a support system, has helped liberate women all over the world.'

38   **There are 99,202,000 women in the United States:** US Bureau of the Census, Washington DC, 1993.

42   **Diana and Actaeon:** Thomas Bulfinch, *The Age of Fable: Or, Beauties of Mythology* (New York: Mentor Books, 1962), pp. 65–7.

43   *The First Wives' Club:* Olivia Goldsmith, *The First Wives' Club* (New York: Pocket Books, 1992). 'What does it take for you to say "enough"?' pp. 191–5.

45   **Precedents for the themes:** Margaret Mitchell, *Gone With The Wind* (New York: Avon Books, 1964); Judith Krantz, *Scruples* (New York: Bantam, 1978); Jackie Collins, *Lady Boss* (New York: Pocket Books, 1990); Ivana Trump, *For Love Alone* (New York: Pocket Books, 1992).

48   **'Other Management functions':** *Sunday Times*, 17 March 1993.

48   **Ivana Trump:** 'Ivana Trump Will Write *On My Own*, a financial management and personal growth guide for suddenly single women', *Time*, 28 December 1992, p. 75.

55   **Helena Kennedy, QC:** *Guardian*, 31 December 1991.

59   **The master's tools:** in 'Master's Tools', Audre Lorde, *Sister Outsider: Essays and Speeches by Audre Lorde* (Freeman, CA: The Crossing Press, 1984), p. 112: '(S)urvival ... is learning how to take our differences and make them strengths. *For the master's tools will never dismantle the master's house*. They may allow it temporarily to beat him at his own game, but they will never bring about genuine change.'

52   **Thomas-Hill hearings:** For essays on the nexus of race and gender in the Hill-Thomas hearings, see Toni Morrison, ed: *Race-ing Justice, En-gendering Power: Essays on Anita Hill, Clarence Thomas, and the Construction of Social Reality*, (New York: Pantheon 1992; London: Chatto & Windus 1992).

55   **A fish to grow feet:** *Observer*, 31 December 1991.

Part 2: What Went Wrong? How So Many Women and Their Movement Parted Ways

63   **'Stopped talking to me':** letter from reader Linda Jaques, San Gabriel, California, 18 February 1993.

63   **Hill had been sexually harassed:** Eloise Salholz, 'Did America Get It?', *Newsweek*, 28 December 1992, pp. 20–2; see also Jill Abramson, 'Reversal of Fortune: Image of Anita Hill Brighter in Hindsight, Galvanizes Campaigns', *Wall Street Journal*, 5 October 1992, p. 1.

63   **'Women's right organizations'**: Jane Gross, 'Patricia Ireland: Does NOW's New President Speak for Today's Women?', *New York Times*, 1 March 1992.

63–4   **A 1992 Ms. Foundation survey**: 'Many women report that they are personally uncomfortable with the term "feminist" even while they applaud the goals of the women's movement', 'Women's Voices '92: A Polling Report', a joint project of the Ms. Foundation for Women and the Center for Policy Alternatives, September 1992, p. 31.

64   **1989 Time/CNN Yankelovich poll**: Claudia Wallis, 'Onward, Women!', *Time*. 4 December 1989. pp. 80–9.

64   **1987 . . .1986**: Fund for the Feminist Majority pamphlet, 'Empowering Women in Business', The Empowering Women series, No. 1, Arlington, VA, 1991, p. 8.

64   **Claimed to be feminists**: British Psychological Association Annual Conference, cited in *Guardian*, 17 August 1992.

64   **Negative feelings**: Sarah Lonsdale, 'Feminists Feel the Backing of Opinion', *Observer*, 4 April 1993; see also, Paula Kamen, *Feminist Fatale: Voices from the 'Twentysomething Generation' Explore the Future of the 'Women's Movement'* (New York: Donald I. Fine, 1991), pp. 23–101.

       Kamen condenses a reply from her core group of 103 'non-activists' interviewed: 'What do you associate with the word 'feminist'?

       'I imagine: bra-burning, hairy-legged, amazon, castrating, militant-almost-antifeminine, communist, Marxist, separatist, female skin-heads, female supremacists, he-woman types, bunch-a-lesbians, you-know-dykes, man-haters, men-bashers, wanting-men's-jobs, wanting-to-dominate-men, wear-short-hair-to-look-unattractive, bizarre-chicks-running-around doing kooky things, i-am-woman-hear-me-roar, uptight, angry, white-middle-class radicals.'

       '. . . Even those who fiercely denied that they were feminists or never before heard the word voiced strong support for women's rights in general. Most said that they appreciated the women's movement and believed in what they described as its most basic goals and principles.

       'What was generally missing in their thinking was a sense of connection and commitment to feminism itself. Most didn't identify with feminism or want to be associated with it on a personal or political level. The great irony is that although feminism has generally made a tremendous difference in the perceptions and opportunities in many of these people's lives, it is something that they almost universally shun.' Kamen, ibid, pp. 23–4.

64   **'What Women Really Think'**: *Guardian*, 7 March 1991.

65   **Had not changed**: *Guardian*, 7 March 1991.

65   **ICM Poll**: 'Men and Women', *Guardian*, 9 January 1992, p. 1.

66   **'Who wouldn't define themselves as feminists'**: *Guardian*, 23 April 1992.

67   **'Up-front, provocative'**: *Guardian*, 5 August 1992.

67   **'My freedom is restricted'**: *Guardian*, 24 March 1993.

67   **'You've gotta fight'**: *Guardian*, 19 June 1993.

69   **Christine Bellini**: personal correspondence, 1992.

73   **Left of the 1960s**: For an account of the rebirth of feminism in the 1960s out of radical revolutionary groups like Students for A Democratic Society, see Alice Echols, *Daring To Be Bad: Radical Feminism in America, 1967–1975*, (Minneapolis: University of Minnesota Press, 1989).

75   **'Sexual abnormality'**: Lillian Faderman, *Surpassing the Love of Men: Romantic Friendship and Love Between Women from the Renaissance to the Present* (New York: William Morrow, 1981), p. 335.

75   **Modus operandi**: ibid., p. 336.

75   **Scare women away**: ibid., p. 337.

75   **'Lesbian sickness'**: ibid., p. 339.

76   **'NOW is a militant fringe'**: Jane Gross, 'NOW's Patricia Ireland: Does She Speak for Today's Women?' *New York Times*, 1 March 1992, p. 16; see also Nina J. Easton, *Los Angeles Times Magazine*: feminism has a 'sometimes overweening emphasis on lesbian issues [which] is . . . troubling for Middle America.

... Plenty of women who don't consider themselves homophobic worry that the concerns of a small minority are dominating.... To many, the term feminist still evokes images of hairy-legged, humorless extremists who view men as the enemy.' Cited in Donna Minkowitz, 'The Newsroom Becomes a Battleground', *Advocate*, 12 March 1992, pp. 31–7; see also Sally Quinn, 'Who Killed Feminism? Hypocritical Movement Leaders Betrayed Their Own Cause', *Washington Post*, 19 January, 1992, p. C1.

80   **Eileen Waters was brutally raped:** *Guardian*, 6 February 1993.

81   **'It's too early yet':** *Guardian*, 29 January 1992.

81   **'I owe nothing to women's lib':** J. Green, *The Book of Political Quotes* (London: Angus & Robertson, 1982), p. 180.

83   **'Women Are Revolting':** Marcia Cohen, *The Sisterhood: The Inside Story Of The Women's Movement and the Leaders Who Made It Happen*, (New York: Fawcett Columbine, 1988), p. 205. Cohen details the Second Wave's continual struggles with the media in her chapter. 'Who is the Enemy?', ibid., pp. 197–216.

84   **'162 US universities':** National Women's Studies Association, Washington, DC, 1993.

85   **'Is what you cannot see':** Linda Ellerbee, *'The News, As If All People Mattered'*, Women, Men and Media pamphlet, Unabridged Communications, September 1992, p. 15.

86   **Significant change:** *Equal Times*, No. 4, January 1992.

86   **Board of Management:** BFI figures, March 1993.

86   **BBC documentaries:** Fay Weldon, 'Testosterone, the Key to Success in Television', *Guardian*, 7 June 1993.

86   **Not one is held:** BFI figures, March 1993.

86   **'Skill Search' survey:** Scott Blum et al., *Skill Search: Television, Film and Video Industry Employment Patterns and Training Needs: Part I: The Key Facts*, IMS Report No. 171, Institute of Manpower Services, Brighton, August 1989.

86   **Men were twice as likely:** *Mail on Sunday*, 7 June 1992.

86   **Channel 4:** Weldon, op. cit., *Guardian*, 7 June 1993.

87   **LWT:** *Stage, Screen and Radio*, May 1993, p. 9.

87   **Survey of the Australian film ...:** Eva Cox and Sharon Laura, '"What Do I Wear for a Hurricane?" Women in Australian Film, Television, Video and Radio Industries', report commissioned by the Australian Film Commission and the National Working Party on the portrayal of Women in the Media, November 1992.

87   **79 per cent of the newsmakers:** Women, Men and Media survey, 'The News: looking Like America? Not Yet...', Unabridged Communications, 5 April 1992, pp. 1–3 (study based at the University of Southern California and New York University).

87   **17 per cent of other newsmakers:** John Carmody, 'Women, Minorities Still Shut Out', *Washington Post*, 16 June 1993, p. B8, reporting Cultural Indicators Research Team study, Annenberg School of Communications.

87   **H. Ross Perot:** *1992 Transcript/Video Index: A Comprehensive Guide to Television and Radio ... Programming* (Denver: Journal Graphics, Inc., 1992), Vol. 5, No. 13. See under 'Women', pp. 1055–65, and 'Perot, H. Ross', pp. 738–49.

89   **Opportunity to fail:** *Daily Telegraph*, 17 May 1991.

90   **'Perfectly disgraceful':** *Guardian*, 23 September 1992.

90   **'28 of those appearances':** Lesley Abdela, 'Do Not Adjust Your Sets', *Guardian*, 20 November 1992.

90   **'Maastricht would affect women':** Lesley Abdela, *Guardian*, 20 November 1992.

90   **She also structured:** BBC conference report, op cit., p. 6

91   **'Or does not see':** *Independent*, 4 September 1991.

91   **'Worryingly high proportion':** *Stage and Television Today*, 7 May 1992.

91   **'Interests they don't share':** Rees-Mogg quoted in *Guardian*, 9 July 1992.

91   **'Women running for office'**: Women, Men and Media study, Unabridged Communications, 30 September 1992, pp. 1–3.

91   **White House press corps**: Stephen Hess, 'All the President's Reporters', *Society*, March/April 1992.

91   **Female references in news stories**: Junior Bridge, 'Year of the Woman ... Not!', Women, Men and Media survey, Unabridged Communications, 30 October 1992.

93   **'22 per cent of total staff employed'**: Report of the Hansard Society Commission, *Women at the Top*, London, July 1992.

93   **Women editors**: *Women at the Top*, Hansard report, 1990.

93   **'Kind of media'** *Guardian*, October 1992.

94   **Mainly as a joke**: *Ms*, January/February 1993.

94   **'Prime Minister of Canada'**: Peter Benesh, 'Should a Lonely Divorcee be PM for Canada?', *Observer*, 13 June 1993. See also note to p. 11 above.

94   **Score of 21 per cent**: Women in Publishing, *Reviewing the Reviews* (London: Journeyman, 1987), p. 58

94   **Reviewers were women**: WIP, February 1992.

94   **'20 per cent of the UK's published authors'**: Dale Spender, *The Writing or the Sex?* (Oxford and New York: Pergamon Press, 1989), p. 45.

95   **'Women editors on the staff'**: Nicolette Jones, 'A Way with Words', *Guardian*, 30 May 1991.

95   **British publishing**: ibid.

95   **Publishing directors**: *Women at the Top*, Hansard report.

95   **High earners**: *Twice As Many, Half as Powerful*, Women in Publishing Report, February 1989.

96   **75 per cent of the interviewees were male**: Tracy Quinn, 'The News: Looking Like America? Not Yet...' , Women, Men and Media survey, Unabridged Communications, January 1993, p. 3.

96   **The sexes performing equally**: 'How Schools Shortchange Girls: A Study of Major Findings on Girls and Education', The American Association of University Women, (Wellesley, MA., 1992), p. 24.

97   **'White male bastion'**: Anne Thompson, 'Hollywood Is Taken to Task by Its Women', *New York Times*, 17 January 1993, C25.

97   **'As people not women'**: quoted in Rosalind Coward, *Our Treacherous Hearts: Why Women Let Men Get Their Way* (London: Faber, 1992), p. 12.

97   **'Witty and opinionated pieces'**: ibid, p. 12.

98   **'Career limbo'**: Nan Robertson, *The Girls in the Balcony: Women, Men and the New York Times* (New York: Random House, 1992), p. 215.

98   **Soma Golden**: James Ledbetter, 'O *Times*,, O Mores', *Village Voice*, 30 April 1991, pp. 36 8. Three hundred *Times* staff packed a shop talk discussion on 'How We Write About Rape', National editor Golden, who looked the most distraught, said that the days since the story ran had been 'the most difficult point' in her career. She defended the profile as extremely well reported, said that some 30 per cent of the raciest material had been cut.

99   **'Extra dimension'**: John Carmody, 'The TV Column', *Washington Post*, 15 April, 1993, p. C6.

99   **'"Bossy" woman'**: *Sunday Times*, 10 January 1993

99   **'White guys in suits'**: Howard Kurtz, 'What's Wrong with Newspapers?'. *Washington Post Magazine*, 18 April 1993, p. 11.

101   **Femidon**: *Elle*, September 1992.

101   **'They are running scared'**: *Guardian*, 18 April 1992.

103   **Ritual sexual abuse**: *Ms*, 'Believe It! Cult Ritual Abuse Exists', vol. 3. No. 4, January/February 1993.

103   **'Spare Rib espoused'**: Eileen Fairweather, *Guardian*, 16 June 1992.

106   **'Make feminism look bad'**: Karen Houppert, 'WAC Attacks Itself: Will the Direct Action Group Self-Destruct?', *The Village Voice*, 20 July 1993, p. 28.

110   **Stalin**: transcript, *60 Minutes*, 1 November 1992, pp. 17–19.

110   **Men and women to be the same:** Camille Paglia, 'The Joy of Presbyterian sex', *New Republic*, 2 December 1992, pp. 24-7.

112   **'Self-proclaimed women's advocates':** Alan Dershowitz, 'The Myth of the Super Bowl and Battered Women,' *Los Angeles Times*, 7 February 1993.

113   **Invasion from another planet:** 'Football's Day of Dread', *The Wall Street Journal*, 5 February 1993.

113   **'A climb on Super Bowl Sunday' and 'showed no increase':** 'Portland Hot Line Shelters Vary in Calls on Super Bowl Sunday', *The Oregonian*, 1 February 1993, p. A1.

114   **'Acts of violence':** quoted in the *Guardian*, 5 December 1991.

114   **'Agree to disagree':** Jane Gross, 'Patricia Ireland, President of NOW: Does She Speak for Today's Women?,' *The New York Times Magazine*, 1 March 1992.

121   **Lesbian karate school:** Donna Minkowitz. 'Lesbians Without a Movement,' *The Advocate*, 26 June 1993, p. 17.

121   **'Destroyed many more lesbian groups':** Donna Minkowitz, 'Lesbians Without a Movement,' ibid.

122   **'Recognizing the danger':** Elizabeth Fox-Genovese, *Feminism Without Illusions: A Critique of Individualism* (Chapel Hill: University of North Carolina Press, 1991), p. 243.

124   **Women candidates are turned down:** Lisa Jardine, *Guardian*, 12 May 1993.

124   **Academic World:** ibid.

124   **Dale Spender ... fierce resistance:** Dale Spender, *The Writing or the Sex?*, op, cit., p. 108.

125   **'Menchu':** Dinesh D'Souza, *Illiberal Education* (New York: Simon & Schuster, 1992), pp 71-3. 'Strangely, in the introduction to *I, Rigoberta Menchu*, we learn ... that Rigoberta "speaks for all the Indians of the American continent"'. D'Souza claims that she represents nothing more than 'a projection of Marxist and feminist views on to South American Indian culture'. *Illiberal Education*, p. 72.

125   **Death of a 'white boy':** Justin McKellar, 'Surface Under Attack,' *Queen's Journal*, Queen's College, Canada, 19 March 1993.

126   **Oxbridge first-class degree:** Germaine Greer, quoted in *Guardian*, 12 May 1993.

130   **Curriculum:** See, for an example of the reinvented curriculum, Judith P. Hallett, 'Classics and Women's Studies,' Wellesley College Center for Research on Women, working paper no. 119, Wellesley, Mass, 1983.

131   **Robert Casey visited Cooper Union:** Nat Hentoff, 'The Perennial Face of Fascism', *Village Voice*, 14 October 1992, vol. 37, pp. 22-160.

132   **Susan Brownmiller:** her *Against our Will: Men, Women and Rape* (New York: Simon & Schuster, 1975), p. 16; see e.g. John Stoltenberg, *Refusing to be a Man: Essays on Sex and Justice* (New York: Meridian, 1989).

133   **Catharine MacKinnon:** *Feminism Unmodified: Discourses on Life and Law* (Cambridge, Mass.: Harvard University Press, 1987); '"Sexuality" Toward a Feminist Theory of the State' (Cambridge, Mass.: 1989), pp. 126-54.

133   **Andrea Dworkin:** *Intercourse* (London: Secker & Warburg, 1986): 'The thrusting is persistent invasion ... She is occupied ... Intercourse in reality is a use and abuse simultaneously,', p.122.

133   **Adrienne Rich:** her 'Compulsory Heterosexuality and Lesbian Existence', in Ann Snitow, Christine Stansell and Sharon Thomas (eds), *Powers of Desire: The Politics of Sexuality* (New York: Monthly Review Press, 1983), pp. 177-202.

134   **'Many different paths':** Minette Martin, *London Daily Telegraph*, 18 September, 1992.

136   **On international Women's Day ... 'British feminists rest uneasily':** *Guardian*, 5 March 1993.

136   **Luce Irigaray:** see her *This Sex Which Is Not One* (*Le Sexe qui n'en est pas un*) (Ithaca, NY: Cornell University Press, 1985), p. 79. Amusingly enough, the US publisher provides a note gratefully acknowledging the financial assistance of the French Ministry of Culture in defraying part of the cost of translation.

137 **Academic feminists cannot be blamed:** Russell Jacoby points out in *The Last Intellectuals: American Culture in the Age of Academy* (New York: Farrar, Straus & Giroux, 1987), pp. 16–17, that the intellectuals, access to the public forum has constricted for younger academics in particular: after 1940, he writes, 'The occasion to master a public prose did not arise; consequently, their writings lacked public impact ... They grew up in a world where non-university intellectuals hardly existed.'

138 **If in order to be called a feminist:** see Rebecca E. Klatch, *Women of the New Right* (Philadelphia: Temple University Press, 1987), pp. 119–53, for a penetrating account of conservative women's relationship to feminism: Women of the New Right are not a monolithic group. Nor are all right-wing women antifeminist. They do not all 'fear equality and prefer preferential treatment,' nor are they 'lackeys' of men, suffering from 'false consciousness'. Klatch points out that socially conservative women see feminism as an attack on homemakers, while laissez-faire conservative women oppose feminism primarily insofar as it looks to collective rather than individual solutions.

Part 3: Victim Feminism Versus Power Feminism

147 **Katie Roiphe:** *The Morning After: Sex, Fear and Feminism on Campus* (Boston: Little Brown, 1993).

153 **'A fiesta of whining':** Robert Hughes, 'A Fiesta of Whining', *Time*, 22 March 1993, pp. 68-9.

154 **Violent offences against women:** information from the Home Office, June 1993. (Severe spouse abuse is the single major cause of injury for which women seek medical attention in the US. It is more common than are car accidents, mugging and rape combined. 'Family Violence: An Overview', Office of Health and Human Services, Washington, D.C., 1992.)

154 **Killed by husbands or lovers:** Up to 4,000 women are beaten to death by family members; 30 per cent of women killed in the US are killed by husbands or boyfriends. *FBI Uniform Crime Reports*, US Department of Justice, Federal Bureau of Investigation, Washington D.C., 1992.

154 **60 per cent of battered women:** 60 per cent of battered women are beaten while they are pregnant. 'Myths and Facts About Domestic Violence', Domestic Violence Project, Ann Arbor, Michigan, no date: cited in *WAC STATS: The Facts About Women* (New York: The New Press), p. 58.

154 **Women ... three times more likely:** During the nine-year period of an FBI study, the data showed that "intimates" committed 5.6 million violent victimizations against women, an annual average of almost 626,000. US Department of Justice, 'Female Victims of Violent Crime', Washington D.C., Caroline Wolf Harlow, January 1993, p. 1.

157 **The will to power:** Adrienne Rich, cited in Ynestra King, 'The Ecology of Feminism and the Feminism of Ecology', in Judith Plant (ed.), *Healing the Wounds: The Promise of Ecofeminism* (Philadelphia: New Society Publishers, 1989), p. 23.

157 **'Men Kill':** Meat Eating. Carol J. Adams, *The Sexual Politics of Meat: A Feminist-Vegetarian Critical Theory* (New York: Continuum, 1990), pp. 25–38. Adams's elegant thesis errs on the side of the same totalizing impulses that hobble the less erudite texts.

158 **'Body without a spirit':** Susan Griffin, 'Split Culture', ibid., p. 11.

158 **'They were natural fathers':** Mab Segrest, 'Feminism and Disobedience: Conversations with Barbara Deming', in Pam McAllister (ed.), *Reweaving the Web of Life: Feminism and Nonviolence* (Philadelphia: New Society Publishers, 1982), p. 51.

158 **'Selfishness of patriarchy':** Plant, 'Toward a New World', op. cit., p. 2.

158 **'Their bloody battlefields':** Sharon Doubiago, 'Mama Coyote Talks to her Boys' in McAllister, op. cit., p. 41.

158   **'Nonviolent power be enhanced'**: Marion Bromley, 'Feminism and Nonviolent Revolution', in McAllister, op. cit., p. 154.

159   **'Life-sweet women'**: Ellen Bass, 'Our Stunning Harvest,' in ibid., p. 68.

159   **'We can give death'**: Mab Segrest, 'Feminism and Disobedience: Conversations with Barbara Deming', ibid., p. 52.

159   **'Hiroshimas, Dachaus'**: Joan Cavanaugh, 'I Am a Dangerous Woman', ibid., p. 3.

159   **'Half the human population'**: Pam McAllister, 'Introduction', ibid., p. vi.

159   **'Aggression against life'**: Mary Daly, *Gyn/Ecology*, cited in ibid., p. 17.

159   **'From all that threatens life'**: Barbara Zanotti, 'Patriarchy: A State of War', ibid., p. 19.

159   **Women's testosterone**: Helen E. Fisher, 'Mighty Menopause', *New York Times*, 21 October 1992, p. A23.

162   **'Work to expand our circles'**: Charlene Spretnak, 'Toward an Ecofeminist Spirituality', in Plant (ed.), op. cit., p. 131.

162   **'Firmly and calmly'**: Radha Bhatt, 'Lakshmi Ashram: A Ghandian Perspective in the Himalayan Foothills', ibid., p. 169.

162   **'Saving women's lives'**: Leah Fritz, 'Abortion: A Woman's Rights to Live', in McAllister, op. cit., p. 398.

162   **Genocidal eradication of men**: Sally Miller Gearhart in 'The Future – If There Is One – Is female', ibid., pp. 267–284.

169   **Local 34**: 'A Report to the Community from the Members of Local 34, Federation of University Employees, AFL-CIO', September 1984; see also Craig Charney et al., 'Organizing Yale: A Historical Sketch of Unions and Labor Management Relations at the University', unpublished essay for the Yale Labor Support Group Research Committee: and Molly Ladd-Taylor, 'Women Workers and the Yale Strike', *Feminist Studies*, Vol. 11, No. 3, Fall 1985, pp. 465–90; and 'Economic Discrimination at Yale', Locals 34 and 35, Federation of University Employees, New Haven, January 1988.

173   **Women academics at Oxford University**: *Guardian*, 12 May 1993.

174   **Body Shop founder**: Anita Roddick quoted in *Sunday Times*, 1 September 1991.

174   **Eve Pollard**: quoted in *Guardian*, 8 May 1991.

174   **Lose two novels**: quoted in Guardian, 5 May 1993.

175   **Barbara Follett**: *Guardian*, 25 May 1993.

175   **FemFm**: *Guardian*, 4 March 1992.

175   **Women running their own businesses**: *Guardian*, 13 July 1992.

176   **'If a man left'**: Spencer Stuart, p. 8.

176   **Finland was run by women**: *Guardian*, 5 July 1992.

176   **Ms: reported rapes of Croatian women**: 'Rape after Rape after Rape,' Slavenka Drakulic (ed.), *New York Times*, 13 December, 1992, p. A17.

179   **Make lynching a federal crime**: A'Lelia Perry Bundles, *Madame C. J. Walker, Entrepreneur* (New York: Chelsea House, 1991), p. 81

180   ***A Midwife's Tale***: Laurel Thatcher Ulrich, *A Midwife's Tale: The Life of Martha Ballard, Based on Her Diary 1785–1812*, (New York: Knopf, 1990).

181   **Meddled in public affairs**: Miriam Gurko, *The Ladies of Seneca Falls* (New York: Schocken Books, 1976), p. 188.

181   **'All seems to go well'**: Henry Maudsley quoted in Jane Lewis, *Women in England 1870–1950* (Brighton: Harvester/Wheatsheaf, 1984), pp. 84–5.

181   **'Good and pure'**: Gurko op. cit., p. 256.

182   **By meddling in the affairs of others**: ibid., p. 274.

183   **'To complete man-made legislation**: Lewis op. cit., p. 89.

183   **'In the political world'**: Lewis op. cit., p. 90.

183   **'Sacrifices her own sex'**: Gurko op. cit., p. 267.

183   **Harbinger**: Nancy F. Cott (ed.), *Root of Bitterness: Documents of the Social History of American Women* (New York: Dutton, 1972), pp. 239–42.

184   'A moral, responsible being': Gurko, op. cit., p. 6.
184   'No woman can call herself free': quoted in Alice S. Rossi (ed.), *The Feminist Papers: From Adams to de Beauvoir*, (New York: Bantam Books, 1974), pp. 520–1.
184   'Passion as the flame of love': Carol Dyhouse, *Feminism and the Family in England, 1880–1939* (London: Basil Blackwell, 1989), p. 157.
184   'As powerful a force in women': ibid., p. 171.
184   'General openness': ibid., p. 177.
184   'Women's greater pleasure': ibid., p. 184.
184   'Hangdog dowdies': Camille Paglia, 'Madonna: Finally, a Real Feminist', *New York Times*, December 1990.
185   'Understand what you believe': Gurko, op. cit., p. 32.
185   'Amenable to argument': ibid., p. 32.
185   'Reasoning powers wholly uncultivated': ibid., p. 300.
185   'Most honorable to himself': ibid., p. 308.
186   'Public exercises with men': ibid., p. 133.
186   'Feminine virtues': ibid., p. 42.
186   'Social justice do not apply': ibid., p. 138.
186   'Criminals, Idiots, Women': *Fraser's Magazine*, 8 December 1868.
187   'No true freedom for women': Gurko, op. cit., p. 174.
187   'Raising their own status': ibid., p. 79.
187   'Womanliness in woman': quoted in Lewis, op. cit., p. 95.
188   Exemplary behaviour and gentle entreaties: For additional histories of the 'separate sphere' ideology and the First Wave of feminism among white, middle-class American and British women, see Nancy F. Cott (ed.), *Root of Bitterness: Documents of the Social History of American Women* (New York: Dutton, 1972), especially the chapter 'Nineteenth-Century Alternatives: Pioneers and Utopians' (pp. 217–60); Sherna Gluk (ed.), *From Parlor to Prison: Five American Suffragists Talk About Their Lives* (New York: Vintage, 1976); Elizabeth Griffith, *In Her Own Right: The Life of Elizabeth Cady Stanton* (Oxford: Oxford University Press, 1984); Elizabeth K. Helsinger, Robin Lauterbach Sheets and William Veeder, *The Woman Question: Society and Literature in Britain and America, 1837–1883*, Literary Issues, Vol. 3 (Chicago: University of Chicago Press, 1983); Elaine Showalter, *A Literature of Their Own: British Women Novelists from Brontë to Lessing* (London: Virago, 1984); Barbara Ehrenreich and Deirdre English. *For Her Own Good: 150 Years of the Experts' Advice to Women* (New York: Anchor, 1979); Nancy F. Cott, *The Bonds of Womanhood: 'Woman's Sphere' in New England, 1780–1835* (Hew Haven, Conn.: Yale University Press, 1977); Ann Douglas, *The Feminization of American Culture* (New York: Anchor, 1988); Janet Murray, *Strong Minded Women and Other Lost Voices From 19th-Century England* (New York: Pantheon, 1982); Sandra M. Gilbert and Susan Gular, *The Madwoman in the Attic* (New Haven, Conn.: Yale University Press, 1979); Lynda Nead, *Myths of Sexuality: Representations of Women in Victorian Britain* (Oxford: Blackwell, 1988), especially the chapters. 'The Prostitute as Social Victim (pp. 138–55), and 'Woman's Mission to Women' (pp. 196–209); and Keith E. Melder, *Beginnings of Sisterhood: The American Woman's Rights Movement, 1800–1850* (New York: Schocken Books, 1977), especially the chapters, 'New Bonds of Sisterhood' (pp. 30–49), and 'A Network of Female Societies' (pp. 62–76).
188   Difference feminism: For essential reading on the 'equality feminism/difference debate', see also Susan Faludi, 'Carol Gilligan: Different Voices or Victorian Echoes?', *Backlash* (New York: Doubleday, 1991), pp. 325–32.
       Other texts that have developed related 'difference' themes include: Sara Ruddick, *Maternal Thinking: Towards a Politics of Peace* (New York: Ballantine, 1990), which 'develops a feminist peace politics' based on the activity of mothers; Adrienne Rich, *Of Woman Born: Motherhood as Experience and Institution*, which urges women to integrate mind and flesh and '*think through the*

body' to oppose 'the death-culture of qualification, abstraction and the will to power,' (pp. 284–8), and Mary Field Belenley, Blythe McVicker Clinchy, Nancy Rule Goldberger and Jill Matuck Tarule, *Women's Ways of Knowing: The Development of Self, Voice and Mind* (New York: Basic Books, 1986), which seeks to explain women's distrust of abstraction and logic.

190 **'Male' power:** See Joan L. Griscom for an overview in 'Women and Power: Definition, Dualism and Difference', *Psychology of Women Quarterly*, Vol. 16, 1992, pp. 389–414. She traces this 'power-over' view to Alfred Adler's 1966 essay. 'The Psychology of Power': 'The will to power' in Adler's essay, 'leads to neuroticism, crime, suicide, patriarchal family relations, and war; in this essay power is virtually poison.'

Jean Baker Miller points out that women fear using power because they fear being destructive or selfish, and that the use of power threatens 'a core sense of identity'. Her conclusion is that women are most comfortable in a world in which they are 'enhancing the power of other people while simultaneously increasing [their] own power'. She acknowledges that this is not how the 'real world' defines power, but contends simply that 'women would function more comfortably within such a context. . . . Frankly, I think women are absolutely right to fear the use of power as it has generally been conceptualized and used.' (pp. 2–3. Jean Baker Miller, 'Work in Progress: Women and Power', Stone Center, Wellesley College, Wellesley, Mass. 02181, 1 November 1982).

191 **'Child sexual abuse':** 'Women who have been abused show a higher concern for status and power – and more blocks and fears about acquiring it,' according to this provocative essay, which suggests that early experiences of powerlessness teach women to have a toxic relationship to power – to be compulsively drawn to it and to express an aversion toward it. Joan Huser Liem et al., 'The Need for Power in Women Who Were Sexually Abused as Children: An Exploratory Study', *Psychology of Women Quarterly*, Vol 16, 1992, pp. 467–80, 'Results indicated a higher need for power and greater fear of power than those of nonabused women.'

192 **'Identification with the tormentor':** Donna Minkowitz, 'My Father, Myself', *Village Voice*, 6 April 1993. p. 17.

192 **'If the woman was married':** *Guardian*, 19 April 1993.

192 **'Woman raped by a stranger':** *Sydney Morning Herald*, 19 May 1993.

193 **Dr Margaret Jenvold:** Alisa Solomon, 'Girl Crazy? Psychiatry Tries to Make PMS a Mental Illness', *Village Voice*, 6 April 1993, p. 33.

193 **Victim feminism;** Many feminist theorists have addressed these issues. Bell hooks's *Feminist Theory: From Margin to Center* (Boston: South End Press, 1984), on sisterhood, victim culture, 'trashing' and difference has been influential.

See bell hooks also on victim consciousness: 'Bonding as "victims", white women liberationists were not required to assume responsibility for confronting the complexity of their own experience. They were not challenging one another to examine their sexist attitudes towards women unlike themselves or exploring the impact of race and class privilege on their relationships to women outside their race/class groups. Identifying as 'victims', they could abdicate responsibility for their role in the maintenance and perpetuation of sexism, racism and classism, which they did by insisting that only men are the enemy.' bell hooks, op. cit., p. 46.

See bell hooks also on the fallacy of viewing women as nonviolent: 'By equating militarism and patriarchy, women who advocate feminism often structure their arguments in such a way as to suggest that to be male is synonymous with strength, aggression and the will to dominate and do violence to others; to be female is synonymous with weakness, passivity, and the will to nourish and affirm the lives of others. Such dualistic thinking is basic to all forms of social domination in Western society. Even when inverted and employed for a meaningful purpose such as nuclear disarmament, it is nevertheless dangerous because it reinforces the cultural basis of sexism and other forms of group oppression. It promotes a stereotypical notion of inherent differences between men and women, implying that women by virtue of their sex have played no crucial role in supporting and upholding imperialism. . . . Even if one argues that men have been taught to equate masculinity with the ability to do violence and women have been taught to equate femaleness with nurturance, the fact remains that many women and men do not conform to these stereotypes. Rather than clarifying for women the power we exert in the maintenance of systems of domination and setting forth strategies for resistance and change, most current discussion of women and militarism further mystifies women's role.' bell hooks, 'Feminist Movement to End Violence', ibid., p. 126.

194 'Any sensual indulgence': Lynda Nead, *Myths of Sexuality: Representations of Women in Victorian Britain* (Oxford: Basil Blackwell, 1988), p. 19.

194 Gary Hart: Suzannah Lessard, 'The Issue Was Women: Philandering, Not "Judgment" Got Hart in Trouble', *Newsweek*, 18 May 1987, pp. 32–4.

196 Clinton/Flowers: Congressional Record US Government Printing Office, 23 September 1992, p. H9262–9263.

197 Cline: Sally Cline, *Women, Celibacy and Passion* (London: Deutsch, 1993); see also Deborah Moggach, 'Women, Just Say No', *Sunday Times*, 7 March 1993, p. 11; Janet Watts, 'Celibacy: Exploding the Genital Myth', *Observer*, 7 March 1993, p. 49.

205 'Women kept all their rights': Paul Gray, 'Thou Shalt Not Kill', *Time*, 22 March, 1993, pp. 44–5; see also Larry Rohter, 'Doctor Is Slain During Protest Over Abortions', *New York Times*, 11 March 1993, p. A1.

208 She herself was flat chested: Richard Cohen, 'The Wide Net of Sexual Harassment', *Washington Post*, 15 June 1993, p. A21.

208 The Parishioner accused him of sexual abuse: Laurie Goodstein, 'Women's Anger Reaches Beyond Amorous Priest', *Washington Post*, 31 May 1993, p. A1.

208 A waitress: Stacey Wilkins, 'Stop Ordering me Around', *Newsweek*, 4 January 1993, p. 10.

209 Sexual harassment in school: Anita Manning, 'Schoolgirls Sexually Harassed', *USA Today*, 24 March 1993, p. A1, citing the NOW Legal Defense and Education Fund/Wellesley College Center for Research on Women Survey. 'May offend others and is heterosexist': 'Kindergarten Cops', *Harper's*, June 1993, p. 14, quoting from 'Examples of Hostile Environment Sexual Harassment: Student to Student', Minnesota Department of Education; the guidelines were developed in response to an anti-sexual harassment law that applies to all public school students from kindergarten up. See also Ruth Shalit, 'Romper Room', *New Republic* 29 March 1993, p. 13.

210 'Loved a creep too much': Deborah Solomon, characterizing others' views, 'The Uses of Adversity', *Women's Review of Books*, Vol. 9, No. 8, May 1992, p. 12.

212 'Scorned her': *New York Post*, 30 January 1992, p. 15.

212 'Cad and mouse': *New Republic, 3 March 1981.*

212 'The things she did for love': Walter Isaacson, *Time*, 9 February, 1981, p. 29. See also James Feron, 'Scarsdale Diet Doctor Slain; Headmistress Charged', *New York Times*, 12 March 1980, p. A1; Richard D. Lyons, 'School Staff Expresses Support for Murder Suspect', *New York Times*, 12 March 1980, p. B4; James Feron, 'Gun Used in Slaying of Doctor Is Linked to Suspect', *New York Times*, 13 March 1980, p. A1; James Feron, 'Uncertainty About Charges Delays Harris Court Hearing', *New York Times*, 13 March 1980, p. B1; James Feron, 'Officer in Tarnower Case Tells of Arrival on Scene', *New York Times*, 15 March 1980, p. B21; James Feron, 'Suspect's Lawyers Seek to Quash Order for Letter in Tarnower Case', *New York Times*, 16 March 1980, p. B38; James Feron, 'Accused Slayer of Doctor Given Psychiatric Care', *New York Times*, 17 March 1980, p. B3; James Feron, 'Both Sides Gather Their Evidence', *New York Times*, 23 March 1980, p. B1; James Feron, 'Judge Demands Tarnower Letter from Attorney', *New York Times*, 25 March 1980, p. B1; James Feron, 'Suspect

Indicated in Tarnower Death', *New York Times*, 26 March 1980, p. A1; James Feron. 'Mrs. Harris, in Court, Denies Guilt in Killing', *New York Times*, 29 March 1980, p. A1; Charlotte Evans, 'Attorney for Mrs. Harris Rules Out Insanity Plea', *New York Times*, 19 August 1980, p. B2; James Feron, 'Officer Testifies Mrs. Harris Said She Was Slayer', *New York Times*, 10 October 1980, p. B1 (According to the officer, Mrs. Harris had driven up from Virginia 'with the hope of having Dr. Tarnower kill her'; 'I've been through so much hell with him. He slept with every woman he could, I'd had it.'); James Feron, 'Housekeeper's Statement Cited in Tarnower Inquiry', *New York Times*, 11 October 1980, p. A26; James Feron, 'Lawyer's Warning to Mrs. Harris Cited at Hearing', *New York Times*, 21 October 1980, p. B3; James Feron, 'Patrolman Tells Court of Admission by Mrs. Harris', *New York Times*, 29 October 1980, p. B5. James Feron, 'Witness Recalls a Remark Made to Dying Doctor', *New York Times*, 31 October, 1980, p. B2; James Feron, 'Tarnower Jury Told Mrs. Harris Admitted Shooting', *New York Times*, 6 December 1980, p. A1; James Feron, 'Witness Terms Tarnower's Wounds Inconsistent with Struggle for Gun', *New York Times*, 19 December 1980, p. A1; James Feron, 'Pharmacist Tells of Prescriptions Mrs. Harris Got', *New York Times*, 27 January 1981, p. B1; James Feron, 'Mrs. Harris Gives Jury Her Version of What Led to Death of Tarnower', *New York Times*, 30 January 1981, p. A1; James Feron, 'Mrs. Harris Tells Court She Wanted Her Suicide to Be "a Private Death"', *New York Times*, 31 January 1981, p. A1; James Feron, 'Mrs. Harris Found Guilty of Murder and She Is Removed Quickly to Jail', *New York Times*, 25 February 1981, p. A1; James Feron, 'Defiant Jean Harris Sentenced to Mandatory 15 Years', *New York Times*, 21 March 1981, p. A1.

'How Murder Trial Split a Community', *New York Times*, 29 December 1986.

Feminist reactions: Ann Jones. 'Why Are We So Fascinated by the Harris Case?', *New York Newsday*, 8 November 1981, section 22, p. 24. For Mrs. Harris's own account, see Jean Harris, *Stranger in Two Worlds* (New York: Zebra Books, 1986), pp. 204–25.

214 **Amy Fisher: Amy Fisher with Sheila Weller,** *My Story* (New York: Pocket Books, 1993).

215 **'Presence of her husband':** Gurko, op. cit., p. 308.

215 **Azalea Cooley:** Rachel Zimmerman, 'The Perfect Victim', *Willamette Week*, Vol. 19, No. 5, 26 November–2 December, 1992, p. 12.

218 **'Trashing Geraldine Ferraro':** cited in Alison Mitchell, 'Holtzman Draws Criticism from Feminists over Ads', *New York Times*, 27 August 1992, p. 36.

218 **'Women will change the nature of power...'** : see Todd S. Purdum, 'Holtzman-Ferraro Venom Poses Questions for New Era', *New York Times*, 30 August 1992. See also Alison Mitchell, 'For Ferraro, Cheers of '84 Are Still Resonating', *New York Times*, 1 September 1992, p. B2; Todd S. Purdum, 'Lawyer for Ferraro Clears Her on Finances', *New York Times*, 1 September 1992, p. B1; Todd S. Purdum, 'Democrats Race to Take on D'Amato', *New York Times*, 16 September 1992, p. Al; Sam Howe Verhovek, 'Behind the Allegations in the Senate Campaign', *New York Times*, 14 September 1992, p. B5; Ralph Blumenthal, 'Ferraro's Husband Is Said to Have Met Mob Figure', *New York Times*, 12 September 1992, p. 24; Todd S. Purdum, 'Tone Shrill, Barbs Sharp, Senate Race Nears End', *New York Times*, 13 September 1992, p. 54; Todd S. Purdum, 'Debate and a Last-Minute Flurry Enliven New York's Senate Race', *New York Times*, 14 September 1992, p. A1; Sarah Lyall, 'Ferraro and Holtzman Meet, That's All', *New York Times*, 5 September 1992, p. B22; Sam Howe Verhovek, 'Senate Rivals Assail Ferraro over Ethics', *New York Times*, 20 August 1992, pp. B1 and B4; James Dao, 'Holtzman Hits Road to Attack Ferraro', *New York Times*, 15 August 1991, p. 21; Wayne Barrett and William Bastone, 'Ace in the Hole', *Village Voice*, 15 September 1992, p. 15.

Alison Mitchell, 'For Feminists, It Wasn't What They Had in Mind', *New*

York Times, 17 September 1992, p. B5; Wayne Barrett and William Bastone, 'Gerry and the Mob', *Village Voice*, 25 August 1992, p. 11; Wayne Barrett and William Bastone, 'Ethnics and Ethics', *Village Voice*, 8 September 1992, p. V1; endorsement, 'Holtzman for U.S. Senate', *Village Voice*, p. 22, 'Back to the Future', *Village Voice*, 8 September 1992, p. 27.

218   **Ruth W. Messinger:** Todd S. Purdum, 'For Ferraro, Charges Buzz Just out of Reach', *New York Times*, 23 August 1992, p. A24; regarding the allegations, '[M]ost politicians consider it all but inevitable that such questions would eventually surface in the campaign.' Todd S. Purdum, 'Ferraro and Foes Clash Over Ethics', *New York Times*, 11 September 1992, p. A1; Ralph Blumenthal, 'Ferraro Releases Tax Returns for 2 Missing Years to Offset Attacks by Rivals', *New York Times*, 11 September 1992; Ferraro called for scrutiny of her rivals' tax returns in response to her own being scrutinized, not only by her opponents but by several newspapers that also called for her to reveal her 1984 and 1985 tax returns.

218   **'Feminist ideology':** Catherine S. Manegold, 'Holtzman and Ferraro Fought Double Standard as Well as Each Other', *New York Times*, 16 September 1992, p. B6.

218/9   **Pogrebin and Abzug:** Alison Mitchell, 'Holtzman Draws Criticism from Feminists over Ads', *New York Times*, 27 August 1992, p. B4. According to Letty Cottin Pogrebin, 'Women are promising to do it differently and do it better. With her sleazy campaign, Liz Holtzman has betrayed that promise.' The women's movement,' said former representative Bella S. Abzug, 'has tried for a considerable time to make the point that we need women in political power in order to change things. It's very sad to see antifeminist standards being used, and I believe they are, in trashing Geraldine Ferraro.' Ferraro's camp retaliated by creating an ad that cited Anita Hill as another woman victim of 'smears', and claiming that Holtzman attacked Ferraro not because she was the front-runner, but because she was the only other woman. Todd S. Purdum, 'Ferraro: Answering Mob Charges', *New York Times*, 28 August 1992, p. B4; Alison Mitchell, 'For Ferraro, Cheers of '84 Are Still Resonating', *New York Times*, 1 September 1992, p. B2.

219   **'In the name of feminism':** Todd S. Purdum, 'The Feminist Paradox: Holtzman-Ferraro Battle Tests Idea of Women in Politics', *New York Times*, 30 August 1992, p. A33.

219   **'Tool of a Republican man':** James C. McKinley, Jr, 'Holtzman, After the Flood: Trying to Heal the Wounds from Her Own Attack', *New York Times*, 7 March 1993, p. A37. Abrams also attacked Ferraro: 'Four Senate Challengers Excerpts from the Democrats' Debate', *New York Times*, 11 September 1992; Todd S. Purdum, 'Ferraro and Foes Begin Vying for the Viewer Vote', *New York Times*, 26 August 1992, p. B1.

219   **Abrams also levelled charges:** Todd S. Purdum, 'Ferraro and Abrams Exchange Complaints', *New York Times*, 9 September, 1992, p. B5; Todd S. Purdum, 'Final Push Begins in Race for Senate', *New York Times*, 8 September 1992, p. B1; Todd S. Purdum, 'Ferraro Foes Strive to Take High Ground', *New York Times*, 6 September 1992, p. 49.

221   **Rosalind Coward:** see her *Our Treacherous Hearts*, p. 62.

223   **Said a friend:** Barbara Whitaker, 'She's Come a Long Way in a Year, Friends Say', *New York Newsday*, 24 October 1988: According to Nussbaum friend Larry Weinberg, 'Because Hedda had this gentle nature, this sensitive soul, and some self-doubts that I don't think were greater than any other person's ... he [Steinberg] was able to overwhelm her', See also an unsigned editorial, 'Battered Enough', *New York Times*, 12 November 1987, p. A30. 'The public may feel conflicted about Hedda Nussbaum, charged with complicity in the beatings of a little girl. But she is also a victim.'; Timothy Clifford, 'Nussbaum Readied for Stand', *New York Newsday*, 14 November 1988, p. 3: 'Prosecutors ... will try to show the jury that Steinberg so dominated [Nussbaum] that she was not

criminally responsible for Lisa's death. . . . Prosecutors maintain Nussbaum was under Steinberg's "domination", leaving her physically and psychologically unable to commit any crime"; Timothy Clifford, 'Judge Agrees to Another Delay on Start of Nussbaum Case', *New York Newsday*, 6 October 1988, p. 31: According to Nussbaum's attorney, 'Our position remains that she was not in any physical or mental condition to prevent that death from being caused.'

Barbara Whitaker, 'Steinberg's "Godlike Powers"', *New York Newsday* 3 December 1988, p. 4; trial transcript, 'Hedda Nussbaum on the Stand', *New York Newsday*, 3 December 1988, pp. 5–13; Marianne Yen, 'Former Lover Testifies to Control by Steinberg', *Washington Post*, 3 December 1988, p. A3; Ronald Sullivan, 'Nussbaum Testimony Is Called a Risk', *New York Times* 4 December 1988, p. A54.

223   **'No ability or will to save her own daughter':** George Hackett, 'A Tale of Abuse', *Newsweek* 12 December 1988, p. 56.

For other Nussbaum material, see Barbara Whitaker, 'Emerging Symbol of Abuse: Hedda Gets Activists' Attention', *New York Newsday*, 4 December 1988, p. 7; Timothy Clifford, 'Nussbaum Ties Together Key Elements', *New York Newsday*, 4 December 1988, p. 7; Timothy Clifford, 'Hedda's View of "Beatings": Joel Did It to Help Her, Sources Say She Told Doctor', *New York Newsday* 5 December 1988, p. 5; identifications with Hedda Nussbaum, William Glaberson, 'Why Hedda Nussbaum Fascinates: Most Can Identify', *New York Times*, 9 December 1988, p. B1; Ellen Goodman, 'Hedda's Hurt Is Too Close for Our Comfort', *New York Newsday*, 9 December 1988, p. 94; Ronald Sullivan, 'Defense Tries to Show Nussbaum Liked Pain', *New York Times*, 9 December 1988, p. B2; Marianne Yen, 'Testimony Stirs Troubling Questions About Responsibility for Child's Death', *Washington Post*, 11 December 1988, p. A3; George Hackett, 'A Tale of Abuse', *Newsweek*, 12 December 1988, p. 56; Marianne Yen, 'Defense Prods Nussbaum on Failure to Aid Child', *Washington post*, 13 December 1988, p. A18; Ronald Sullivan, 'Nussbaum Says She Lied to Help Steinberg', *New York Times*, 14 December 1988, p. B1; Richard Cohen, 'When Weakness Becomes an Alibi', *Washington Post*, 21 December 1988, p. A19; Marianne Yen, 'Nussbaum's Account of Action Contradicted by Police Officer', *Washington Post*, 21 December 1988, p. A2; Mary Cantwell, 'Close to Home', *New York Times*, 29 December 1988; Marianne Yen, 'Jurors Told Nussbaum Struck Lisa Steinberg', *Washington Post*, 7 January 1989, p. A3; Ronald Sullivan, 'Nussbaum Seen by a Witness as Competent', *New York Times*, 13 January 1989, p. B3 ('Dr. Eshkenazi's testimony was intended to counter prosecution statements that Ms. Nussbaum was so battered by Mr. Steinberg that she was incapable of inflicting the blows that killed Lisa or of taking any action afterward to save her life.'); Patricia Volk, 'Scenes from a Tragedy', *New York Times Magazine*, 15 January 1989, p. 22; Richard Lacayo, 'A Question of Responsibility', *Time* 13 February 1989, p. 68; Timothy Clifford, 'Steinberg Asks to Question Hedda', *New York Newsday* 10 March 1989, p. 6; Ellis Henican, 'Steinberg Gets Top Term', *New York Newsday*, 25 March 1989, p. 10; Robert Coles, 'The Death of a Child', *New York Times Book Review*, 9 April 1990, p. 1; Emily Sachar, 'Nussbaum Says Joel Drove Her Insane', *New York Newsday*, 7 September 1990. p. 27.

223   **Many women saw themselves:** Barbara Whitaker, 'Feminists: Don't Blame the Victims', *New York Newsday* 25 March 1989, p. 11: '[Gloria] Steinem likened battered women to prisoners in concentration camps who behave in various ways to adapt to their situation.'

224   **'Had been her God':** Murray Kempton, 'A Tormented Soul Confronts Reality', *New York Newsday*, 2 December 1988, p. 4.

224   **Susan Brownmiller:** Susan Brownmiller, 'Hedda Nussbaum, Hardly a Heroine', *New York Times*, 2 February 1989, p. A25; Andrea Dworkin, 'Living in Terror, Pain: Being a Battered Wife', *Los Angeles Times*, 12 March 1989, p. VI; Anne Summers, 'The Hedda Conundrum', *Ms.*, April 1989, p. 54; Susan

Brownmiller, 'Madly in Love', ibid., p. 56; Marilyn French, 'A Gothic Romance', ibid., p. 60; Hedda Nussbaum, 'Hedda Speaks Out', ibid., p. 12; Jane Caputi, 'The Sexual Politics of Murder', *Gender & Society*, Vol. 3, No. 4, December 1989, pp. 437–56; Sheila Anne Feeney, 'Hedda's Secret: What No One Understands About Abused Women', *Mademoiselle*, March 1989, p. 242.

224   **'Though she did not kill that child'**: Nadine Brozan, 'Unresolved Issue: Is Nussbaum Culpable?', *New York Times*, 24 January 1989, p. B1, cites Ellen Jacobs: 'The issue is the death of an innocent child. She was an adult, a college-educated woman who had access to the system, who understood what was available and chose not to use it. This case affirms passivity as a defense.'

224   **'And ultimately, to men'**: Susan Brownmiller, 'Hedda Nussbaum: Hardly a Heroine', *New York Times*, 2 February 1989, p. A25.

224   **'Third century, BC**: Marilyn French *Ms.*, April 1989, p. 60.

225   **'Battered-woman syndrome'**: Holly Maguigan, 'Battered Women and Self-defense: Myths and Misconceptions in Current Reform Proposals'. *University of Pennsylvania Law Review*, Vol. 140, No. 2, December 1991, pp. 379–486.

226   **Children to death**: Ann Jones, 'Children of a Lesser Man', *Lear's*, May 1993, p. 30.

226   **'Need to be changing ourselves'**: Tamar Lewin, 'Feminists Wonder If It Was Progress to Become "Victims"', *New York Times*, 10 May 1992, p. D6.

227   **Helena Kennedy**: see her *Eve Was Framed* (London:Chatto & Windus, 1992), p. 202.

227   **'Prescribed for their sex'**: Jennifer Nadel, *Observer*, 25 April 1993.

227   **'Pin-ups or physical contact'**: OEC 1988.

228   **A 'reasonable person' would find offensive**: Linda Greenhouse, 'Justices to Decide if Psychological Injury is Needed to Prove Sex Harassment', *New York Times*, 2 March 1993, p. A17.

228   **No Pity**: Joseph P. Shapiro, *No Pity: People with Disabilities Forging a New Civil Rights Movement* (New York Times Books, 1993).

228   **A growing body of research**: see William B. Swann, Jr, Alan Stein-Serouss and Shawn E. McNulty, 'Outcasts in a White Lie Society: The Enigmatic Worlds of People With Negative Self-Concepts', *Journal of Personality and Social Psychology*, Vol. 62, No. 4, 618–26, 1992: The findings show that people with negative views of their own potential send cues that keep them deprived of 'corrective feedback'. See also Robert A. Josephs, Hazel Rose Markus and Roemin W. Tafarodi, 'Gender and Self-Esteem', *Journal of Personality and Social Psychology*, Vol. 63, No. 3, 391–402, 1992.

229   **Disdain ... self-help**: see Wendy Simonds, *Women and Self-Help Culture: Reading Between the Lines* (New Brunswick, N.J. Rutgers University Press, 1992).

230   **Firearms-buying American public**: Peggy Tartaro, 'Fish on Bicycles', *Women & Guns*, September 1991, p. 50. 'Twelve million women own guns': Sonny Jones, 'From the Editor', *Women & Guns*, September 1991, p. 7.

230   **With a knife or a firearm**: Survey, *Women & Guns*, March 1992, p. 4.

230   **Self-defence**: highlights of *Women & Guns*, 1991 readers' survey, February 1992, p. 25.

231   **Only 3 per cent ... succeeded**: Shielah Dawson, 'Letters to the Editor', *Women & Guns*, March 1992, p. 4.

231   **Annual incomes of between $25,000 and $50,000**: ibid., p. 25.

231   **'I still see the violence'**: Maria M. C. Esling, San Diego, California, 'Letters to the Editor', *Women and Guns*, February 1992, p. 4.

232   **'I know I'll be glad to have presented my friends'**: Barbara Healy, Rochester, New York, 'Letters to the Editor', *Women & Guns*, December 1991, p. 4.

232   **'Ability to inflict abuse'**: author, 'Sisters of the Gun', *Women & Guns*.

232   **'There is a lot of talk about "women's liberation"'**: Karen MacNutt, 'Perpetuating the Victim Status of Women', *Women & Guns*, December 1991, p. 7.

233   'Fired five times at the windshield': *Women & Guns*, December 1991, p. 6.

233   'Be Safe, Feminine and Stylish!': Love Leathers advertisement, *Women & Guns*, March 1993, p. 5. An example of *Women & Guns'* self-defence features is in Marshall J. Brown, 'True Life Self Defense: A Woman Fights Back', *Women and Guns*, March 1993, p. 28: Two teenage burglars told Willeen Lansberry, 'Go ahead and shoot!': 'I grabbed his shirt and said, "You're not leaving – all I have to do is pull this trigger and your blood will be all over the walls . . . I'm counting to three!' The youth sat down. 'He knew I wasn't fooling – I would have shot him at that point', said Lansberry. An example of *Women & Gun's* Cosmo-like fashion presentation is the caption, 'Graciella Casillas demonstrates the feasibility of wearing an ankle holster beneath a full-length evening dress', *Women & Guns*, April 1992, p. 3.

233   'The Armed Women's Aptitude Test': Massad Ayoob, *Women & Guns*, December 1991, p. 38.

234   'Never slave for anybody': Chuck Sudetic, 'In Sarajevo, War Also Means Battle of the Sexes', *New York Times*, 6 June 1993, p. A12.

235   'I felt great': Richard Ellis, 'Blacks Join in the White Fight for Survival', *Sunday Times*, 7 March, 1993.

235   32 per cent of women in prison . . . for violent crime: Mimi Hall and Tom Watson, 'Survey Show Prisons Aren't Curbing Crime', *USA Today*, 20 May 1993.

235   Violent crime: Prison data suggests that women are far less reactable than their reputation pretends: see Meda Chesney-Lind, 'Patriarchy, Prisons and Jails: A Critical Look at Trends in Women's Incarcerations', paper presented at the International Feminist Conference in Women, Law and Social Control, Mont Gabriel, Quebec, July 1991. Meda Chesney-Ling, 'Women and Crime: The Female Offender', *Signs: Journal of Women in Culture and Society*, Vol. 12, No. 1, Autumn 1986.

235   'Other maltreatment': American Association for Protecting Children highlights of official child neglect and abuse reporting, Denver, Colorado, 1986, p. 29; see also Deborah Daro, and Karen McCurdy, 'Current Trends in Child Abuse Reporting and Fatalities: The Results of the 1991 Fifty-State Survey', working paper 808, April 1992.

236   'Quite without concern for her infant': Jane Goodall, *In the Shadow of Man* (Boston: Houghton Mifflin, 1971), p. 148.

238   'Zines': *Bad Attitude*, Vol. 8, No. 2, Winter 1992, Cambridge, Mass.; see also Julie Doucet, 'Dirty Plotte', *Drawn & Quarterly*, No. 5, May 1992; Eve Gilbert, 'Dangerous Pussy', San Francisco: Manic D Press, 1993, 'Dear Good Abby/Bad Abby', *On Our Butts*, No. 1, March 1993, San Francisco, p. 14; Hothead Paisan, 'Our Favorite Lesbian Terrorist', *Brat Attack (The Zine for Leatherdykes and Other Bad Girls)*, San Francisco, p. 26.

238   Aileen Wuornus: Cris Gutierrez, 'Aileen Wuornos, Hothead Paisan, and Me,' *Frighten the Horses: a Document of the Sexual Revolution*, No. 11, Winter 1993, p. 9.

239   Elimination of the male: Nancy Friday, 'Angry Women, Sadistic Fantasies', *Women on Top: How Real Life has Changed Women's Sexual Fantasies* (New York: Pocket Books, 1991), pp. 161–75.

239   Sexual harassment: Bill Hewitt and Nancy Matsumoto, 'Trading Places: Sexually Harassed at Work, a California Man is Awarded $1 Million', *People*, 7 June 1993, pp. 99–100.

240   'Rip off my underwear': *New York Times*, 21 February 1993, p. 3; see also pornography for women, *Women Only: For Women Who Want More*, Vol 1, No. 4, and *For Women: The Magazine for the Sensual Woman*, London, 1993, Vol. 1, No. 10.

243   'Bad girl': '90210's Shannen Doherty: Out of Control!', *People,*, 14 June 1993, cover.

243   'Child abuse the Vatican ignores': *Guardian*, 1 May 1993.

243   'Who dressed in black: *New York Times*, 14 February 1993.
243   'Huggy Bear are the most badly behaved: *Guardian*, 24 March 1993.
244   Catwoman: Mindy Newell, *The Catwoman: Her Sister's Keeper* (New York: D. C. Comics, 1991).

Part 4: Towards a New Psychology of Female Power

251   'Particular advantages': Coward, op. cit., p. 41.
251   'Frightened by success': Sue Butterworth, quoted in *Guardian*, 23 April 1993.
251   'Wanted to be powerful': Jill Tweedie, *Guardian*, 12 May 1993.
255   Audre Lorde: Audre Lorde, 'The Transformation of Silence into Language and Action', *Sister Outsider* (Trumansburg: The Crossing Press, 1984), p. 71.
260   If they do not apply: Hansard, *Women at The Top*, op. cit.
260   'Missed opportunities': *Equal Times*, No. 8, January 1993.
260   'Accessible to you': Lord Mackay, quoted in *Guardian*, 22 April 1993.
260   Such deprecatory descriptions: Anne Karpf, 'Convincing a worker that she's as good as her word', *Guardian* 15 June 1993.
262   'A rich bitch': Anita Roddick quoted in the *Sunday Times*, 1 September 1991.
265   Treated them like idiots: *Guardian*, 24 September 1991.
265   'Dependent ... on men for their wealth': *Business Age Magazine*, September 1992.
267   Tannen: Deborah Tannen: *You Just Don't Understand: Women and Men in Conversation* (New York: William Morrow, 1990)
267   Gilligan ... first book: Carol Gilligan, *In a Different Voice: Psychological Theory and Women's Development* (Cambridge, Mass.: Harvard University Press, 1982).
267   Underground: Carol Gilligan and Lyn Mikel Brown, *Meeting at the Crossroads* (Cambridge, Mass.: Harvard University Press, 1992).
272   'Ridicule': Shulamith Firestone, *The Dialectic of Sex: The Case For Feminist Revolution* (London: The Women's Press, 1979). p. 32; see also Carol Hymowitz and Michaele Weissman, *A History of Women in America* (New York: Bantam, 1978), p. 285.
274   'Seem to get worse': Jean Baker Miller, *Toward a New Psychology of Women* (Boston: Beacon Press, 1986), p. 93.
274   'Follow through on the new course': ibid., p. 93.
276   'What feels bad or wrong': Carol Gilligan, Lyn Mikel Brown, op cit., p. 52.
278   Chodorow: Nancy Chodorow, *The Reproduction of Mothering, Psychoanalysis and The Sociology of Gender*, (Berkeley: University of California Press, 1978).
279   Erikson: Erik H. Erikson, *Childhood and Society* (New York: W. W. Norton, 1963), pp. 97–108.
280   Evelyn Fox Keller: *Reflections on Gender and Science* (New Haven, Conn.: Yale University Press, 1985).
282   Madeline: Ludwig Bemelmans, *Madeline* and *Madeline's Rescue* (New York: Simon & Schuster, 1939).
285   'I care about it and they don't': Frances Hodgson Burnett, *The Secret Garden* (New York: HarperCollins, 1991), p. 106.
285   Harriet: Louise Fitzhugh, *Harriet the Spy* (New York: HarperCollins, 1964).
286   Louisa May Alcott: *Little Women* (New York: Puffin Books, 1953), p. 11.
289   Leadership and Egotism: Carol J. Eagle and Carol Colman, *All That She Can Be: Helping Your Daughter Achieve Her Full Potential and Maintain Her Self-esteem During the Critical Years of Adolescence* (New York: Simon & Schuster, 1993).
289   'To care about somebody else': ibid., p. 141.
293   'Ultimate means of social control': Deborah Tannen, *You Just Don't Understand: Women and Men in Conversation* (New York: Ballantine, 1990), p. 108.
293   'Submerge her own feelings': Eagle and Colman, op. cit., p. 149.

294　'Makes them uncomfortable': ibid., pp. 142–3; see also this conversation with young women at Virginia Tech, a state college. Katie, Tonya, Joetta, and Kari are Caucasian, and Renée is African-American. Their parents are teachers, pharmacists, and homemakers:

TONYA: 'The master's tools will never dismantle the master's house.' Is there something inherently wrong with buying into those hierarchies and appropriating them or should we be trying to dismantle them? When we begin working in the system we become part of it.

KATIE: It's easier to renounce the power if you're close to it.

RENEE; Maybe [women] are scared they'll be so criticized if they take that power they'll be knocked back down. Even if they get that far, they think it's just luck, and maybe if they take that last step, then luck will run out.

NW: What's wrong with failing?

JOETTA: It's so ingrained that we'll fail. You're afraid if you do try, and you fail, they'll say, 'see, it failed because it was never supposed to be.'

TONYA: You'll be ridiculed. You're ridiculed when you're trying to achieve, then you're ridiculed when you do achieve.

KATIE: I think a lot of women feel just fraudulent.

TONYA: We didn't want to list your credentials because women are only listened to if they have male educational credentials. Power is very dangerous if you don't keep aware of it. Sometimes you have to step away from it so you don't abuse it.

KARI: So many people are afraid of hierarchy, when sometimes hierarchies are good. Sometimes someone has to lead. It doesn't mean they are lord or king.

295　'Lifeblood ran in different directions': Tannen, op. cit., p. 26.

295　'Compromise and evasion': ibid., p. 45.

298　'Cooperative nature of human existence': Miller, op cit., p. 41.

298　'Women's lives are organized': ibid., p. 61.

298　'May not apply': ibid., p. 73.

298　'Conquest and destruction': ibid., p. 78.

298　'Distortion': Gilligan, op cit., p. 23.

299　'Threats to rapport': Tannen, op cit., p. 274.

299　Salary or position: Miller, op cit., p. 223.

299　'Suffering as a result': ibid., p. 178.

299　'End in ... embarrassment': Tannen, op cit., p. 177.

299　'Troubles talk': Tannen, op cit., p. 100.

299　'Equal in status': Miller, op. cit., p. 155.

299　Ms M.: ibid., p. 133.

299　'Worry about offending': ibid., p. 131.

300　Jake: Gilligan, op. cit., p. 29.

301　'Gossip': Tannen, op. cit., p. 110.

303　'Control or submerge others': Miller, op. cit., p. 96.

303　'Control or restrict them': ibid., p. 116.

Part 5: What Do We Do Now? Power Feminism in Action

308　'Nay, we are in truth': 'Letter from the Union of Women for Association,' cited in Nancy F. Cott (ed.), *Root of Bitterness* (New York: Dutton, 1972), pp. 239–41.

See bell hooks on sisterhood: 'Women who are exploited and oppressed daily cannot afford to see themselves solely as "victims" because their survival depends on continued exercise of whatever personal powers they possess. It would be psychologically demoralizing for these women to bond with other women on the basis of shared victimization. They bond with other women on the basis of shared strengths and resources. This is the woman bonding [the] feminist movement should encourage. It is this type of bonding that is the essence of Sisterhood.'

Also: '[White women's] version of Sisterhood dictated that sisters were to "unconditionally" love one another; that they were to avoid conflict and minimize disagreement; that they were not to criticize one another, especially in public. For a time these mandates created an illusion of unity suppressing the competition, hostility, perpetual disagreement, and abusive criticism (trashing) that was often the norm in feminist groups. Today many splinter groups who share common identities (e.g. Wasp working class; white academic faculty women; anarchist feminists, etc.) use this same model of sisterhood, but participants in these groups endeavor to support, affirm and protect one another while demonstrating hostility (usually through excessive trashing) towards women outside the chosen sphere. . . . Rather than bond on the basis of shared victimization or in response to a false sense of a common enemy, we can bond on the basis of our political commitment to a feminist movement that aims to end sexist oppression.'

310   **[Men] form alliances:** Jean Baker Miller, *Toward a New Psychology of Women* (Boston: Beacon Press, 1976), p. 135.

317   **Farmers, producers and traders:** Sharon Capeling-Alakija, Director, Unifem, Unifem Annual report, 1991, p. 3.

318   **One in four of all self-employed:** *Guardian*, 13 July 1992.

318   **Male counterparts:** 'Facts of the Matter', *Good Weekend*, March 1993.

318   **'With clenched fists':** Claudia Wallis, 'Onward. Women!', *Time*, 4 December 1989, p. 4.

321   **1,373 won:** Center for American Women and Politics.

321   **Incomes between $40,000 and $49,000:** Fund for the Feminist Majority, pamphlet, 'Empowering Women in Philanthropy'.

330   **Faculty was female:** AUT figures, May 1993.

330   **92 per cent of lecturers were men:** *Guardian*, 2 September 1992.

331   **16 per cent of promotions:** Hansard, *Women at the Top*; and AUT.

331   **Just 7 per cent of women:** AUT, reported in *Guardian*, 19 May 1993.

337   **Charlotte Woodward:** Miriam Gurko, *The Ladies of Seneca Falls: The Birth of the Women's Rights Movement* (New York:Schocken Books, 1976), pp. 99–100.

[See Selected Bibliography for current UK editions of works, where available.]

Selected Bibliography

A Comprehensive Guide to Television and Radio New and Public Affairs Programming. Transcript: Video Index. Denver, Col.: Journal Graphics, 1992.

Alcott, Louisa M. *Little Women.* New York: Puffin Books, 1953. Harmondsworth: Penguin Books, 1989.

Andersen, Margaret L., and Patricia Hill Collins. *Race, Class, and Gender. An Anthology.* Belmont, Calif.: Wadsworth Publishing Co., 1992.

Anderson, Bonnie S., and Judith P. Zinsser. *A History of Their Own: Women in Europe from Prehistory to the Present, Vol. II.* New York: HarperCollins, 1988.

Anzaldua, Gloria, ed. *Making Face, Making Soul (Haciendo Caras): Creative and Critical Perspectives by Women of Color.* San Francisco: Aunt Lute Books, 1990.

Aufderheide, Patricia. *Beyond P.C.: Toward a Politics of Understanding.* St. Paul: Graywolf Press, 1992.

Barnett, Rosalind C. *Women in Management Today.* Wellesley, Mass.: Working Papers Series, Wellesley Center for Research on Women, No. 249, 1992.

Belenky, Mary Field, et al. *Women's Ways of Knowing: The Development of Self, Voice, and Mind.* New York: Basic Books, 1986.

Bem, Sandra Lipsitz. *The Lenses of Gender: Transforming the Debate on Sexual Inequality.* New Haven: Yale University Press, 1993.

Berman, Paul, ed. *Debating P.C.: The Controversy Over Political Correctness on College Campuses.* New York: Bantam Doubleday Dell, 1992.

Berry, Mary Frances. *The Politics of Parenthood: Child Care, Women's Rights, and the Myth of the Good Mother.* New York: Viking, Penguin, 1993.

Breitman, George, ed. *Malcolm X Speaks: Selected Speeches and Statements.* New York: George Weidenfeld, 1965. London: Secker & Warburg, 1966.

Bright, Susie. *Susie Sexpert's Lesbian Sex World.* Pittsburgh: Cleis Press, 1991.

Brock, David. *The Real Anita Hill: The Untold Story*. New York: The Free Press, 1993.

Brownmiller, Susan. *Against Our Will: Men, Women, and Rape*. New York: Simon & Schuster, 1975. London: Secker & Warburg, 1975.

Capeling-Alakija, Sharon. *Unifem Annual Report 1991*. New York: United Nations Development Fund for Women, 1991.

Card, Emily. *The Ms. Money Book: Strategies for Prospering in the Coming Decade*. New York: Dutton, 1990.

Chesler, Ellen. *Woman of Valor: Margaret Sanger and the Birth Control Movement in America*. New York: Summit Books, 1992.

Chesler, Phyllis, and Emily Jane Goodman. *Women, Money, and Power*. New York: Bantam, 1977.

Cohen, Marcia. *The Sisterhood: The Inside Story Of The Women's Movement and the Leaders Who Made It Happen*. New York: Fawcett Columbine, 1988.

Collins, Patricia Hill. *Black Feminist Thought: Knowledge, Consciousness, and the Politics of Empowerment*. New York: Routledge, 1991. London: Unwin Hyman, 1991.

Davis, Angela Y. *Women, Race, and Class*. London: The Women's Press, 1982. New York: Vintage, 1983.

Davis, Flora. *Moving the Mountain: The Women's Movement in America Since 1960*. New York; London: Simon & Schuster, 1981.

Diebold, Elizabeth, Idelisse Malave, and Marie Wilson. *Mother-Daughter Revolution: From Betrayal to Power*. New York: Addison-Wesley Publishing, 1993.

Demac, Donna A. *Liberty Denied: The Current Rise of Censorship in America*. New Brunswick; London: Rutgers University Press, 1990.

Deutsch, Helene, M.D. *The Psychology of Women: A Psychoanalytic Interpretation*. New York: Grune & Stratton, 1944.

Dinnerstein, Dorothy. *The Mermaid and the Minotaur: Sexual Arrangements and Human Malaise*. New York: Harper Colophon, 1977. London: Souvenir Press, 1978.

D'Souza, Dinesh. *Illiberal Education: The Politics of Race and Sex on Campus*. New York: Vintage, 1992.

'Drugs Play Major Role in Female Jail Population Increase,' Department of Justice Release, Washington D.C.: Bureau of Justice Statistics, March 1992.

Dworkin, Andrea. *Intercourse*. London: Secker & Warburg, 1986. New York: The Free Press, 1987.

——. *Mercy*. London: Secker & Warburg, 1990. New York: Four Walls Eight Windows, 1991.

——. *Woman Hating: A Radical Look at Sexuality*. New York: Dutton, 1974.

Dyhouse, Carol. *Feminism and the Family in England, 1880–1939*. Oxford: Basil Blackwell, 1989.

Echols, Alice. *Daring to Be Bad: Radical Feminism in America, 1967–75*. Minneapolis: University of Minnesota Press, 1989.

Ehrenreich, Barbara. *The Hearts of Men: American Dreams and the Flight from Commitment*. New York: Anchor, 1983. London: Pluto Press, 1983.

——, and Deirdre English. *For Her Own Good: 150 Years of Experts' Advice to Women*. New York: Anchor, 1979. London: Pluto Press, 1979.

——, Elizabeth Hess, and Gloria Jacobs. *Re-Making Love: The Feminization of Sex*. New York: Anchor, 1986. London: Pluto Press, 1987.

Elshtain, Jean Bethke. *Women and War*. New York: Basic Books, 1987. Brighton: Harvester Press, 1987.

Epstein, Cynthia. *Deceptive Distinctions: Sex, Gender, and the Social Order*. New Haven; London: Yale University Press, 1988.

Erikson, Eric H. *Childhood and Society*. New York: W. W. Norton & Co., 1963. Harmondsworth: Penguin Books, 1965.

Faderman, Lillian. *Surpassing the Love of Men: Romantic Friendship and Love Between Women from the Renaissance to the Present*. New York: William Morrow & Co., 1981.

Faludi, Susan. *Backlash: The Undeclared War Against American Women*. New York: Crown, 1991. London: Chatto & Windus, 1992 [as *Backlash: The Undeclared War Against Women*].

Firestone, Shulamith. *The Dialectic of Sex: The Case for Feminist Revolution*. London: The Women's Press, 1979.

Fisher, Helen E. *Anatomy of Love: The Natural History of Monogamy, Adultery, and Divorce*. New York: W. W. Norton, 1992.

Fitzhugh, Louise. *Harriet the Spy*. New York: Harper & Row, 1964; London, 1966.

Foucault, Michel. *The History of Sexuality: An Introduction, Volume 1*. New York: Vintage, 1990. Harmondsworth: Penguin Books, 1984.

Fox-Genovese, Elizabeth. *Feminism Without Illusions: A Critique of Individualism*. Chapel Hill; London: University Of North Carolina Press, 1991.

Friday, Nancy. *Women on Top: How Real Life has Changed Women's Sexual Fantasies*. New York: Simon & Schuster, 1991. London: Hutchinson, 1991.

Friedan, Betty. *The Second Stage*. New York: Summit Books, 1981. London: Abacus Books, 1983.

Giddings, Paula. *When and Where I Enter: The Impact of Black Women on Race and Sex in America*. New York: Bantam Books, 1985.

Gilligan, Carol. *In a Different Voice: Psychological Theory and Women's Development*. Cambridge, Mass.; London: Harvard University Press, 1982.

——, and Lyn Mikel Brown. *Meeting at the Crossroads: Women's Psychology and Girls' Development*. Cambridge, Mass.: Harvard University Press, 1992.

'Girls in Our Schools: A Bibliography of Research on Girls in U.S. Public Schools, Kindergarten Through Grade 12.' Wellesley, Mass.: Wellesley Center for Research on Women, September 1992.

Gluck, Sherna, ed. *From Parlor to Prison: Five American Suffragists Talk About Their Lives*. New York: Hippocrene Books, 1976.

Goldsmith, Olivia. *The First Wives' Club*. New York: Pocket Books, 1993. London: Heinemann, 1992.

Goodall, Jane. *In the Shadow of Man*. Boston: Houghton Mifflin, 1988. London: Weidenfeld & Nicolson, 1989.

Gordon, Vivian, M.D. *Black Women, Feminism, and Black Liberation: Which Way?*. Chicago: Third World Press, 1987.

Greenfield, Lawrence A., and Stephanie Minor-Harper. *Women in Prison*. Washington, D.C.: Bureau of Justice Statistics Special Report, U.S. Department of Justice, March 1991.

Griffin, Susan. *Woman and Nature: The Roaring Inside Her*. New York: Harper & Row, 1978. London: The Women's Press, 1984.

Grimshaw, Jean. *Philosophy and Feminist Thinking*. Minneapolis: University of Minnesota Press, 1986.

Gurko, Miriam. *The Ladies of Seneca Falls: The Birth of the Women's Rights Movement*. New York: Schocken Books, 1976.

Hahn, Emily. *Once Upon a Pedestal*. New York: NAL, 1975.

Haley, Alex, and Malcolm X. *The Autobiography of Malcolm X*. New York: Grove Press, 1964.

Helgasen, Sally. *The Female Advantage: Women's Ways of Leadership*. New York: Doubleday, 1990.

Helsinger, Elizabeth K., Robin Lauterbach Sheets, and William Veeder. *The Woman Question: Society and Literature in Britain and America, 1837–1883, Volume 3*. Chicago: University of Chicago Press, 1983. Manchester: Manchester University Press, 1983.

Hentoff, Nat. *Free Speech for Me – But Not for Thee: How the American Left and Right Relentlessly Censor Each Other*. New York: HarperCollins, 1992.

hooks, bell. *Black Looks: Race and Representation*. Boston: South End Press, 1992.

——. *Feminist Theory: From Margin to Center*. Boston: South End Press, 1984.

——. *Talking Back: Thinking Feminist, Thinking Black*. Boston: South End Bress, 1989. London: Sheba, 1989.

Hull, Gloria T., Patricia Bell Scott, and Barbara Smith. *All the Women Are White, All the Blacks Are Men, But Some of Us Are Brave: Black Women's Studies*. New York: The Feminist Press, 1982.

Hymowitz, Carol, and Michaele Weissmann. *A History of Women in America*. New York: Bantam, 1978.

Irigaray, Luce. *This Sex Which Is Not One*, trans. Carolyn Burke. Ithaca: Cornell University Press, 1985.

Jacoby, Russell. *The Last Intellectuals: American Culture in the Age of Academe*. New York: Farrar, Straus & Giroux, 1987.

Johnston, Jill. *Lesbian Nation: The Feminist Solution*. New York: Touchstone, 1974.

King, Martin Luther, Jr. *Strength to Love*. Philadelphia: Fortress Press, 1981.

——. *Why We Can't Wait*. New York: Mentor Books, 1964. London: Hodder & Stoughton, 1964.

Kleiman, Carol. *Women's Networks*. New York: Harper & Row, 1980.

Kraditor, Aileen S. *Up from the Pedestal: Selected Writings in the History of American Feminism*. New York: Quadrangle, 1968.

——. *The Ideas of the Woman Suffrage Movement, 1880–1920*. New York; London: W. W. Norton & Co., 1981.

Langer, Marie. *Motherhood and Sexuality*, trans. Nancy C. Hollander. New York: The Guilford Press, 1992.

Leone, Bruno, ed. *Sexual Harassment*. San Diego: Greenhaven Press, 1992.

Lerner, Gerda. *Black Women in White America: A Documentary History*. New York: Vintage, 1973.

Lieberman, Annette, and Vicki Lindner. *Unbalanced Accounts: Why Women Are Still Afraid of Money*. New York: Penguin, 1988.

Lorde, Audre. *Sister Outsider: Essays and Speeches*. Trumansburg: The Crossing Press, 1984.

——. *Zami: A New Spelling of My Name*. Freedom, Calif.: The Crossing Press, 1983. London: Sheba, 1984.

MacKinnon, Catharine A. *Feminism Unmodified: Discourses on Life and Law*. Cambridge, Mass.; London: Harvard University Press, 1987.

Macurdy, Grace Haroet. *Hellenistic Queens: A Study of Woman-Power in Macedonia, Seleucid Syria, and Ptolemaic Egypt*. Baltimore: The Johns Hopkins University Press, 1932. Oxford: Oxford University Press, 1932.

Maguigan, Holly. "Battered Women and Self Defense: Myths and Misconceptions in Current Reform Proposals." *University of Pennsylvania Law Review*, vol. 140, no. 2, December 1991.

Mead, Margaret. *Male and Female: A Study of the Sexes in a Changing World*. New York: Dell, 1967. Harmondsworth: Penguin Books, 1962.

Miller, Jean Baker, MD *Toward a New Psychology of Women*. Boston: Beacon Press, 1986. Harmondsworth: Penguin Books, 1988.

Moraga, Cherrie, and Gloria Anzaldua, eds. *This Bridge Called My Back: Writings By Radical Women of Color*. New York: Kitchen Table: Women of Color Press, 1984.

Morgan, Robin. *The Anatomy of Freedom: Feminism, Physics, and Global Politics*. Oxford: Robertson, 1983. New York: Anchor, 1984.

——, ed. *Sisterhood Is Powerful: An Anthology of Writings from the Women's Liberation Movement*. New York: Vintage, 1970.

Morrison, Toni, ed. *Race-ing Justice, En-Gendering Power: Essays on Anita Hill, Clarence Thomas, and the Construction of Social Reality*. New York: Pantheon, 1992. London: Chatto & Windus, 1992.

Nead, Lynda. *Myths of Sexuality: Representations of Women in Victorian Britain*. Oxford: Basil Blackwell, 1988.

Newell, Mindy. *The Catwoman: Her Sister's Keeper*. New York: DC Comics, 1991.

Nietzsche, Friedrich. *On the Genealogy of Morals*, trans. Walter Kaufman. New York: Vintage Books, 1989.

Ornstein, Norman, Andrew Kohut, and Larry McCarthy. *The People, the Press and Politics: The Times-Mirror Study of the American Electorate*. Reading, Mass.: Addison-Wesley, 1988.

Ostrander, Susan A. *Women of the Upper Class*. Philadelphia: Temple University Press, 1984.

Phelan, Shane. *Identity Politics: Lesbian Feminism and the Limits of Community*. Philadelphia: Temple University Press, 1989.

Phelps, Timothy M., and Helen Winternitz. *Capitol Games: The Inside Story of Clarence Thomas, Anita Hill, and a Supreme Court Nomination*. New York: HarperCollins, 1992.

Redstockings. *Feminist Revolution*. New York: Random House, 1978.

Rich, Adrienne. *Of Woman Born: Motherhood as Experience and Institution*. London: Virago Press, 1986.

——. *On Lies, Secrets, and Silence: Selected Prose, 1966–1978*. London: Virago Press, 1980.

Richardson, Diane, and Vicki Robinson, eds. *Thinking Feminist: Key Concepts in Women's Studies*. New York: Guilford Press, 1993.

Robertson, Nan. *The Girls in the Balcony: Women, Men, and The New York Times*. New York: Random House, 1992.

Ruddick, Sara. *Maternal Thinking: Toward a Politics of Peace*. New York: Ballantine, 1990. London: The Women's Press, 1990.

Sanders, Marlene, and Marcia Rock. *Waiting for Prime Time: The Women of Television News*. New York: HarperCollins, 1990.

Schneider, Susan Weidman, and Arthur Drache. *Head and Heart: A Woman's Guide to Financial Independence*. Pasadena: Trilogy Books, 1991.

Shapiro, Joseph P. *No Pity: People with Disabilities Forging a New Civil Rights Movement*. New York: Times Books, 1993.

Shreve, Anita. *Women Together, Women Alone: The Legacy of the Consciousness-Raising Movement*. New York: Viking Penguin, 1989.

Smith, Barbara, ed. *Home Girls: A Black Feminist Anthology*. New York: Kitchen Table: Women of Color Press, 1983.

Snell, Tracy J. *Women in Jail, 1989*. Washington, D.C.: Bureau of Justice Statistics Special Report, March 1992.

Sterling, Anne Fausto. *Myths of Gender: Biological Theories About Women and Men*. New York: Basic Books, 1986.

Stein, Nan, Nancy L. Marshall, and Linda R. Tropp. *Secrets in Public: Sexual Harassment in Our Schools*. Wellesley, Mass.: Center for Research on Women, NOW Legal Defense and Education Fund, March 1993.

Stoltenberg, John. *Refusing to Be a Man: Essays on Sex and Justice*. New York: Meridian, 1989. London: Fontana Books, 1990.

Stone, Merlin. *When God Was a Woman*. New York: Harvest Books, 1978.

Stratton, Joanna L. *Pioneer Women: Voices from the Kansas Frontier*. New York: Simon & Schuster, 1982.

Tannen, Deborah. *You Just Don't Understand: Women and Men in Conversation*. New York: William Morrow, 1990. London: Virago Press, 1991.

Thomas, William I. *The Unadjusted Girl*. New York: Harper & Row Torch Books, 1967.

Travis, Carol. *The Mismeasure of Woman: Why Women Are Not the Better Sex, the Inferior Sex, or the Opposite Sex*. New York: Simon & Schuster, 1992.

Trump, Ivana. *For Love Alone*. New York: Pocket Books, 1992. London: Century, 1992.

Tuttle, Lisa. *Encyclopedia of Feminism*. New York: Facts on File, 1986. Harlow: Longman, 1986.

Ulrich, Laurel Thatcher. *A Midwife's Tale*. New York: Alfred A. Knopf, 1990.

Wall, Ginita. *Our Money, Our Selves: The Guide for Women at Financial Crossroads*. Yonkers, N.Y.: Consumer Reports Books, 1992.

Weldon, Fay. *The Life and Loves of a She-Devil*. London: Coronet Books, 1983.

Williams, Patricia J. *The Alchemy of Race and Rights: Diary of a Law Professor*. Cambridge, Mass.; London: Harvard University Press, 1992.

Wolf, Deborah Goleman. *The Lesbian Community*. Berkeley; London: University of California Press, 1979.

Women's Action Coalition Staff, ed. *WAC Stats: The Facts about Women*. New York: The New Press, 1993.

Index

INDEX

Concerned Women for America 76
conflict, fear of 120–2, 252–3, 302–4
  see also competition
Conley, Dr Frances 33
consciousness-raising groups 120,308
contraception 139–40, 141–2
Cooley, Azalea Althea 216–17
Cosmopolitan (UK) 64
Couric, Katie 176
Coward, Rosalind 97–8, 251
  Our Treacherous Hearts, 221
Crowley, Senator Rosemary xv
Cox, Eva 87
Coyle, Angela 90
Coyne, Judy 136
Crawford, Cindy 177
Crimewatch (TV) 90
Crisp, Wendy Reid 318
criticis.n, fear of 268, 270, 271
'cross-targeting' 322–3
Cuomo, Governor Mario 213, 214
Currie, Edwina 89, 102

Daily Telegraph 94
Daly, Mary 69, 159, 203
D'Amato, Al 218, 219
Darling, Lynn 23
date rape 25, 110, 116, 120, 125, 208
  media coverage of 107, 117, 147–8, 175,
    206–7, 211
debate, feminist:
  blocked by the media 110–14, 118, *see also*
    television
  collective process of 128–9, 165–6
  fear of 120–2, 185, 252–3
  and inflexibility of thought 119–20, 129–32,
    137–8, 143
  at universities 73, 127–31, 135–8
Deep Throat (film) 115
Delalic, Jasna 234
Democratic Party 6, 7, 9
  see also Emily's List
demographic statistics 17, 18, 19, 38
Dershowitz, Alan 112
Designing Women (TV) 46
Diana, Princess of Wales 48
Diana principle, the 41, 42
'difference feminism' 110, 188–90
  and power 277, 298–301, 302
DiMassa, Diane 238
disability-rights movement 228
Dixon, Senator Alan 6
domestic violence 21, 22, 25, 152, 153, 154,
    177
  and charity donations 328
  and legal system 56, 120, 222–7
Donahue, Phil 8, 204
Doubiago, Sharon 158
Doucet, Julie 239
Douglass, Frederick 59, 204

D'Souza, Dinesh 125
Dunwoody, Gwyneth 94
Dworkin, Andrea 109–10, 154, 156, 194, 200,
    202, 203
  Intercourse 133
  Mercy, 237
dyke-baiting 72, 74–8
  see lesbians

Eagle, Carol J., and Colman, Carol: *All That
    She Can Be* ... 289, 292, 293, 294
earnings *see* employment, women's
Eberhard, Dr E. F. W. 75
Echols, Alice: *Daring to Be Bad: Radical
    Feminism 1967–1975* 73
education *see* universities and colleges
electioneering *see* politics
Elle (magazine) 101
Ellerbee, Linda 85
Ellis, Bret Easton: *American Psycho* 116, 173
Ellis, Edith 184
Ellis, Richard 235
Emily's List xiv, 33, 38, 53, 89, 175, 318,
    371–?
Emily's List, UK xv, 10, 175
employment, women's (*see also specific
    activities and spheres*):
  'cross-targeting' and 322–3
  and earnings/power relationship 44–8, 49,
    256–7, 260–6, 321–2
  earnings statistics of 16, 86, 321
  feminists and 72, 79–82, 189
  in film industry 96–7
  in the media 85–7, 89–93, 95–6, 97–9,
    104–5, 268–9
  and power feminism 310–19
  in publishing 94–5
  running of own businesses 10, 47, 49, 175,
    263, 318
  and self-denigration 251, 257, 258–9, 260,
    287
  sexual harassment and 56, 80, 81
  women in top positions 47–8, 259–60, 265,
    321
Engel, Peter H. 24–5
Erikson, Erik H. 279
Esquire (magazine) 23
Everywoman (magazine) 108
Extremities (film) 237

Face the Nation (TV) 88
Faderman, Lillian 74, 75, 76, 77
Fagan, Debbie 67
FAIR (Fairness and Accuracy in Reporting)
    112–13
Fairchild, Morgan 88
Fairweather, Eileen 103
Falling Down (film) 23
Faludi, Susan 14, 19
  Backlash 69, 153, 273

INDEX